Windows
6 in 1

by Jane Calabria, et al.

A Division of Macmillan Computer Publishing
201 West 103rd Street, Indianapolis, Indiana 46290 USA

Library of Congress Catalog No.: 97-075462

ISBN: 0-7897-1486-8

00 99 98   6 5 4 3 2 1

Interpretation of the printing code: The rightmost double-digit number is the year of the book's printing; the rightmost single-digit number, the number of the book's printing. For example, a printing code of 98-1 shows that the first printing of the book occurred in 1998.

Screen reproductions in this book were created using Collage Plus from Inner Media, Inc., Hollis, NH.

Composed in *Palatino* and *Helvetica* by Que Corporation.

Director of Editorial Services
Carla Hall

Executive Editor
Grace Buechlein

Development Editor
Sandy Doell

Technical Editor
Jeff Perkins

Project Editor
Tom Lamoureux

Indexer
Chris Barrick

Production Team
Brad Lenser
Sossity Smith

Contents

Part I: Navigating Windows 98

1 What's New in Windows 98 3
For Windows 95 Users 3
Making Windows 98 Work Like Windows 95 8
For Windows 3.1 Users 8

2 Navigating the Windows Desktop 11
What Is Windows 98? 11
Starting Windows 98 11
Understanding the Windows Desktop 13
Using the Mouse 15
Using the Start Button 16
Using the Taskbar 18
Shutting Down Windows 98 20

3 Working with a Window 22
What Is a Window? 22
Windows Contents 25
Opening a Window 25
Sizing a Window with Maximize, Minimize, and Restore 26
Sizing a Window's Borders 27
Using Scroll Bars 28
Moving a Window 29
Viewing a Window's Contents 29

4 Using Menus 32
Using Toolbar Buttons 32
What Is a Menu? 33
Choosing Menu Commands 34
Reading a Menu 35
Using Shortcut Keys Instead of Menus 36
Using Shortcut Menus 37

5 Using Windows 98 Help 39

Getting Help in Windows 98 39

The Help Window 40

Using Windows On-Line Help 40

      Using the Contents Feature 41

      Using the Index Feature 42

      Using the Search Feature 44

Using Web Help 46

6 Using Dialog Boxes 48

What Is a Dialog Box? 48

Using the Components of a Dialog Box 49

Using the What's This? Feature 51

Using Text Boxes 52

Using List Boxes 54

Using Option Buttons 54

Using Check Boxes 55

Using Command Buttons 56

Using Property Sheets and Tabs 57

Part II: Working with Files, Folders, and Disks

1 File Management in Windows 98 61

Categorizing Your Files 61

Creating Folders 63

Looking at Folders 65

2 Using My Computer 67

What Is My Computer? 67

Browsing Folder Options 71

The My Computer Menu 76

The My Computer Toolbars 77

Changing the Appearance of the Folder Window 79

      Creating an HTML Document 80

      Selecting a Background Picture 80

      Removing Folder Customization 81

3 Managing Files with My Computer 82

Selecting Files and Folders 82

Moving Files and Folders 83

Copying Files and Folders 84

Deleting Files and Folders 85
Renaming Files and Folders 86
Creating Shortcuts 86
Finding Files 87

4   The Recycle Bin.. 91
What Is the Recycle Bin? 91
Opening the Recycle Bin 91
Emptying the Recycle Bin 92
Selected Files 93
All Files 93
Restoring Files 93
Recycle Bin Properties 94

5   Understanding the Windows Explorer............................. 96
What Is the Windows Explorer? 96
Opening the Explorer 96
Understanding the Explorer Window 97
Using File Viewing Options 101

6   Navigating Explorer 103
Changing Displays..103
Using the Explorer Toolbar...107
Using the Menu 109
Searching for a File 110
Closing Explorer 113

7   Managing Files with Explorer 114
Selecting Files and Folders...114
Moving Files and Folders..115
Copying Files and Folders 116
Deleting Files and Folders 117
Renaming Files and Folders 118
Creating Shortcuts..119

8   File Properties.. 120
File Names 120
File Size 121
File Creation Date and Time...123
File Attributes 123
Viewing Properties...124

9   **Registering Files** **127**
    What Is File Association? 127
    Registering a New File Type 128
    Editing an Existing File Type 131
    Removing a File Type 132
    Changing the Icon for a File Type.......................................133

10 **Using Task Scheduler and Backing Up**........................... **135**
    What Is Backing Up?...135
    Backing Up Data 135
    Restoring Files 142
    Scheduling Tasks 145

11 **Disk Management** **150**
    Understanding Disk Management 150
    Cleaning Up Your Disk 151
    Using Disk Defragmenter 152
    Using DriveSpace 155
    Using FAT32 159
    Using ScanDisk 161
    Using the System File Checker Utility 164
    Using Maintenance Wizard 165

12 **Working with Floppy Disks** **167**
    Formatting Floppy Disks 167
    Copying Disks 169
    Naming Disks 171

Part III: Customizing and Maintaining Windows 98

1   **Understanding the Control Panel**.................................... **175**
    What Is the Control Panel? 175
    What Can You Accomplish in the Control Panel? 177
    Selecting a Screen Saver 180

2   **Customizing the Active Desktop**...................................... **183**
    Creating Shortcuts...183
    Arranging Icons 187
    Choosing Colors and Backgrounds 189
        Colors 189
        Schemes 190

Wallpaper 190

Patterns 191

Desktop Themes 192

Changing Fonts 194

3 Customizing the Taskbar **196**

Positioning the Taskbar 196

Sizing the Taskbar 197

Hiding the Taskbar 198

Using Taskbar Properties 199

Showing the Clock 199

Creating Custom Toolbars 200

4 Customizing the Start Menu **204**

Using the Start Menu Properties 204

Adding and Removing Programs 205

Organizing the Start Menu 208

Customizing the Favorites Entries 209

Clearing the Document Menu 211

Adding Programs to the Startup Window 212

5 Adding and Removing Software and Hardware **213**

When You Buy Software 213

Preparing to Install 215

Installing Software 216

Removing Programs 218

Adding New Hardware 218

Adding Windows 98 Components 220

6 Sharing Workstations and Setting Passwords **223**

Why Use a Password? 223

Setting Up a Password 224

Changing Your Password 225

Configuring for Multiple Users 226

7 Configuring Peripheral Devices and Sound Options **229**

Configuring Video Options 229

Configuring for Multiple Monitors 233

Configuring Sound Options 234

Configuring Multimedia Devices 235

Configuring Your Keyboard and Mouse 237

8   Configuring a Modem **240**
What Is a Modem? 240
Adding a Modem 240
    Modifying Dialing Properties 242
    Changing Modem Properties 244

9   Understanding and Using the Device Manager **246**
What Is the Device Manager? 246
Finding Information on Your Hardware 247
Printing Device Information 249

10   Managing Fonts **251**
What Are Fonts? 251
Adding Fonts 254
Removing Fonts 255
Using Character Map 256

11   Computer Viruses **258**
What Is a Computer Virus? 258
    Curing and Preventing Computer Viruses 259

12   Rebooting, Restarting, and Disaster Planning **261**
Using Ctrl+Alt+Del 261
Restarting Windows 98 262
Disaster Planning 263
    Backing Up the Entire Hard Drive 263
    Creating a Startup Disk 264
    Using Your Startup Disk 264

13   Printing in Windows 98 .... **267**
Installing a Printer 267
Printing from an Application 268
Working with the Print Folder 270
Controlling the Print Job 271
    Pausing and Resuming the Queue 271
    Deleting a Print Job 272
Using Drag-and-Drop Printing 272

14   Accessibility Options **273**
Using the Accessibility Wizard 273
Using Accessibility Properties 277

Part IV: Working with Windows Applications

1   Starting and Exiting Windows Applications **281**
Opening a Windows Application 281
Viewing an Application's Window 283
Exiting an Application 284

2   Working with Multiple Windows **285**
Arranging Windows on the Desktop 285
    Cascading Windows 285
    Tiling Windows 286
    Minimizing All Windows 287
Moving Between Applications 288
Moving Between Windows in the Same Application 288

3   Copying and Moving Information Between Windows **291**
What Is the Clipboard? 291
Selecting Text for Copying or Moving 293
Selecting Graphics 294
Copying Information Between Windows 294
Moving Information Between Windows 294

4   Using WordPad **296**
What Is WordPad? 296
Moving the Text Insertion Point 298
Inserting and Deleting Text 298
Selecting, Cutting, Copying, and Pasting Text 299
Formatting a Document 299
Formatting Text 300
Aligning Text 301
Adjusting Page Margins 302
Saving a Document and Exiting WordPad 303

5   Using Paint **305**
What Is Paint? 305
Drawing in Paint 307
Adding Text to a Graphic 308
Saving a Drawing 310

6 Using Windows 98 Entertainment Features 311
What Is Multimedia? 311
Using the Sound Recorder 313
Recording Sounds 313
        Playing Sounds 314
        Editing and Working with Effects..314
Operating the CD Player 315
Using the Media Player 316
Using the ActiveMovie Player 317
Placing a Multimedia File in a Document 317
Using WebTV for Windows 318

7 OLE: Linking Data to Different Applications 320
Sharing Information Between Applications 320
Understanding Linking 322
Creating Links 322
Understanding Embedding 325
Embedding Objects 325

Part V: Windows 98 and the Internet

1 Understanding the Internet and the Web 331
What Are the Internet and the World Wide Web? 331
Clients and Servers 332
Grasping Protocols 332
Hypertext: The Heart of the Web 334
What's an Intranet? 335

2 Configuring for Internet Access 337
What Is an Internet Service Provider? 337
        Indirect Access 337
        Dial-Up Connection 338
        Persistent Connection 338
Using Connection Wizard 339
        Choosing an ISP 339
        Connecting to an Existing Internet Account 340

3 Understanding the Internet Explorer 4 Window 345
Starting Internet Explorer 4 345
Navigating the Internet Explorer 4 Window 347
The Internet Explorer 4 Toolbars 348
Navigating a Web Page 351

4 Visiting a Web Site **352**
Reading URLs 352
Visiting a Web Site 354
Understanding Caching 356
Understanding Links 358
    Graphic Links 358
    Gopher Links 358
    FTP Links 360
    Mailto Links 360
    Hypertext Links 361
    Image Maps 361

5 Web, Site, and Document Searching **363**
Understanding Searches...363
    Searching the Web 363
    Searching a Web Site 365
    Searching a Web Page 365
Creating a Web Search...365
    Following Search Results...368
    Visiting a Search Engine Site..369
Searching for Text on a Web Page 370

6 Working with Web Pages.. **372**
Returning to a Previously Viewed Page 372
Changing How Text Is Displayed...374
Using the Favorites Folder 377
    Adding a Page to Favorites 377
    Displaying a Favorite Page 378
    Managing Your Favorites..379
Downloading Files from a Web Page 380

7 Customizing Internet Explorer 4 .... **382**
Customizing the Start Page 382
Adding Buttons to the Links Toolbar......................................384
Changing the Size of the Toolbar Buttons 385
Creating a Desktop Shortcut...385
Using a Graphical Image as Wallpaper 386
Fast Loading Your Web Pages 386
    Adjusting the Cache 386
Setting Up Security Zones...387
Censoring Internet Sites 390
Selecting Default Programs 391

8 Subscribing to a Channel, a Web Site, or an Active Desktop Item **392**
What Is a Subscription? 392
Using the Channel Bar 393
Subscribing to a Channel 394
Subscribing to a Web Site 396
Subscribing to an Active Desktop Item 397

9 Managing Subscriptions and Working Offline **399**
Managing Subscriptions 399
Modifying Subscriptions 399
Canceling Subscriptions 402
Updating Subscriptions 403
Working Offline 403

10 Configuring Outlook Express **405**
What Is Outlook Express? 405
Using the Connection Wizard to Configure Email and News 406

11 Using Outlook Express Mail **410**
Opening and Closing Outlook Express Mail 410
The Outlook Express Mail Window 411
Sending a Message 412
Setting Priorities, Attaching Files, and Other Options 415
Using the Windows Address Book 415
Addressing a Message with the Address Book 417
Retrieving and Reading Your Messages 418
Saving a File Attached to a Message 419
Replying to a Message 419
Deleting Old Messages 420

12 Using Outlook Express News **421**
What Is Outlook Express News? 421
Opening and Closing Outlook Express News 422
Retrieving a List of Newsgroups 422
Subscribing to and Unsubscribing from Newsgroups 422
Reading Messages 424
Posting Your Own Messages 425

13 Understanding FrontPage Express **427**
What Is FrontPage Express? 427
The FrontPage Express Tools 428
Creating a Web Page 431

Editing an Existing Web Page 432
Formatting Text 433
Changing the Page Properties 434
Adding Hypertext, Images, and WebBot Components 435
    Creating Links 435
    Adding Graphics 436
    Inserting WebBots 437

14 Using HyperTerminal **439**
What Is HyperTerminal? 439
Creating a Connection 440
Dialing Into a Computer 442
Connecting to a Bulletin Board 442

15 Web Integration and My Computer/Windows Explorer **444**
How the Single-Click (Web Style) Option Affects Windows 444
    Customizing the Single-Click (Web Style) Option 446
Displaying the Contents of a Folder Using HTML 447
    Turning on Web Style for a Single Folder 448
    Creating an HTML Folder Page 449
Adding a Graphic Background to a Folder 452
Removing Folder Customization 453
Browsing the Web with My Computer/Windows Explorer 453

Part VI: Networking and Mobile Computing with Windows 98

1 Using Network Neighborhood **457**
What Is a Network? 457
About Clients and Servers 458
What Is Network Neighborhood? 459
Logging on to a Network 461
Accessing Network Neighborhood 462
    Understanding the Network Neighborhood Window 462
    Creating Shortcuts to Network Resources 464
    Closing Network Neighborhood 465
Logging Off a Network 465
    Changing Your Password 465

2 Navigating Network Neighborhood **468**
   Changing Displays 468
   Using the Network Neighborhood Toolbar 471
   Using the Menu 472
   Exploring Network Neighborhood 474
   Finding a Computer or File on the Network 475

3 Sharing Your Folders, Files, and Printers **478**
   Sharing Folders on Your Computer 478
   Configuring Your PC to Share Resources 479
   Sharing a File, Folder, or Drive 479
   Sharing Your Printer 483
   Mapping Drives 483

4 Attaching to Network Printers **485**
   Working with Network Printers 485
   Printing from Applications 485
      Drag-and-Drop Printing 486
      Adding a Network Printer 486

5 Working on a Laptop Computer **489**
   Undocking Your PC 489
   Managing Power Consumption 490
      Setting Power Management Options 491
      Receiving Calls While on Standby 494
   Direct Cable Connection 494
   Traveling with Laptops and Notebooks 495
      Obtain Local Access Numbers 495
      Buy the Right Case 495
      Charge the Batteries 496
      Remember the Supplies and Peripherals 496
   Protect Yourself from Theft 497
      Understand and Respect Airport Security and FAA
         Regulations 498

6 Using My Briefcase **499**
   What Is My Briefcase? 499
   Creating a Briefcase Folder 500
   Adding Files to the Briefcase 500
   Moving My Briefcase to a Floppy Disk 501
   Checking File Status 502
   Updating Files 503
   Removing Sync Links 504

7 Connecting to a Network from a Remote Location **505**

Dial-Up Networking Basics 505

Preparing Your Computer 506

Making a Dial-Up Connection 507

Modifying a Connection 508

Connecting to the Dial-Up Network 510

Part VII: Appendixes

A Installing Windows 98 .... **515**

Before You Start 515

Upgrading from Windows 95 516

Upgrading from Windows 3.1 517

Installing from MS-DOS 517

Setup Options 518

B DOS and Legacy Applications **520**

What Is DOS? 520

Understanding DOS File Naming Rules 521

Using the DOS Prompt 522

Windows DOS Sessions 523

MS-DOS Mode 524

Booting Directly to DOS 524

Running DOS Applications 525

Installing DOS Applications 527

Programs That Will Run in a DOS Virtual Machine 528

Programs That Won't Run in a DOS Virtual Machine 528

Programs That Won't Tolerate Windows or DOS Memory
    Management 529

Making the Boot Menu Appear When Your Computer
    Starts Up 530

Booting Directly to DOS 531

C Sharing and Using a Fax Modem **533**

Microsoft Fax Basics 533

Using Microsoft Fax 533

D Glossary of Terms **535**

Index **551**

Dedication

To Tom Burke for putting up with Dorothy's long hours and for his support and encouragement. Also, to Steven Klotz and Hannah and Caroline Kirkland for a wonderful experience "In Search of the Castle Beltzhoover," an experience we shall never forget.

Jennifer would like to dedicate this book to the newest member of her family, her daughter, Katerina.

Acknowledgments

Jane, Rob, and Dorothy would like to thank Jennifer Fulton for her contribution to this book. We are fortunate to be teaming up with such an experienced author and look forward to future collaborative efforts.

In the wee hours of the morning, we write this in Jane's office, while no fewer than five computers and four bodies are crammed in what used to be more-than-adequate space. The "other" two of those four bodies are Janet Crawford and Carol Manieri, without whom this book could not have found its way into your hands. We thank them for their long hours and hard work checking, double-checking, and body checking us through this new release of Windows.

It is our good fortune to work with the talented and dedicated folks at Que who developed and delivered the *Windows 98 6 in 1*. We are thrilled to be working with Sandy Doell, our Development Editor. We wish great luck and success to John Gosney, who began the development of this book but followed a path that took him from the publishing industry. We will miss working with you, John. Thanks to Tom Lamoureux, our Production Editor, without whom, we believe, no books would ever make it to completion! We are deeply indebted to Jill Byus, Angie Wethington, and Grace Buechlein, Acquisition Editors, for bringing this opportunity our way.

Jennifer would like to acknowledge her co-authors, Jane, Rob, and Dorothy, whose dedication, intelligence, and fine writing style made them so easy to work with. In addition, she'd like to thank everyone at MCP (especially Jill Byus, Angie Wethington, Grace Buechlein, and Sandy Doell) who helped make this book such a pleasurable project on which to work.

About the Authors

Jane Calabria

Jane has authored or contributed to no fewer than 15 Que books, which include the *Windows 95 6 in 1*, *Lotus Notes 6 in 1*, and *Internet 6 in 1*. She has been an independent consultant, trainer, and speaker for seven years. Jane is a Certified Lotus Notes Professional (Principal Application Developer) and is a Microsoft Office User Specialist. In addition to her writing and consulting, Jane and her husband Rob Kirkland travel the country delivering seminars and classes about Lotus Notes and Windows.

Dorothy Burke

Dorothy started life as a technical magazine editor. She has been an independent consultant and trainer for many years. Her books include the *Ten Minute Guide to Lotus Notes Mail 4.6*, and she has contributed to several other Que books, including *Special Edition, Using Power Point*. As a trainer, Dorothy teaches desktop publishing, operating systems, spreadsheets, and graphics programs as well as Lotus Notes and Domino. As a consultant, Dorothy works with Lotus Notes and Domino, developing applications.

Rob Kirkland

Rob is a Certified Lotus Notes Instructor (CLI), a Certified NetWare Engineer (CNE), and a Microsoft Certified Product Specialist (MCPS) for Windows NT. He co-authored the *Professional Developers Guide to Domino 4.5* with Jane Calabria and is a contributing author of several Que books including *Using Windows NT Workstation*, *Intranet Publishing*, *Running a Perfect Intranet*, and *Intranet HTML*. Rob began his computer teaching career as a word processing and desktop publishing guru. Today, Rob also teaches Lotus Notes, Novell NetWare, Windows NT, numerous application programs, and hardware management. As a consultant, he sets up networks, designs applications, and subdues unruly hardware and software. In his spare time, Rob picked up a law degree.

Jane and Rob have teamed up successfully on several Que books, including the *Professional Developers Guide to Domino 4.5* and, with Dorothy Burke, have authored Que's *Using Word*. Jane and Dorothy have teamed up on seven Que books including the *10 Minute Guide to Lotus Notes 4.6*, *Microsoft Works 6 in 1*, *Microsoft Windows 95 6 in 1*, *Microsoft Word 97 Exam Guide*, *Microsoft PowerPoint 97 Exam Guide*, and *Microsoft Excel 97 Exam Guide*.

Jennifer Fulton

Jennifer Fulton is a computer trainer, consultant, and best-selling author of over 50 books covering many areas of computing, including DOS, Windows 3.1, Windows 95, and Windows 98. Jennifer is a self-taught veteran of computing, which means that if something can happen to a computer user, it has happened to her at one time or another. As a computer veteran, Jennifer brings what's left of her sense of humor to her many books, including: *Sams Teach Yourself Windows 98 in 10 Minutes, Big Basics Book of Windows 95, Netscape Navigator 6 in 1, Ten Minute Guide to Excel 97, Big Basics Book of Office 97, Easy Outlook, Big Basics Book of PCs,* and *Computers: A Visual Encyclopedia, 20th Century Computers and How They Worked (The Official Starfleet History of Computers).*

Jennifer began her writing career as a staff writer for Alpha Books, a former division of Macmillan Computer Publishing, before escaping to the life of a freelance author.

Jennifer lives in Indianapolis with her husband, Scott, who is also a computer book author. They live together in a small home filled with many books, some of which they have not written.

We'd Like to Hear from You!

Que Corporation has a long-standing reputation for high-quality books and products. To ensure your continued satisfaction, we also understand the importance of customer service and support.

Tech Support

If you need assistance with the information in this book or with a CD or disk accompanying the book, please access Macmillan Computer Publishing's online Knowledge Base at **http://www.superlibrary.com/general/support**. If you do not find the answer to your questions on our Web site, you may contact Macmillan Technical Support by phone at **317/581-3833** or via email at **support@mcp.com**.

Also be sure to visit Que's Web resource center for all the latest information, enhancements, errata, downloads, and more. It's located at **http://www.quecorp.com/**.

Orders, Catalogs, and Customer Service

To order other Que or Macmillan Computer Publishing books, catalogs, or products, please contact our Customer Service Department at **800/428-5331** or fax us at **800/882-8583** (International Fax: 317/228-4400). Or visit our online bookstore at **http://www.mcp.com/**.

Comments and Suggestions

We want you to let us know what you like or dislike most about this book or other Que products. Your comments will help us to continue publishing the best books available on computer topics in today's market.

Que Corporation
201 West 103rd Street, 4B
Indianapolis, Indiana 46290 USA
Fax: 317/581-4663

Please be sure to include the book's title and author as well as your name and phone or fax number. We will carefully review your comments and share them with the author. Please note that due to the high volume of mail we receive, we may not be able to reply to every message.

Thank you for choosing Que!

Introduction

Whether you are using a computer at home, at work, or both, odds are good that you are using—or you're about to use—Microsoft Windows 98. A powerful and flexible operating system, Windows 98 offers multitasking (the ability to work with many applications open at one time), a consistent look and feel across programs designed to run in Windows, the ability to integrate a variety of servers, 16- and 32-bit applications and easy network access to other computers files, printers, and the Internet. Windows is designed to make computing easier, and this introduction is designed to help you decide if this book can make Windows 98 easier for you to work with and understand.

Who Should Use This Book

Windows 98 6 in 1 is for anyone who:

- Is new to Windows 98.
- Is new to Internet Explorer 4.
- Is new to the Internet.
- Is new to computers.
- Wants to expand their Windows 98 skills.
- Wants to learn the new features of Windows 98.
- Wants to learn or reference tasks in short, concise lessons.

Why *This* book?

We present to you, in a reasonable and concise method, the tools and information you need to understand the most powerful software installed on your computer—your operating system. We help you to make Windows work for you—not against you.

This book is written using a proven and popular format. The authors are experienced writers on many software products, having also taught computer applications, operating systems, hardware, networking, and programming classes for many years.

How This Book Is Organized

Windows 98 6 in 1 has lessons ranging from the basics to some more advanced features. Each lesson is intended to take 10 minutes or less of your time. You can work through the book lesson by lesson, building upon your skills, or you can use the book as a quick reference when you want to perform a new task.

Following is a brief description of each part of *Windows 98 6 in 1:*

- *Part I, Navigating Windows 98*   The book begins with an overview of Windows 98—what's new and what's different from previous versions of Windows. You'll learn how to move around the Windows desktop, open and close windows, get help, use dialog boxes, and use menus.

- *Part II, Working With Files, Folders, and Disks*   Learn why you want to use the new file management functions in Windows 98 as well as how to use them. Manage files with My Computer, work with the Windows Explorer, understand File Properties, and more.

- *Part III, Customizing and Maintaining Windows 98*   Here, you learn how to use the Control panel, customize your Active Desktop, install new software and hardware, configure modems and printers, and customize the Start Menu.

- *Part IV, Working with Windows Applications*   If you are new to computers, this invaluable section teaches you how to work with Windows applications, copy and move information between applications, and use Paint and WordPad.

- *Part V, Windows 98 and the Internet*   Internet Explorer 4 (IE4) is introduced in this section, from configuring to surfing the Net. Learn about the new capabilities of IE4 and even learn the basics of the Internet and the Web.

- *Part VI, Networking and Mobile Computing with Windows 98*   If you're new to networks, you'll gain some important skills from Part VI. Learn how to attach to an existing network, map drives, share printers and files, use dial-up networking, remotely access computers, and navigate Network Neighborhood.

- *Appendix A: Installing Windows 98*   A must for upgraders!

- *Appendix B: DOS and Legacy Applications*   For those who need to run DOS applications under Windows 98.

- *Appendix C: Sharing and Using a Fax Modem*   For those upgrading from Windows 95 who want to retain its fax capabilities.

- *Appendix D: Glossary*   Review some of the terms that have been discussed in the chapters.

Conventions Used in This Book

Commands, directions, and explanations in this book are presented in the clearest format possible:

> Titles of windows and dialog boxes will be capitalized to distinguish them from regular text. For example, the Custom Conventions box refers to an onscreen box whose title bar reads "Custom Conventions."

> A series of menu selections that you much click will be separated by commas. For instance, "Select **Start**, **Programs**, **Excel**," means that you click the Start button, the Programs menu choice, and then the Excel option.

> As a further help, commands you are directed to type will also be in **bold** type so you can see them clearly.

> You might also be directed to hold down several keys simultaneously, as in the command "Press **Ctrl+F2**." The two keys that you press will be connected with the plus sign (+).

Some information is offset in sidebars to draw your attention.

TIP   **Tips**   These provide timesaving shortcuts and workarounds to potential trouble spots.

Cautions   These warn you of situations that can land you in trouble.

CAUTION

TERM   **Terms**   These give definitions for jargon that you are not expected to know but which will be useful as you master Microsoft Windows 98.

SKILLS TRANSFER   **Skills Transfer Tips**   These highlight procedures that you learn in Windows but can apply to other Windows programs.

Navigating Windows 98

What's New in Windows 98

In this lesson you get a quick overview of what's new in Windows 98. If you're brand new to Windows, you can skip this lesson. Here, we highlight the new features of Windows 98 for those who are upgrading from Windows 95 or Windows 3.1.

For Windows 95 Users

The first change that you'll notice in Windows 98 is the new Active Desktop. The new desktop has a similar *look* but a very different *feel* from Windows 95. Desktop shortcuts look the same as they did in Windows 95, but you only need to point at one to see that they don't act the same. Point at a desktop icon and a hand appears (see Figure 1.1). The icon is immediately selected, and you have to click only once to activate the shortcut. This is not the only Desktop interface available. You can learn more about customizing the Desktop in Part III, Lesson 2, "Customizing the Active Desktop." If you're familiar with the Internet and have "surfed" the Web, you'll recognize that shortcuts have become hyperlinks. If you're new to the Internet, see Part V, "Windows 98 and the Internet," for more information on Internet Explorer and hyperlinks.

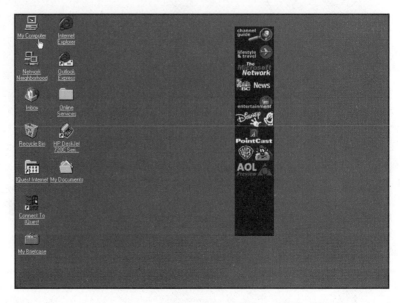

Figure 1.1 Shortcuts have become hyperlinks in Windows 98. Watch your pointer turn to a hand as you hold your mouse over a shortcut.

The Active Desktop gives you the ease of use of a Web browser. For a full rundown of the Active Desktop features, see Part I, Lesson 2, "Navigating the Windows Desktop."

Internet Explorer 4 ships with Windows 98 and is integrated into Windows 98 so that many windows have a Web browser feel. You'll find new navigation buttons and address bars, making it easy for you to browse files on your computer or browse Web sites without having to change windows or programs. You can browse your computer with Internet Explorer, or connect to a Web site by typing a Web address into the address bar of My Computer (see Figure 1.2). My Computer and Windows Explorer look very much like Internet Explorer (see Figure 1.2). You can add a Web view to any folder in Windows 98 and open the folder from Internet Explorer 4.0.

The Start menu has a new Favorites choice, so you can quickly go to your favorite Web sites and customize the taskbar by adding a Windows toolbar. If you have used Windows 95, you are undoubtedly familiar with the taskbar. If you are upgrading from Windows 3.1, you can learn about the taskbar in Part I, Lesson 2, "Navigating the Windows Desktop." Also see Part III, Lesson 3, "Customizing the Taskbar," to learn how to add items to the taskbar.

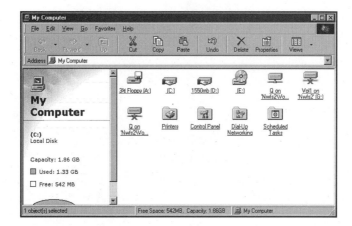

Figure 1.2 My Computer looks and feels like a Web browser.

Figure 1.3 shows the Start menu with some customization, so your Start menu may look at little different. In this example, the Start menu includes items for Microsoft Office, which were added by Office when it was installed.

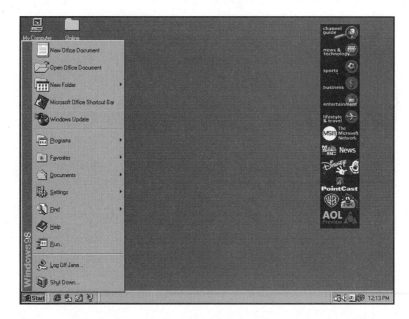

Figure 1.3 The Start menu can tell you who is logged in, and it has a new Favorites folder and Windows Update button.

It may take you a little time to become accustomed to the single click. If you find it difficult, you can switch back to the double-click world of Windows 95; the following section explains how. If you aren't having problems with the single click, you can learn more about working in Active Desktop in Part I, Lesson 2, "Navigating the Windows Desktop."

Other new features include

- **Internet Explorer 4.0** Web browser is packaged with Windows 98. Learn more about Explorer in Part V, "Windows 98 and the Internet."

- **Outlook Express** uses open Internet standards and allows you to read your e-mail and address books created in other programs. For more information on Outlook Express, See Part V, "Windows 98 and the Internet."

- **NetMeeting** provides Internet collaboration in real time. Using data, audio, and even video, you can share information, work together, and exchange files during conferences. For more information on NetMeeting, see Part V, "Windows 98 and the Internet."

- Secure your PC with **zones.** Zones allow you to assign security options to Web sites, requiring approval when you open a file or run a program from the Internet. For more information on zones, see Part V, "Windows 98 and the Internet."

- Using **channels**, you can open a full screen window to a Web site and schedule updates to the channel. For more information on channels, see Part V, "Windows 98 and the Internet."

- **Streamlined setup for users upgrading from Windows 95.** Learn more about upgrading to Windows 98 in Appendix A, "Installing Windows 98."

- **Multiple display support for PCI machines.** If you have a PCI machine and two PCI display adapters and monitors, when you click a hypertext line in your email, the browser pops up on the adjacent monitor. Learn more about using multiple monitors in Part III, Lesson 7, "Configuring Peripheral Devices and Sound Options."

- **A unified driver model for Windows 95 and Windows NT** means that all the "old" drivers for your hardware will continue to work even though you've upgraded your operating system.

- **Increased performance and disk space utilization**, including improved system boot time, a FAT 32 conversion utility, improved application load time, and faster system shutdown time. You can learn more about disk space management in Part II, Lesson 11, "Disk Management."

- Incorporated **full window dragging**, font smoothing, and other interface enhancements formerly available only with Microsoft Plus!, which was an add-in to Windows 95. You see examples of enhancements throughout all of Windows 98.

- **Windows Maintenance Wizard** automatically schedules tune-up jobs to maintain your computer. Learn more about the Maintenance Wizard in Part II, Lesson 11, "Disk Management."

- **Internet Connection Wizard** steps you through configuring your Internet connections, helps you sign up with an Internet Service Provider, and configures custom software provided by your service provider. To learn about the Internet Connection Wizard, see Part V, Lesson 2, "Configuring for Internet Access."

- **Start Menu Organizer Wizard** helps you add and remove programs from the Start menu. To learn how to use this Wizard, see Part III, Lesson 4, "Customizing the Start Menu."

- **System File Checker** utility helps you track changes to Windows 98 system files and restore original files when necessary. For more information on the System File Checker utility, see Part II, Lesson 11, "Disk Management."

- A new backup applet and **Task Scheduler** that support SCSI tape and other backup devices. Learn more about backing up and Task Scheduler in Part II, "Working with Files, Folders, and Disks."

- **Multimedia enhancements** for improved gaming.

- **Software to broadcast-enable your computer** to blend television with Web pages and computer content. With broadcast reception hardware, you'll be able to receive data broadcasts of Web pages, multimedia streams, and data packets from television stations and networks.

- To learn more about the WebTV for Windows, see Part IV, Lesson 6, "Using Windows 98 Entertainment Features."

- A new and improved **Windows Help**, which includes new contents and **Web Help** (when you are connected). Learn more about Windows Help in Part I, Lesson 5, "Using Windows 98 Help."

Making Windows 98 Work Like Windows 95

It may take awhile for you to become accustomed to the single-click Active Desktop. Should you want to become familiar with Windows 98 using the old double-click process, you can disable the single-click Web look of the desktop. To do so:

1. Click the **Start** button and choose **Settings, Folder Options**.
2. On the General tab, click **Classic Style**.
3. Click **OK**.

This will restore your desktop so that you will need to double-click when you open files.

To learn more about customizing Active Desktop, see Part III, Lesson 2, "Customizing the Active Desktop."

For Windows 3.1 Users

Windows 98 looks and feels more like a Web browser than the 3.1 operating system you are accustomed to—if in fact you have been using a Web browser. If both Windows 98 and Web navigation are new to you, you may find yourself using this book more like the tutorial it was meant to be than the reference book you thought you'd like to have around "just in case." Table 1.1 contains a brief roadmap of Windows 3.1 tasks and shows you how to perform them in Windows 98 to get you up and running. The following is a list of items found in Windows 3.1 and their replacement features or items in Windows 98:

- The Program Manager is replaced by the Start button and taskbar. See Part I, Lesson 2, "Navigating the Windows Desktop," to learn more about the Start button and taskbar.

- Groups are gone, but programs that are grouped together are indicated as such under the Programs menu. Click the Start button and select Programs to see your old "groups."

- File Manager is replaced by My Computer and Windows Explorer. Unlike File Manager, Windows Explorer will display all your drive connections in one window. To learn more about Windows Explorer and My Computer, see Part II, "Working with Files, Folders, and Disks."

- The Minimize button has been repositioned and its look has changed. Also, the maximize/restore icons have been combined and are changed in appearance. A new Close button (represented by an X) now appears at the top right of every window. This Close button will close your application. When first using Windows 98, you will undoubtedly close applications that you meant to minimize. For more information on minimizing, maximizing, and restoring, see Part I, Lesson 3, "Working with a Window."

Table 1.1 Performing Windows 3.1 Tasks in Windows 98

To:	Do This:	For More Information, See:
Start a Program	Use the Start Button: Click Start, slide your mouse to Programs, and click the program you want to start.	Part I, Lesson 2, "Navigating the Windows Desktop."
Copy and paste files	Right-click on the file and choose Copy. Right-click on the folder you want to place the copy in, and choose Paste. This works the same as copying and pasting text in Windows 3.1.	Part II, Lesson 3, "Managing Files with My Computer."
Switch between windows	Click the icon representing the opened window on the taskbar.	Part I, Lesson 2, "Navigating the Windows Desktop."
Open an MS-DOS window	Click the Start button, slide your mouse to Programs, and click the MS-DOS prompt.	Appendix B, "DOS and Legacy Applications."
Run a program from the DOS command line	Choose Start, Run and type your command in the dialog box.	Appendix B, "DOS and Legacy Applications."

continues

Table 1.1   Continued

To:	Do This:	For More Information See:
Access the Control Panel	Choose Start, Settings, Control Panel.	Part III, Lesson 1, "Understanding the Control Panel."

In this lesson you got a brief introduction to what's new in Windows 98. In the next lesson you'll learn how to navigate the Active Desktop.

Navigating the Windows Desktop

In this lesson, you learn to start and shut down Windows, work with the parts of the Windows desktop, and use a mouse to manipulate items on the desktop.

What Is Windows 98?

Windows 98 is an *operating system*. It controls the hardware of your computer and interprets the instructions from your software and operating systems to the hardware. When you use a menu command such as File, Save, Windows 98 is the driving force that writes the file to your disk or hard drive.

Windows 98 includes such features as *multitasking*, or the ability to run more than one program at a time. It uses a *graphical user interface (GUI)*, which allows you to get up and running through the use of pictures and graphics, instead of having to type out long commands to the operating system. Programs designed to run under Windows 98 (such as Word or Lotus) use similar keyboard and mouse operations to select objects and choose commands. Video and graphics applications run smoothly on Windows 98, enabling multimedia programs to run quickly and efficiently. Windows 98 also incorporates *hyperlinks* and Web functions into the desktop.

Starting Windows 98

To start Windows 98, you turn on your computer and monitor. As your computer *boots*, Windows loads the files it needs to run. You'll notice the Windows 98 logo screen and several black screens with white type.

After the operating system is loaded, you may see a password dialog box asking for your *user name* and your *password*. If you are a member of a network, you must use the exact user name and password assigned to you by your network administrator; if you are not sure what to enter in this dialog box, ask your administrator. You should use the same user name and password each time you *log on* to Windows so that your desktop, applications, and customization settings will always be the same. By default, Windows displays the Log On dialog box if you're on a network. If you don't see a Log On dialog box, you don't have to enter a user name or password to work in Windows.

Boot   A term used to describe a computer's starting up process, during which the operating system and configuration files are loaded into the computer's memory.

User Name and Password   Identifies you to your computer or to the network server, and protects your computer from illegal entry.

Log On   Attaching to the network so you can use its resources—files, printers, and so on.

Follow these steps to open the Windows program if you're on a network:

1. Enter the following information:

User Name   The name by which you are identified to your computer or the network.

Password   Your personal watchword for logging in to the computer or network.

2. Press **Enter** or click **OK** to start Windows.

Error Message!   Many different errors could occur at this point. For example, a message might appear on your screen telling you a connection could not be restored or that you're not a valid user. First, make sure you've typed your password correctly and used the appropriate case when typing. If you still have a problem connecting to the network, see your network administrator for help.

For more information on working with Windows in a networked environment, see Part VI, "Networking and Mobile Computing with Windows 98."

TIP **Should I Press Enter or Click OK?** Pressing Enter in a dialog or message box is the same as choosing the OK button; pressing the Escape key is the same as choosing the Cancel button.

Understanding the Windows Desktop

After Windows 98 starts, you will see various items on the screen, as shown in Figure 2.1. The items you see enable you to open applications, manage files, send and receive mail, and perform many other tasks throughout your work day. Depending on your installation, you may or may not see all of the items shown in the following figure. If you upgraded from Windows 95, you may see additional icons on your Desktop.

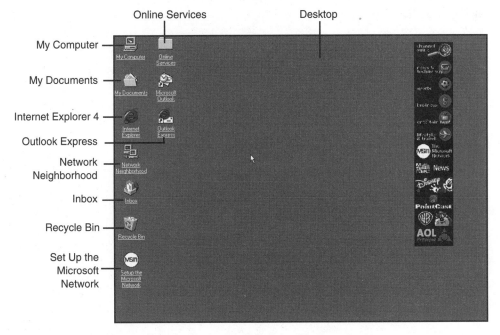

Figure 2.1 Common components of the Windows screen.

The components of the Windows screen include:

- **Desktop** This is the background on which all other elements appear. You can think of the Windows desktop like the top of your own traditional office desk. Just as you can move papers around, hide certain items in drawers, and add and remove things on your desk, you can manipulate items on your Windows desktop.

- **Icons**   Icons arepictures that represent programs (the Internet, Word for Windows, Excel, and so on), folders, files, printer information, computer information, and so on, in both Windows 98 and programs designed to run under Windows. Most often, you use icons to open folders and files.

- **My Computer**   The My Computer icon represents the contents of your computer, including the hard drive, floppy and CD drives, applications, folders, files, and so on. Double-click an icon to open it and view its contents.

- **Network Neighborhood**   This icon displays other computers connected to your computer on a Microsoft or other type of network, such as NT or NetWare.

- **Outlook Express**   The Outlook Express program works with Internet Explorer and allows you to send email, participate in chat groups, and work in newsgroups over the Internet.

- **Recycle Bin**   The Recycle Bin is a place in which deleted objects remain until you empty the trash. You can retrieve items—files, programs, pictures, and so on—from the Recycle Bin after you delete them. Once you empty the trash, however, you can no longer retrieve items from the bin.

- **Online Services**   This folder icon enables you to quickly and easily sign up for any of the online services it contains, including America Online, AT&T WorldNet, and CompuServe. You must have a modem connected to your computer and configured before using one of these services.

- **Set Up**   The Microsoft Network is a step-by-step guide to configuring your computer and connecting to Microsoft's special Internet network. Again, you need a modem to use this feature.

- **Taskbar**   The taskbar contains the Start button, any open application or window buttons, and the time. You can click a taskbar button to open the window or application it represents. Use the Start button to open programs, documents, help, and so on.

- **Start Button**   The Start button displays a menu from which you can choose to open an application, open a document, customize Windows, find a file or folder, get help, or shut down the Windows 98 program.

- **Folder** A folder contains files, programs, or other folders on your computer; for example, the Online Services folder contains programs that let you sign up for an online service like CompuServe. A folder is the same thing as a directory.

- **Pointer** The pointer is an on-screen icon (usually an arrow) that represents your mouse, trackball, touchpad, or other selecting device. You use it to select items and choose commands. You move the pointer by moving the mouse or other device across your desk or mouse pad. You learn how to use the mouse in the next section.

Using the Mouse

You use the mouse to perform many actions in Windows and in Windows applications. With the mouse, you can easily select an icon, folder, or window, among other things. Selecting involves two steps: pointing and clicking. You can move an item by clicking and dragging it.

To point to an object (icon, taskbar, Start button, and so on) move the mouse across your desk or mouse pad until the on-screen mouse pointer touches the object. You can pick up the mouse and reposition it if you run out of room on your desk. To click, point the mouse pointer at the object you want to select, and then press and release the left mouse button. If the object is an icon or window, it opens. When following steps in this book, click the left mouse button unless the directions specify otherwise.

The right mouse button can be used when you want to display a shortcut, or a quick menu. To right-click, point the mouse pointer at an object—folder, taskbar, desktop, and so on—and click the right mouse button. A shortcut menu that presents common commands relating to the object appears. If, for example, you right-click a folder, the menu might offer these commands: Open, Explore, Create Shortcut, and Properties. The items on the menu depend on the object you're right-clicking.

When you double-click an item, you point to the item and press and release the left mouse button twice quickly. Double-clicking is often a shortcut to performing a task. Double clicking is usually reserved for use within Windows applications, such as Word or Excel.

You can use the mouse to move an object (usually a window, dialog box, or icon) to a new position on-screen. You do this by clicking and dragging the object. To drag an object to a new location on-screen, point to the object, press and hold the left mouse button, move the mouse to a new location, and release the mouse button. The object moves with the mouse cursor as you drag it. If you want some practice with the mouse, open the Solitaire game and play a round or two; choose Start, Programs, Accessories, Games, and then Solitaire. Solitaire will also help you practice double-clicking. If Solitaire is not installed on your computer and if you have the Windows 98 installation CD, you can add Solitaire to your games list. To learn how to install programs, see Part III, Lesson 5, "Adding and Removing Software and Hardware."

You also can perform certain actions, such as selecting multiple items or copying items, by performing two additional mouse operations. Shift+click means to press and hold the Shift key and then click the left mouse button while pointing to various objects; Ctrl+click means to press and hold the Ctrl key, and then click the left mouse button. The result of either of these actions depends upon where you are in Windows.

Using the Start Button

The Windows Start button provides access to programs and documents, the help feature, find feature, and many other elements in Windows 98. You use the Start button to perform most tasks in Windows.

To use the Start button, follow these steps:

1. Point the mouse at the **Start** button, located on the taskbar, and click the button. The Start menu appears (see Figure 2.2). Your Start menu may display more options than the one in the figure, depending on what is installed on your computer.

2. Click the task or command you want to display, as follows:

   - **Windows Update**   A shortcut (you must have Internet Access) to the Microsoft Web site where you can learn what's new with Windows 98, download updated files and seek technical support.

   - **Programs**   Displays a submenu (also called a "cascading" or "secondary" menu) that includes Windows Accessory programs, Online Services, the Internet Explorer, and other programs on your computer.

- **Favorites**   Displays Web sites or programs you add to the Favorites folder, making access to those pages quick.

- **Documents**   Displays up to 15 of the most recently opened documents; for quick and easy access, click the document name and the application. The document opens, ready to work.

- **Settings**   Displaysa secondary menu that includes the Control Panel and Printers folders, and the taskbar command for customizing your Windows setup. For more information, see Part III, "Customizing and Maintaining Windows 98."

- **Find**   Enables you to search for specific files, folders, or computers. You can search your own hard drive, a network drive, or the Internet. You can also search your address books to locate a person using the People selection.

- **Help**   Displays help for performing tasks and procedures in Windows as well as finding Windows Help on the Internet. For more information, see Lesson 5.

- **Log Off**   Allows you to log off or on to Windows 98 so that another user can log on.

- **Run**   Enables you to enter a command line (such as a:\install) to run a program from hard, floppy, or CD disks.

- **Shut Down**   Displays the Shut Down dialog box in which you prepare your computer before turning it off.

- **Eject and Suspend**   If you are running Windows 98 on a laptop with a docking station you may see the additional items, Eject and Suspend. To learn more about these Start Menu items, see Part VI, "Networking and Mobile Computing with Windows 98."

 TIP   **Submenu**   An arrow after any menu command designates another menu, called a submenu (or sometimes a "cascading" or "secondary" menu). It will appear if you choose that command. Windows supplies as many as four submenus starting from the Start menu.

For more information about using menus, see Lesson 3. To learn how to customize the Start Menu see Part III, Lesson 4, "Customizing the Start Menu."

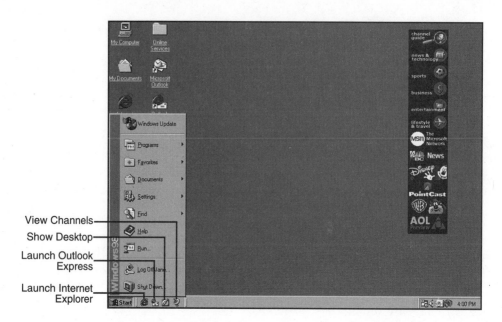

View Channels
Show Desktop
Launch Outlook
Express
Launch Internet
Explorer

Figure 2.2 The Start menu provides easy access to programs.

Using the Taskbar

In addition to the Start button, the TaskBar contains a Quick Launch toolbar as shown in Figure 2.3. The Quick Launch toolbar contains four items that act as shortcuts, eliminating the need to use the Start menu to launch programs or to create shortcuts on your desktop:

- Launch Internet Explorer Browser: Launches Internet Explorer 4.
- Launch Outlook Express: Launches Outlook Express.
- Show Desktop: Launch Outlook ExpressMinimizes all open programs and windows. Once clicked, the button remains depressed. Click the depressed button to restore all windows and programs.
- View Channels: Launches Internet Explorer 4 Channels.

Figure 2.3 The Quick Launch toolbar can launch Internet Explorer, Outlook Express, or Channels, or it can be used to minimize all open windows and programs.

The taskbar also displays buttons representing open windows and applications. You can quickly switch between open windows by clicking the button on the taskbar. Figure 2.4 shows the taskbar with three buttons representing open and minimized programs—Microsoft Word and two Network Neighborhood windows.

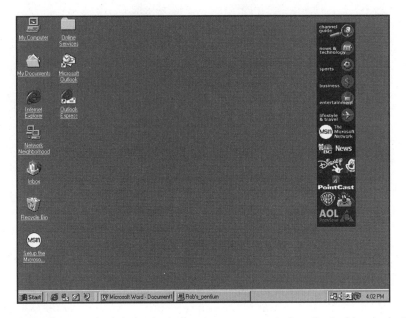

Figure 2.4 Open and minimized windows are represented on the taskbar by buttons and the window's name.

You can move the taskbar to the top, left, or right side of the screen to customize your workspace. Additionally, you can hide the taskbar until you need it.

To move the taskbar, click the mouse anywhere on the bar—except on a button—and drag the taskbar to the right, the left, or the top of the screen. As you drag, the taskbar relocates to that area. You can easily drag the taskbar back to the bottom if you prefer it there.

To hide the taskbar, follow these steps:

1. Click the **Start** button.
2. From the Start menu, click **Settings** and then click **Taskbar**.
3. Choose the **Auto Hide** check box by clicking that box; then press Enter to close the dialog box. The taskbar slides off of the screen.

19

When you need the taskbar, move the mouse to where the taskbar last appeared; you may have to slide the mouse off of the screen. The taskbar reappears.

CAUTION

I Can't Display the Taskbar! If you move the mouse to where the taskbar should be and the taskbar doesn't display, press **Ctrl+Esc** to display the taskbar and open Start menu. On newer keyboards, you can press the windows key.

To show the taskbar all the time, click **Start**, **Settings**, **Taskbar** and click the **Auto Hide** check box so no check mark appears. Press **Enter** to close the dialog box. For more on working with the taskbar, see Part III, Lesson 4 "Customizing the Taskbar."

Shutting Down Windows 98

Before you turn off your computer, you must shut down Windows to ensure you don't lose any data or configuration. You also can shut down Windows and restart the computer, in Windows 98 or MS-DOS mode. Following are the Shut Down options available to you in the Shut Down Windows dialog box:

- **Shut Down the Computer** Choose this option when you're finished using your computer for the day. When Windows displays a message telling you to shut off your computer, you can safely turn off the machine.

- **Restart the Computer** Choose this option to shut down and then restart the computer in Windows mode. You use this option when you've changed configuration in the Control Panel, for example, and you want that configuration to take effect.

- **Restart the Computer in MS-DOS Mode** This option shuts down Windows and starts the computer back in DOS mode, with a black screen, white type, and a C-prompt, or command prompt. From the command prompt, you can enter many familiar DOS commands or install DOS applications. For more information on DOS, see Appendix B, "DOS and Legacy Applications."

- **Cancel** Choose if you change your mind and do not want to restart the computer.

CAUTION

Soft shutdown   Before you turn off your computer, always shut down Windows 98 by clicking the Start button and choosing Shut Down. This results in a safe shutdown and helps to prevent files from being corrupted or damaged.

To shut down Windows, follow these steps:

1. From the Desktop, click **Start, Shut Down**.

2. When the Shut Down Windows dialog box appears, choose one of the options previously described. To quit working on the computer, choose Shut Down the Computer. Then choose **Yes**.

3. Do not turn the computer off until Windows displays the message telling you that it's okay to turn off your computer (some computers turn off automatically, so this message isn't displayed).

In this lesson, you learned to start and shut down Windows, work with the parts of the Windows desktop, and use a mouse to manipulate items on the desktop. In the next lesson, you learn to work with windows.

Working with a Window

In this lesson, you learn to open, resize, move, view, and close a window, and how to use scroll bars to view more of a window.

What Is a Window?

A window is a boxed area in which you view programs, files, folders, drives, icons representing programs, files or folders, and other elements. Figure 3.1 shows a window in which a program is running (Microsoft Word). Figure 3.2 shows a window displaying the contents of a file folder—in this case, Microsoft Office and some of its components. Many of these components are the same for all windows in Windows 98 and Windows applications, which makes it easy for you to manage your work. Keep in mind that although most windows are similar, some will not have all of the following components.

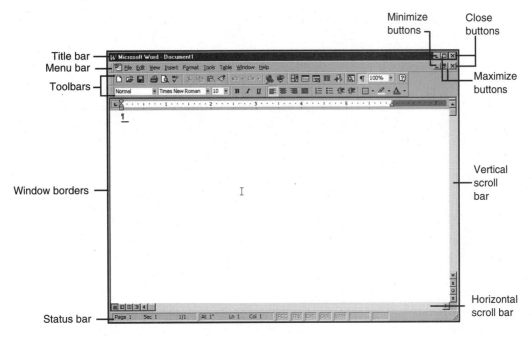

Figure 3.1 Microsoft Word running in a window.

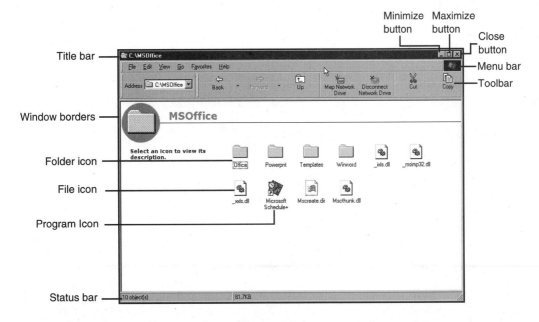

Figure 3.2 A window displaying the contents of a folder.

Most windows can be opened, closed, sized, reduced, enlarged, moved, or positioned on the desktop. Whether a window is open to run a program or display the contents of a file or the elements of your computer, some window elements remain constant. Table 3.1 briefly describes the common elements of windows.

Table 3.1 Window Elements

Element	Description
Title bar	Contains the window's name, the Control menu, and the Minimize, Maximize or Restore, and Close buttons.
Menu bar	Contains menus with related commands and options that help you control the window and its contents. See additional information about menus in Part I, Lesson 4.
Control menu button	Contains menu commands that help you manage the window itself. Can be used in lieu of Mimimize, Maximize, Restore, and Close buttons. Can also be used to size and move a window.
Toolbar	Displays graphic tool buttons that represent shortcuts to various menu commands.
Minimize button	Reduces the window to a button on the taskbar.
Maximize button	Enlarges the window to full screen.
Close button	Closes the window and, if a program is running in the window, exits the program.
Folders	Icons within windows that represent directories; folders can hold other folders and files.
Files	Icons representing documents, spreadsheets, databases, program files, and other files stored in folders on a drive or floppy disk.
Windows border	A rim around a window that you can use to resize the window.
Status bar	A bar across the bottom of the window that describes the contents of the window, such as free space, number of objects or files in a window, and so on.
Scroll bar	A vertical or horizontal bar that enables you to move the internal viewing area of a window.

CAUTION

No Toolbar or Status Bar Showing? If a window doesn't display the toolbar, choose **View**, **Toolbar**; to display the Status bar, choose **View**, **Status Bar**.

Windows Contents

Windows 98 is made up of a series of windows that often contain different items. When opened, each icon on your desktop, for example, displays different contents just as various folders, files, and applications display various contents. Additionally, after you open a window, you can usually open items within the window, such as icons, folders, programs, and documents. Often, you can open a window within a window within a window, and so on, until your desktop is filled with windows. Be aware, however, that having a lot of windows open (especially program windows) may slow down the operation of your computer.

Following is an example of a set of windows you can open from the My Computer icon:

- **My Computer window** Displays hard drive icons, floppy disk and CD icons, the Control Panel folder, and the Printers folder. Often this window also includes the Dial-Up Networking icon.
- **Hard drive icon** Displays all folders (or directories) on that drive, plus any files found on the root directory (usually C).
- **Program Files folder** Displays folders representing programs included with Windows, such as Accessories, Internet Explorer, Online Services, and so on.
- **Internet Explorer folder** Includes the Internet Explorer program and files needed to run the program, plus several text files you can read to get more information about Internet Explorer.

Opening a Window

To open a window from an icon, click the icon. For example, point to the My Computer icon and click. If you do it correctly, the My Computer icon opens into the My Computer window.

There is another method you can use to open a window. Just point to the icon and right-click once, and a shortcut menu appears. Select Open from the menu to open the window.

Sizing a Window with Maximize, Minimize, and Restore

You may want to increase the size of a window to see its full contents, or you may want to decrease a window to a button on the taskbar in order to make room for other windows. One way to resize a window is to use the Maximize, Minimize, and Restore commands found on the Control menu. If you use the mouse, you will use the Maximize, Minimize, and Restore buttons located at the right end of the window's title bar. The Restore button and the Maximize button will appear interchangeably on the title bar of a window. For example, if you maximize a window, the Restore button replaces the Maximize button, and you can then minimize or restore a window (see Figure 3.3). If you restore a window, the Maximize button replaces the Restore button. Figure 3.3 displays the title bar of a maximized window. Figure 3.4 displays the title bar of a restored window.

Figure 3.3 When a window is maximized, the Restore button replaces the Maximize button.

Figure 3.4 When a window is restored, the Maximize button replaces the Restore button.

The buttons and commands work as described here.

Click the Maximize button, or command, to enlarge the window. A maximized window fills your entire screen, hiding any of the desktop in the background.

Click the Minimize button, or command, to reduce the window to a button on the taskbar.

Click the Restore button, or command, to return a window to the size it was before it was maximized

To maximize, minimize, or restore a window with the mouse, click the appropriate button in the title bar of the window. To maximize, minimize, or restore a window using the Control menu, follow these steps:

1. Click the Control menu button to open the window's **Control** menu; alternatively, press **Alt+Spacebar**.

2. Click the command (Restore, Minimize, or Maximize) you want to initiate. Alternatively, use the down arrow to move to and highlight the command, and then press Enter.

Sizing a Window's Borders

At some point, you'll need a window to be a particular size to suit your needs. For example, you might want to fit two or more windows on-screen at the same time. You can drag the window's frame, or border, to change the size of the window. A window's border appears only on a restored window, not on a maximized or minimized window.

To use the mouse to size a window's borders, follow these steps:

1. Place the mouse pointer on the portion of the border that you want to resize: left or right side, top or bottom. When the mouse is positioned correctly, it changes shape to a double-headed arrow.

   Use the vertical double-headed arrow (on the top or bottom of the window border) to resize the window's height by dragging the frame up or down.

   Use the horizontal double-headed arrow (on the left or right window border) to resize the window's width by dragging the frame left or right.

   Use the diagonal double-headed arrow (on any of the four corners of the window border) to resize the window's height and width proportionally by dragging the corner diagonally.

2. Click and drag the border toward the center of the window to reduce the size of the window, or away from the center to enlarge the window.

3. When the border reaches the desired size, release the mouse button.

Using Scroll Bars

Scroll bars appear along the bottom or the right edge of a window when the window contains more text, graphics, or icons than it can display.

Using scroll bars, you can move up, down, left, or right in a window (see Figure 3.5). Because all of the hard drive window's contents are not fully visible in the window, the scroll bars are present on the right side and the bottom of the window.

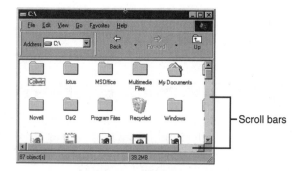

Figure 3.5   Use scroll bars to move within the window.

 TERM   **What Is a Scroll Bar?**   A scroll bar is a bar that contains three items: two scroll arrows and a scroll box. You use the scroll arrows and the scroll box to move around in the window, scrolling a line at a time, or even a page at a time.

The following steps show you how to use the scroll bars to view items not visible in the window:

1. To see an object that is down and to the right of the viewable area of the window, point at the down arrow located on the bottom of the vertical scroll bar.

2. Click the arrow, and the window's contents move up.

3. Click the scroll arrow on the right side of the horizontal scroll bar, and the window's contents shift to the left.

To drag the scroll box and move quickly to a distant area of the window (top or bottom, left or right), use this technique:

1. Point to the scroll box in the scroll bar and press and hold the left mouse button.

2. Drag the scroll box to the new location.

3. Release the mouse button.

Moving the scroll bar is a quick way to move through the contents of a window. To slow down the process, use a mouse click method and click the down or up arrows inside the scroll bar to move a line at a time.

Empty Windows?   Don't worry if text, graphics, or icons don't appear in a window. Use the scroll bar to bring them into view. Items in any window appear

CAUTION   first in the upper-left corner.

Moving a Window

When you start working with multiple windows, moving a window becomes as important as resizing one. For example, you may need to move one or more windows to make room for other work on your desktop, or you may need to move one window to see another window's contents. You can move a window easily with the mouse.

To move a window, point at the window's title bar, press and hold the left mouse button, and drag the window to its new location.

Viewing a Window's Contents

By default, Windows displays the contents of a window in icon form; for example, elements in the My Computer window are represented by pictures of a hard drive, floppy drive, and folders. Other windows, such as your hard drive window, display elements as folders and files.

Default   The initial settings of a program. In other words, how a program will look and respond without intervention on your part. Many program defaults can be changed. For example, in Microsoft Word you can change the default font or the default color scheme.

The default view for displaying *the contents of a window is *Large Icons*. You can change the default by selecting one of the following choices:

- **Small Icons**   Contents are displayed with a small icon next to the file or folder name; small icons represent the application in which a file was created, a folder, or an executable program.
- **List**   Similar to small icons, but the icons are even smaller.
- **Details**   Lists icon, file or folder name, file size, file type, and last date modified. When in Details view, you can click the heading button—Name, Size, Type, or Modified—to automatically sort the contents by that heading. For example, when you click Name, folders list in alphabetical order followed by file names listed alphabetically.

Figure 3.6 shows four windows, each with a different view of the window's contents: Large Icons, Small Icons, Details, and List. Please note that you cannot re-create this image on your screen without customizing your Windows 98 defaults. By default, Windows 98 will display only one window at a time while you are viewing the contents of My Computer and will not open four windows as shown in Figure 3.6. See Part III, "Customizing and Maintaining Windows 98," for more information on changing the defaults in Windows 98.

To change the view of a window's contents, click the View menu and then select Large Icons, Small Icons, List, or Details.

When you're finished working with a window, you should close it. This often helps speed up Windows, conserve memory, and keep your desktop from becoming cluttered.

To close a window, you can do any of the following:

- Click the Control menu button and choose Close.
- Click the Close button in the title bar.
- Press **Alt+F4**.
- Choose **File**, **Close**.
- Double-click the window's Control menu button.

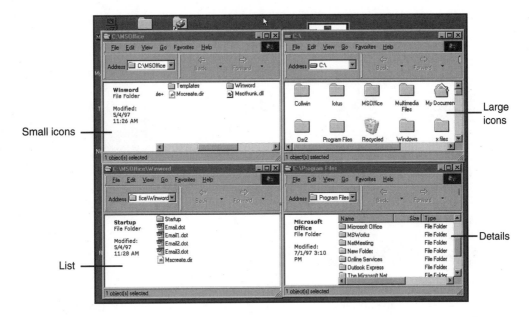

Figure 3.6   Display the contents of a window in a different view so you can easily identify files or folders.

   Quickie Close   To quickly close several related open windows, hold the Shift key while clicking the Close button on the last window you opened.

Closing Windows in Applications   These methods of closing Windows apply when you close other programs, such as Word or Lotus 1-2-3, with some small differences. **File**, **Close** will close a file or document, keeping the program opened. All of the other keystrokes described will close the actual application.

In this lesson, you learned to open, resize, move, view, and close a window, and how to use scroll bars to view more of a window. In the next lesson, you will learn to use menus and toolbar buttons.

Using Menus

In this lesson, you learn how to use toolbar buttons, select menus, open menus, choose menu commands, and use menu shortcuts.

Using Toolbar Buttons

Most windows and Windows programs offer a toolbar containing various buttons you can use as shortcuts. Toolbar buttons represent common commands you often use in Windows, such as cut, copy, undo, and so on. The tools that are available to you depend on the window or application you're using. Figure 4.1 shows the toolbar for the My Computer window. By default, the icons are displayed on the toolbar with descriptive text beneath them. To learn more about the toolbar shown here, see Part II, Lesson 2, "Using My Computer."

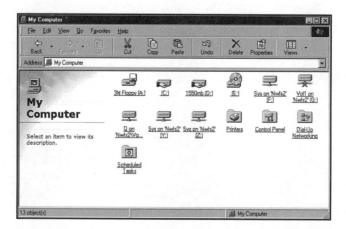

Figure 4.1 Use toolbar buttons to speed up your work.

To use a button, click it. Just like commands, any of a variety of results may occur. If, for example, you select a folder or file and choose the Copy button, a duplicate of the folder or file moves to the Windows Clipboard for pasting to another area later. For more information on using Cut, Copy, and Paste, see Part IV, Lesson 3, "Copying and Moving Information Between Windows." If you choose the Undo button, the last action you performed is reversed. You learn more about the buttons on toolbars throughout this book.

What Is a Menu?

A menu is a list of related commands that you use to perform tasks in Windows and in Windows applications (tasks such as copying or deleting selected items in a window). Menu commands are organized in logical groups. Menus are context-sensitive—that is, different menu options and different menus themselves will appear within the menu depending on the task you are currently performing. For example, if you haven't cut or copied text or files, the Paste command on the Edit menu is not available (it's grayed out). Once you have copied or cut something, the Paste command is available.

You find menus on the menu bar and you also see menu when you right-click an item. When you right-click an item, a shortcut menu pops up on the screen (hence the name pop-up menu). Shortcut menus are context-sensitive too, and depending on the program you are in and the item that you right-click, you will see different pop-up menus at different times.

Items on the menu bar, are organized to help you find the command you want. For example, all the commands related to arranging and opening windows are found on the Windows menu. Items that relate to editing functions, such as cut, copy, and paste, are found on the Edit menu. Opening files, closing windows, and exiting programs are options that are found on the File menu.

 Programs designed to run with Windows 98 (such as games, word processing, and other programs) follow the same layout of menu items. When File is a menu, it is always the first menu on the menu bar, and you will always find the option to exit the program on the File menu. When you can open more than one window within a program, the word Window appears on the menu bar. Help is usually the last item on the menu bar.

This book uses the format *menu title, menu command* to tell you
to choose a command from a menu. For example, the phrase "choose **File,
Properties**" means to open the File menu and select the Properties command.

 TERM   **Pull-Down Menu**   A menu that appears to "pull down" from the menu bar.
You access the menu by clicking its name in the menu bar. You then have
several options to choose from within the pull-down menu.

Choosing Menu Commands

To choose a menu command with the mouse, follow these steps:

1. Click the menu title in the menu bar. The menu opens to display the
available commands.

2. To choose a particular command, simply click it. For example, to see the
View commands available for the My Computer window, click the **View**
menu in the menu bar. The View menu appears (see Figure 4.2).

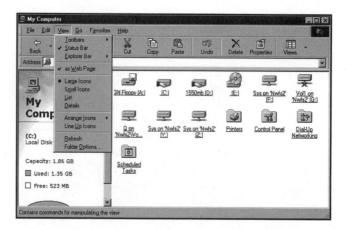

Figure 4.2   Click any menu to view its contents.

3. To make the menu disappear, click anywhere outside the menu.

To choose a command on the menu, move the mouse to that command and
click. What happens next depends on the menu and the command.

Want to Use the Keyboard? If you want to use the keyboard to choose menu commands, press the Alt key to activate the menu bar of the active window. Use the left and right arrow keys to highlight the menu you want; then use the up and down arrows to highlight the command you want. Press Enter to activate the highlighted command. You could, alternatively, press Alt + the underlined letter to activate a menu. Press Alt+F, for example, to open the File menu, and then press the underlined letter in the command you want to activate.

Reading a Menu

Windows menus contain a number of common elements that indicate what will happen when you choose a command, provide a shortcut, or limit your choice of commands. Some menus, for example, may contain commands that are dimmed or grayed out. However, most commands perform some sort of task when you select them.

CAUTION

Grayed-Out Commands If a command appears grayed out, you cannot currently use that command. Grayed-out commands are only available for use under certain circumstances. For example, you cannot choose the Copy command or the Delete command if you have not first selected an object to copy or delete.

Depending on the type of command you select, one of four things will happen:

- An action will take place. For example, choosing **File**, **Delete** erases the selected icon or file.
- A dialog box will appear. Any command followed by an ellipsis (...) displays a dialog box containing related options (see Part I, Lesson 6, "Using Dialog Boxes," for more information).
- A submenu will appear. A command followed by an arrow displays a second menu offering related commands.
- A feature will be turned on. A check mark or bullet appears to the left of the option on the menu, and that option remains active until you either select a different bulleted option in the same menu or deselect the checked option by clicking it a second time.

TIP   **Separator Lines Give You a Clue**   Commands on most menus are grouped and divided by separator lines. When bulleted option commands are grouped, you can select only one option in the group. When checked commands are grouped, you can choose as many or as few options as you want.

Figure 4.3 shows common menu elements: the ellipsis, the check mark, the option bullet, an arrow with a submenu, and a separator line.

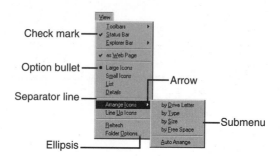

Figure 4.3   Indicators let you know what will happen before you select the command.

To practice using menu commands, follow these steps:

1. In the My Computer window, choose **View, Toolbars**. The Toolbar menu displays, showing you the options available for displaying toolbars. Items with check marks are currently selected. To select a new option, click it. To deselect an option, click it once, which removes the check mark.

2. Choose **View, Folder Options** (notice the ellipsis after the Options command). A dialog box appears. Click on each tabbed page in the dialog box to review folder options. To cancel the dialog box, choose the Cancel button.

Using Shortcut Keys Instead of Menus

Until you become familiar with Windows and your various Windows applications, you'll need to use the menus to view and select commands. However, after you've worked in Windows for a while, you'll probably want to use shortcut keys for commands you use often. Shortcut keys enable you to select commands without using the menus. Shortcut keys generally combine the Alt,

Ctrl, or Shift key with a letter key (such as W). If a shortcut key is available, it is listed on the pull-down menu to the right of the command.

For example, Figure 4.4 shows the Edit menu from the hard drive window on My Computer. As you can see, the shortcut key for Cut is Ctrl+X. You cannot use the shortcut key while the menu is open; you must either choose a command or cancel the menu. You can, however, remember the shortcut key and use it instead of opening the menu the next time you need to cut a file or folder.

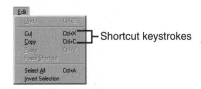

Figure 4.4   Use shortcut keys to save time.

Using Shortcut Menus

Windows supplies a variety of shortcut, or quick, menus that contain common commands you often use. You can display a shortcut menu by right-clicking an object such as the desktop, a window, a folder or file, and so on. The commands that a shortcut menu displays depend on the item and its location. These menus are also often referred to as pop-up menus.

To display and use a shortcut menu, point the mouse at the object you want to explore, cut, open, or otherwise manipulate, and right-click the mouse. The shortcut menu appears; move the mouse to the command and click again. Cancel a shortcut menu by clicking the mouse anywhere outside the menu.

Figure 4.5 displays a shortcut menu resulting from right-clicking the Windows 98 desktop.

In this lesson, you learned how to use toolbar buttons, open menus, choose menu commands, and use menu shortcuts. In the next lesson, you'll learn to access Help in Windows.

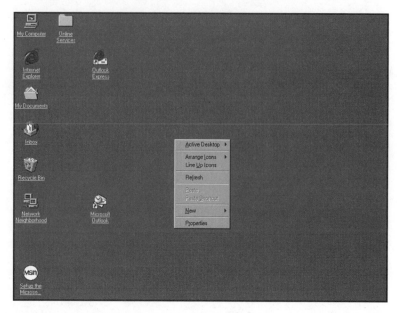

Figure 4.5   Quickly access a command with a right-click.

Using Windows 98 Help

In this lesson, you learn how to get help, use the Help feature's shortcut buttons, and use Web Help.

Getting Help in Windows 98

Windows 98 offers several ways to get online help—instant on-screen help for menu commands, procedures, features, and other items. Online help is information that appears in its own window whenever you request it. Windows 98 also features Web Help. If you are connected to the Internet, you can go directly to the Microsoft site, which has information on Windows 98, new features, tips and tricks, and so on.

Windows' Help feature offers four ways to seek help: Web Help, on-line Contents features, Index, and Search. To access Windows help in one of the following ways:

- Click the **Start** Button
- Press the **F1** key

TIP   Tutorial Help   Windows 98 includes an on-line tutorial program called the Windows 98 Getting Started Book. If you are new to Windows, you may want to take the time to look at this book. To access it, click the Start button and choose Help. Click the Contents tab and click Getting Started Book-Online help.

The Help Window

When you access Windows Help through the menu, the Windows Help screen appears. The toolbar includes five buttons: Hide, Back, Forward, Options, and Web Help. Table 5.1 describes each of these buttons.

Table 5.1   Windows Help Toolbar Buttons

Button	Description
Hide	Displays or hides the left pane of the Help window. The right pane (or preview pane) is always visible. If you hid the left pane, the icon changes to read "Show." Click Show, and the left pane reappears.
Back	Displays the previous page. Like a Web browser, the Back button will only work as far back as the first page you viewed when you opened the Windows Help program.
Forward	After you have clicked the Back button, the Forward button will move you ahead through pages you have viewed, in the order you have viewed them.
Options	Displays a menu containing the following commands: Back, Forward, Stop, Refresh, Customize, and Print.
Web Help	If you are connected to the Internet, Web Help will display the Microsoft Web site containing information and help for Windows 98.

Using Windows On-Line Help

Windows on-line help is designed to provide local (files found on your PC) help for using Windows 98. Three views are available within the Help program: the Contents, the Index, and the Search view.

The Contents view displays a list of topics, such as Introducing Window 98 and What's New in Windows 98. The Index feature enables you to access specific categories of topics—such as adapters, disk configuration, copying, and so on. Search lets you search for specific words and phrases—such as Copy, Memory, Printing, and so on.

Windows help text often contains links to other documents and more information. These links are identified by underlined text, and usually appear in blue on your screen. Click the underlined text to access additional information (see Figure 5.1).

 TIP **Setting Up Help** The first time you choose Search in Windows Help, Windows runs a Search Setup Wizard that compiles every word from the Help files into a database you will use to find subjects. Follow the directions, and the Wizard will guide you through this process.

 Fast Help In Windows 98, as well as within other programs such as Word and Excel, pressing the F1 screen will activate the Windows Help dialog box.

Using the Contents Feature

You can get help with common procedures using Help's Contents feature. The Contents feature displays a list of collapsed categories such as Welcome and Printing. Categories are represented by a closed book. To view the contents of a category, click once on the book. Expanded categories are represented by an open book. Documents or pages that contain help information are represented by a document with a question mark, as shown in Figure 5.1. When you click on a document, its contents display in the preview pane on the left of the screen.

Follow these steps to use Help's Contents feature:

1. Choose the **Start** button and then choose **Help**. The Windows Help window appears; select the Contents tab if it is not already selected.

 TIP **Pick a Tab** The last tab in the Help Topics window that you accessed is the one that appears the next time you open Help.

41

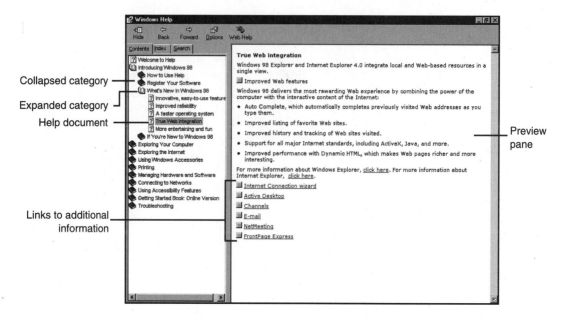

Figure 5.1   Click on a category (book) to expand it; click again to collapse the category.

2. In the Contents list, click the book icon in front of the topic you want to view. The book opens, and related topics appear in a list of books or documents.

3. Click a document icon to view information about that topic.

4. When you finish with the Help topic, you can choose one of the following buttons:

   - Close (X) to close the Help window and return to the Desktop
   - Back to display the previously viewed Help window
   - Options to print or otherwise set preferences for the Help window

Using the Index Feature

Help's Index feature provides a list of Help topics arranged alphabetically on the Index tab of the Help Topics window. You can enter a word for which you are searching, or you can scroll through the list to find a topic. Figure 5.2 shows the Index tab of the Help Topics: Windows Help dialog box.

To use the Help Index, follow these steps:

1. In the Windows Help window, click the Index tab.

2. Click in the text box located directly under the Index tab. Type the topic or word you want help with. As you type, Windows moves to the topics beginning with the first letters you enter.

3. Click the display button to view the topic information in the preview pane, as shown in Figure 5.2.

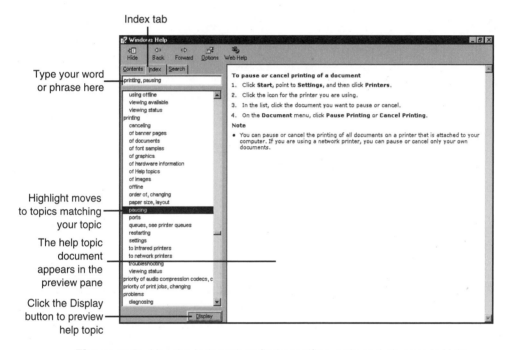

Figure 5.2 Use the Index tab to find specific words and phrases in Help.

 TIP   **Browse the List**   You can scroll through the index list to see what other topics are available.

4. In the list of topics, select the topic you want to view and choose Display, or simply double-click the topic. Display will either display a document in the preview screen or display a Topics Found window containing choices regarding your topic, as shown in Figure 5.3. If the dialog box appears, highlight a topic and click Display.

Figure 5.3 Depending on the topic you search for in Help, an interim Topics Found window may appear.

5. Depending on the topic you have chosen, the preview pane document will display the information you are seeking, or it may display information for obtaining more detailed data on your topic.

6. When you're finished with the Help topic, you can choose another option, or you can close the Help windomenu commands by pressing **Alt+F4**.

Using the Search Feature

To search for specific words and phrases within a Help topic instead of searching for a Help topic itself, use the Search feature. The Search feature requires that the Help database be indexed—that is, the text contained within the Help documents themselves can be searched. Therefore, the first time you use the Search feature you will need to instruct Windows to create a list that contains the words from your Help files. You only create this list once, and it could take a few moments. It might be a good idea to use Search and build the list before you actually need it. This way, when you are working on a project and need to search the database, you won't have to wait for the index to build.

The Search feature is especially useful when you cannot find a particular Help topic in Help Contents or on the Index tab's list of topics.

To use the Search feature, follow these steps:

1. In the Windows Help window, choose the Search tab. If you have used Search before, skip to step 3. If you haven't previously set up the Help topics, the Search Setup Wizard dialog box appears. Continue with these steps.

2. In the Search Setup Wizard dialog box, choose one of the following:

- Minimize Database Size creates a short, limited word list (recommended because it takes less hard disk space).

- Maximize Search Capabilities creates a long, detailed word list.

- Customize Search Capabilities enables you to create a shorter word list, including only the Help files you want to use. Use this option if you have limited disk space. If you select this option, choose Next, and then choose the topics you want to include.

3. Click the **Finish** button to create the word list.

When Windows finishes creating the word list, the Search tab contains a text box, a word list, and a topic list, as shown in Figure 5.4.

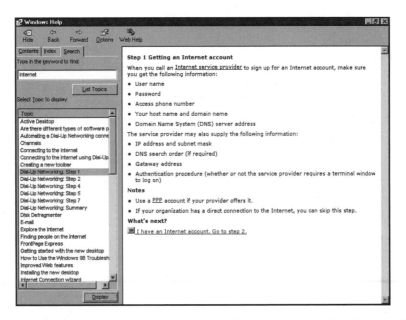

Figure 5.4 Search for words or phrases within Help documents using the Search feature.

To search for words or a phrase in Help, follow these steps:

1. Type the word or phrase you want to find in the keyword text box on the Search page. Then click the **List Topics** button or press **Enter**.

2. A list of available topics appears in the Topic pane (see Figure 5.4). Select the topic you wish to display and click the Display button.

TIP   **Topic List**   Instead of typing something in the text box, you can scroll through the word list and select the word you want from the list. If you want to find words similar to the words in a Help topic, click the Find Similar button.

3. When you finish with the Help topic, you can close the Help window or select another option, as described in the preceding section "Using the Index Feature."

CAUTION

Rebuild the List   If you don't want to use the first list that Windows creates, you're not stuck with it. You can rebuild the list to include more words or to exclude words. Click the Rebuild button and choose a word list option to re-create the word list.

Using Web Help

Web Help connects you to the Microsoft site containing help on Windows 98. Here, you find information not available in the Help files provided with Windows. Use this when you want to see the most current Windows 98 information. Don't use this for simple Help topics, such as how to minimize windows or copy files. To use Web Help, you must be connected to the Internet. For information on connecting to the Internet, see Part V, "Windows 98 and the Internet."

If you have an active connection to the Internet, access Web Help by clicking the Web Help button on the Windows Help toolbar. Ultimately, your Web broswer will open and you will be immediately connected to the Microsoft site. The Web page will be displayed in the preview pane of the Windows Help window, as shown in Figure 5.5.

Like all good Web sites, the Microsoft site updated frequently. Once the Windows Web Help page is displayed in the preview pane, follow the instructions on the Microsoft site page. As you move around the site, Web pages will be displayed in the preview pane, and your Windows Help window acts like a Web browser. For more information on using Web browsers, see Part V, "Windows 98 and the Internet."

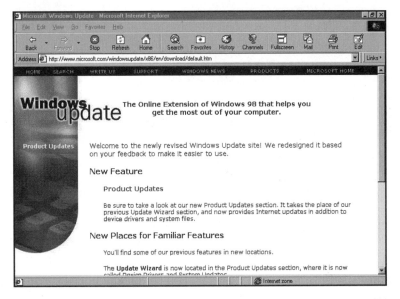

Figure 5.5   Using Web Help, you can surf the Microsoft Windows 98 Help site.

CAUTION

The first time you access Web Help, you may receive a security warning asking you to run "Registration Verification Control" for the Microsoft Corporation. You can learn more about security in Part V, "Windows 98 and the Internet." If you are unsure of what to do at the Security Warning dialog box, you can click the No button to bypass the dialog box.

In this lesson, you learned how to access Help and use Search, Contents, Index, and Web Help. In the next lesson, you'll learn to start and exit applications in Windows.

Using Dialog Boxes

In this lesson, you learn about dialog boxes and their components.

What Is a Dialog Box?

Windows and Windows applications use dialog boxes to exchange information with you. As you learned in Part I, Lesson 4, "Using Menus," a menu command followed by an ellipsis (…) indicates that a dialog box will appear. A dialog box asks for related information the program needs in order to complete the operation.

In this exchange of information, a dialog box may warn you about a problem (such as `File already exists, Overwrite?`) or confirm that an operation should take place (`In Are you sure you want to send "Shortcut to Printers" to the Recycle Bin?`) or provide check boxes or text boxes in which you give instructions.

TIP **Why Is My Computer Beeping at Me?**   If a dialog box won't go away and your computer beeps at you when you try to continue your work, don't worry. That beep is Windows' way of telling you that you must always respond to a dialog box before you can continue. You can press Enter or choose OK to accept the message or changes in the dialog box, or you can press the Esc key or choose Cancel to cancel the message or changes in the box.

Using the Components of a Dialog Box

Dialog boxes vary in complexity depending on the program, the procedure, and the number of options in the actual box. Some simply ask you to confirm an operation before it is executed; others ask you to choose, for example, a drive, folder, file name, file type, network path, or any of numerous other options.

The following list briefly explains the components of a dialog box. Not all dialog boxes contain all components. The dialog box in Figure 6.1 is from the Microsoft Word program. We chose this box for our example because it contains many of the components that can be found in dialog boxes, and to represent the fact that dialog boxes are found in Windows applications as well as in Windows 98 itself.

- **Text box**   A text box provides a place to type an entry, such as a file name, path (drive and directory), font, or measurement.
- **List box**   A list box presents a slate of possible options from which you can choose. Scroll bars often accompany a list box so you can view the items on the list. In addition, a text box is sometimes associated with a list box; you can either choose from the list or type the selection yourself.
- **Drop-down list box**   This box is a single-line list box with a drop-down arrow button to the right of it. When you click the arrow, the drop-down list box opens to display a list of choices. You can often scroll through a drop-down list as you do a list box.
- **Option buttons**   Option buttons present a group of related choices from which you can choose only one. Click the option button you want to select, and all others become deselected.
- **Check box**   A check box enables you to turn an option on or off. You might find a single check box or a group of related check boxes. A check mark appears in the box next to any option that is active (turned on). In a group of check boxes, you can choose none, one, or any number of the options.
- **What's This?**   The What's This? feature provides a handy way for you to get more information about dialog box options. You activate this feature by selecting the ? icon that appears at the right end of the title bar in some (but not all) Windows dialog boxes.

TIP **Dialog Box Options** Circles such as those found in option buttons are often referred to as radio buttons. When a dialog box presents radio buttons, you can select only one. Check boxes are square, and when they appear in dialog boxes, you may choose none, any, or all of the selections. This applies to all of Windows 98 and programs designed to run under Windows.

- **Command button** When selected, a command button carries out the command displayed on the button (Open, Help, Quit, Cancel, or OK, for example). If there is an ellipsis on the button (as in Option…), choosing it will open another dialog box.

- **Tabs** Tabs represent multiple sections, or pages, of a dialog box. Only one tab is displayed at a time, and each tab contains related options. Choosing a tab changes the options that appear in the dialog box.

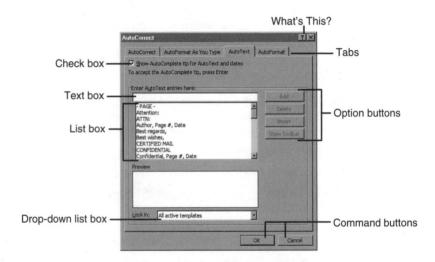

Figure 6.1 The components of a dialog box: Not all dialog boxes contain all components.

Using the What's This? Feature

The What's This? feature of dialog boxes is designed to supply a description of the options in a dialog box. For example, if a dialog box appears asking you to provide information in a text box and you aren't certain of the kind of information to supply, use the What's This? feature to help you.

The following steps tell you how to use the What's This? feature:

1. Click the ? icon in the upper-right corner of the Windows dialog box. A large question mark appears next to the mouse pointer, as shown in Figure 6.2.

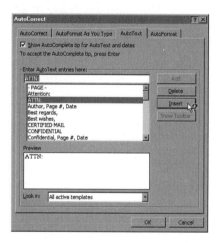

Figure 6.2   The mouse pointer changes to a question mark when you use the What's This? feature.

2. Click any option in the dialog box, and Windows displays a box containing a short description of the item you selected (see Figure 6.3).

51

Figure 6.3   What's This? provides additional descriptions and help for dialog box options.

3. When you finish reading the Help information, click anywhere on the screen to close the Help box.

Using Text Boxes

Use text boxes to enter the information that Windows or a Windows application needs in order to complete a command. This information might be a file name, folder name, measurement, style or font name, or other information related to the original menu and command. Figure 6.4 shows a text box and list boxes in the Open dialog box (accessed from the Windows WordPad File menu).

Figure 6.4   Use text boxes and list boxes to specify your preferences.

To activate a text box using the mouse, position the mouse over the text box (the mouse pointer changes to an I-beam) and click. The I-beam pointer shape indicates that the area you're pointing to will accept text. Look for the I-beam when you want to enter text in a dialog box. Notice that the insertion point (a flashing vertical line) appears in the active text box.

TIP **Save Time and Trouble** If you want to replace text that's already in a text box, drag your mouse I-beam over the text (to highlight text) and start typing. When you type the first character, the original text is deleted. Often when you first open a dialog box containing a text box, there is already text present and highlighted; if you start typing, you automatically delete the current text.

To activate a text box using the keyboard, press Alt+selection letter. (The selection letter is the underlined letter in a menu, command, or option name. The combination of Alt+selection letter is called a hotkey.) After you have activated a text box and typed text into it, you can use several keys to edit the text. Table 6.1 outlines these keys.

Table 6.1 Editing Keys for Text Boxes and Other Text

Key	Description
Delete	Deletes the character to the right of the insertion point
Backspace	Deletes the character to the left of the insertion point
End	Moves the insertion point to the end of the line
Home	Moves the insertion point to the beginning of the line
Arrow keys	Moves the insertion point one character in the direction of the arrow
Shift+End	Selects the text from the insertion point to the end of the line
Shift+Home	Selects the text from the insertion point to the beginning of the line
Shift+Arrow key	Selects the next character in the direction of the arrow
Ctrl+C	Copies the selected text to the Clipboard
Ctrl+V	Pastes the selected text from the Clipboard

Clipboard The Clipboard is a tool provided by Windows that holds any cut or copied text for you so you can paste it to another location, document, or application. For more information, see Part II, Lesson 3, "Managing Files with My Computer."

Using List Boxes

Use list boxes to select from multiple available options. For example, you use the Look in list box in the Open dialog box to select the drive that contains the file you want to open.

To select an item from a list box using the mouse, click the appropriate list item and click OK. You can also select more than one item in many list boxes by holding the Shift key as you click. The item you select automatically appears in the linked box above the list box.

 TIP

Quick Close Double-click an item in a list box to select the item and close the dialog box as if you had clicked OK.

To select an item from a drop-down list box, open the list box by clicking the down-arrow, and then click the appropriate item.

Using Option Buttons

Option buttons enable you to make a single choice from a group of possible command options. For example, the Print Range options displayed in Figure 6.5 enable you to choose which pages of your document you want to print. The active option (the All option in Figure 6.5) has a filled-in circle. The figure is from WordPad using the **File**, **Print** command.

To select an option button, click the circle for the option you want. (If you have trouble pointing into the circle, click the accompanying text instead.)

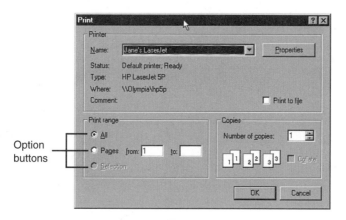

Option buttons

Figure 6.5 You can choose only one option in a group.

Using Check Boxes

For options that you can select (activate) or deselect (deactivate), Windows and Windows applications usually provide check boxes. When a check box is selected, an X or a check mark appears in the box, indicating that the associated option is active (see Figure 6.6). This figure is from WordPad using the **Format**, **Font** command.

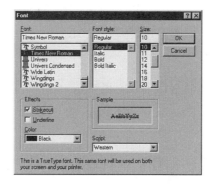

Figure 6.6 A check mark indicates the active, or selected, option.

To select or deselect a check box, click the box.

Using Command Buttons

You use command buttons to either accept or reject the changes you've made in a dialog box, to get help, or to access another related dialog box. To select a command button, simply click it.

Figure 6.7 shows the two most common command buttons: OK and Cancel. Select the **OK** command button to accept the information you have entered or to verify an action and close the dialog box. Select the **Cancel** command button to leave the dialog box without putting into effect the changes you made in the dialog box.

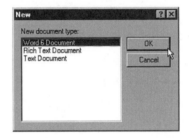

Figure 6.7   Common command buttons.

 TIP   **Quick and Easy**   You can press the Enter key in a dialog box to quickly accept the changes and close the dialog box. Similarly, you can press the Esc key to cancel the changes made to the dialog box and close the box at the same time.

 CAUTION   **Look Before You Click**   If you accidentally select the Cancel command button in a dialog box, don't worry. You can always reenter the changes to the dialog box and continue. However, you need to be more careful when you select OK in a dialog box. The instructions you enter in the dialog box will be executed, and changing them back may be a bit harder than canceling changes.

 TIP   **Close Means Cancel**   Choosing the Close button in a dialog box is the same thing as canceling it.

Using Property Sheets and Tabs

As noted previously, property sheets are similar to dialog boxes in the components they contain: check boxes, list boxes, text boxes, command buttons, and so on. Figure 6.8 shows the Taskbar Properties sheet.

Figure 6.8 Choose a tab that represents the options you want to change.

In a property sheet containing more than one tab, choose options within the sheet and then click the Apply button to accept the changes. Depending on the properties box you are working in, after you click Apply, you can then select the other tabs and make other changes, or the choices are applied and the dialog box closes. Once you've chosen the Apply button, however, you cannot cancel those changes using the Cancel command button; you must go back to the tab and change the options.

To select a tab, click it with the mouse pointer.

In this lesson, you learned how to use the various dialog box components.

Working with Files, Folders, and Disks

File Management in Windows 98

In this lesson, you'll find out how to organize your files and folders on your hard drive, just as you would organize your paperwork in a file cabinet.

Categorizing Your Files

When you install Windows-based software, the installation program creates a folder (directory) for the program to reside in on your hard drive. Microsoft Office, for example, is automatically placed in a folder called "Microsoft Office." This is done to keep the software separate from other programs you may have loaded on your computer. Figure 1.1 shows the contents of the Microsoft Office folder as viewed in the Windows Explorer. For more information on using Windows Explorer, see Part II, Lesson 7, "Managing Files with Explorer."

When you create a document, spreadsheet, database, or any other type of file, you determine where it will reside on your hard drive when you save it. If you have Office 97 installed, Office 97 creates a default folder called "My Documents." When you save a document using one of the Windows 97 products, such as Word or Excel, those documents will be saved in the "My Documents" folder unless you instruct the program otherwise. With or without this folder, you may want to create more folders for your files. Some examples:

- **Categorize your files by software**   You can create folders to store your files based on the software used to create them. For example, a folder called "Documents" to store files created with your word processor, "Spreadsheets" for files created with your spreadsheet software, and so forth. Figure 1.2 shows an example of this categorization method.

Figure 1.1   The Microsoft Office folder.

Figure 1.2   Explorer view—folders by software type.

- **Categorize your files by date**   If you track your sales and general business activity by quarter, you can create folders for all four quarters of the year, and place subfolders inside them, for each month in the quarter (see Figure 1.3).

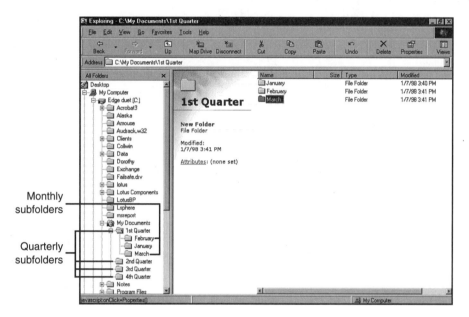

Monthly subfolders

Quarterly subfolders

Figure 1.3   Explorer view—folders by date.

- **Categorize your files by client name**   If you sell to a few major customers, create a folder for each one, and then store any documents, spreadsheets, and other files for a particular client in that client's folder. Figure 1.4 shows a set of four client folders. If you have a group of less-active clients, you can store all the files pertaining to them in a "catchall" folder entitled "Misc Clients," for example.

Creating Folders

If you were creating a new folder for your paperwork in a file cabinet, you'd write a name or phrase on the tab of a manila folder, and put the papers in it. You might write "1st Quarter" or "Letters" on the tab, and that would tell you what to put in it, and help you find your paperwork later. Creating folders in Windows 98 is similar.

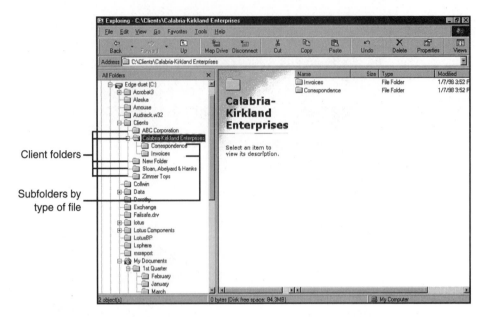

Client folders —

Subfolders by
type of file

Figure 1.4   Explorer view—folders by client name.

Use either My Computer or Explorer to create a new folder:

1. Be sure that you're in the folder that will contain your new folder. You can
   check the title bar, **Address** box, or the folder icon in the Folder pane to
   determine which folder is open.

2. From the **File** menu, choose **New, Folder**. A folder icon appears in the
   window (or in the Contents [right] pane in Explorer) with a box around it
   and the text "New Folder" highlighted.

 TIP   **Right-Clicking to Create Folders**   When you right-click in an open folder
window or on the Windows 98 desktop, a shortcut menu appears. Choose **New,
Folder**.

3. Type the name you want for your new folder. The text you type replaces
   the text "New Folder." Windows 98 allows you to use up to 255 characters,
   including spaces, for your folder's name. You may not use any of the
   following characters, which have special meaning to the operating system:
   \ / : * ? " < > |. Windows 98 usually warns you that you can't use these
   characters if you accidentally include one in your folder name.

4. Press Enter. Your new folder, with the name you assigned it, now appears in the window.

TIP **What if I Put the Folder in the Wrong Place?** That's easy to fix! Click and hold the mouse on the folder you want to move, and drag it to the folder that you want to place it in. When the target folder highlights, release the mouse. Or, if the mistake was just made and the new folder is still empty, delete the new folder and re-create it in the right place.

Looking at Folders

To see the contents of a folder, click on it. A window appears with the contents of the folder displayed.

You can view the icons in the window a number of ways, as shown in Figure 1.5. These views are available as choices on the **View** menu, or to cycle through the different views keep clicking on the View icon on the toolbar until the folders are displayed in the view you want. The available views are:

- **Large icons** show the icons scattered in the window. Only the names of the files or folders appear below the icons.
- **Small icons** show the icons in reduced size, lined up in rows alphabetically.
- **List** looks like small icons except that it's organized vertically.
- **Details** displays small icons listed vertically, with each row providing information on the size (in kilobytes) of the file, the type of file or folder, and the date and time last modified. You can click the column headers to sort the files by the information in that column. Click once for ascending order (A–Z) and again for descending order (Z–A).

The icons are generally shown in alphabetical order, but you can change the order. Choose **View, Arrange Icons** and select the order you want: **By Drive Letter**, **By Name**, **By Type** (file type), **By Size** for files (in kilobytes), **By Free Space** for drives, **By Date**, or **Auto Arrange** to let Windows 98 arrange them for you.

If you accidentally move the icons around and you want them put in straight lines again (especially in the large icon view), choose **View, Line Up Icons**. This option is only available for the Large Icon and Small Icon views.

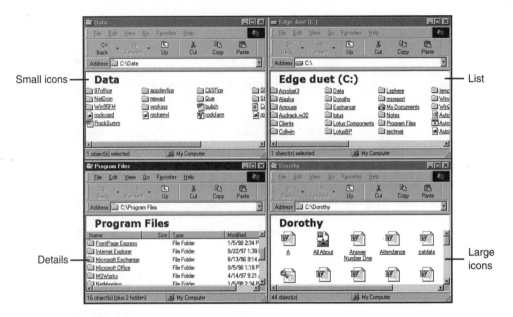

Small icons

List

Details

Large icons

Figure 1.5 The four ways to view icons.

If you make changes to the folder you're viewing and they haven't appeared yet, choose **View, Refresh** to bring the window up to date.

To learn more about creating and viewing foldf-s, see Part II, Lesson 3, "Managing Files with My Computer," and Lesson 7, "Managing Files with Explorer."

In this lesson you learned the basics of organizing your files into folders and viewing what each folder contains. In the next lesson, you'll learn about working with My Computer.

Using My Computer

In this lesson, you learn about My Computer: what it is, how to browse files, what's on the menu, how to use the toolbar, how to open drives and folders, and how to work with more than one window open at a time.

What Is My Computer?

My Computer is a way to quickly see everything on your computer—files, folders, and drives—and how files and folders are organized.

To open My Computer, click its icon on the desktop (see Figure 2.1).

 — My Computer icon

Figure 2.1   The My Computer icon on the desktop.

 TIP   **My Window Doesn't Have All Those Things!**   The icons that appear in the My Computer window vary from computer to computer. Depending on what components are installed on your computer, you may see different icons than those shown in Figure 2.2.

When you click the My Computer icon, the My Computer window appears (see Figure 2.2).

Some of the icons in the My Computer window represent drives; in this case, A: represents the floppy drive, C: the computer's hard drive, and D: the CD-ROM drive. Your driver letters might be assigned differently. Icons for those items will also appear in this window.

Figure 2.2 The My Computer window.

There are also icons within folders. The Control Panel icon opens the Control Panel window. You use the icons in that window to configure your computer. For more information on using the Control Panel, see Part III, Lesson 1, "Understanding the Control Panel."

The Printers icon opens the Printers window. Use the icons in that window to control print jobs and set up new printers. For information on installing printers, see Part III, Lesson 13, "Printing in Windows 98."

In Figure 2.2 you also see a Dial-Up Networking folder icon. Use that icon when you want to connect one computer to another using a modem. For more information on dialing into another computer, see Part VI, Lesson 8 "Connecting to a Network from a Remote Location."

At the top of the window is the *title bar*, which indicates the name of the currently opened window, drive, or folder. You can move the entire window on your screen by dragging the title bar.

Beneath the title bar is the *menu bar*, which contains the options available for this drive or folder.

Below the menu bar is the *toolbar*. If your toolbar is not showing, choose **View, Toolbars, Standard Buttons** from the menu. The toolbar contains icons to quickly execute common commands used in My Computer.

The *address bar* appears below the toolbar. The address bar shows your current path and location. A *path* is a roadmap showing the location of a file. For more information about DOS, paths, and naming conventions, see Appendix B, "DOS and Legacy Applications."

The address bar can also indicate a Web page address or URL (Uniform Resource Locator). If you enter a Web page address, you can view a Web page without opening your Web browser. For more information on viewing Web pages in My Computer, See Part V, Lesson 15, "Web Integration and My Computer/Windows Explorer."

To turn the display of the address bar on or off, choose **View, Toolbars, Address Bar** from the menu.

 Path The path is the full name of a file combined with the drive letter, folder, and subfolders that make up its specific location. For example, the spreadsheet file JanTax.xls is located in the January subfolder of the 1st Quarter folder, which is a subfolder of the My Documents folder that resides on the C: drive. The full path for this file is C:\My Documents\1st Quarter\January\JanTax.xls.

At the bottom of the screen is the *status bar*. In My Computer, the status bar displays the number of objects (files and folders) and the size (disk space) of those objects. If you are connected to a network, the Status bar displays a message indicating your connection, such as "local intranet zone." If you select one or more files, the status bar changes to display the number of selected files and the total number of bytes or storage space they use. If you don't see the status bar on your window, choose **View, Status Bar** from the menu.

There are several ways to open the drives or folders displayed in My Computer:

- Click the drive or folder icon.
- Select the drive or folder icon by pointing to it or using the arrow keys to move around the window to highlight the icon you want. Press **Enter** to open the highlighted drive or folder.
- Select the drive or folder icon by pointing to it or using the arrow keys to move around the window to highlight the icon you want. Choose **File, Open**.
- Point at the drive or folder icon and click the right mouse button. From the pop-up menu, select **Open**.

TIP **Starting Programs** You can start programs from My Computer by clicking the program icon.

Opening Files Files saved by applications (such as word processing documents or spreadsheets) also bear a program icon with a piece of paper behind it. If you click one of these file icons, you'll start up the program with that document opened and ready for work.

Viewing Files If you have installed QuickView (an optional install component of Windows 98), you can double click a file to view its contents quickly without launching the program.

When you click one of the drive icons in the My Computer window, another window appears showing a listing of folders and files for that drive (see Figure 2.3). The My Computer window remains open but the new window is the *active* window.

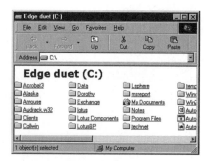

Figure 2.3 The window for the hard drive (C:).

To switch between open windows:

- To switch quickly to another window, click whatever portion of it you can see to make it the active window and bring it to the top.

- Each open window is represented by an icon on the taskbar. Click the icon for the window you want to see.

- Hold down the **Alt** key and press **Tab** to bring up the switching window (see Figure 2.4). Each time you press Tab, it cycles to the next window. Release the Alt key when the title of the window you want to see appears in the switching window.

Figure 2.4   The switching window.

Should you practice opening windows and end up with many windows open, try one of these skills to reduce the clutter on your screen:

- Close any unnecessary windows by choosing **File, Close** or by clicking the Close button on the title bar.
- Minimize any windows you don't need immediately but don't want to close by clicking the Minimize button on the title bar. The minimized windows are represented by icons on the taskbar, and you can click the appropriate icon to open the window again.
- To see more than one window at the same time, point at a blank area of the taskbar and click the right mouse button. From the pop-up menu, choose **Cascade Windows** to see the all the open windows piled on top of each other with the title bar of each window visible. Choose **Tile Windows Horizontally** to have all the open windows divide up the screen with the windows showing one below the other. Choose **Tile Windows Vertically** to have all the open windows divide up the screen with each window beside the other.
- Click the Show Desktop icon on the Taskbar to minimize all windows at one time.

Browsing Folder Options

In Windows 98, folder views have Web-style characteristics. For example, you just point to an icon to select it and you click once to open it. Some users who upgraded from Windows 95 or Windows 3.1 may be uncomfortable with this style, preferring to double-click to open folders and files.

To turn the Web "look" on or off for a folder in My Computer, choose **View, as Web Page** from the menu or click the down arrow next to the Views button on the toolbar and select **as Web Page**. When you do this, the Web-style graphics disappear and the window looks as it would have in Windows 95 (see Figure 2.5), but you still have the Web single-click functionality. Also, this affects only the current window.

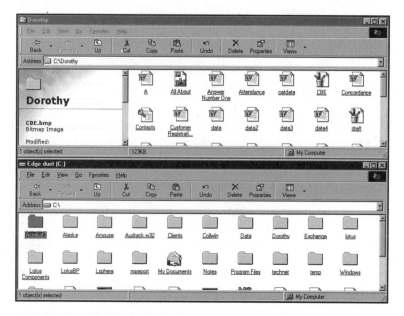

Figure 2.5   The top window is viewed as a Web page and the bottom window is not.

In order to change the functionality of the folder window, you need to set the folder options.

1. Choose **View, Folder Options** from the My Computer menu, or choose **Settings, Folder Options** from the Start menu. The Folder Options dialog box appears (see Figure 2.6).

2. Click the **General** tab, if it's not already displayed.

3. Select **Web style** to make the folder and your desktop look and work like a Web page (point to select icons, single click to open files and folders or run items). Click **Classic style** if you want the folder and your desktop to work as they did in Windows 95 (single click selects icons, double-click opens files and folders or runs items). To individually specify the settings you want to use, choose **Custom** and then click **Settings**.

4. (Optional) When you click Settings, the Custom Settings dialog box appears (see Figure 2.7). Make the selections you want to have your folders and desktop act and look the way that best suits you. Then click **OK** to return to the Folder Options dialog box.

Figure 2.6 The Folder Options dialog box.

Figure 2.7 The Custom Settings dialog box.

- **Active Desktop** If you want your desktop to look and act like a
  Web page, click **Enable all web-related content on my desktop**.
  Click **Customize** to close the Folder Options dialog box and open the
  Display Properties box instead, where you can set options to custom-
  ize the display. To have your desktop resemble the Windows 95
  desktop, select **Use Windows classic desktop**.

- **Browse folders as follows**   Each time you open a folder in My Computer, that folder will open as another separate window if you select **Open each folder in its own window**. If you don't want several windows opened each time you look through folders, select **Open each folder in the same window**.

- **View Web content in folders**   To display all folders as Web pages, so you can add information, change fonts, or set backgrounds, click **For all folders with HTML content**. If you want only those folders you specify to act like Web pages, select **Only for folders where I select "as Web Page" (View menu)**.

- **Click items as follows**   To set the number of clicks required to select or open items, select either **Single-click to open an item (point to select)** or **Double-click to open an item (single-click to select)**. If you opted to single-click, you need to choose whether you want the icons always underlined or underlined only when you point at them.

5. Click **OK** to save your settings and close the dialog box, **Cancel** to close the dialog box without saving your settings, or **Apply** to save your settings without closing the dialog box.

The Folder Options dialog box also gives you control over which files are displayed in the folders, whether you see the file extensions, and how you see some files and folders. These options are all available on the View tab of the Folder Options dialog box (see Figure 2.8). Table 2.1 provides a brief description of these items.

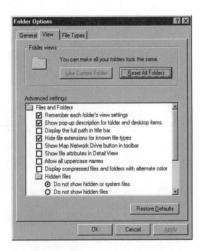

Figure 2.8   The View tab of the Folder Options dialog box.

Table 2.1 Folder Options Advanced Settings

To	*Check*
Retain the view settings for the folder so you see them when you reopen the folder	Remember each folder's view settings
Have a brief description of a desktop item or folder appear in a pop-up window whenever you point at it (doesn't affect pages that are displayed as Web pages; the description appears in the left pane of the window instead)	Show pop-up description for folder and desktop items
Display the full path (location) of the folder in the title bar instead of just the folder name	Display the full path in the title bar
Not see the file extensions (familiar to DOS and Windows 3.1 users) that define the type of file	Hide file extensions for known file types
Be able to assign drive letters to network drives	Show Map Network Drive button in toolbar
Display file attributes such as read-only or system as one of the columns in the Detail view	Show file attributes in Detail View
Not have your filenames changed to all lowercase when you type them with uppercase letters	Allow all uppercase names
Show compressed files with a different color	Display compressed files and folders with alternate color
Prevent all your system files from being accidentally changed or deleted	Do not show hidden or system files
Prevent your hidden system files from being accidentally changed or deleted	Do not show hidden files
Display all system or hidden files	Show all files
Remove all icons from the desktop when it's viewed as a Web page (only HTML and taskbar items are visible)	Hide icons when desktop is viewed as Web page
Have computer fill in any jagged edges on your screen fonts	Smooth edges of screen fonts
See the window and its contents when you are moving the window to another location (instead of seeing just the outline of the window)	Show window contents while dragging

You may want to experiment with some of these settings to see if you like them. Don't worry about getting the options back to their original settings. Click the **Restore Defaults** button in the Folder Options dialog box.

After you've set the options for your folder, you may decide you'd like all the folders to look the same. Click the **Like Current Folder** button in the Folder Options box. To set the folder view options back to the original specifications in place after installation, click **Reset All Folders**.

For more information on files and file properties, see Part II, Lesson 8, "File Properties."

The My Computer Menu

The menu bar on the My Computer window offers four choices: File, Edit, View, and Help.

The **File** menu changes depending on what you may have selected. In the File menu are commands pertaining to file management, such as creating new folders, creating shortcuts, deleting and renaming files or folders, checking file and folder properties, and closing the window.

The **Edit** menu contains editing functions. Here, the Undo command will undo your last action. Use Cut to remove a file or folder and store it in the Windows Clipboard, Copy to store a duplicate of a file or folder and store it in the Clipboard and Paste to put the contents of the Clipboard in the selected window. Choose **Select All** to select all of the files and folders in the window, and Invert Selection to select all the files and folders not selected while deselecting the currently selected files. Select all is helpful when you are deleting, copying or moving several files at one time. To learn more about Cut, Copy, and Paste, see Part II, Lesson 3, "Managing Files with My Computer."

Under the **View** menu are a series of options (discussed in Part II, Lesson 1, "File Management in Windows 98") for viewing files and folders with differently sized icons or in a different order.

Use the **Go** menu to move forward or backward to the most recently viewed folders or to move up one level in the folder hierarchy. Using the Go menu, you can also visit a home page (if you set a start page), search the Web (opens your browser), open the Channel Guide Web page, open your Internet email program or Internet Call and Meeting program, or open your contact manager (address book). For more information on the Internet options found in My Computer, see Part V, Lesson 15, "Web Integration and My Computer/Windows Explorer"

Favorites contains commands to add Web pages, folders, or files to your Favorites folder and lists the items already in the Favorites folder.

The **Help** menu offers a way to open the Help Topics window, as well as open the About Windows 98 dialog box. About Windows 98 tells you the version of Windows you're using, its copyright date, the name of the licensee, the amount of memory available to Windows 98, and the percentage of system resources that are available. To learn how to use Windows Help effectively, see Part I, Lesson 5, "Using Windows 98 Help."

The My Computer Toolbars

To see the *Standard Buttons* toolbar (see Figure 2.9), choose **View, Toolbars, Standard Buttons** from the menu. Table 2.2 provides a short description of each button.

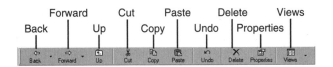

Figure 2.9 The My Computer Standard Buttons toolbar.

Table 2.2 The My Computer Toolbar buttons

Click	To
Back	Return to the previously opened folder
Forward	Go to the next folder on the recently opened folder list
Up	Go up one level in the folder hierarchy
Cut	Remove a selected item from the folder and store it in the Windows Clipboard
Copy	Store a duplicate of a selected item in the Windows Clipboard
Paste	Place a duplicate of Clipboard contents in the folder

continues

Table 2.2   Continued

Click	To
Undo	Undo the last action you performed
Delete	Remove a selected item from the folder and send it to the Recycle Bin
Properties	Display the Properties dialog box for the selected item
Views	Cycle between the Large Icon, Small Icon, List, and Detail views (click the down arrow next to views to select one of these views from a list or choose to view the folder as a Web page)

A text label at the bottom of the button identifies each button on the toolbar. To make these text labels visible or invisible, choose **View, Toolbars, Text Labels**.

 TIP   **Quickly Display or Close Toolbars**   Right-click on any toolbar to see a list of available toolbars. The currently displayed toolbars have check marks in front of them. Select the toolbar you want to display or close.

The My Computer window also has an *Address Bar*, which lists the path of the current folder. To view another folder, enter the path in the Address box and press Enter. The Address Bar stores a list of your most recently visited folders or Web pages that you may select from the drop-down list instead of typing the address you want. However, if you do start to type a previously entered address, AutoComplete will finish the address for you. To display the Address Bar, choose **View, Toolbars, Address Bar** from the menu.

The Address Bar also lets you open programs by typing the path and file name of the executable file that starts the program (such as C:\Program Files\Microsoft Office\Office\Winword.exe) and then pressing Enter.

If you're connected to an intranet or to the Web, enter the address of a Web page in the Address box (such as www.microsoft.com) and press **Enter** to open Internet Explorer and search for that page. Another way to use the Address Bar is to search for Web sites. Type **Find, Go,** or **?** followed by the word or phrase for which you want to search. Then press **Enter**. When the search results appear, click a link to open that Web page.

When you use My Computer in conjunction with Internet Explorer, you might want to add the *Links* toolbar to your windows by choosing **View, Toolbars, Links**. The Links toolbar has buttons that act as shortcuts to Web pages. You don't have to open Internet Explorer first to open the Web pages available from the Links toolbar.

Changing the Appearance of the Folder Window

Windows 98 lets you design your own look for your folders with the help of the Customize This Folder wizard. To start the wizard, do the following:

1. Choose **View, Customize this Folder** from the menu.

2. When the Customize this Folder dialog box appears (see Figure 2.10), make one of three choices:

- **Create or edit an HTML document** makes it possible to fully customize the appearance of your folder using an HTML document as the basis.
- **Choose a background picture** lets you select a picture to appear in the background, behind the icons, of your folder.
- **Remove customization** restores the folder to its original appearance.

3. Click **Next** to proceed with the next step of the wizard. When you have completed your task, click **Finish**.

   HTML (Hypertext Markup Language)   HTML is the coding used to mark formatting in Web page design.

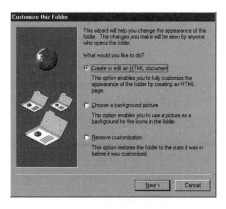

Figure 2.10   The Customize this Folder dialog box.

Creating an HTML Document

In order to add your own formatting, text lines, or layout to the folder window, you need to create an HTML document. Windows 98 accesses this document each time it displays the folder and sets up the view based on the code in the document.

To create the HTML document, follow steps 1 and 2 of "Changing the Appearance of the Folder Window." When you click **Next**, the wizard informs you that it's going to open your Hypertext Template editor, in which you will edit the document, save it, and then close it. This, of course, implies that you have and know how to use a Hypertext Template editor or that you're able to edit HTML code in a text editor such as Notepad.

After you complete your changes and save the file, the wizard returns and notes the changes that you made to the folder view. Click **Finish**. See Part V, Lesson 15 "Web Integration and My Computer/Windows Explorer" for more details on customizing folders by creating an HTML document.

Selecting a Background Picture

Windows 98 lets you personalize your folder backgrounds by adding pictures or drawings. For example, you may want your logo to appear as the background of your folders, behind the file and folder icons.

To add a background graphic to your folder view, follow steps 1 and 2 of "Changing the Appearance of the Folder Window." When you click **Next**, the wizard offers a set of graphic files that are found in the Windows directory. Most are wallpaper artwork.

1. Click on the name of a picture to see a preview on the left side of the dialog box (see Figure 2.11).

   To view other picture files found elsewhere on your computer system, click **Browse**. From the **Look In** drop down list, select the drive and folder where your picture files are stored. Then select the name of the file and click **Open**.

2. Select the colors for the text that appears beneath your icons from the Icon caption colors section. Click the color box for **Text**, select a color swatch, and then click **OK**. If you want a background color behind the letters, check **Background** and then click the background swatch and choose a color.

Figure 2.11 Select the name of the picture file to display a sample.

3. Click **Next**. The wizard confirms your choice of picture.

4. Click **Finish** (click Back if you need to return to a previous step).

Although personalizing your folders is fun, you are more likely to use this feature when working with Web pages. To learn more about adding custom backgrounds to folders, see Part V, Lesson 15 "Web Integration and My Computer/Windows Explorer"

Removing Folder Customization

To remove the customization you added to your folder by creating an HTML document or by adding a graphic to the background, follow steps 1 and 2 of "Changing the Appearance of the Folder Window." When you click **Next**, the wizard tells you that the file Folder.htt that you created when you made an HTML document and the Desktop.ini file will be moved into the Recycle Bin. That will remove any customization you made to the folder.

Click **Next** to remove the customization or **Cancel** to exit the dialog box without removing the customization. If you clicked Next, the wizard confirms your choice. Then click **Finish**.

In this lesson you learned how to change what folders and files appeared in the window, how to open them, what choices were available on the menu and toolbars, and how to customize the appearance of the folder. In the next lesson you'll learn how to manage your files from My Computer.

Managing Files with My Computer

In this lesson you learn how to select, move, copy, delete, and rename files and folders. You'll also find out how to create shortcuts, as well as how to find files.

Selecting Files and Folders

Before you can perform an operation on a file or folder, you must select (or highlight) the item so Windows knows which one you want to use.

To select files or folders:

- **Single file or folder**   Point to the file or folder icon, or use the arrow keys to move the highlighting to the file or folder icon you want to select.

- **Multiple contiguous files or folders**   Point to the first file or folder icon, hold down the Shift key, and point to the last file or folder icon. This method selects all the files between. You can also hold down the Shift key and use an arrow key to move down to the final icon in the group you want.

- **Multiple non-contiguous files or folders**   Point to the first file or folder icon, hold down the Ctrl key, and point to each of the additional file or folder icons you want.

- **All the file or folder icons in the window**   Choose **Edit, Select All** from the menu or press **Ctrl+A**.

- **All except the file or folder icons you have currently selected**   Choose **Edit, Invert Selection** from the menu.

When you select a file or folder, the name and type of the file or folder appears on the left side of the window, along with the last modified date. For files, the size of the file is also displayed.

CAUTION **I Didn't Mean to Select That File** When you're selecting multiple files with either the Shift or Ctrl keys, it's very easy to accidentally highlight a file or folder you don't want to include in your selection. After you have selected your files, hold down the Ctrl key and point at the files (one at a time) that you don't wish to include in your selection.

Moving Files and Folders

Windows 98 lets you move files and folders to different folders or different drives. You can do this by copying and pasting the files or folders, or by using your mouse to drag and then drop the files or folders in a new location. To use the drag-and-drop method:

1. Open the drive or folder window where the file or folder is stored. This is the *source* window.

2. Open the drive or folder window where you want to put the file or folder. This is the *destination* window.

3. If the windows you have open are for folders on the same drive, you can just drag the file or folder icon from the source window to the destination window.

Dragging from a window on one drive to a window on another drive copies the file, so you have to delete the original icon in the source window if you do this.

TIP **My Icon Disappeared When I Released the Mouse Button** Be careful as you drag the icon into the destination window that you do not drop it over a folder icon. When you do this, the icon gets moved into that folder and not into the destination window. To fix it, choose **Edit, Undo** from the menu and redo the drag and drop, or open the folder you dropped the icon into and then drag the icon to the original destination window.

To move files or folders using the cut and paste method:

1. Open the drive or folder window where the file or folder is stored.

2. Select the files or folders you want to move.

3. Choose **Edit, Cut** from the menu or click the Cut button on the toolbar. This removes the icon(s) from the current window and stores them in the Windows Clipboard (a temporary holding place).

4. Open the drive or folder window where you want to put the file or folder.

5. Choose **Edit, Paste** from the menu or click the Paste button on the toolbar.

TIP   **Cut and Delete Have Different Results!**   When you delete a file, text, or an item in Windows, you are either deleting it permanently or sending it to the Recycle Bin, depending on your Windows default settings. Items that you cut—using the menu command Cut, the Cut icon found on many toolbars, or the keystroke shortcut Ctrl+V—are sent to the Windows Clipboard and retained there until you replace the Clipboard contents with something new.

When using the cut and paste method, be careful not to copy or cut another item before you paste your icon in its new location, as the new item you cut or copy will replace the item you already had stored in the Clipboard.

Copy and Paste   These are skills that you can use in other Windows programs such as Microsoft Works, Microsoft Excel, and other programs that are not Microsoft programs but are designed to run under Windows. Keyboard shortcuts are Cut (Ctrl+X), Copy (Ctrl+C), and Paste (Ctrl+V).

Copying Files and Folders

Copying files and folders to different folders or different drives is similar to moving files and folders. To copy files and folders using the drag-and-drop method:

1. Open the drive or folder window where the file or folder is stored. This is the source window.

2. Open the drive or folder window where you want to put the file or folder. This is the destination window.

3. If the windows you have open are for folders on different drives, you can just drag the file or folder icon from the source window to the destination window.

Dragging from a window on a drive to another window on the same drive moves the icon. You need to hold down the Ctrl key as you drag to copy the icon.

To copy files and folders using the copy and paste method:

1. Open the drive or folder window where the file or folder is stored.

2. Select the files or folders you want to copy.

3. Choose **Edit, Copy** from the menu or click the Copy button on the toolbar. This places a duplicate of the selected files or folders in the Clipboard.

4. Open the drive or folder window where you want to put the file or folder.

5. Choose **Edit, Paste** from the menu or click the Paste button on the toolbar.

TIP **Copying to the Floppy Disk**   A quick way to copy selected files or folders from one of your drives to your floppy disk is to click the selected icons with the right mouse button. Then choose **Send To, 3¹/₂ Floppy (A)** from the pop-up menu.

Deleting Files and Folders

When you delete files or folders from your hard disk or a network drive, they are removed from their current window and placed in the Recycle Bin. If necessary, you can recover them from the Recycle Bin (see the next lesson for more information on the Recycle Bin). However, if the file is on a floppy disk it doesn't go to the Recycle Bin, so be very sure you want to delete files from a floppy disk.

I Lost All the Files in That Folder!   Be careful, too, when deleting folders. If you delete a folder, you're also deleting the contents of the folder. The folder doesn't have to be empty before you delete it, as in MS-DOS. Be

CAUTION   sure you move any valuable files or folders to other locations before deleting a folder.

To delete a file or folder:

1. Select the files or folders to be deleted.

2. Press the **Delete** key, click the Delete button on the toolbar, or choose **File, Delete** from the menu.

3. A Windows 98 alert box appears, asking if you are sure you want to send the selected files or folders to the Recycle Bin. If you are certain, select **Yes**. If not, select **No** and the operation will cease.

 TIP **A Quick Way to Delete Files or Folders** Drag the file or folder icon from the My Computer window to the Recycle Bin. When Windows 98 highlights the Recycle Bin, release the mouse button.

Renaming Files and Folders

To give a different name to a file or folder:

1. Select the file or folder you want to rename.

2. Choose **File, Rename** from the menu, or click on the icon with the right mouse button and choose **Rename** from the pop-up menu. The name gets a box around it and the text is highlighted (see Figure 3.1).

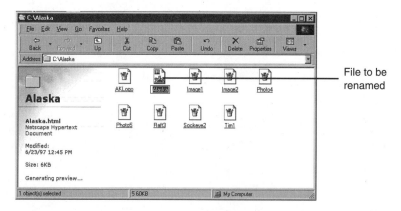

Figure 3.1 The file name when ready for renaming.

3. Enter the text for the new name.

4. Press **Enter**.

Creating Shortcuts

Shortcuts provide you with easy access to files and programs. Once you place a shortcut icon on the desktop, you can click that icon to start up a program or open a file or folder that you use frequently.

To create a shortcut from My Computer:

1. Open **My Computer**.

2. Select the drive, folder, or file for which you want to create the shortcut.

3. Choose **File, Create Shortcut**, or right-click and choose **Create Shortcut** from the shortcut menu.

4. A copy of the icon appears in the window with the words "Shortcut To" in front of the name. Drag that icon from the folder onto the desktop.

 TIP   **Quickly Create Shortcuts for the Desktop**   A quick method to create a shortcut you want to put on the desktop is to use the right mouse button when you drag the icon from the folder to the desktop. When you release the mouse button a menu appears. Select **Create Shortcut(s) Here**.

It's also possible to create shortcuts directly from the Start menu. You point to a program or document entry on the Start menu and right-click. Choose **Create Shortcut** from the shortcut menu. The shortcut appears on the menu, so you need to drag it off and onto the desktop.

Some shortcuts are created when you install programs. To remove unwanted shortcuts from the desktop, drag them over the Recycle Bin and release the mouse button when the Recycle Bin icon is highlighted.

Finding Files

What do you do if you aren't sure of a file name or the folder where it's stored? My Computer has a Find feature to help you search for the file.

1. Open the My Computer window.

2. Select the drive you want to search, such as C:.

3. Choose **File, Find** from the menu. The Find: All Files dialog box appears (see Figure 3.2).

4. In the Named box, enter the name of the file you want to find. If you don't know the complete name, use an asterisk (*) to substitute for the beginning or end of the name (such as *97 to find all file names that end in 97); use a question mark (?) to substitute for a character you don't know. Choose **Options, Case Sensitive** from the menu if you want to find a file that's in uppercase but not find a file with the same name that's in lowercase.

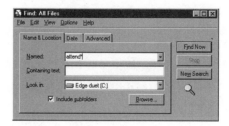

Figure 3.2   The Find: All Files dialog box.

5. The Look In box should already show the name of the drive you selected.

6. To search through all the folders in the specified drive, check **Include Subfolders**.

7. If you want to look in a specific folder, click **Browse** to open the Browse for Folder dialog box (see Figure 3.3) and select the folder you want to search.

Figure 3.3   The Browse for Folder dialog box.

8. Click **Find Now**.

9. When the search is complete, a list of files or folders matching your search criteria appears at the bottom of the dialog box (see Figure 3.4). Click the file that you want to open.

10. Click **New Search** to clear the search criteria so you can search for another file.

TIP   **Plan Now to Find Later**   When you save files, use naming conventions that you will remember and understand later, particularly when you need to find a file. For example, name files you need for your tax information with the word

TAX followed by a date (1/17/98) or account number. Next March when you are looking for all of your tax records you can search for TAX*98*.

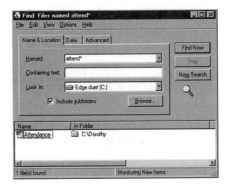

Figure 3.4   The search results appear at the bottom of the Find window.

You can also search for files based on the created or last modified date:

1. Follow steps 1 through 7 for finding a file, but don't enter a file name in the **Named** box.

2. Click the Date tab of the Find dialog box (see Figure 3.5).

Figure 3.5   The Find dialog box with the Date tab selected.

3. Select **Find all files**. From the drop-down list select **Created, Modified**, or **Last Accessed**.

4. Choose one of three options. Select **Between** (and enter the starting and ending dates) to look for all files created, modified, or last accessed between those dates. Select **during the previous x month(s)** (where x is the number of months) to return a list of files created, modified, or last accessed in the specified number of previous months. Or select **during the previous x day(s)** (where x is the number of days).

5. Click **Find Now**.

89

Use the advanced options of search to look for files by type, files that contain text strings, or files that are of a particular size.

1. Follow steps 1 through 7 for finding a file, but don't enter a file name in the **Named** box.

2. Click the Advanced tab of the Find dialog box (see Figure 3.6).

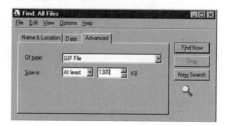

Figure 3.6 The Find dialog box with the Advanced tab selected.

3. From the **Of type** drop-down list, select the type of file or folder you are seeking. The list depends on the types of applications or other programs you have loaded on your computer.

4. To find a file within a specific size range, enter the minimum number of kilobytes in the first **Size is** box or choose **At Least** or **At Most**, and then enter the number of kilobytes in the **KB** box.

5. Click **Find Now**.

In this lesson you learned how to create, move, copy, and rename files. You also learned how to find files. In the next lesson you will learn about the Recycle Bin.

The Recycle Bin

In this lesson, you look at the Recycle Bin and find out what it is, how to open it, how to empty it, how to restore files from it, and how to look at its properties.

What Is the Recycle Bin?

The Recycle Bin is a temporary storage area on your hard disk (drive C:). When you delete a file or folder from your hard drive (as described in the previous lesson), Windows 98 moves it into the Recycle Bin. However, the file or folder still takes up space on the hard disk, since it is essentially just moved to the Recycle Bin. You must empty the Recycle Bin to remove the file or folder from the drive.

This means that you still have a second chance to get that file or folder back before it's gone forever. You can restore it back to its former position from the Recycle Bin.

Opening the Recycle Bin

The Recycle Bin icon on the desktop differs slightly depending on whether it is empty, as in Figure 4.1, or if files have been placed in it and the bin appears full, as in Figure 4.2.

Figure 4.1   The Recycle Bin icon (empty).

Figure 4.2   The Recycle Bin icon (with files in it).

To open the Recycle Bin, click the Recycle Bin icon on the desktop, select it using the arrow keys, and then press Enter, or right-click the icon and choose **Open** from the pop-up menu.

The Recycle Bin window then opens (see Figure 4.3). The Recycle Bin window has the same look and much of the functionality as My Computer (see Part II, Lesson 2, "Using My computer"). Except for the network buttons, the toolbar is the same (if you can't see your toolbar choose **View, Toolbar** from the menu). The status bar at the bottom of the screen shows the number of objects in the window or the number of selected items and the total amount of disk space they use.

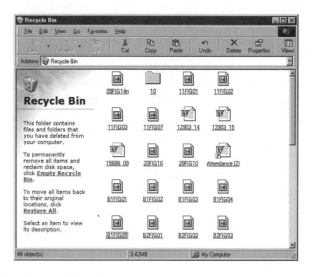

Figure 4.3   The Recycle Bin window.

Emptying the Recycle Bin

To keep your hard disk drive "lean and mean," you're going to have to empty the Recycle Bin from time to time, especially if you get an error message when you try to save a file saying that there is insufficient disk space.

CAUTION

Do You Have Enough Room?   You should check your hard disk space occasionally to make sure you have enough room to add more files. If you don't have much space left on the drive, then you should empty your Recycle Bin. To check your available disk space, open the My Computer window, click the hard drive icon to select it, and then check the amount of free space listed on the status bar.

Selected Files

You may not want to remove all the files from the Recycle Bin, especially if you think you might need some of them again.

To remove only specified files from the Recycle Bin:

1. Select the files you want to delete (see Part II, Lesson 3, "Managing Files with My Computer," to learn how to select files).

2. Press the Delete key, click the Delete button on the toolbar, or choose **File, Delete** from the menu.

 TIP   **What's in a File?**   Before you permanently delete a file from your hard drive, you may want to check its contents first. To open a file from the Recycle Bin, drag the icon to the desktop and then click it.

All Files

To remove all the files from the Recycle Bin, choose **File, Empty Recycle Bin** from the menu or click Empty Recycle Bin in the left pane of the window.

If you don't have the Recycle Bin window open, you can empty the Recycle Bin from the desktop by clicking the icon with the right mouse button and selecting **Empty Recycle Bin** from the pop-up menu.

Restoring Files

Once you have put a file or folder into the Recycle Bin, how do you get it out?

1. Select the file(s) or folder(s) that you want to restore. The original location of the file is listed in the left pane of the Recycle Bin window (see Figure 4.4).

2. Choose **File, Restore** from the menu, or right-click the icon and choose **Restore**, or click **Restore** in the left pane of the Recycle Bin window. The file or folder is returned to the location on your computer where it was before it was deleted.

Figure 4.4   The original location of the selected file shows in the left pane.

Recycle Bin Properties

To customize your Recycle Bin and how files are deleted on your system, you need to open the Recycle Bin Properties box (see Figure 4.5).

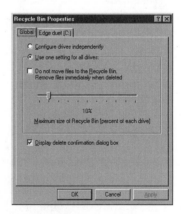

Figure 4.5   The Recycle Bin Properties box.

To open the Recycle Bin Properties box, click the **Recycle Bin** icon with the right mouse button and choose **Properties** from the pop-up menu.

You can choose to make your Recycle Bin settings work for all the drives on your computer by selecting **Use one setting for all drives**. Otherwise, select **Configure drives independently**. If you choose the latter, you have to click each of the other tabs in the Properties box that bear the names of your drives and make the settings on each one.

There are three properties to set for the Recycle Bin:

- **Configure drives independently**   Click to use separate settings for each drive on your system.
- **Use one setting for all drives**   Click to have the settings on the current tab apply to all your drives.
- **Do not move files to the Recycle Bin. Remove files immediately when deleted**   If you check this option, your deleted files will not be stored in the Recycle Bin but will disappear from the drive. This means you won't be able to restore the files. However, if you're tight on disk space, you may want to do this rather than buying a second or larger disk drive.
- **Maximum size of Recycle Bin (percent of each drive)**   Use the slide indicator to set the maximum size to which the Recycle Bin can grow. Making it smaller will conserve disk space.
- **Display delete confirmation dialog box**   Check this to be asked if you really want to delete the files every time you do a deletion. If you're tired of seeing the dialog box and having to click **Yes** every time you want to delete files, remove the check mark from this option. If you enable this option, just be sure in the future that you really want to delete the files, because you'll no longer be getting a warning.

Once you've selected your options in the Property box, click **OK**.

In this lesson, you learned what the Recycle Bin is and how to use it to remove and restore files to your drives. In the next lesson, you'll learn what the Windows Explorer is and how it differs from My Computer.

Understanding
the Windows
Explorer

In this lesson, you find out what the Windows Explorer is, how to open the Explorer, what the features of the Windows Explorer window are, and what the file viewing options are.

What Is the Windows Explorer?

As with My Computer (see Part II, Lesson 2, "Using My Computer"), you use the Windows Explorer to view and organize your drives, folders, and files.

Unlike My Computer, the Explorer doesn't show you the contents of just one folder at one time. Instead, everything is contained within one window. The list of all the drives and folders on your system or network is on the left, and the contents of the selected folder or drive are on the right. This arrangement makes it easier to navigate when you need to look at different drives and folders.

Opening the Explorer

To open the Windows Explorer:

1. Click the **Start** button on the taskbar.

2. Select **Programs** from the Start menu.

3. Click **Windows Explorer** (see Figure 5.1).

 TIP **Right-Click to Start**   Another method for opening the Windows Explorer is to right-click the Start button and choose **Explore** from the pop-up menu. The Windows Explorer opens with the Start Menu folder selected.

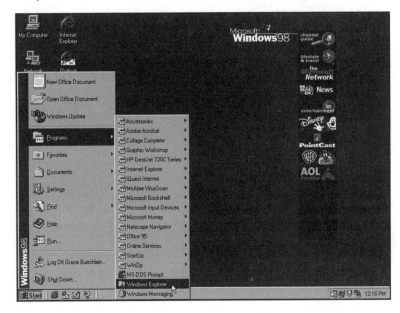

Figure 5.1 Starting Windows Explorer.

Understanding the Explorer Window

The Explorer window (see Figure 5.2) is divided into two panes. On the left is the list of drives and folders. The right pane displays the contents of the selected drive or folder.

At the top of the window is the *title bar*, which tells you the name of the window you have open. You move the window by dragging the title bar.

Beneath the title bar is the *menu bar*, which contains commands that you may give to the program.

Below the menu bar is the *toolbar*. If your toolbar is not showing, choose **View, Toolbars, Standard Buttons** from the menu. The toolbar has buttons that perform menu commands without your having to open the menu.

The *address bar* appears below the toolbar. To turn the display of the address bar on or off, choose **View, Toolbars, Address Bar** from the menu. The address bar shows your current location. Enter or select a new path and press Enter to go to that site, including a Web page address. By entering a Web page address, or URL (Uniform Resource Locator), you bypass the first step of opening the Internet Explorer browser.

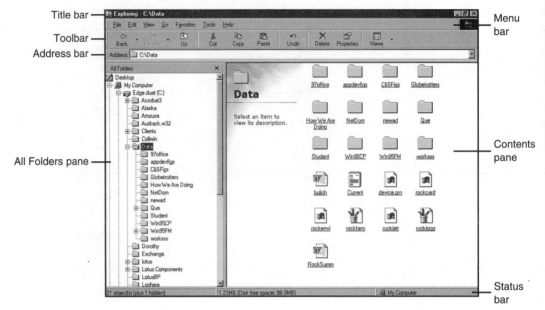

Figure 5.2   The Windows Explorer window.

 TIP   **Quickly Display or Close Toolbars**   Right-click on one of the toolbars to see a shortcut menu listing the available toolbars. Check marks appear before the toolbars being currently displayed. Click on the toolbar name to display or close it.

At the bottom of the screen is the *status bar*. The status bar displays the number of objects (files and folders) in the window and the number of bytes they take up in memory space. If you select one or more files, the status bar changes to display the number of selected files and how many bytes of memory they total. If you don't see the status bar on your window, choose **View, Status Bar** from the menu.

Because Windows 98 incorporates features of Internet Explorer into all folders, it's possible to reach Web pages from the Windows Explorer. One way to make this easier is to open one of the Explorer bars by choosing **View, Explorer Bar** from the menu. Then choose one of the following to place in the left pane of the Explorer window:

- **Search**   When the Search Explorer bar appears, type a phrase or word you want to look for on the Web, Usenet News, or both (choose which from the **Search** list box). To select an Internet search engine, click on your choice in the **Select provider** list box.

- **Favorites**   When the Favorites Explorer bar appears, it displays a list of folders or Web pages that you added to your Favorites folder. These locations are the ones you visit most frequently.

- **History**   A list of your most recently visited Web pages appears in the History Explorer bar, separated by the days on which you visited them. The number of days displayed is set in the Internet options of Internet Explorer.

- **Channels**   The Channels Explorer bar displays a list of channel categories. When you click a category, the available channels in that category are listed. A *channel* is a Web site to which you can subscribe to receive information.

- **All Folders**   The All Folders Explorer bar is the default view. It shows the hierarchy of drives and folders on your system.

- **None**   Choose None to remove the Explorer bar from the Explorer window.

The default Explorer bar is the *All Folders* pane, which normally appears on the left side of the Explorer window. Some of the icons in the All Folders pane represent drives, such as a floppy drive (A:), a hard drive (C:), or a CD-ROM drive (D:) (remember, your drive letter designations could be different). If you have a tape drive or an additional floppy drive, icons for those items will also appear in this window. You'll also see icons for the Recycle Bin, My Briefcase, and Network Neighborhood (if you have a network).

The remaining icons in the All Folders pane look like manila folders because they're folder icons. When you create documents with an application such as a word processor, you save those documents as files. In order not to have the files haphazardly scattered across your hard drive, you store them in folders. Your program files are also stored in folders. Some folders contain other folders.

The All Folders pane shows you the hierarchy of drives and folders (sometimes referred to as the "tree"). It's like an organization chart turned sideways or like a computer's family tree. Here you can see clearly which folders reside inside other folders because the inside folders (called "subfolders") are indented under the main folder and are tied to the main folder by a line.

In front of some of the folder and drive icons in the All Folders pane you'll see plus (+) and minus (-) signs. A plus means the folder or drive has folders inside it but you can't see the list at the moment because it is collapsed. Click the plus to expand that folder or drive, and then you'll see the folders listed below it. A minus sign will appear in front of the drive or folder icon. To collapse the folder or drive so you no longer see the folders under it, click the minus sign.

To see the full contents of a drive or folder, click it. The folder opens up. Look to the right side of the window, to the *Contents* pane, to see the folders and files that the selected folder or drive contains. The files have different icons depending on what type of file they are and what program they represent or were created by.

If you need more room in either pane, point to the dividing border between them until you see the mouse pointer become a two-headed arrow (see Figure 5.3), and then drag left or right to increase the size of the left or right pane.

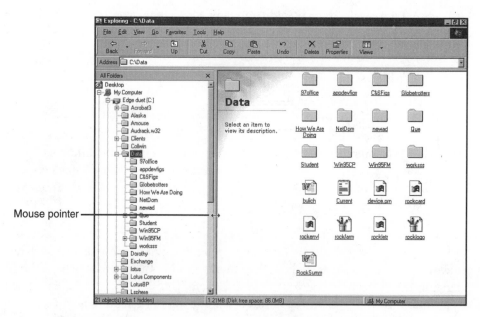

Mouse pointer

Figure 5.3   Drag the dividing border to change the pane size.

Using File Viewing Options

Not all files are displayed when you open a folder. Some system files are hidden. Also, if you are accustomed to DOS, you probably noticed that no file extensions appear in Windows 98.

To change how and what files the Explorer displays:

1. Choose **View, Folder Options** from the menu. The Folder Options dialog box opens.
2. Click the **View** tab to select it (see Figure 5.4).

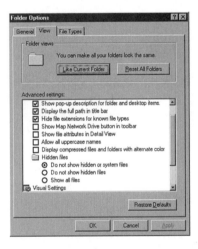

Figure 5.4 The Folder Options dialog box with the View tab selected.

3. Under Hidden files in the Advanced settings box, select **Show all files** to see hidden and system files when you open a folder. To see only the system files that aren't hidden, click **Do not show hidden files**. Choose **Do not show hidden or system files** to make those files invisible to the user, so they don't get accidentally deleted.

CAUTION

Deleting Hidden Folders If a folder contains files that are hidden, it may appear empty. If you should delete the folder, Windows will prompt you to confirm whether you want to delete the folder and its contents. You will see that same message whether a folder is genuinely empty, has files, or has hidden files. If you suspect the folder might contain hidden files, don't delete it until you choose to show the hidden files.

4. Check **Display the full path in title bar** if you would like the Explorer title bar to show C:\Data\Student instead of displaying just Student.

5. If you don't care about seeing the file extensions with every file name (file extensions are three-letter descriptions of the file type), check **Hide file extensions for known file types**.

6. To identify the file attributes (such as read-only or system) when you open the files in Detail view, enable Show file attributes in Detail View. A separate column appears on the far right in the Detail view and displays the first letter of the file attribute type.

7. Click **OK**.

For a more detailed description of the folder options, see Part II, Lesson 2, "Using My Computer."

TIP   **Explore My Computer or Network Neighborhood**   If you like the look and feel of Windows Explorer, you can view My Computer or Network Neighborhood in the same way. Instead of clicking to open My Computer or Network Neighborhood, *right click* their icons and choose Explore from the pop-up menu.

In this lesson, you learned what the Windows Explorer is, how it differs from My Computer, what the elements of the Explorer window are, and how to set the file viewing options. In the next lesson, you'll learn more about the Explorer and changing views, using the toolbar and menus, and searching for files.

Navigating Explorer

*In this lesson you go deeper into the Explorer window. You
learn how to change the way files are viewed by using the
toolbar and menus. You also learn how to search for a file and
close the Explorer. If you are new to the Windows Explorer, you might want to review Part II,
Lesson 5, "Understanding the Windows Explorer," before you complete this lesson.*

Changing Displays

Windows 98 gives you the option of displaying your windows as Web pages or
in the style of Windows 95 views. When viewed as Web pages, the Contents
pane has background color, the files or folders are opened by a single click, and
information about a selected file or folder appears on the left side of the pane
(see the top of Figure 6.1). When not viewed as a Web page, only the folders and
files appear, without a background (see the bottom of Figure 6.1). You double-
click to open files and folders. Information about selected files is not displayed
in the Contents pane.

Many of the skills you use in Windows Explorer and many of the features of
Explorer are similar or identical to those found in My Computer. If you are very
familiar with My Computer, you may find you can skip over some of the information in this lesson.

To turn the Web look on or off, choose **View, as Web Page** from the menu or
click the down arrow next to the **Views** button on the toolbar and select **as Web
Page**. This affects only the current window.

In order to change the functionality of the folder window, you need to set the
folder options.

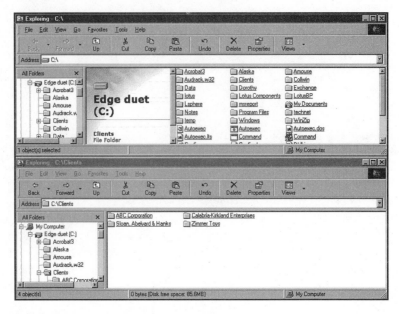

Figure 6.1   The top window is viewed as a Web page and the bottom window is not.

1. Choose **View, Folder Options** from the Explorer menu, or choose **Settings, Folder Options** from the Start menu. The Folder Options dialog box appears (see Figure 6.2).

Figure 6.2   The Folder Options dialog box.

2. Click the **General** tab, if it's not already displayed.

3. Select **Web style** to make the folder and your desktop look and work like a Web page (point to select icons; single-click to open files and folders or run items). Click **Classic style** if you want the folder and your desktop to work as they did in Windows 95 (single-click selects icons; double-click opens files and folders or runs items). To individually specify the settings you want to use, choose **Custom** and then click **Settings**.

4. (Optional) When you click **Settings**, the Custom Settings dialog box appears (see Figure 6.3). Make the selections you want to have your folders and desktop act and look the way that best suits you. Then click **OK** to return to the Folder Options dialog box.

- **Active Desktop** If you want your desktop to look and act like a Web page, click **Enable all web-related content on my desktop**. Click **Customize** to close the Folder Options dialog box and open the Display Properties dialog box instead, where you can set options to customize the display. To have your desktop resemble the Windows 95 desktop, select **Use Windows classic desktop**.

- **Browse folders as follows** Each time you open a folder in My Computer, that folder will open as another separate window if you select **Open each folder in its own window**. If you don't want several windows opened each time you look through folders, select **Open each folder in the same window**.

- **View Web content in folders** To display all folders as Web pages so that you can add information, change fonts, or set backgrounds, click **For all folders with HTML content**. If you want only those folders you specify to act like Web pages, select **Only for folders where I select "as Web Page" (View menu)**.

- **Click items as follows** To set the number of clicks required to select or open items, select either **Single-click to open an item (point to select)** or **Double-click to open an item (single-click to select)**. If you opt to single-click, you need to choose whether you want the icons always underlined or underlined only when you point at them.

5. Click **OK** to save your settings and close the dialog box, **Cancel** to close the dialog box without saving your settings, or **Apply** to save your settings without closing the dialog box.

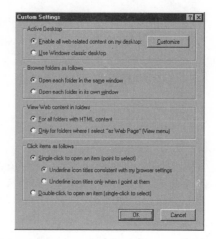

Figure 6.3   The Custom Settings dialog box.

There are four ways to view the icons in the Contents pane, as shown in Figure 6.4. Available choices on the **View** menu are:

- **Large Icons** shows the icons scattered in the window. Only the names of the files or folders appear below the icons.
- **Small Icons** shows the icons in reduced size lined up alphabetically.
- **List** looks like small icons except that it's organized vertically.
- With **Details**, the small icons are listed vertically, with each row providing information on the size of the file (in kilobytes), the type of file or folder, and the date and time last modified. You can click the column headers to sort the files by the information in that column. Click once for ascending order (A–Z) and again for descending order (Z–A).

The icons are generally shown in alphabetical order, but you can change the order by choosing **View, Arrange Icons** from the menu and then selecting the order you want—**By Drive Letter, By Name, By Type** (file type), **By Size** for files (in kilobytes), **By Date**, or **Auto Arrange** to let Windows 98 arrange them for you.

If you've accidentally moved the icons around and you want them put in straight lines again, choose **View, Line Up Icons**. This option is only available for the large and small icon views.

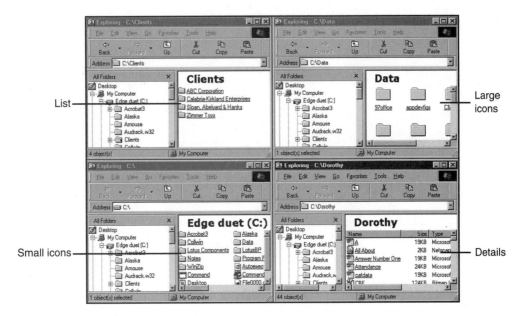

List
Small icons
Large icons
Details

Figure 6.4 Available views of icons in the Contents pane.

If you've made changes to the folder you're currently viewing and they haven't appeared yet, choose **View, Refresh** from the menu to bring the window up to date.

Using the Explorer Toolbar

To see the toolbar (see Figure 6.5), choose **View, Toolbars, Standard Buttons** from the menu or right-click a toolbar and then select **Standard Buttons** from the shortcut menu. Table 6.1 lists the buttons and what they do.

Figure 6.5 The Windows Explorer toolbar.

A text label at the bottom of the button identifies each button on the toolbar. To make these text labels visible or invisible, choose **View, Toolbars, Text Labels**.

Table 6.1   The Explorer Toolbar Buttons

Click	To
Back	Return to the previously opened folder
Forward	Go to the next folder on the recently opened folder list
Up	Go up one level in the folder hierarchy
Cut	Remove a selected item from the folder and store it in the Windows Clipboard
Copy	Store a duplicate of a selected item in the Windows Clipboard
Paste	Place a duplicate of Clipboard contents in the folder
Undo	Undo the last action you performed
Delete	Remove a selected item from the folder and send it to the Recycle Bin
Properties	Display the Properties dialog box for the selected item
Views	Cycle between the Large Icon, Small Icon, List, and Detail views (click the down arrow next to Views to select one of these views from a list or choose to view the folder as a Web page)

The Windows Explorer window also has an *Address Bar*, which lists the path of the current folder. To view another folder, enter the path in the Address box and press Enter. The Address Bar stores a list of your most recently visited folders or Web pages that you may select from the drop-down list instead of typing the address you want. However, if you do start to type a previously entered address, AutoComplete will finish the address for you. To display the Address Bar, choose **View, Toolbars, Address Bar** from the menu.

The Address Bar also lets you open programs by simply typing the path and file name of the executable file that starts the program (such as C:\Program Files\Microsoft Office\Office\Winword.exe) and then pressing Enter.

If you're connected to an intranet or to the Web, enter the address of a Web page in the Address box (such as www.microsoft.com) and press Enter to open Internet Explorer and search for that page. Another way to use the Address Bar is to search for Web sites. Type **Find, Go,** or **?** followed by the word or phrase for which you want to search. Then press Enter. When the search results appear, click a link to open that Web page.

When you use Windows Explorer in conjunction with Internet Explorer, you might want to add the *Links* toolbar to your windows by choosing **View,**

Toolbars, Links. The Links toolbar has buttons that act as shortcuts to Web pages. You don't have to open Internet Explorer first to open the Web pages available from the Links toolbar.

As you read here about Windows Explorer menus and toolbars, you will see references to Internet exploring options. To learn more about Windows Explorer and the Internet, see Part V, Lesson 15, "Web Integration and My Computer/ Windows Explorer."

Using the Menu

The menu bar on the Explorer window offers seven choices: File, Edit, View, Go, Favorites, Tools, and Help. The following list explains these menu items:

- **File** The File menu changes depending on what you may have selected. It contains commands pertaining to file management. Creating new folders, creating shortcuts, deleting and renaming files and folders, checking file and folder properties, and closing the window are all commands found on the File menu.

- **Edit** The Edit menu includes the **Undo** command, which is used to undo your last action. Here you also find **Cut** to remove a file or folder and store it in the Clipboard, **Copy** to store a duplicate of a file or folder and store it in the Clipboard, and **Paste** to put the contents of the Clipboard in the selected window. Use **Select All** to select all the files and folders in the window and **Invert Selection** to select all the files and folders not selected while de-selecting the currently selected files.

- **View** Under the View menu are a series of options for looking at the files and folders with differently sized icons or in a different order. See the "Changing Displays" section earlier in this lesson for more information.

- **Go** Use the Go menu to move forward or backward to the most recently viewed folders, go up one level in the folder hierarchy, or visit a home page (if you set a start page). You can search the Web (which opens your browser), open the Channel Guide Web page, open your Internet email program or Internet Call and Meeting program, or open your contact manager (address book).

- **Favorites** Favorites contains commands to add Web pages, folders, or files to your Favorites folder. It also lists the items already in the Favorites folder.

- **Tools**   Use the Tools menu to find files or folders, map network drives, and disconnect network drives.

- **Help**   The Help menu offers a way to open the Help Topics window as well as the About Windows dialog box. About Windows tells you which version of Windows you're using, its copyright date, the name of the licensee, the amount of memory available to Windows 98, and the percentage of system resources that are available.

Searching for a File

Use the Explorer to search a drive, to find a file or folder, or to search for a computer by name if you have a network.

To find a file:

1. Open the Explorer.
2. Select the drive you want to search.
3. Choose **Tools, Find, Files or Folders** from the menu. The Find dialog box appears (see Figure 6.6).

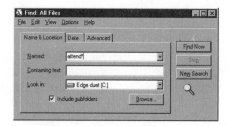

Figure 6.6   The Find dialog box.

4. In the **Named** box, enter the name of the file you want to find. If you don't know the complete name, use an asterisk (*) to substitute for the beginning or end of the name (such as *97 to find all file names that end in 97); use a question mark (?) to substitute for a character you don't know. Choose **Options, Case Sensitive** from the menu if you want to find a file that's in uppercase but not find a file with the same name that's in lowercase.

5. If you want to search for a file that contains specific text, enter some of that text in the **Containing text** box.

6. The **Look in** box should already show the name of the drive you selected.

7. To search through all the folders in the specified drive, check **Include subfolders**.

8. If you want to look in a specific folder, click **Browse** to open the Browse for Folder dialog box (see Figure 6.7) and select the folder you want to search.

Figure 6.7   The Browse for Folder dialog box.

9. Click **Find Now**.

10. When the search is complete, a list of files or folders matching your search criteria appears at the bottom of the dialog box (see Figure 6.8). Click the file that you want to open.

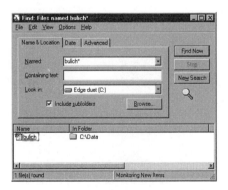

Figure 6.8   The search results appear at the bottom of the Find window.

11. Click **New Search** to clear the search criteria so you can search for another file.

You can also search for files based on the created or last modified date:

1. Follow steps 1 through 7 for finding a file, but you don't need to enter a file name in the **Named** box.

2. Click the Date tab of the Find dialog box (see Figure 6.9).

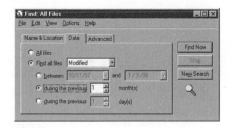

Figure 6.9   The Find dialog box with the Date tab selected.

3. Select **Find all files**. From the drop-down list select **Created, Modified**, or **Last Accessed**.

4. Choose one of three options:

- To find all files created, modified, or last accessed between two dates, use between and enter the starting and ending dates.

- To find files that were created, modified, or last accessed during a specified number of previous months, choose during the previous x month(s), where *x* is the number of months.

- To find files that were created, modified, or last accessed during a specified number of previous days, choose during the previous x day(s), where *x* is the number of days.

5. Click **Find Now**.

Use the advanced options to look for files of a certain type, files that contain text strings, or files that are of a particular size.

1. Follow steps 1 through 7 for finding a file, but you don't need to enter a file name in the **Named** box.

2. Click the Advanced tab of the Find dialog box (see Figure 6.10).

3. From the **Of type** drop-down list, select the type of file or folder you are seeking. The list depends on the types of applications or other programs you have loaded on your computer.

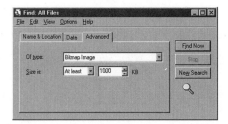

Figure 6.10 The Find dialog box with the Advanced tab selected.

4. To find a file within a specific size range, enter the minimum number of kilobytes in the first **Size is** box or choose **At least** or **At most,** and then enter the number of kilobytes in the **KB** box.

5. Click **Find Now**.

Closing Explorer

To close the Windows Explorer, choose **File, Close** from the menu or click the **Close** button on the title bar.

In this lesson, you learned how to use the Explorer to look at the files and folders on your computer, how to change the views, how to use the toolbar and menus, and how to search for files. In the next lesson, you will explore file management as you create folders and move, copy, delete, and rename files and folders using Windows Explorer.

Managing Files with Explorer

In this lesson, you learn to use Explorer to manage your drives, folders, and files by copying, moving, deleting, and renaming files and folders. You'll also find out how to create shortcuts to put on the desktop.

Selecting Files and Folders

Before you can perform an operation on a file or folder, you must select (or highlight) the item so Windows knows which one you want to use.

To select files or folders:

- **Single file or folder**   Point to the file or folder icon, or use the arrow keys to move the highlighting to the file or folder icon you want to select.

- **Several files or folders that are together**   Point to the first file or folder icon, hold down the Shift key, and point to the last file or folder icon. This method also selects all the files between. You can also hold down the Shift key and use an arrow key to move down to the final icon in the group you want.

- **Several files or folders that are not together**   Point to the first file or folder icon, hold down the Ctrl key, and point to each additional file or folder icon you want selected.

- **All the file or folder icons in the window**   Choose **Edit, Select All** from the menu or press Ctrl+A.

- **All except the file or folder icons you have currently selected**   Choose **Edit, Invert Selection** from the menu.

When you select a file or folder, the name and type of the file or folder appears on the left side of the Contents pane, along with the last modified date. For files, the size of the file is also displayed.

 Many of the skills you use in Windows Explorer and many of the features of Explorer are similar or identical to those found in My Computer. If you are very familiar with My Computer, you may find you can skip over some of the information in this lesson.

To quickly move to the file(s) you want to select, you may find it helpful to press Home to select the first item in the folder or End to select the last item. When you press the first letter in the item name, Explorer selects the first file or folder that begins with that letter. Combine Shift with Home or End to select all the files between the currently selected item and the beginning or end of the list. Press Tab to move from the Contents pane to the All Folders pane, and vice versa.

To learn how to create folders, see Part II, Lesson 1, "File Management in Windows 98."

Moving Files and Folders

There are two ways to move files and folders to different folders or different drives. One method is called *drag and drop*:

1. From the All Folders pane, open the drive or folder where the file or folder you want to move is stored by clicking on the drive or folder icon.

2. Drag the file or folder icon from the Contents pane to the drive or folder icon in the All Folders pane where you want to put it. Don't release the mouse button until the destination drive or folder is highlighted.

Dragging from a file or folder on one drive to another drive copies the file, so you have to delete the original icon in the Contents pane if you do this.

TIP   **My Icon Disappeared When I Released the Mouse Button**   Be careful as you drag the icon into the destination window that you do not drop it over a folder icon. When you do this, the icon gets moved into that folder and not into the destination window. To fix this, choose **Edit, Undo** from the menu and redo the drag and drop, or open the folder you dropped the icon into and then drag the icon to the original destination window.

The second method is to use cutand paste:

1. From the All Folders pane, open the drive or folder where the file or folder you want to move is stored.

2. From the Contents pane, select the file or folder you want to move.

CAUTION

Cut and Delete Have Different Results!   When you delete a file, text, or item in Windows, you are either deleting it permanently or sending it to the Recycle Bin, depending on your Windows default settings. Items that you cut—using the menu command Cut, the Cut icon found on many toolbars, or the keystroke shortcut Ctrl+V—are sent to the Windows Clipboard and retained there until you replace the Clipboard contents with something new.

3. Choose **Edit, Cut** from the menu or click the **Cut** button on the toolbar. This removes the icon(s) from the current folder or drive and stores the item(s) in the Windows Clipboard (a temporary storage area). Be careful not to copy or cut another item before you paste the icons, or you will lose them.

4. In the All Folders pane, open the drive or folder where you want to put the file or folder.

5. Choose **Edit, Paste** from the menu or click the **Paste** button on the toolbar. The contents of the Clipboard appear in the folder or drive.

Copying Files and Folders

Copying files and folders to differentfolders or different drives is similar to moving. To do this using the drag and drop method:

1. In the All Folders pane, open the drive or folder where the file or folder you want to copy is stored. Just click the drive or folder icon to open it.

2. Hold down the Ctrl key and drag the file or folder icon you want to copy from the Contents pane to the drive or folder icon in the All Folders pane, where you want to put it.

3. Release the mouse button when the destination drive or folder is highlighted.

If you are dragging the file or folder from one drive to another, you don't need to hold down the Ctrl key.

To copy files or folders using the cut and paste method:

1. In the All Folders pane, open the drive or folder where the file or folder you want to copy is stored.

2. In the Contents pane, select the files or folders you want to copy.

3. Choose **Edit, Copy** from the menu or click the **Copy** button on the toolbar. This places a duplicate of the selected files or folders in the Clipboard.

4. In the All Folders pane, open the drive or folder where you want to put the duplicate file or folder.

5. Choose **Edit, Paste** from the menu or click the **Paste** button on the toolbar. Be careful not to copy or cut another item before you paste the icons, or you will lose them.

 TIP **Copying to the Floppy Disk**   If you want to copy selected files or folders from one of your drives to your floppy disk, click the selected icons with the right mouse button. Choose **Send To, 3½ Floppy (A)** from the pop-up menu.

Deleting Files and Folders

When you delete files or folders from your hard disk or a network drive, they are removed from their current folder and placed in the Recycle Bin. If necessary, you can recover them from the Recycle Bin (see Part II, Lesson 4, "The Recycle Bin," for more information about the Recycle Bin). However, if the file is on a floppy disk it doesn't go to the Recycle Bin. Be very sure you want to delete files from your disk.

Be careful, too, when deleting folders. If you delete a folder, you're also deleting the contents of the folder. The folder doesn't have to be empty before you delete it, as in MS-DOS. Be sure you move any valuable files or folders to other locations before deleting a folder.

To delete a file or folder:

1. Select the files or folders to be deleted.

2. Press the Delete key, click the **Delete** button on the toolbar, or choose **File, Delete** from the menu.

3. A Windows 98 alert box appears, asking if you are sure you want to send the selected files or folders to the Recycle Bin. If you are, select **Yes**. If not, select **No** and the operation will cease.

TIP   **A Quick Way to Delete Files and Folders**   Drag the file or folder icon from the Explorer window to the Recycle Bin. When Windows 98 highlights the Recycle Bin, release the mouse button.

Renaming Files and Folders

To give a different name to a file or folder:

1. Select the file or folder you want to rename.

2. Choose **File, Rename** from the menu, or click the icon with the right mouse button and choose **Rename** from the pop-up menu. The name gets a box around it and the text is highlighted (see Figure 7.1).

File to be
renamed

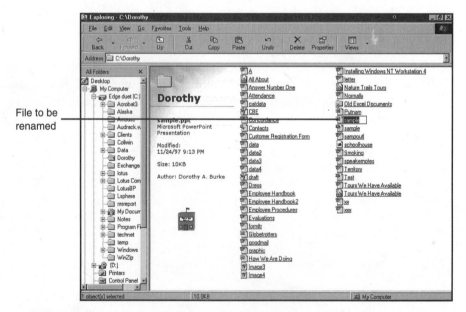

Figure 7.1   The file name when ready for renaming.

3. Enter the text for the new name.

4. Press Enter.

Creating Shortcuts

Shortcuts provide you with easy access to files and programs. Once you place a shortcut on the desktop, you can double-click that shortcut icon to start a program or open a file or folder.

To create a shortcut:

1. Open the Explorer.

2. Select the drive, folder, or file for which you want to create the shortcut.

3. Choose **File, Create Shortcut**.

4. A copy of the icon appears in the window with the words "Shortcut to" in front of the name. Drag that icon onto the desktop.

 TIP **Quickly Create Shortcuts for the Desktop** A quick method to create a shortcut you want to put on the desktop is to use the right mouse button when you drag the icon from the Explorer window to the desktop. When you release the mouse button a menu appears. Select **Create Shortcut(s) Here**.

It's also possible to create shortcuts directly from the Start menu. You point to a program or document entry on the Start menu and right-click. Choose **Create Shortcut** from the shortcut menu. The shortcut appears on the menu, so you need to drag it off and onto the desktop.

Some shortcuts are created when you install programs. To remove unwanted shortcuts from the desktop, drag them over the Recycle Bin and release the mouse button when the Recycle Bin icon is highlighted.

For more information on creating shortcuts for the desktop, see Part III, Lesson 2, "Customizing the Active Desktop."

In this lesson, you learned to manage your files by moving, copying, renaming, and deleting them. You saw how to add shortcuts to your desktop. In the next lesson, you'll learn about file properties.

File Properties

In this lesson, you learn about properties and how to view the properties of a particular file.

File Names

Files needed to run programs are generally installed on your hard disk when you install the programs. You create new files in your application programs when you save documents, spreadsheets, databases, pictures, and so forth.

When you save a file in an application, you assign a name to the file. Files stored in the same folder must have unique file names. Any file name longer than eight characters is considered a long file name, although a name that includes a space or a comma is also considered a long file name. Windows 98 allows you to use up to 255 characters when you name a file, but remember you must include the full path of the file in that number. For example, the full name of the Profits spreadsheet you stored in the January subfolder of the My Documents folder is C:\My Documents\January\Profits.xls, which is 35 characters.

CAUTION

Old Eight-Character Names   When you work with other computers, either by sharing files on disks or on a network, you should avoid long file names (over eight characters) when working with MS-DOS machines or some application programs that have difficulty reading long names. Windows 98 will automatically convert your long names to an MS-DOS-compatible format, such as converting January Profits to Januar~1.xls. This is for MS-DOS computers but may not be acceptable in all situations. For information on DOS naming conventions, see Appendix B, "DOS and Legacy Applications."

Windows 98 has few restrictions on the characters used in file names. The characters you must not use in file names are / \ :*?<>|. Spaces and other punctuation marks are allowable. Be careful with periods, however, because a period marks the beginning of a file extension. In MS-DOS file names, the eight-character file name was followed by a period and a three-letter extension that defined the type of file. Even if you can't see those extensions in My Computer or Windows Explorer, Windows 98 does store that information. You can display it using folder options (see Part II, Lesson 2, "Using My Computer," for a full explanation of folder options).

A practical consideration in naming files is being able to find them later. Although long file names give you the advantage of a more descriptive name, you have to keep in mind that a name like "Letter to Paul Jones" will be lost in a group of similar file names beginning with "Letter to." To make it easier to locate later, you might want to name this file "Paul Jones" Letter.

Long file names also consume memory storage space, so you may want to avoid long names where storage is critical. One place to be careful is in your root directory (C:\), because the root directory is limited to 512 names (unless you are using the FAT32 file system, as explained in Part II, Lesson 11, "Disk Management"). Very long file names may consume more than one entry, which would further cut down the number of files you can store in the root directory. The easy solution is to move some of these files to other folders, where the number of entries is unlimited.

File Size

All storage media (hard disks, floppy disks, CDs) measure their capacity in bytes. A byte is approximately the size of one character. Roughly a thousand bytes is a kilobyte (1024 bytes), abbreviated K or KB, a million bytes is a megabyte (abbreviated MB, called "meg"), and a billion bytes is a gigabyte (abbreviated GB, called "gig").

File sizes are measured in bytes. That doesn't mean that a 1,000-character essay equals 1000 bytes. All the formatting directions in a document also take up space. You can see the size of your files by looking in My Computer or the Windows Explorer, where the size of the selected file is displayed on the left side of the My Computer window or Explorer Contents pane. When you use the Details view (see Figure 8.1), the size of all the files is listed.

If you know the size of the files you want to store and you know the storage capacity of the disk you want to store them on, you can tell if the disk is large enough to hold all the files. You have to take into account whatever files are already on the disk. It's the *free space* of the disk that must be large enough to hold your files. When you select a drive in My Computer or Windows Explorer, the capacity of the drive and the amount of free space appear on the status bar and on the left side of the My Computer window (see Figure 8.2) in Web style mode.

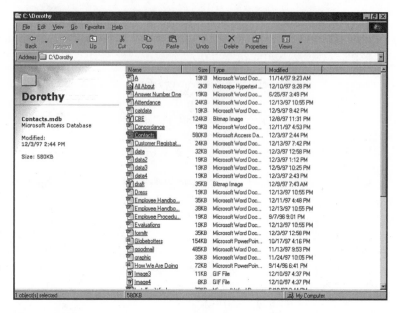

Figure 8.1 My Computer using the Details view.

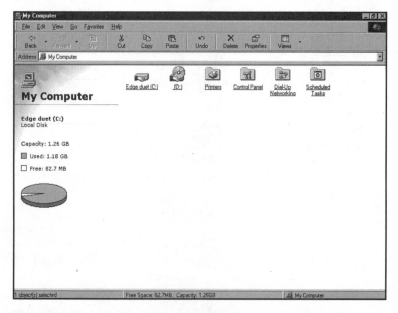

Figure 8.2 The disk capacity and free space appear on the status bar.

File Creation Date and Time

When you first save a file, Windows automatically records the date and time that you saved it. When you open the file again and make changes, the date and time you save it are again recorded as the modified date. You can see the modified date in the details view of My Computer (as shown in Figure 8.1) or the Windows Explorer.

You need to know the modified date to determine which file is the most recent. Backup programs use that information to determine which files have been modified since the last backup. Also, if you know the date you last modified a file but can't remember the name, you can search for that file by date (see Part II, Lesson 6, "Navigating Explorer").

The date and time are dependent on the system clock, so be sure to set yours for the correct time (by selecting the Date/Time icon in the Control Panel, as explained in Part III, Lesson 1, "Understanding the Control Panel").

File Attributes

There are four attributes that can be assigned to files:

Read-only   You can open a read-only file and read it or print it, but you cannot change it or delete it. This protects the original file from being changed.

Archive   Some programs use this option to determine which files are to be backed up. In most cases, if the file is not read-only, it has an Archive attribute.

Hidden   Some files are not visible in file listings, and you can't use them unless you know the name of the file. Program files may be hidden to keep you from moving or deleting them accidentally.

System   Certain files are necessary to the operation of your system; these are system files. When you open My Computer or the Windows Explorer in Details view, you can see which files are system files under the Attributes column, if you enabled that option in folder options (see Figure 8.3).

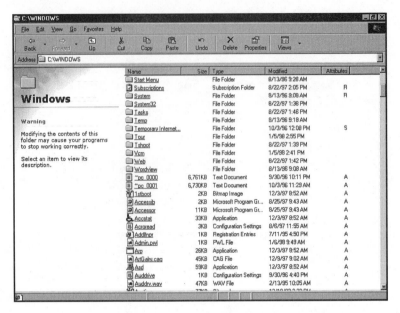

Figure 8.3 The My Computer Details view displaying file attributes.

Viewing Properties

To see the properties of a file—whether you are in My Computer, Windows Explorer, or Network Neighborhood—you must first select the file and then do one of the following:

- Choose **File, Properties**.
- Click the right mouse button and choose **Properties** from the pop-up menu.
- Click the **Properties** button on the toolbar.
- Click the **Attributes** link on the left side of the Windows Explorer Contents pane or the My Computer window. The Properties dialog box for the selected file opens (see Figure 8.4).

The Properties dialog box provides you with information about the file:

- File name
- Type (of file)
- Location (what drive and folder it's in)
- Size (in kilobytes and actual number of bytes)

- MS-DOS name (includes extension)
- Created (date and time the file was created)
- Modified (date and time the file was last modified)
- Accessed (date the file was last opened)
- Attributes (Read-only, Archive, Hidden, System)

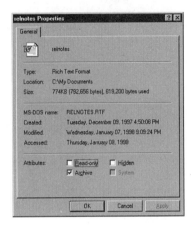

Figure 8.4   The Properties dialog box for a file.

Except for System files, you can change the attributes of selected files by checking the attributes you want to assign to them. For example, if you want to provide a file to several users for reference but you don't want them to change the file, change the file attribute to Read-only.

Click **Apply** to change an attribute without closing the Properties dialog box; click **OK** to accept the changes.

If you open the Properties dialog box for a document, you may see two additional tabs in the box: Summary and Statistics.

- The Summary page, shown in Figure 8.5, contains information entered by the program that created it. For instance, in many word processors you can create a summary sheet and add information about the file. That information would appear in this Properties dialog box.
- The Statistics page not only contains creation and modification dates and times but has the name of the person who last modified the file (see Figure 8.6). The Statistics page also lists the number of revisions and contains

information about the number of pages and so forth. The information on this page may vary widely from application document to application document.

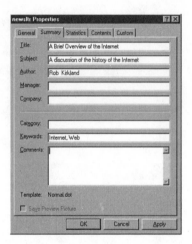

Figure 8.5 The summary page of the Properties dialog box.

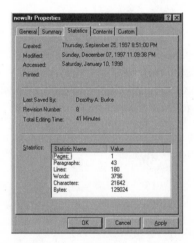

Figure 8.6 The Statistics page of the Properties dialog box.

In this lesson, you learned the various properties of a file: size, date, and time, and attributes. You learned how to find the properties of a selected file and how to change the attributes. In the next lesson, you'll learn about registering files.

Registering Files

9

In this lesson, you learn how to associate files with programs, so that clicking on a file opens the file in its designated program.

What Is File Association?

In Windows version 3.1 you could *associate* files with particular applications. This allowed you to double-click a document file icon in the File Manager and have it automatically open in the associated application. For example, double-clicking the icon for a Word document would automatically start Word for Windows and open the document.

 TERM **Document File** Document files are not just word processing documents. In Windows terms, a document file is any file created by an application—spreadsheet, database, drawing, or word processing document. Other types of files are program files that are necessary to run programs and executable files that start programs. System files are program files necessary to run the operating system.

Registered files in Windows 95 and Windows 98 work the same way. If you click a document file icon in My Computer, Windows Explorer, or Network Neighborhood, the file opens in its associated application. Registering goes beyond association because you can also specify which program controls the printing of a file. This is helpful when you want to open a file from Windows Explorer or My Computer, because you don't have to start a program first.

If you click a file icon and it isn't registered, it's probably because it wasn't created by one of the applications on your computer. Instead of opening a program, a dialog box appears, asking which program to associate with the file (see Figure 9.1).

Figure 9.1   The Open With dialog box.

In the case of Figure 9.1, the Open With dialog box appeared because the file was originally created in CorelDRAW! on another computer. CorelDRAW! is not loaded on this computer, so no program can automatically open it. Select another program that can open the file (check **Always use this program to open this file** if you want to make the association permanent) and click **OK**.

In selecting a program to associate with a file type, select a program that is capable of opening and reading the file. For example, if you open a CorelDRAW! file in WordPad, all you will see is a series of unusual characters representing the code in the file. WordPad is a program that deals with text files, but CorelDRAW! is a graphics program.

If you already know that a file has an extension that won't open automatically into one of your current applications when you click it, open My Computer or Windows Explorer, select the file, and choose **File, Open with** from the menu. The Open With dialog box appears, and you can select the appropriate application in which to open the file.

Registering a New File Type

Since most of the files you deal with are created on your own computer, you rarely need to create new file types. Instead, you associate any unknown file extensions with current file types. However, you may have a special occurrence when you need a new file type.

For example, in WordPerfect for DOS you could assign any three-letter file extension to a document, such as the initials of the author or a project code. You may want to retain that system after you switch to another word processor, or you may still be sending files to a WordPerfect for DOS user who requires those extensions. To help Windows 98 identify which application to open when it encounters those new extensions, assign a new file type to each different extension.

To register a new file type:

1. From either My Computer or the Windows Explorer, choose **View, Folder Options** from the menu. From the Start menu, choose **Settings, Folder Options**. The Options dialog box appears.

2. Select the **File Types** tab (see Figure 9.2). Check the **Registered file types** list to be sure the file type isn't already listed, which means you don't have to create a new type. For each file type listed, the file type details display the extension and the application it opens with.

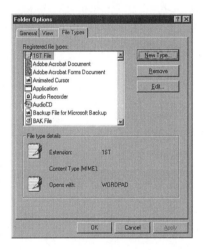

Figure 9.2 The Folder Options dialog box with the File Types tab selected.

3. Click **New Type**. The Add New File Type dialog box appears (see Figure 9.3).

4. In the **Description of type** box, enter the brief description that appears under Type when you choose the Details view in My Computer or the Windows Explorer.

129

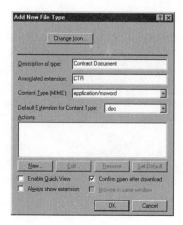

Figure 9.3 The Add New File Type dialog box.

5. In the **Associated extension** box, specify the three-letter file extension for this file type. Any files bearing this extension will automatically get the same icon and commands as in this dialog box.

6. From the **Content Type (MIME)** drop-down list, select the appropriate MIME type or enter the name in the box. If you don't know the MIME type, or if you don't intend to attach this type of file to an Internet message, leave this option blank.

 MIME (Multipurpose Internet Mail Extensions) An Internet browser or Internet mail viewer associates a MIME type with a file type, which gives information about which program should run when you open the file over the Internet.

7. Once you select the MIME type, an entry may appear automatically in the **Default Extension for Content Type** box. If not, select one from the list or enter one. You would select the extension that would normally be associated with files of this type.

8. The **Actions** box lists commands that have been defined for the selected file type. You can set up as many commands as you want and give them any name you want. To add a new command, click **New**.

9. The New Action dialog box appears (see Figure 9.4). In the **Action** box, enter the name of the command (such as Open or Print) that will appear on the shortcut menu for this type of file. If you want to specify a character as an accelerator key, precede it with an ampersand (&).

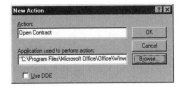

Figure 9.4 The New Action dialog box.

Accelerator Key One letter in each menu command is underlined. This means you can use this letter in combination with the Alt key as a keyboard shortcut.

10. In the **Application used to perform action** box, specify the command file and path that performs the action you want. For example, if the action you entered was Open Solitaire, enter SOL.EXE here, which is the executable file for Solitaire. Click **Browse** to help locate the correct file.

11. If you know that the program or file type uses Dynamic Data Exchange (DDE) to link data, check **Use DDE** and complete the fields that appear. Click **OK**. The action appears in the **Actions** box.

Dynamic Data Exchange (DDE) A communications protocol that lets you share data between two open applications. DDE is an older technology, so most programs in Windows and OS/2 support it.

12. If you know that the application supports Quick View, check **Enable Quick View**.

13. If you always want the file extension to show on this type of file, check **Always show extension**.

14. Click **Close** to return to the Folder Options dialog box.

Editing an Existing File Type

To edit an existing file type:

1. Choose **View, Folder Options** from the My Computer or Windows Explorer menu, or choose **Settings, Folder Options** from the Start menu. The Options dialog box appears.

2. Select the **File Types** tab (refer to Figure 9.2).

3. Under **Registered file types**, select the type you want to edit.

4. Click **Edit**. The Edit File Type dialog box appears (see Figure 9.5).

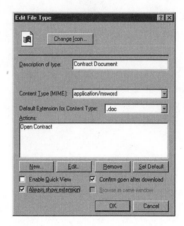

Figure 9.5 The Edit File Type dialog box.

5. Make any modifications you want. Use the **New**, **Edit**, or **Remove** buttons to add, change, or delete actions.

6. Click **OK** to return to the Folder Options dialog box.

7. Click **OK** to close the Folder Options dialog box.

Removing a File Type

To remove a file type:

1. Choose **View, Folder Options** from the My Computer or Windows Explorer menu, or choose **Settings, Folder Options** from the Start menu. The Options dialog box appears.

2. Select the **File Types** tab (see Figure 9.6).

3. Under **Registered file types**, select the file type you want to remove.

4. Click **Remove**.

5. Windows requests a confirmation that you want to remove the file type (see Figure 9.7). Click **Yes**.

6. Click **Close**.

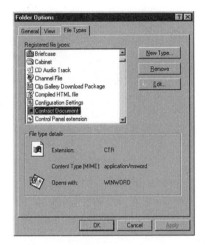

Figure 9.6 The Options dialog box with the File Types tab selected.

Figure 9.7 Confirm that you want to remove the file type.

Changing the Icon for a File Type

Every file type has an icon associated with it. To change the icon for an existing file type:

1. Choose **View, Folder Options** from the My Computer or Windows Explorer menu, or choose **Settings, Folder Options** from the Start menu. The Options dialog box appears.
2. Select the **File Types** tab (refer to Figure 9.2).
3. Under **Registered file types**, select the type you want to edit.
4. Click **Edit**. The Edit File Type dialog box appears (refer to Figure 9.5).
5. Click **Change Icon**. The Change Icon dialog box appears (see Figure 9.8).
6. Select one of the icons in the **Current icon** box or click **Browse** to search for another icon file.

133

Figure 9.8 The Change Icon dialog box.

7. Click **OK** to close the Change Icon dialog box and then **OK** to close the Edit File Type dialog box.

8. Click **OK** to exit the Folder Options dialog box.

In this lesson, you learned what registering files means, how to register a file type, how to edit it, and how to remove it. You also learned how to change an icon for a file type. In the next lesson, you'll learn about backing up and using the Task Scheduler to maintain your system.

Using Task Scheduler and Backing Up

In this lesson you will learn how to use Windows 98 to back up your files and how to schedule disk maintenance tasks.

What Is Backing Up?

What's the difference between copying and backing up files? Although the terms are sometimes used interchangeably, backing up is making a special copy of your files that can easily be restored should something happen to your hard drive or in case your files are damaged or lost. Backing up makes a set of files, so you're not copying a file here or a folder there. Also, you can schedule your backups so they occur automatically.

You can back up your files to floppy disks, a tape drive, or another computer on your network. If you have a read-write CD-ROM device, you could also back up to CD-ROM.

You should back up your hard drive on a regular basis. At a minimum, once a week is recommended. If you're working on a network, the network drive is probably being backed up for you. If you're keeping any files on your own hard drive, it is your responsibility to back them up.

Backing Up Data

Windows 98 has a built-in backup utility that you can use, although you may have backup software that was packaged with your tape drive (if you have one).

To back up files the first time with Windows 98 Backup, follow these steps:

1. Choose **Programs, Accessories, System Tools, Backup** from the **Start** menu.

2. When the Microsoft Backup dialog box appears (see Figure 10.1), select **Create a new backup job** and click **OK**.

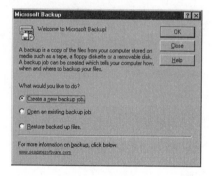

Figure 10.1   The Microsoft Backup dialog box.

3. The Backup Wizard dialog box opens (see Figure 10.2). To back up all the files on your hard disk (make sure you have adequate storage space to do this), select **Back up My Computer**. To back up only parts of your hard drive, such as your data files, click **Back up selected files, folders and drives**. Then click **Next** to go on to the next step.

   If you chose to back up your entire hard disk, skip to step 5.

 TIP   **Back Up Only What You Need**   Once you have created a backup of programs, you need only back up your data files on an ongoing basis. When you install new software, you'll have the original CD or disks, so you probably don't need to back up new software unless you have customized the installation.

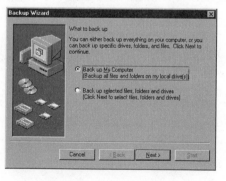

Figure 10.2   The Backup Wizard dialog box.

4. If you chose to back up only specified files, the Backup Wizard displays a screen that resembles the All Folders pane in the Windows Explorer (see Figure 10.3), except that the folders have check boxes in front of them. Click the check boxes in front of the items you want to include in your backup. Click **Next** (click **Back** to go back to the previous step).

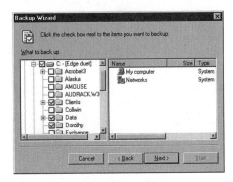

Figure 10.3 Check the folders you want to include in the backup.

5. Click **All selected files** to have all files backed up or **New and changed files** to back up only the files that are new or have been modified since your last backup. Click **Next**.

6. Select the type of backup you're making and then enter the location where you want to store your backup files in the second text box (see Figure 10.4). To select the location by browsing, click the button to the right of the text box to open the Where to back up dialog box (see Figure 10.5). Choose the computer, drive, or folder where you want the backup files stored. Then enter a **File name**, if you don't want the file to be named MyBackup, and click **Open**. Click **Next**.

7. Set your preferences on how you want the backup performed (see Figure 10.6) by checking **Compare original and backup files to verify data was successfully backed up** and/or **Compress the backup data to save space** (don't choose this option if your data files are already compressed). Click **Next**.

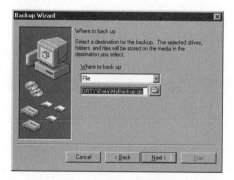

Figure 10.4   Select the type of backup you're making and then enter the location.

Figure 10.5   Where to back up dialog box.

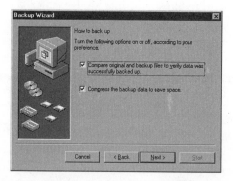

Figure 10.6   Select the options to set how you want the backup done.

8. Enter a name for these backup settings in the **Type a name for this backup job** box (see Figure 10.7).

9. Click **Start**. The backup process begins.

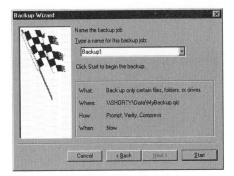

Figure 10.7 Enter a name for your backup settings.

10. An alert box appears when the operation is completed. Click **OK**.

11. The Backup Progress dialog box appears (see Figure 10.8), showing the status of the backup, how many files were processed, and what the total size of the backup was. Click **OK**.

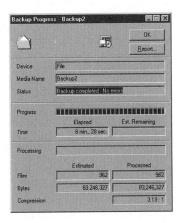

Figure 10.8 The Backup Progress box.

12. The Microsoft Backup window appears. Close the window by choosing **Job, Exit** from the menu or by clicking the Close button.

Be sure to carefully mark and store the backup tapes or disks you created. You may also want to test your backup files, at least the first time, by restoring the set to see that there are no problems with the files that you stored (see the next section for information on how to restore files).

CAUTION

I Don't See Backup Under System Tools!   It is possible that the Backup component wasn't installed when Windows 98 was put on your computer. You'll need the Windows 98 CD you used to install your program. Then choose **Settings, Control Panel** from the **Start** menu and then click the **Add/Remove Programs** icon. Click the **Windows Setup** tab. Under **Components**, check **System Tools** and click **OK**. Follow the on-screen instructions.

When you need to run the backup job again, do the following:

1. Choose **Programs, Accessories, System Tools, Backup** from the **Start** menu.

2. When the Microsoft Backup dialog box appears (refer to Figure 10.1), select **Open an existing backup job** and click **OK**.

3. The Open Backup Job dialog box appears (see Figure 10.9). Select the backup job you want to run and click **Open**.

Figure 10.9   The Open Backup Job dialog box.

4. The Microsoft Backup window appears (see Figure 10.10). The current settings for the job listed in the Backup Job box are displayed. To change what files you want backed up, select **All selected files** under **What to back up** to copy all the designated files or **New and changed files** to update only the backup files.

5. To change what drives and folders are backed up, check the boxes in front of the drives or folders listed below **What to back up**. Click in a box to add or remove the check mark.

6. To modify the location where your backup files will be stored, change the type and location under **Where to back up**.

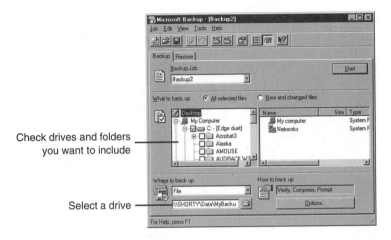

Check drives and folders
you want to include

Select a drive

Figure 10.10 The Microsoft Backup window.

7. Click **Options** to specify new choices for how you want your files backed up—whether you want to backup files compared for verification, whether you want the data compressed and how, and whether you want to automatically overwrite current backup files or have that choice during the backup (see Figure 10.11). Click **OK** to return to the Microsoft Backup window.

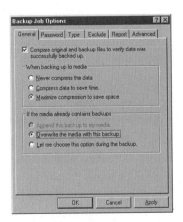

Figure 10.11 The Backup Job Options dialog box.

8. If you made changes to the job settings, you must save them before you do the backup. Choose **Job, Save** from the menu or click the Save Job button on the toolbar.

9. Click **Start** to begin the backup. The Backup Progress dialog box shows the status of the backup, the elapsed time, what is being processed, and the number of files and bytes being processed (refer to Figure 10.8).

10. Microsoft Backup alerts you when the operation is complete. Click **OK**.

11. Click **OK** to close the Backup Progress dialog box.

12. The Microsoft Backup window appears. Close the window by choosing **Job, Exit** from the menu or by clicking the Close button.

CAUTION

Backing Up Windows   When choosing folders and files to back up, always make a point of backing up your Windows folder. Most of the files that determine what your user preferences are and how your system is configured are contained in the Windows folder. You don't want to lose them.

Restoring Files

The worst day of your life inevitably arrives, and your hard disk crashes or the temp filling in during your vacation accidentally deletes all your correspondence files. Once you have your hard disk repaired or you discover your loss of vital files, it's time to restore your backup files to your hard disk.

To restore your files:

1. Choose **Programs, Accessories, System Tools, Backup** from the **Start** menu.

2. When the Microsoft Backup dialog box appears (refer to Figure 10.1), click **Restore backed up files** and then click **OK**.

3. The Restore Wizard opens (see Figure 10.12). In the **Restore from** box, select the type of backup you made and then indicate the location of the backup in the box below (such as another network computer, as shown in Figure 10.12). Click the button on the right side of the box to browse your system for the file location. Click **Next**.

4. The Restore Wizard locates all backup files at the indicated location (see Figure 10.13). To select a set of backup files to restore, check the box in front of the backup set name. Then click **OK**.

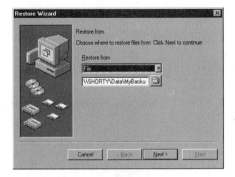

Figure 10.12   The Restore Wizard.

Figure 10.13   Select the backup set you want to restore.

5. After a short logging process, the What to restore screen appears (see Figure 10.14). This screen displays the list of drives, folders, and files you backed up in the specified set. Select the ones you want to restore by clicking the check box in front of the drive or folder to place a check mark there. Click **Next**.

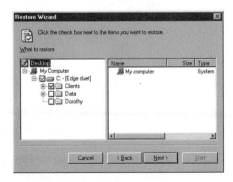

Figure 10.14   Specify what you want to restore.

143

6. In the Where to restore box (see Figure 10.15), indicate **Original Location** or **Alternate Location** as the place where you want to put the restored files. If you chose Alternate Location, specify that location in the box below. Click **Next**.

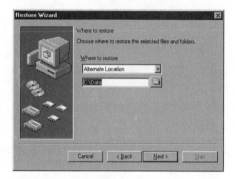

Figure 10.15   Specify the location where you want to place the restored files.

7. You must decide how you want to replace existing files during the restore process (see Figure 10.16).You have three options: Replace a file only if the file on the computer is older than the backup version, automatically replace all the files even if the file on the computer is newer than the backup file, or don't replace any of the files. Choose one of the first two options and then click **Start**.

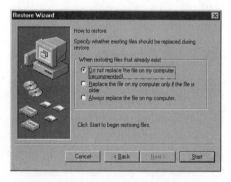

Figure 10.16   Determine how you want to restore files.

8. The Restore Wizard lists the required media (file, disk, or tape) needed for the backup. If you used a tape or floppy disks for backups, be sure to select the correct one before inserting it into your tape or floppy drive. If you used a network drive, be sure that drive is available. Then click **OK**.

9. When the operation is complete, Microsoft Backup alerts you. Click **OK**.

10. The Restore Progress dialog box appears showing the status of the restore and the number of files and bytes restored. Click **OK**.

11. The Microsoft Backup window appears. To close the window, choose **Job, Exit** or click the Close button.

Scheduling Tasks

Ideally, you should back up your computer files on at least a weekly basis. However, not all of us remember to do this—or any of the other routine maintenance tasks required to keep your system in peak working order. Windows 98 includes a task scheduler to automatically run these tasks for you.

To schedule a new task:

1. Choose **Programs, Accessories, System Tools, Scheduled Tasks** from the **Start** menu to open the Scheduled Tasks folder (see Figure 10.17).

Figure 10.17 The Scheduled Tasks folder.

2. Click on the **Add Scheduled Task** icon to open the Scheduled Task Wizard.

145

3. Click **Next**. Select the task you want to run from the list of applications (see Figure 10.18). If the task you want to run is not listed, click **Browse** to locate the application's executable file (the program file that runs the application), select the file, and click **Open** to return to the wizard.

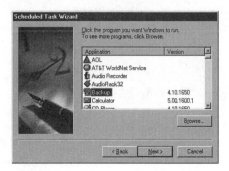

Figure 10.18   Select the application you want to schedule.

4. Click **Next** (click **Back** to return to the previous step). Enter a name for the task (see Figure 10.19) and then select how often the task should run (daily, weekly, monthly, one time only, when your computer starts, or when you log on). Remember, your computer must be on for the scheduled task to run, so pick your schedule with that in mind. Also, if your computer has energy-saving features that put it in suspend mode after a period of inactivity, be aware that some automated tasks may not run until full power is restored.

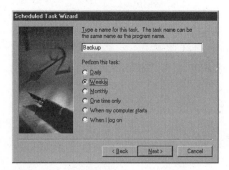

Figure 10.19   Give a name to the task and determine how often it should run.

5. Click **Next**. If you chose to run the task daily, weekly, or monthly, you need to set the scheduled time and days; otherwise, skip to step 6. In the **Start time** box (see Figure 10.20), enter the time of day when the task should run. Then complete the following settings depending on your choice of timing:

> **Daily scheduling** Choose whether to run the task every day, just on weekdays, or at an interval of specified days (enter **2** for every other day, for example). Then select a starting date by clicking in the **Start date** box and picking a date from the pop-up calendar.

> **Weekly scheduling** Enter a number for the weekly interval in the **Every *x* weeks** box (where *x* is the number of weeks between runs of the task) and then check the days of the week on which you want to run the task.

> **Monthly scheduling** Specify the day of the month when you want the task to run by clicking **Day** and then entering the day of the month, or by clicking **The** and then selecting a week and day of the week from the drop-down lists (such as "first" and "Tuesday"). Check the months of the year during which you want the task to run.

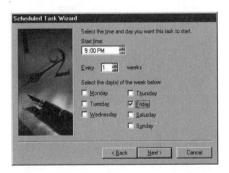

Figure 10.20 To set a weekly schedule, choose a weekly interval and a day of the week to run the task.

6. Click **Next**. The wizard confirms your choices. If you need to set additional options, check **Open advanced properties for this task when I click Finish**.

7. Click **Finish** to add the task to your schedule.

If you checked **Open advanced properties**, the properties box for the task opens. Every scheduled task has properties, which you view by right-clicking the icon and choosing **Properties** from the pop-up menu, or by selecting the icon and then choosing **File, Properties** from the menu. You use the Properties box to view or change the settings for a scheduled task.

The properties box for a scheduled task has three tabs (see Figure 10.21). The **Task** tab lists the filename and path of the scheduled task, the executable file for the application, the name of the folder where the program file or any related files are stored, and a space for comments.

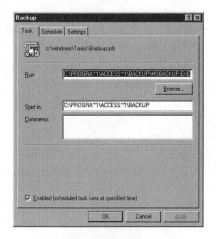

Figure 10.21   The properties for a scheduled backup.

The **Schedule** tab (see Figure 10.22) displays how often the task is scheduled, at what times, and on what days or weeks or months. Click **Advanced** to enter starting and ending dates for the task. Check **Show multiple schedules** to create mixed schedules or more complicated schedules.

Select the **Settings** tab (see Figure 10.23) to set a completion time for the task, tell the scheduler to run the task during the idle times of the computer, or keep the task from running if the computer is running on batteries.

Make any changes to the settings for the scheduled task in the properties box and then click **OK**.

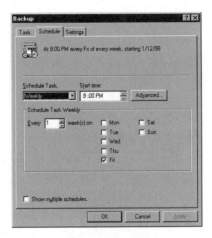

Figure 10.22   The Schedule tab of the properties box.

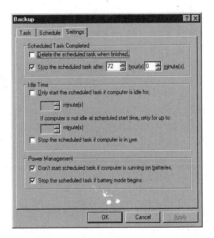

Figure 10.23   Use Settings to run the task only during idle times or only when the battery isn't running.

In addition to scheduling your backups, the task scheduler can run the disk maintenance tasks such as disk defragmenter and ScanDisk, which are discussed in the next lesson.

In this lesson you learned how to set up and run a backup job, how to restore files that you backed up, and how to schedule routine tasks. In the next lesson you'll learn to manage your disk space.

Disk Management

In this lesson, you learn about the utility programs of Windows 98 that help you manage your disk storage capacity and performance.

Understanding Disk Management

How well your system performs is greatly dependent upon your hard drive performance. All of your files—the ones that run your programs as well as your data files—are stored on disks. You must be able to access these files easily and quickly, and you must have sufficient disk space when you add new programs and data files. You also need sufficient disk space for programs that create and use temporary files while they are working (this space is referred to as the *swap file* or *virtual memory*). Without sufficient space for the virtual memory, you may experience errors when trying to run your applications.

One way to maintain disk space is to remove any files you no longer need. Old letters, last year's spreadsheets, last month's newsletter, and so forth can all be archived by storing them on floppy disks or backup tapes. After you've copied the files to disks or backed them up to tape, remove the originals from your hard disk.

Remember to empty your Recycle Bin routinely. The files you place in the Recycle Bin may be out of your other folders, but they still take up space on the hard disk.

In addition to deleting and backing up files, fine-tune your disk. The Windows 98 utilities can help you compress files, make better use of space allocation on the disk, keep files together for quick access, and detect, repair, or replace damaged files.

CAUTION

Always Back Up! Before you do anything to your hard disk (moving files, compressing files, scanning for damaged files, and so on), always back up your files. If any problem occurs, you may need to restore files. For more information on backing up, see Part II, Lesson 10, "Using Task Scheduler and Backing Up."

Some of these utilities aren't automatically loaded when you install Windows 98. If you can't find them, consult Help for instructions on how to load the Windows 98 components, or refer to Part III, Lesson 5, "Adding and Removing Software and Hardware."

Cleaning Up Your Disk

The temporary files that many programs write to your hard disk are no longer needed after you close the session with your application, but unfortunately not all will be deleted when you close a session. If you use the Internet, your hard disk may also be cluttered with files you downloaded or with items cached by your Web browser. You need to routinely remove these from your hard disk. With Internet files, your browser program settings can assist with file cleanup, but Windows itself also writes temporary files to disk.

Fortunately, Windows 98 provides a utility program to help you with this process. This program is called Disk Cleanup.

To use Disk Cleanup, follow these instructions:

1. Open My Computer or the Windows Explorer, select the drive you want to clean up, and then right-click the drive icon. From the pop-up menu, select **Properties**. When the Properties box appears, select the **General** tab and then click **Disk CleanUp**.

Or, select the drive icon in My Computer or the Windows Explorer and then choose **File, Properties** from the menu or click the Properties button on the toolbar. When the Properties box appears, select the **General** tab and then click **Disk CleanUp**.

Or, choose **Programs, Accessories, System Tools, Disk Cleanup** from the Start menu.

2. Disk Cleanup calculates the space you should be able to free on your disk. Then the Disk Cleanup dialog box appears (see Figure 11.1).

Figure 11.1 The Disk Cleanup dialog box.

3. In the **Files to remove** box, a list of file types that may need removing appears. Each file type has a check box in front of it. Click to check the boxes for the file types you want to clear off your disk, such as Temporary Internet Files, Downloaded Program Files, or Temporary Files. When you select a file type, information about the file type appears in the **Description** area of the dialog box. To see the files involved, click **View Files**.

4. Click **OK** to begin the disk cleanup. Disk Cleanup will ask you if you want to delete the files. Click **Yes**.

5. A small dialog box displays the progress of the cleanup process. When the process is complete, this box disappears.

Using Disk Defragmenter

When files are stored on new disks, they are written one after another. As time goes by, one file gets deleted, leaving a "hole," and then another, and so on. The "holes" are scattered all over the disk. As the disk becomes filled, the new files are stored on the disk filling up the "holes" left by the deleted files. However, one "hole" may not be enough for a file, so part of it is stored there and another part is stored on another part of the disk.

Over time, your files become scattered or *fragmented* across the disk. When a program retrieves a file, it takes longer to put the file's pieces together if the file has become fragmented. You see the whole file but may not realize that it's fragmented. Slow access time to retrieve the file alerts you that the file might be fragmented.

The Disk Defragmenter reorganizes the files on the disk and puts the fragmented files together. This speeds up your file retrieval, so you get your files faster. It also frees up larger chunks of space for future file storage.

The Disk Defragmenter Wizard takes this one step further by analyzing which programs you use most frequently. It creates a log file that records your most commonly used files, and then it uses this information to store these files in one location on your disk for quicker access.

You should close all your open applications when you're running the Defragmenter. Although the Disk Defragmenter can run in the background (meaning you should be able to run other applications at the same time you're defragmenting your disk), you run the risk of having one of your applications write to your disk, which causes the process to start all over again. It's best to run the Disk Defragmenter when you won't need to use your computer, such as after hours or on the weekend. The Task Scheduler can schedule the Disk Defragmenter for these off times and make sure that the process is run routinely (see Lesson 10).

Defragmenting a large disk can take quite a while. If you need to run an application during defragmentation, click **Pause** to temporarily halt the Disk Defragmenter. This allows the application to run faster. Click **Resume** to continue the defragmentation.

To start Disk Defragmenter:

1. Choose **Programs**, **Accessories**, **System Tools**, **Disk Defragmenter** from the **Start** menu.

   Or, right-click the drive icon in My Computer or Windows Explorer, choose **Properties** from the pop-up menu, select the **Tools** tab, and then click **Defragment Now**. Skip to step 5.

2. When you open the Disk Defragmenter from the Start menu, the Select Drive dialog box appears (see Figure 11.2). Select the drive you want to defragment from the drop-down list.

Figure 11.2   The Select Drive dialog box.

3. (Optional) Click **Settings** to specify how you want the Disk Defragmenter
to work (see Figure 11.3). If you don't want your files arranged in one
contiguous unit, but would rather have your program files optimized for
quick startup, check **Rearrange program files so my programs start faster.**
To have the utility also check your files and folders for errors before
defragmenting your disk, enable **Check the drive for errors.** Then select
whether you want to use the options **This time only** or **Every time I
defragment my hard drive**. Click **OK** to return to the Select Drive
dialog box.

Figure 11.3   The Disk Defragmenter Settings dialog box.

4. Click **OK**. If your disk does not need to be defragmented, a dialog box will
appear, suggesting that you cancel Defragmenter. You can choose to cancel
or continue.

5. When the Defragmenting dialog box appears (see Figure 11.4), click **Stop**
to end the process, **Pause** to temporarily stop the process, **Resume** to
continue the process, or **Show Details** to see the details of the process as
it's happening.

Figure 11.4 The Defragmenting dialog box.

6. When the Defragmenter is finished, a dialog box will alert you that the process is complete.

Using DriveSpace

Need more space for your files? DriveSpace can free up space on hard and floppy disks. It compresses data on the disk, giving you 50% to 100% more free space. By using DriveSpace, you can also configure drives that have already been compressed with DoubleSpace or previous versions of DriveSpace.

Before using DriveSpace on your disks, there are some considerations about when you want to use this utility:

- **Compressed files** If you have a lot of ZIP files or other compressed files on your disk, you may not want to use DriveSpace. DriveSpace cannot further compress these files.

- **Dual Boot** Don't use DriveSpace if your system is set to also boot into other operating systems besides Windows 98 (such as Windows NT or OS/2), because DriveSpace isn't compatible with these operating systems and they won't be able to read the disk.

- **Large Disk** DriveSpace produces the best results on disks that are smaller than 512MB. If your disk is larger than 2G and isn't partitioned into more than one drive (the entire disk is assigned to one drive letter), you can't use DriveSpace.

- **FAT32** If you have converted your disk to FAT32 (see the next section "Using FAT32"), you can't use DriveSpace on the same disk.

- **Slower Performance** DriveSpace can slow the performance of your disk. Most of the time, this slowness is not noticeable.

- **Disks** If you use DriveSpace on a floppy disk, you'll only be able to use that disk with systems that have Windows 95 or Windows 98 and have DriveSpace loaded.

- **Applications**   Some applications do not work well on disks that use DriveSpace. Check your application manuals first before using DriveSpace.

Compressing a drive can take quite a bit of time. You want to do this when you won't be using the computer for other tasks.

To compress a drive:

1. Choose **Programs, Accessories, System Tools, DriveSpace** from the **Start** menu. The DriveSpace window opens (see Figure 11.5).

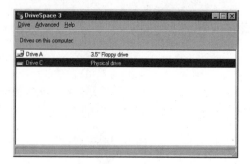

Figure 11.5   The DriveSpace 3 window.

2. Select the drive you want to compress.

3. Choose **Drive, Compress** from the menu. The Compress a Drive window appears (see Figure 11.6). The left side of the window shows the current free space on the disk; the right side shows the projected free space after compression.

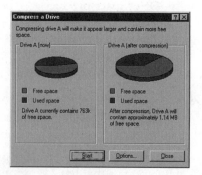

Figure 11.6   The Compress a Drive window.

4. Click **Start**.

5. (Optional) If you haven't backed up your files, click **Back Up Files** and follow the instructions on the screen (or use the instructions in Part II, Lesson 10, "Using Task Scheduler and Backing Up").

6. Click **Compress Now**.

7. Windows may prompt you to restart your computer. Click **Yes**. Otherwise, the Compress a Drive window reappears, reporting the amount of space gained by the compression. Then click **Close**.

 TIP **Maximum Compression** To get the maximum compression from DriveSpace, choose **Advanced, Settings** from the DriveSpace menu and select **HiPack compression**. Then click **OK**. When you use HiPack compression, you get more available space on your disk, but you do sacrifice system speed.

After you run DriveSpace, you will see two drives listed in the DriveSpace window. If you compressed drive C, one is the "compressed drive C" and the other is the "host drive" for drive C.

The compressed drive isn't really a drive—it's an artificial designation. It appears as a drive to Windows and to your programs, but the entire contents of the compressed drive are really stored in a single file called a *compressed volume file* (CVF). The compressed volume file is located on the host drive. The default drive assignment for the host drive is **H**, although you can change that by clicking **Options** in the Compress a Drive window and changing the drive letter assigned to the host drive. The host drive also contains any necessary system files needed to access the compressed files and run DriveSpace.

The host drive doesn't appear in My Computer or the Windows Explorer. It's hidden unless it has more than 2MB of free space.

After you have used DriveSpace on your disk, you can use the Compression Agent to change the level of compression to give you even more space on your disk. DriveSpace applies a standard compression to your files, although you can opt for HiPack compression. The Compression Agent applies UltraPack compression. To use the Compression Agent to recompress your files:

1. Choose **Programs, Accessories, System Tools, Compression Agent** from the **Start** menu.

157

2. When the Compression Agent opens (see Figure 11.7), click Settings to choose the level of compression you want to apply and what files you want recompressed.

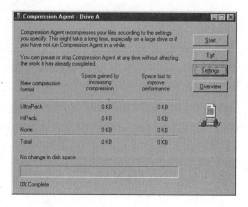

Figure 11.7   The Compression Agent window.

3. The Compression Agent Settings dialog box appears (see Figure 11.8). Select an option to determine which files receive UltraPack compression—none, all, or those not used in the specified time period (you specify the number of days). Then choose whether you want HiPack compression applied to the remainder of the files or not. Click **OK**.

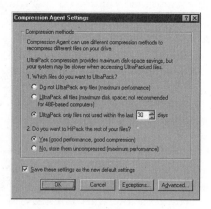

Figure 11.8   The Compression Agent Settings dialog box.

4. Click **Start**.

5. When the recompression is complete, the Compression Agent dialog box displays the amount of space gained. Click **Exit** to close the window.

To uncompress a drive:

1. From the DriveSpace window, click on the drive you want to uncompress.

2. Choose **Drive, Uncompress** from the menu.

3. Click **Start**.

4. Click **Uncompress Now**.

5. Click **Yes** to remove the compression driver from memory (which means you can't run DriveSpace again but you'll save disk space) or **No** to keep it.

6. When the drive has been uncompressed, click **Close**.

7. Close the DriveSpace window.

Using FAT32

Computers using MS-DOS and Windows as their operating systems use a *file allocation table* (FAT) to track and control the allocation of space on the disks. The FAT allocates a certain amount of space to each file. If the file doesn't use the entire allotment, the rest is unused disk space that can't be reassigned to another file. Unfortunately, as the size of disks grew, MS-DOS and then Windows had difficulty keeping up with them, so the allocation was expanded for each file to meet the larger size of the disk—using as much as 32K of disk space for a one-byte file. This wasted a lot of disk space.

Another problem of the older FAT and FAT16 systems was that the maximum size of a drive was limited to 2 gigabytes. You were forced to partition any larger disk into two or more drives.

The FAT32 system eliminates the 2GB barrier and uses smaller allocation units so you can store more files in the same amount of space. Instead of allocating 32K of disk space for a one-byte file, FAT32 allocates about 4K of space.

There are some things to keep in mind when you consider converting your drive to FAT32:

- After you convert your disk to FAT32, you can't convert it back to FAT16 without partitioning the drive and reformatting it. This also would make it necessary to reinstall Windows 98 (unless the drive was not your boot drive).

- You can't convert a disk you've compressed with DriveSpace to FAT32. You also can't run DriveSpace on a disk that has been converted to FAT32.

- If you convert a floppy or removable disk to FAT32, you can't use it with another operating system.

- Do not use FAT32 on a disk drive if you dual-boot the computer (use it sometimes with another operating system, such as Windows NT or OS/2).

- There is little benefit in converting a disk under 512MB to FAT32. Use DriveSpace to gain more disk space on a drive that small.

- You can't uninstall Windows 98 if you convert to FAT32.

- Hibernate features, such as suspend to disk, won't work on a FAT32 drive.

- Some of your disk utilities might not work as well with FAT32. Contact the manufacturer for a version that is compatible with FAT32. The disk utilities in Windows 98 have already been upgraded to be compatible with FAT32.

- There will be a slight performance loss after you convert to FAT32, although you may not notice it.

Close all open applications, save your files, and back up your disk before conversion. To convert your disk to FAT32, do the following:

1. Choose **Programs, Accessories, System Tools, Drive Converter** (FAT32) from the **Start** menu.

2. The Drive Converter wizard appears. Click **Next** to begin the process.

3. Select the drive you want to convert (see Figure 11.9). Click **Next**.

Figure 11.9   Select the drive you want to convert.

4. A warning appears to let you know that the Converter must reboot your system. Click **Next**. (Until the conversion is complete, you won't be able to use your system).

After the FAT32 conversion, the Disk Defragmenter will run on the drive the next time you reboot your computer. Be aware that your system performance may not be up to par until after this process has been run. So, if you stop the process so you can work on an application, make sure you run it as soon as possible after you complete your tasks on the computer.

CAUTION

Working with Anti-Virus Programs The conversion requires updating of your partition table and boot record. If the anti-virus program detects the changes to the partition table and boot record during rebooting, *do not* allow the anti-virus software to restore the boot record or partition table. Your drive will become inaccessible.

Using ScanDisk

Your hard disk can harbor damaged files, partial files, or unnecessary files. Part of the hard disk itself may be defective. Check your files and folders for data errors by using ScanDisk. ScanDisk will also check the physical surface of your drive.

To start ScanDisk:

1. Choose **Programs, Accessories, System Tools, ScanDisk** from the **Start** menu, or from My Computer or Windows Explorer, right-click the drive icon, choose **Properties** from the pop-up menu, select the **Tools** tab, and click **Check Now**. The ScanDisk window appears (see Figure 11.10).

2. Select the drive you want to scan for errors.

3. Under **Type of test**, choose which type of test you want to run. Select **Standard** to check files and folders for data errors. Choose **Thorough** to go beyond the Standard test and scan the disk surface for errors as well.

4. If you selected the Thorough test, click **Options** to specify how you want ScanDisk to scan the disk surface. The Surface Scan Options dialog box opens (see Figure 11.11). Select the options for the test and click **OK** to exit the dialog box.

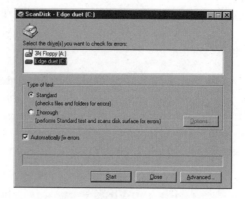

Figure 11.10   The ScanDisk window.

Figure 11.11   The Surface Scan Options dialog box.

You can choose to scan the System area only, the Data area only, or both the System and data areas.

When ScanDisk checks a disk, it reads the contents of every sector and then writes the contents back. By doing this, it verifies that the drive can be read from and written to. **Check Do not perform write-testing** if you don't want ScanDisk to write the contents back.

ScanDisk repairs bad sectors on your disk. Data in a bad sector gets moved to a valid location. Problems may arise with system and hidden files if they are moved, because some programs require that these files be stored in a specific location. Moving the files may cause serious problems. To protect the location of these files, check **Do not repair bad sectors in hidden and system files**.

Check **Automatically fix errors** to have ScanDisk repair your data errors.

5. Click **Start**.

6. When the process is complete, ScanDisk reports the bad sectors, how many files are on the disk, how many allocation units are on the disk, how many bytes in each allocation unit, and so forth. Click **Close** to close the dialog box.

You can specify how ScanDisk works by clicking the **Advanced** button before clicking **Start**. The Advanced Options dialog box appears (see Figure 11.12). In the Advanced Options dialog box, you specify what to check files for and what files should be replaced, copied, or deleted, as well as telling ScanDisk to provide a summary or keep a log of its activities. Select the options you want and then click **OK**.

Figure 11.12 The Advanced Options dialog box.

ScanDisk automatically runs if you shut off the operating system without going through Shutdown (a major cause of disk errors). This gives ScanDisk the opportunity to immediately repair any damage caused by improper shutdown.

You should run ScanDisk on a routine basis. Use the Task Scheduler to set a schedule for it to run (see Part II, Lesson 10, "Using Task Scheduler and Backing Up") or add ScanDisk to the StartUp folder (see Part III, Lesson 4, "Customizing the Start Menu").

When ScanDisk finds errors, such as file fragments, it presents you with choices about what to do with the damaged file. One choice is to discard the file fragment and recover lost disk space. Another is to convert the fragment into a file, which usually is saved as File0001 or File0002. The last choice is to ignore the error and continue.

Using the System File Checker Utility

The System File Checker deals only with system files needed to run the operating system. These files have extensions such as com, dll, drv, hlp, inf, ocx, and vxd. The utility verifies that these files haven't been corrupted or modified, restores them if they are corrupted, or extracts the necessary compressed files from your installation disks to replace damaged ones.

To run the System File Checker:

1. Choose **Programs, Accessories, System Tools, System Information** from the **Start** menu.

2. Choose **System File Checker** from the **Tools** menu.

3. The System File Checker opens (see Figure 11.13). You can do two different things with the System File Checker. Choose **Scan files for errors** to scan the system files for possible corruption or modification, or click **Extract one file from installation disk** if you need to pull a compressed file from the installation disk onto your hard drive. If you chose the latter, enter the name and path of the file in the **File to extract** box or click **Browse** to select the file.

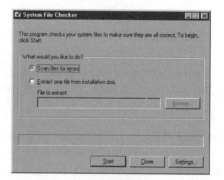

Figure 11.13 The System File Checker window.

4. Click **Settings** to set options for the system file scan. These options include specifying an automatic backup before restoring the files, whether to log the results, choosing what to check for (deleted or changed files or both), what drives and folders to scan, and what file types to check. Make your selections and click **OK**.

5. Click **Start**.

6. If you're extracting a file, insert the installation disk in the disk drive. The file is uncompressed and copied to your hard disk.

If you're scanning files and the System File Checker identifies a file that may be corrupted, the File Corrupted dialog box appears (see Figure 11.14). You are offered three choices: choose **Update verification information** if you know a newer version of this file is available, **Restore file** to restore the uncorrupted file from the installation disks, or **Ignore** to ignore the warning this time. Click **OK** to continue.

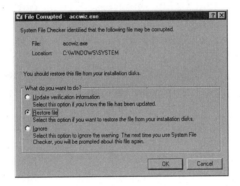

Figure 11.14 The File Corrupted dialog box.

7. When the scan is finished, a dialog box appears. Click **OK**.

8. Click **Close** to exit the System File Checker.

Using Maintenance Wizard

The Maintenance Wizard helps you make your programs run faster, check your hard disk for problems, and free up hard disk space. It does this by running Disk Defragmenter, ScanDisk, and Disk Cleanup for you. Plus, it schedules when these utilities should run.

To run the Maintenance Wizard:

1. Choose **Programs, Accessories, System Tools, Maintenance Wizard** from the **Start** menu.

2. If you have already set up Maintenance Wizard, you will get a dialog box asking if you want to perform maintenance now or change your maintenance settings or schedule. Choose **Change your maintenance settings or schedule**.

3. Click **Next**. If you chose **Express**, choose a schedule for the tune-ups: Nights (midnight to 3:00 a.m.), Days (noon to 3:00 p.m.), or Evenings (8:00 p.m. to 11:00 p.m.. Click Next.

If you selected **Custom**, select **Days**, **Nights**, **Evenings**, or **Custom** for the schedule. When you select Custom, you may later change the schedule for any specific task.

4. The last window in the Maintenance Wizard displays the tasks **usually Speed up your most frequently used programs, Check hard disk for errors**, and **Delete unnecessary files from hard disk**, which you have set up (see Figure 11.15). Click **Finish** to accept the work you have done or **Back** to change settings.

Figure 11.15   The last window of the Maintenance Wizard.

The tasks you set up will run when you scheduled them. If you used this method, you don't have to do Disk Cleanup, ScanDisk, or Disk Defragmenter individually.

In this lesson, you learned how to maintain your disk by compressing its files or using a new file allocation table to make more room, defragmenting files to consolidate free space, and scanning the disk for data errors. In the next lesson, you'll learn about working with floppy disks.

Working with Floppy Disks

In this lesson you learn how to format a floppy disk, copy the entire contents of one disk to another, and name a disk.

Formatting Floppy Disks

One way to store your files or take them with you is to copy them onto floppy disks, or diskettes. A floppy disk today is usually a high-density $3^1/_2$-inch disk that stores about 1.44MB of data.

Reliable preformatted floppy disks are available for little more than the price of unformatted disks, so the need to format your floppies is not as prevalent as it once was. However, you may prefer to format your own or want to format a previously used disk to thoroughly erase it and start fresh.

 TERM   **Formatting**   Formatting divides a disk into tracks and sectors so that the operating system can find and identify the files stored on the disk.

Formatting erases all of the files on a disk, so be sure to check the disk contents thoroughly before you format it.

To format a floppy disk:

1. Open My Computer or the Windows Explorer. Close all other windows that display information about or are using the drive you are about to format.
2. Select the floppy disk drive (usually A:, although some computers may also have a second floppy disk drive that is B:).
3. Right-click the drive icon and choose **Format** from the pop-up menu. The Format dialog box appears (see Figure 12.1).

Figure 12.1 The Format dialog box.

4. From the **Capacity** drop-down list, select **720Kb (3.5")** if your disk is low-density or **1.44Mb (3.5")** if your disk is high-density (usually has an HD on the disk or label).

5. Select a **Format type**:

- Quick removes all the files from the disk without scanning for bad sectors. Use this type format only on disks that have been previously formatted.

- Full removes any files that are on the disk and scans for any bad sectors, in addition to preparing the disk to receive information.

- Copy system files only should be used on a disk that is already formatted. You make this choice if you are copying system files to a boot disk (one that you can use to start your computer if you are unable to start it from the hard disk). The resulting boot disk is also called a system disk, and it's a good idea to have one in case of hard disk emergencies.

6. (Optional) To give a name to the disk that helps identify it, type a name in the **Label** box. You can use up to 11 characters in the name.

7. If you don't want to name the formatted disk (see step 6), check **No label**.

8. Check **Copy system files** to add those files to the disk after it's formatted, so you can use the disk to start up your computer in case of a failure. However, you will also be able to add other files to the disk if you use this option.

9. Click **Start**.

10. The results of the formatting appear when the process is complete (see Figure 12.2). Click **Close** to close the dialog box.

Figure 12.2 The results of the formatting process.

11. The Format dialog box remains open, in case you want to format another disk. If you do, repeat steps 4 through 10. If not, click **Close**.

Copying Disks

You learned how to copy files in Part II, Lesson 3, "Managing Files with My Computer." Copying a disk is not the same thing. When you copy a disk, you make an exact duplicate of the original disk, including hidden, compressed, and system files. For MS-DOS users, this method is the same as using the Diskcopy command.

Most often the reason you copy disks is to make duplicates of installation disks, in case one of the disks gets damaged during the installation process.

When you copy disks, you must copy from and to the same type of disk (for example, from one high-density $3^1/_2$-inch disk to another). Any existing data on the target disk (the disk you're copying to) will be erased.

To copy a disk, do the following:

1. Insert the disk you want to copy into your disk drive.

2. In My Computer or Windows Explorer, select the drive icon for the disk you want to copy.

3. Right-click the icon.

4. From the pop-up menu, select **Copy Disk**. The Copy Disk dialog box opens (see Figure 12.3). The disk you selected is listed in the **Copy from** box (also called the *source*). In the **Copy to** box, select the drive to which you will copy the duplicate (also called the *target*). You can specify the same drive for both disks.

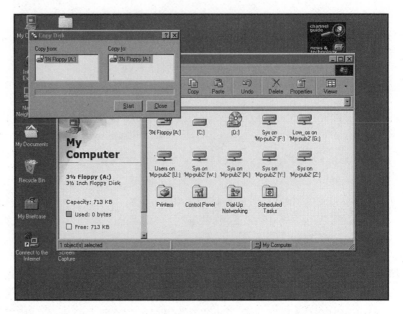

Figure 12.3   Select the drive where you want to put the duplicate disk.

5. Click **Start**.

6. The copying process begins by reading the source disk. When asked to insert the destination disk into the drive, remove the source disk and insert the target disk into the drive. Then click **OK**.

7. Windows 98 begins writing to the destination disk. When the writing is complete, the Copy Disk dialog box returns. If you need to copy another disk, insert the new source disk in the disk drive and follow steps 5 and 6. If you don't want to copy another disk, click **Close**.

If you were used to working with the Diskcopy command in MS-DOS, you remember having to trade disks back and forth—first putting in the source disk, then the target disk, then the source disk again, and then the target disk again. Because Windows 98 stores the entire contents of the source disk in memory after reading it, you will rarely have to put the disks in for a second pass in order to read and write the entire contents. To learn more about MS-DOS, see Appendix B, "DOS and Legacy Applications."

Naming Disks

As explained in "Formatting Floppy Disks" earlier in this lesson, you name a disk by applying a label to it during the formatting process. Many people don't apply labels to their disks because they frequently change the contents. They prefer to rely on the paper label on the outside of the disk.

To give a disk a name or label, or to change its current label, do the following:

1. In My Computer or Windows Explorer, select the disk you want to name.

2. Choose **File, Properties** on the menu or right-click the icon and select **Properties** from the pop-up menu.

3. The Properties box appears (see Figure 12.4). Enter or change the name of the disk by changing the text in the **Label** box. The name cannot be longer than 11 characters.

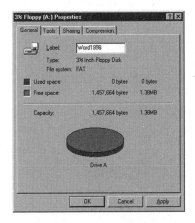

Figure 12.4 Enter the name of the disk in the Label box.

4. Click **OK**.

In this lesson you learned to format floppy disks, duplicate disks, and name them. In Part III, "Customizing and Maintaining Windows 98," you'll learn how to set up Windows 98 to suit yourself, beginning with finding out about the Control Panel.

Customizing
and
Maintaining
Windows 98

Understanding the Control Panel

In this lesson, you will find out how to access and use elements found in the Control Panel.

What Is the Control Panel?

Access the Control Panel to change the appearance of your desktop, choose a screensaver, change your default font, the time and date, and so forth. From the Control Panel you can configure your Windows environment to work the way you want it to.

Access the Control Panel one of these ways:

- From the taskbar, click the Start button and then choose **Settings**, **Control Panel**. The Control Panel window appears (see Figure 1.1).
- From the desktop, click My Computer and then click the Control Panel folder icon. The Control Panel window appears (see Figure 1.1).
- From Windows Explorer, click the Control Panel folder found in the left pane of the window. The contents of the Control Panel appear in the right panel (see Figure 1.2). These are the same icons that are displayed in the Control Panel window.

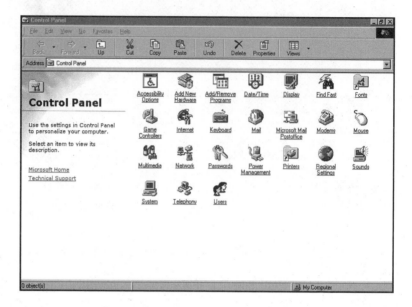

Figure 1.1   Access settings to change how your hardware and software work from the Control Panel.

Figure 1.2   The Control Panel in Windows Explorer.

CAUTION

My Control Panel Isn't Like the One in the Book!   Don't be alarmed if the icons in your Control Panel don't match the ones you see in these figures. Some of them, such as the mouse, will differ depending on the peripheral equipment you have and who manufactured it.

Once the Control Panel is open, you click the icon that represents the feature you want to change. A dialog box or properties box opens and displays options that affect that feature.

What Can You Accomplish in the Control Panel?

The Control Panel contains a set of icons indicating the different areas that you can modify to customize your computer configuration. In this book we only discuss the most commonly used features of the Control Panel. They include:

- **Set Accessibility Options**   Some disabilities can make computer operation difficult. Accessibility options provide ways to adjust computer hardware to make computing easier for impaired operators. For example, you can set the keyboard to slow it down, or ignore repeated keystrokes, or play tones when you press Caps Lock, Num Lock, or Scroll Lock. You can set visual warnings to replace sound warnings, display captions for computer speech and sounds, add more contrast to the screen for easier reading, and transfer command of the mouse pointer to the numeric pad of the keyboard. To learn more about using and setting accessibility options, see Part III, Lesson 14, "Accessibility Options."

- **Add New Hardware**   Windows 98 detects most new hardware automatically. This capability is referred to as the plug and play feature of Windows 98. When Windows 98 fails to detect your new hardware, use the Add New Hardware feature to start a wizard. The wizard searches for and identifies the new hardware so Windows 98 can work with it properly. For more information, see Part III, Lesson 5, "Adding and Removing Software and Hardware."

TERM

Wizard   A program within Windows that helps you perform a specific task. Wizards ask you questions about the task and then automatically perform operations that complete the task for you.

- **Add or Remove Programs**   Install or uninstall software with the help of a Wizard. Here too you can add or remove components of Windows 98 itself, such as games and Web TV for Windows. For more information, see Part III, Lesson 5, "Adding and Removing Software and Hardware."

- **Set the System Date and Time**   Although the internal clock of your computer maintains the current date and time, you may occasionally have to adjust it for a new time zone or to turn off Daylight Savings settings when you're in a particular area. Learn how to change the system date and time in Part III, Lesson 3, "Customizing the Taskbar."

- **Change Desktop Colors and Backgrounds**   Add colors or patterns to the background of your desktop and change the look of the windows and pick new window themes. To learn how to change desktop colors and backgrounds, see Part III, Lesson 2, "Customizing the Active Desktop."

- **Add or Switch Screen Savers**   Screen savers preserve your monitor quality, and you can select the one you want to use. Learn how to change screen savers later in this lesson.

- **Add or Remove Fonts**   Add new fonts, remove old fonts, and view fonts with this option. For more information on working with fonts, see Part III, Lesson 10, "Managing Fonts."

- **Change Settings on Your Keyboard**   You can change the character repeat speed of your keyboard. This is the speed at which a character repeats when you hold down the key on your keyboard. You can also set the length of delay interval before a key repeats, to give you time to move your finger off a key before you get a repeat of the same character. To customize your keyboard, see Part III, Lesson 7, "Configuring Peripheral Devices and Sound Options."

- **Configure Your Modem**   Adjust the settings on your modem. See how to configure a modem in Part III, Lesson 8, "Configuring a Modem."

- **Adjust the Settings for Your Mouse**   Set the speed of the mouse pointer and the double-click, as well as swap buttons for left-handed users. For instructions on adjusting your mouse, see Part III, Lesson 7, "Configuring Peripheral Devices and Sound Options."

- **Change Settings for Multimedia Devices**   If you are using audio or video devices with your computer, you adjust the settings for those devices through the Control Panel. Learn more about multimedia devices in Part IV, Lesson 6, "Using Windows 98 Entertainment Features."

- **Set or Change Passwords**   Protect your computer from unauthorized people by assigning passwords. You can set or change your password from the Control Panel. To set or change a password, see Part III, Lesson 6, "Sharing Workstations and Setting Passwords."

- **Change Regional Settings**   If you're working outside the United States, you can change the standard settings for how currency, numbers, dates, and times appear. For most average users, it is sufficient to set the country here and there is no need to change or set other regional settings.

- **Modify Internet Settings**   Specify where your temporary Internet files are stored, set parameters for the History folder, select the page to use as your home page, select security options, specify connection types, and set preferred programs. To learn more about Windows 98 and the Internet, see Part V, "Windows 98 and the Internet."

- **Adjust System and Program Sounds**   Certain sounds signify different events, and you can choose which sounds you want to hear. Learn how to assign sound options in Part III, Lesson 7, "Configuring Peripheral Devices and Sound Options."

- **Set up Mail and Fax**   Set up the messaging profiles to send and receive e-mail and faxes. Faxing capability will be available only if you upgraded from Windows 95. Windows 98 doesn't come with its own fax service. For more information on Outlook Express, see Part V, Lesson 10, "Configuring Outlook Express."

- **Configure Your System for Networking**   Make the settings that help you connect your system to a network. To learn more about working with networked computers, see Part VI, "Networking and Mobile Computing with Windows 98."

- **Set Up for Dialing Out**   Enter the settings needed to establish the dialing properties for your system. To see how to configure dial-up properties, see Part VI, Lesson 7, "Connecting to a Network from a Remote Location."

- **Manage the Use of Your Power Resources**   Set alarms and establish standby schemes for your laptop battery. Learn all about laptops running Windows 98 in Part VI, Lesson 5, "Working on a Laptop Computer."

- **Find System Information and Make Advanced Settings**   You can manage the devices in your computer system and view their current settings. See how to use Device Manager in Part III, Lesson 9, "Understanding and Using the Device Manager."

Selecting a Screen Saver

A screen saver is a moving picture or pattern than appears on your screen when you've left the computer idle for a specified number of minutes.

Screen savers can be interesting and fun to watch, but did you know that screen savers are designed to prevent monitor burn-in? When the same image stays on the screen for periods of time without changing, it can leave a ghost image that you can see even when the monitor is turned off. To prevent burn-in, turn off your monitor when you walk away from it, or use a screen saver. Screen savers display constantly moving images to prevent burn in.

Newer computer monitors are not as susceptible to burn-in as older models were. Many of them are equipped with energy-saving or-reducing features that put the monitor on standby mode in which the monitor blanks out until you move the mouse or press a key.

When a screen saver is enabled, or turns on and off automatically, an idle keyboard and mouse trigger the screen saver to start, and touching the mouse or pressing a key on the keyboard deactivates the screen saver.

The screen saver also has an optional security feature in which you can assign a password. Once the screen saver activates, the password is needed to deactivate the screen saver and continue working. Use this feature when you don't want casual passersby or coworkers to have access to your computer when you walk away from your desk.

Windows 98 comes with several screen savers. To select a screen saver:

1. Choose **Settings**, **Control Panel** from the **Start** menu and then click the **Display** icon, or right-click the desktop and choose **Properties** from the pop-up menu.

2. When the Display Properties dialog box appears, select the **Screen Saver** tab (see Figure 1.3).

3. From the **Screen Saver** drop-down list, select a screen saver. A sample appears in the monitor on the dialog box. Click **Preview** to see a full-screen version.

Figure 1.3   The small monitor in the middle of the dialog box previews the selected screen saver.

4. Many screen savers can be customized. With screen savers such as 3D Text and Scrolling Marquis, you need to enter the text that will move across your screen. Other screen savers let you set the speed, the colors, the number of elements, and the shape of the elements. To customize your screen saver, click **Settings**. After you set your options, click **OK** to return to the Display Properties dialog box.

5. In the **Wait** box, enter the number of minutes that represents the amount of time the system is idle before the screen saver activates.

6. If you want to set a password for your screen saver, click **Password protected**. Click **Change** and enter your password in the **New password** box (see Figure 1.4). As you type, you'll only see asterisks, so be careful not to misspell your password. Then type the password again in **Confirm new password** and click **OK**. After you create a screen saver password, you won't be able to turn off the screen saver without entering your password.

Figure 1.4   Enter your new screen saver password.

181

7. For computers with energy-saving features, you adjust the standby and power settings by clicking **Settings** and entering your options in the Power Management Properties box (as explained in Part VI, Lesson 5, "Working on a Laptop Computer").

8. Click **OK** to accept your settings and close the dialog box. Click **Apply** to accept your settings without closing the dialog box. Click **Cancel** to close the dialog box without saving your settings.

In this lesson you learned about the Control Panel and what it can do for you. You also learned how to select and configure a screen saver. In the next lesson you'll learn to customize your desktop.

Customizing the Active Desktop

In this lesson, you learn how to create shortcut icons to your favorite programs or documents, how to arrange the icons on your desktop, how to add color and background patterns to your desktop, and how to change the desktop fonts.

Creating Shortcuts

A shortcut is a quick way to access a program, printer, folder, or document you use often. The shortcut appears as an icon on your desktop that acts as a pointer to that program, printer, or document.

To create a shortcut:

1. From My Computer, Windows Explorer, or Network Neighborhood, select the icon that represents the program or printer for which you will create a shortcut. For example, to create a program shortcut, select the program's executable file (such as the Word icon). To create a printer shortcut, select the appropriate printer. To create a folder icon, select the folder.

TIP   **Executable File**   An executable file is the file that starts a program. You can identify it by the icon, which should match the logo of the software product. These files have an EXE file extension (see Part II, Lesson 2, "Using My Computer," to learn how to display file extensions). To test a file to see if it is the executable file, click its icon. The program should start. To learn more about DOS file extensions, see Appendix B, "DOS and Legacy Applications."

2. From the menu, choose **File, Create Shortcut** or click the right mouse button and select **Create Shortcut** from the pop-up menu.

3. An icon will appear in the window labeled as "Shortcut to" the program, printer, or document you selected. The icon looks the same as the icon you originally selected, except it is smaller and has an arrow in its lower-left corner (see Figure 2.1).

A new shortcut icon ——

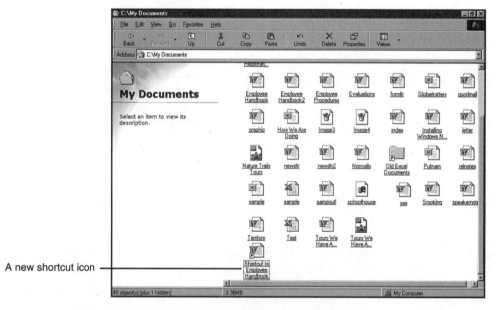

Figure 2.1   A shortcut icon created within My Computer.

4. Drag that icon to the desktop. (You will not be able to drag the printer shortcut, but Windows 98 will ask if you want to put it on the desktop. Click **Yes**.)

5. To rename the shortcut, click once on the name to place your cursor there (or right-click the icon and choose **Rename** from the pop-up menu), enter the name you want to assign to the shortcut, and press the Enter key.

TIP   **Using the Right Mouse Button**   A quick way to make a shortcut is to point to the icon in My Computer or Windows Explorer, hold down your right mouse button, and drag the icon to your desktop. When you release the right mouse button, a pop-up menu opens. Select **Create Shortcut(s) Here**, and the shortcut icon appears on the desktop.

An alternative to creating shortcuts from My Computer or Windows Explorer is to make them from the Start menu for any entry on the Programs, Favorites, or Documents submenu. Point to the entry, hold down the right mouse button, and drag the icon to the desktop. Choose **Create Shortcut(s) Here** from the menu that appears.

Another way to create a shortcut is to right-click an open area of the desktop and choose **New, Shortcut** from the pop-up menu. When the Create Shortcut dialog box opens (see Figure 2.2), enter the path and name of the folder, executable file (for a program), or document file for which you are creating the shortcut. If you aren't sure of the name or location, click **Browse** and select the file or folder from the Browse dialog box. Click **Next** and then enter a name for the shortcut. Then click **Finish**.

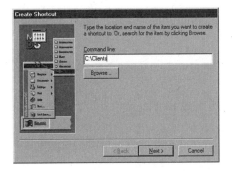

Figure 2.2   Enter the name and location of the file or folder to which you're making the shortcut.

To use a shortcut, click the icon. If the shortcut is to a program, it will start the program. If the shortcut is to a document, it will start the program associated with the document and then open that document. If the shortcut is to a printer, just drag a document icon over the shortcut to print the document. If you drag a document icon over a program shortcut, the program will start and then open that document.

You don't have to be stuck with the icon that automatically appears for the shortcut. Right-click the icon and choose **Properties** from the pop-up menu. On the Shortcut tab of the Properties dialog box, click **Change Icon**. The **Current icon** box (see Figure 2.3) displays the set of available icons for your shortcut (this set may be more limited for program shortcuts or for documents associated with programs). Click an icon to select it (click **Browse** to find icons from other locations, such as the \Windows\System folder) and then click **OK**. Click **OK** to close the Properties dialog box.

Figure 2.3   Select a new icon for your shortcut.

To remove a shortcut icon, drag it to the Recycle Bin or select the shortcut icon and then press the Delete key. If you delete the shortcut, you're not deleting the program, printer, or document—you're only removing the icon from your desktop. However, if you delete or remove the program, document, or printer, the shortcut no longer has anything to point to and clicking it results in an error message to that effect.

Shortcuts aren't confined to the Windows desktop. Try placing a shortcut in a folder that lets you open another related folder. If you use email, drag a file shortcut onto your email message and when the recipients open the message they can click on the shortcut to open the file (this is *embedding* shortcuts, which is discussed more fully in Part IV, Lesson 7, "OLE: Linking Data to Different Applications"). Shortcuts can also be added to the Start menu (see Part III, Lesson 4, "Customizing the Start Menu").

Arranging Icons

When shortcuts are added to the Desktop, they are not arranged neatly. You can control, or arrange the appearance of icons on the Desktop.

To arrange your desktop icons:

1. Click an open area of your desktop with the right mouse button.

2. From the pop-up menu, choose **Arrange Icons**.

3. Select **By Name** to have the desktop icons arranged in alphabetical order, **By Type** to have the icons arranged by type of file, **By Size** to order them by size of file, or **By Date** to have them appear in the order they were created.

To keep your icons from getting scattered all over your desktop, click the right mouse button on the desktop and select **Arrange Icons, Auto Arrange** from the pop-up menu. The icons will always return to the columns at the left side of your screen. Choose this option again to turn it off.

To have each row of your icons align horizontally, right-click the desktop and select **Line Up Icons** from the pop-up menu.

Like the shortcut icons, the appearance of the standard icons on your desktop (My Computer, My Documents, Network Neighborhood, Recycle Bin) can be changed. Right-click a blank area of the desktop and choose **Properties** from the pop-up menu. In the Display Properties dialog box, select the **Effects** tab (see Figure 2.4). From the Desktop icons box, select the icon you want to change and then click **Change Icon**. Select a picture from the icons displayed in the Change Icon dialog box (refer to Figure 2.3), and then click OK. Click **OK** to close the Display Properties dialog box.

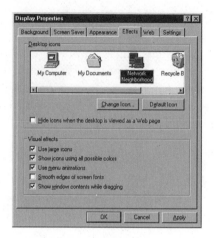

Figure 2.4   Select the icon you want to change and click Change Icon to see the alternatives.

In Windows 98, can view your desktop as a Web page (right-click the desktop and select **Active Desktop, View as Web Page**). If you've selected that option, you may also want to hide the icons so you can't see them on the desktop. Right-click the desktop, select **Properties** on the pop-up menu, select the Effects tab, and then check **Hide icons when the desktop is viewed as a Web page**. Click **OK**. Don't worry that you've lost your icons—right-click the taskbar and choose **Toolbars, Desktop** to add the desktop icons as a toolbar (see Part III, Lesson 3, "Customizing the Taskbar," for more details).

The Effects tab of the Display Properties box has an option to increase the size of all the desktop icons. Click **Use large icons**. This may slow up your processor slightly, so turn off this option if you notice a problem.

To change the way you click on icons (single- versus double-click), adjust the settings in Folder Options, as explained in Part II, Lesson 2, "Using My Computer."

Choosing Colors and Backgrounds

For better viewing or just for variety, you can change the background color of
your screen or choose a pattern or wallpaper for your desktop background.

Colors

The desktop color is applied to the area behind the icons and windows. To
change the color of the desktop:

1. Choose **Settings, Control Panel** from the Start menu.

2. From the Control Panel window, click the **Display** icon. The Display
   Properties dialog box appears.

TIP   **Right-Click the Desktop**   To quickly access the Display Properties box,
right-click an open area on your desktop and select **Properties** from the pop-
up menu.

3. Click the **Appearance** tab (see Figure 2.5).

4. Select **Desktop** from the **Item** drop-down list.

5. Click the down arrow on the **Color** list box to see a selection of background
   colors.

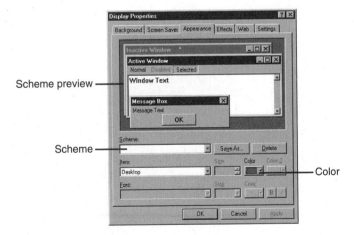

Figure 2.5   Select Desktop as the item and then choose a color.

6. Click the color you want.

7. Click **Apply** to see how the desktop will look in that color.

8. Click **OK** to accept your choice and close the dialog box.

Schemes

Windows 98 also has a series of color schemes from which you can choose. These color schemes not only choose a background color but also set the color for the window title bars, window borders, and on-screen text. If you change the color scheme, it will override your background color choice; you'll have to set the color again if you want it to be different than the one in the color scheme.

The color scheme choices are also located on the Appearance tab of the Display Properties dialog box. Choose one from the Scheme drop-down list. The display will change to show you how your choice will affect the windows and background on your computer.

Wallpaper

Wallpaper makes your desktop interesting and fun. To select a wallpaper for your desktop background:

1. Open the Display Properties dialog box.

2. Select the **Background** tab (see Figure 2.6).

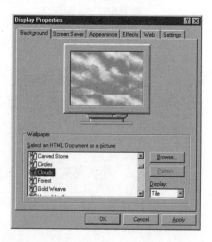

Figure 2.6   When you select a wallpaper, a preview appears in the monitor screen.

3. From the list under **Select an HTML Document or a picture**, select a picture to place on your desktop. It will appear in the monitor picture so you can see how it will look on your screen.

Choose **(None)** to remove all wallpaper from the desktop. The background color fills the screen.

To select a file you created or imported to be the wallpaper, click the **Browse** button. The file must be a *.bmp, *.jpg, *.gif, or *.png file or an HTML page (Web page).

TIP   **Using the Web to Make Wallpaper**   A quick way to use any graphic on a Web page as a wallpaper is to right-click the graphic and choose **Set as Wallpaper** from the menu.

4. To determine how the wallpaper fills your screen, choose one of the following from the **Display** drop-down list (if the choice is unavailable, the picture automatically fills the entire screen):

> **Center**   The wallpaper picture appears in the middle of your desktop. The background color will still show around the outside of the picture.
>
> **Tile**   The picture repeats across the screen until it fills the desktop background.
>
> **Stretch**   The picture fills the entire screen. If your picture isn't the same shape as the screen, stretching it may distort the picture.

5. Click **Apply** to see how the desktop will look with the pattern or wallpaper you selected.

6. Click **OK** to accept your choice and close the dialog box.

Patterns

Wallpapers are usually large and may be distracting or use a lot of memory. Use a pattern as an alternative to wallpaper and you will still add interest to your desktop. To add a pattern to the desktop background:

1. Open the Display Properties dialog box and select the **Background** tab.

2. Choose **(None)** as the wallpaper choice if you want to fill the entire background with pattern.

To combine a wallpaper with a pattern, select the wallpaper and choose **Center** as the Display; the pattern will fill the area around the outside of the wallpaper.

3. Click **Pattern** to open the Pattern dialog box (see Figure 2.7).

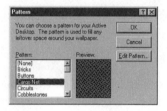

Figure 2.7   A sample of the pattern appears in the Preview box.

4. Under **Pattern**, select the name of the pattern you want to use. Choose **(None)** to remove all patterns from the background of the desktop.

5. (Optional) Click **Edit Pattern** to open the Pattern Editor dialog box where you modify the pattern by changing the pixel colors.

6. Click **OK** to close the Pattern dialog box.

7. Click **OK** to close the Display Properties dialog box.

Desktop Themes

Many of the features of Microsoft Plus! (which you had to buy separately for Windows 95) are incorporated into Windows 98. The desktop themes set up related screen savers, wallpapers (with sounds), and mouse pointers.

To select or change a theme:

1. Choose **Settings, Control Panel** from the Start menu.

2. Click on the **Desktop Themes** icon to open the Desktop Themes dialog box (see Figure 2.8).

3. From the **Theme** drop-down list, select a theme. A preview of how it affects your desktop and windows appears in the dialog box.

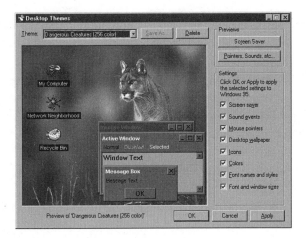

Figure 2.8 Deselect any items you don't want the desktop theme to control.

4. To preview the screen saver, click **Screen Saver** (don't be surprised to hear sounds if you have a sound card).

5. To preview the mouse pointers and sounds, click **Pointers, Sounds, etc**. In the Preview dialog box, click the tab for the category you want to preview and select an item to see its preview (or click the Play button to hear the sound if you have a sound card). Click **Close** to return to the Desktop Themes dialog box.

6. Under **Settings**, deselect any items to which you don't want to apply the theme.

7. Click **Apply** to accept the settings but not close the dialog box (in case you want to apply a different theme once you've seen it). Click **OK** to accept the settings and close the dialog box.

Because the desktop themes are Windows 98 components, you may have to install them on your computer. Look up "Themes, Desktop" in Help for instructions on how to install them. If you have children, there are four "kids" themes. You can get more from your local retailer.

Changing Fonts

To change the size, color, and font of the screen text:

1. Choose **Settings**, **Control Panel** from the **Start** menu and then click **Display**, or right-click the desktop and choose **Properties** from the pop-up menu.

2. Select the **Appearance** tab (see Figure 2.9).

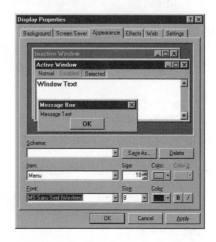

Figure 2.9   You must select a text-related item for the font choices to be available.

3. From the **Item** drop-down list, select the item for which you want to adjust the text, such as Active Title Bar, Icon, Inactive Title Bar, Menu, Message Box, Palette Title, Selected Items, or ToolTip. Unless you pick one of these items, the font choices will not be available.

4. Select the font you want to use from the **Font** drop-down list, the point size from the **Size** drop-down list, and the color of the text from the **Color** list (color is not available for all items). Click the **B** button for boldface and the **I** button for italic.

5. Click **Apply** to see how the desktop will look.

6. Click **OK** to accept your choice and close the dialog box.

In this lesson you learned to create shortcuts on your desktop, arrange your desktop icons, change the color and/or background pictures and patterns of the desktop, and to change the fonts of the items on the desktop. In the next lesson you'll learn about customizing the taskbar.

Customizing the Taskbar

In this lesson, you learn how to move, size, and hide the taskbar. You also learn how to set taskbar properties.

Positioning the Taskbar

The taskbar serves as a program launcher and an application-switching platform. Open applications are represented by buttons on the taskbar. You click a program button to make that program your active window. The taskbar also displays a set of icons that are indicators for utility programs and hardware such as PC cards so that you can check the current status of items or change control settings. The clock appears next to these icons. Toolbars also appear on the toolbar, such as the Quick Launch toolbar, which gives you shortcuts to Internet Explorer, Outlook Express, the desktop, or the channels.

By default, the taskbar appears at the bottom of your screen. You can change its position so that it appears at the top, left, or right of the screen. In Figure 3.1, the taskbar is on the left side of the screen.

To move the taskbar:

1. Point to a spot in the middle of the taskbar where there are no buttons.

2. Hold down your left mouse button.

3. Drag to the side of the screen where you want to position the taskbar.

4. The taskbar jumps to that side of the screen. Keep dragging the taskbar if it doesn't jump to the side you want right away.

5. Release the mouse button when the taskbar appears in the desired position.

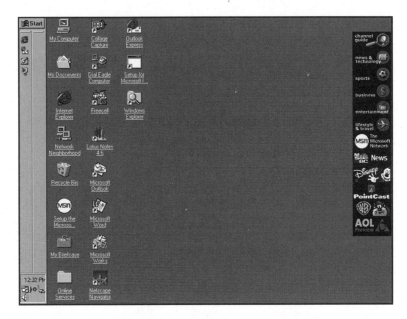

Figure 3.1 The taskbar has been moved to the left side of the screen.

Sizing the Taskbar

If you work with several windows open or minimized at the same time, the taskbar can become crowded. To accommodate the number of buttons on the taskbar, the buttons become smaller and smaller as the number of buttons increases. To make more room for the buttons, you can make the taskbar thicker so that buttons appear stacked and larger than if they were in a single row. Later, when you no longer need the room, you can make the taskbar thinner again.

To change the size of the taskbar:

1. Point to the border on the edge of the taskbar (your mouse pointer will become a two-headed arrow, as shown in Figure 3.2).

Mouse pointer ——

Figure 3.2 The mouse pointer becomes a two-headed arrow as you drag the taskbar border.

197

2. Drag in one of the directions shown by the two-headed arrow to make the taskbar thinner or thicker. The border of the taskbar will jump in increments as you drag.

3. Release the mouse button when the border is where you want it.

TIP   **I Lost My Taskbar!**   Did you make the taskbar so thin you can't find it? If you look closely, there is still a double line at the side of the screen where your taskbar was. Point at that line and then drag it away from the edge of the screen. Release your mouse button, and your taskbar is back.

To readjust the size of the taskbar after you have closed all your application or folder windows, repeat steps 1 through 3 but drag in the opposite direction to narrow the taskbar.

Hiding the Taskbar

You can hide the taskbar to maximize the display of a program. This is useful when you are working in programs such as graphics or desktop publishing programs. To hide your taskbar:

1. Choose **Settings, Taskbar** from the Start menu, or right-click a gray area of the taskbar and choose **Properties** from the pop-up menu. The Taskbar Properties box appears (see Figure 3.3).

Figure 3.3   Check Auto hide to have the taskbar disappear when you aren't using it.

   2. Click the **Taskbar Options** tab if it's not already selected.

   3. Enable **Auto hide**.

   4. Click **OK**.

The taskbar will automatically reduce to a double-line thickness when an application is open and will reappear when you point to the double line.

Using Taskbar Properties

As with most items in Windows 98, the taskbar has properties or options that you can specify. To set the taskbar properties:

   1. Choose **Settings, Taskbar** from the Start menu, or right-click a gray area of the taskbar and choose **Properties** from the pop-up menu. The Taskbar Properties box appears (refer to Figure 3.3).

   2. There are four options in the properties box:

   Always on top   Enable this to be able to see the taskbar even when an application is running fully maximized. Otherwise, the application window will cover the taskbar.

   Auto hide   When this is enabled, the taskbar reduces to a double line once you activate an application. Just point to the taskbar to have it reappear. This feature allows you to see an application fully maximized and to make maximum use of your screen space while still having the taskbar available.

   Show small icons in Start menu   Check this to reduce the size of the Start menu icons (see the sample picture in the properties box to see the difference). The bar along the side of the Start menu that says "Windows 98" disappears when you enable this option.

   Show clock   Check this to have the time show on the taskbar.

   3. Click **OK** to accept the choices and close the properties box.

Showing the Clock

The current time appears on the right side of the taskbar (or at the bottom if your taskbar is on the left or right side of your screen). If you point to the time, a pop-up appears, giving you the current day of the week, month, day, and year (see Figure 3.4).

Figure 3.4 The date appears as a pop-up above the time when you point to the clock.

If your clock isn't showing on your taskbar, do the following:

1. Choose **Settings, Taskbar** from the Start menu, or right-click a gray area of the taskbar and choose **Properties** from the pop-up menu. The Taskbar Properties box appears (refer to Figure 3.3).

2. Check **Show clock**.

3. Click **OK**.

The time on the clock is the system time of your computer. Double-click the clock to open the Date/Time Properties dialog box (see Figure 3.5), where you set the clock. Do any of the following, and then click OK:

- Select the current month from the drop-down list under **Date**.
- In the year box under **Date**, enter the year or use the up and down arrows to select the year.
- To choose the day, click the date on the calendar that appears below the month and year.
- Click in the **Time** text box and enter the correct time, or select each of the time components (hour, minutes, seconds, AM/PM) and use the up and down hours to select the setting.
- Click the **Time Zone** tab and select your time zone from the drop-down list.
- If your area recognizes Daylight Savings Time, check **Automatically adjust clock for daylight saving changes**. Then you won't have to worry about resetting the clock when the time change occurs.

Creating Custom Toolbars

The default settings of Windows 98 provide four toolbars available for display on the taskbar. You can create your own custom toolbars to display on the taskbar.

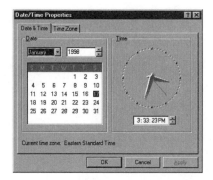

Figure 3.5 Change the time, date, and time zone in the Date/Time Properties box.

To display any of the available toolbars on the taskbar, right-click a gray area of the taskbar, choose **Toolbars** from the pop-up menu, and then select the toolbar you want to display:

- **Address** Skip the first step of going to a Web browser in order to enter a Web page address by typing the URL in the text box on the Address toolbar.

- **Desktop** All of the shortcuts on your desktop appear in this toolbar, which lets you use the desktop to display a Web page, for example.

- **Links** This toolbar lets you quickly open important Web sites without opening your browser first. Each Web site is a separate button.

- **Quick Launch** Quickly open some of your most-frequently used programs or features from the toolbar, which appears on the taskbar by default. The four items displayed on this toolbar are buttons for your Web browser, Outlook Express, the desktop, and channels. Drag a shortcut from the desktop onto this toolbar to add a new item.

 TIP **Clear Your Desktop** When you have several windows open for different folders or applications, you can't see the shortcuts on your desktop. You could choose **Minimize All Windows** from the taskbar menu if you could find an empty gray space to right-click your taskbar. A faster way to clear your desktop and minimize all your windows is to click the **Show Desktop** button on the Quick Launch toolbar on the taskbar.

Windows 98 uses an existing folder or Web page to create a new toolbar:

1. Right-click the taskbar.

2. Choose **Toolbars, New Toolbar** from the pop-up menu.

3. In the New Toolbar dialog box (see Figure 3.6), enter the name of a folder or Web site, or select one from the displayed tree of your folder hierarchy.

Figure 3.6   By selecting the Clients folder, you'll be able to access all the subfolders from a toolbar.

4. Click **OK**.

You can set custom display options for your new toolbar. To change the icon size, text, or title:

- **Icon size**   To make the icons on the toolbar larger or smaller, right-click the toolbar and choose **View, Large** or **View, Small** from the menu.

- **Icon text**   To hide or display the text beneath the icons on the toolbar, right-click the toolbar and choose **Show Text** from the menu.

- **Toolbar title**   To hide or display the title of the toolbar, right-click the toolbar and choose **Show Title** from the menu.

Although you can drag a folder, file, or shortcut onto a toolbar to add it to the toolbar, it's difficult to find enough gray space to add it successfully. Instead, add the item to the folder you used to create the toolbar. It automatically becomes part of the toolbar. If the icon doesn't immediately appear on the toolbar, right-click the toolbar and choose **Refresh** from the menu.

When a toolbar contains many icons, you may not be able to see all of them. A small arrow appears at the end of the toolbar. Click that arrow to scroll across and see the remaining icons.

To change the size of a toolbar on the taskbar, point to the double gray line between the toolbars and drag it to a new position. The mouse pointer changes to a two-headed arrow when you point to the line and that indicates the directions in which you may drag (see Figure 3.7).

Mouse pointer ——

Figure 3.7 Change the size of a toolbar by dragging the double gray line.

Any toolbar can be dragged from the taskbar and put on the desktop as a floating toolbar. Once it's on the desktop, you can size the toolbar to suit your needs. To move the toolbar, point to the double gray line at the left of the toolbar and drag it onto the desktop. Drag it back to the taskbar if you decide you prefer it there.

Right-click the toolbar and choose **Close** to remove the toolbar from the taskbar. A dialog box appears, asking you to confirm your decision to close the toolbar. Click **OK**.

In this lesson, you learned to customize your taskbar by changing its size and position, hiding it, displaying the clock, and adding toolbars. In the next lesson, you'll learn how to customize the menu that appears when you click the Start button.

Customizing the Start Menu

In this lesson you learn how to add and remove items listed on the Start menu, how to organize the Start menu, how to make some programs open automatically when you start up the operating system, and how to clear the Document menu.

Using the Start Menu Properties

When you click the **Start** button on the taskbar and choose Programs, you see a list of available programs. How do these programs get added to the list? If you upgraded your operating system from Windows 3.1, these are the old program groups you had in that version. During Setup, Window 98 adds some program groups, such as Accessories, to the menu. As you install new software, the new programs appear on the Start menu.

To modify the Start menu by changing its properties, do the following:

1. Choose **Settings, Taskbar & Start Menu** from the **Start** menu, or right-click the taskbar and choose **Properties** from the menu.
2. When the Taskbar Properties dialog box opens, click the **Start Menu Programs** tab (see Figure 4.1).
3. Set the options as outlined in this lesson.
4. Click **OK**.

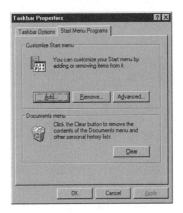

Figure 4.1 Use the Taskbar Properties dialog box to add, remove, and reorganize the Start menu entries.

Adding and Removing Programs

The Start menu may not list every program you use. Some of your programs may be old, some may be located on a network drive or on a CD, or some of them may have been copied to your hard disk but not properly installed (see Part III, Lesson 5, "Adding and Removing Software and Hardware"). If Windows 98 doesn't detect a program during Setup, the program won't be listed on the menu and you'll have to add it to the menu manually.

To add a program to the Start menu:

1. Open the Taskbar Properties and select the **Start Menu Programs** tab.

2. Under **Customize Start menu**, click **Add**. The Create Shortcut dialog box appears (see Figure 4.2).

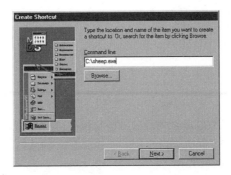

Figure 4.2 Enter the name and location of the program you want to add.

205

3. In the **Command line** text box, enter the path and file name of the program's executable file (the file that starts the program). If you don't know the name, click **Browse**, select the file, and click **OK**.

4. Click **Next**.

5. The Select Program Folder dialog box appears (see Figure 4.3). From the listing in **Select folder to place shortcut in**, select a folder where the new program logically belongs (such as Games for a checkers game). The groupings on the Start menu follow the organization of these folders. Select **Programs** if you don't want your program to appear on a submenu.

   To add a new entry to the Start menu, click **New Folder**, and enter a name for the folder. The folder name becomes the entry on the Start menu, and the program appears as a submenu of that entry.

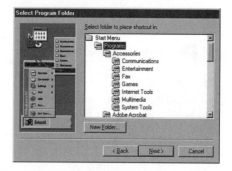

Figure 4.3 Choose the folder for the menu group where you want to put your program.

6. Click **Next**. In the **Select a name for the shortcut** text box, enter the name for the program as you want it to appear on the Start menu.

7. Click **Finish**. If the program doesn't have its own icon, a prompt appears, asking you to choose one from a set of available Windows icons.

TIP **Quick Additions** Adding an item to the Start menu in Windows 98 is easy—use drag-and-drop. Drag the item you want to put on the menu from its folder or the desktop onto the Start button. The item becomes part of the Start menu.

If you delete a program (instead of uninstalling it through the Control Panel), the program may still be seen on the Start menu. Of course, if you click it, nothing happens, because the program files aren't there. You should remove the entry from the Start menu. To remove a program from the Start menu:

1. Open the Taskbar Properties dialog box and select the **Start Menu Programs** tab.
2. Under **Customize Start menu**, click **Remove**.
3. The Remove Shortcuts/Folders dialog box appears (see Figure 4.4). Select the folder or program shortcut and click **Remove**.

Figure 4.4 Select the folder or program name you want to remove.

4. A dialog box asks you to confirm that you want to remove the item. Click **Yes**.
5. Click **Close**.

You may also remove an item from the Start menu by dragging it off the menu. The item may end up on your desktop or in whatever folder you have open. You will have to drag it to the Recycle Bin. Easier yet, right-click the entry and choose **Delete** from the pop-up menu. For more information on using the Recycle Bin, see Part II, Lesson 4, "The Recycle Bin."

Removing from the Start Menu Does Not Remove the Program Removing the program listed on the Start menu does not delete the program files from your computer. You must uninstall the program or delete the program folder. The entry on the Start menu is only a shortcut.

CAUTION

Organizing the Start Menu

The Start menu has several entries that open submenus when you select them. Dealing with submenus is preferable to seeking one program from a long list.

To organize your Start menu into a series of submenus, you need to create folders and subfolders in the Start Menu subfolder of the Windows folder. Then move the program shortcuts into the appropriate folders.

There are several ways to reach the Start Menu folder:

- Open the Taskbar Properties dialog box, select the **Start Menu Programs** tab, and then click **Advanced**.
- Right-click the Start menu button and choose **Explore** from the pop-up menu.
- Open the Windows Explorer by choosing **Programs, Windows Explorer** from the Start menu. Then open the Start Menu subfolder under the Windows folder.
- Open My Computer and then open the Start Menu subfolder under the Windows folder.

Figure 4.5 shows the Start Menu folder displayed in Windows Explorer. Using the features of Windows Explorer, add subfolders to the Programs folder to create the menu titles. Move shortcuts into those folders to create the program entries. To review the skills you need to do this, see Part II, Lesson 7, "Managing Files with Explorer."

TIP **Drag-and-Drop** A quick way to organize the programs on your Start menu is to drag them to new positions on the menu.

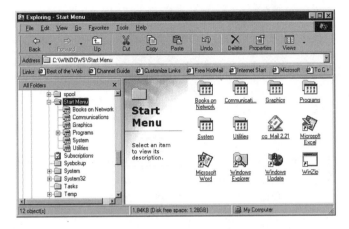

Figure 4.5 Add subfolders to the Programs folders and then move your Program shortcuts to the appropriate subfolders.

Customizing the Favorites Entries

One of the entries on the Start menu is Favorites. The items on the Favorites submenu are the same ones you see in My Computer, Windows Explorer, Network Neighborhood, Control Panel, and the Recycle Bin.

Even though it's designed to give you a shortcut to your most frequently visited Web sites, Favorites can also be a quick way to open folders that you use often.

To add an item to Favorites:

1. Open My Computer, Windows Explorer, or Network Neighborhood.
2. Select the folder(s) or file(s) you want included in Favorites.
3. Choose **Favorites, Add to Favorites** from the menu.
4. The Add Favorite dialog box opens (see Figure 4.6), but most of the options are not available because you are not adding a Web page. The only available option is already selected: **No, just add the page to my favorites**. In the **Name** box, enter a label for the item you're adding.

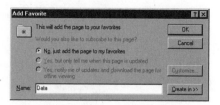

Figure 4.6   Enter the entry label for your item in the Name box.

5. (Optional) Favorites already has submenus for Channels, Imported book-marks, Links, and Software Updates. To add your item to one of those submenus, click **Create in** to expand the dialog box. Then select the appropriate folder from the displayed list. If an appropriate folder isn't listed, click **New Folder**, enter a **Folder name**, and click **OK**.

6. Click **OK**.

To organize the entries for the Favorites submenu, follow these steps:

1. Open My Computer, Windows Explorer, or Network Neighborhood.

2. Choose **Favorites**, **Organize Favorites** from the menu.

3. When the Organize Favorites dialog box appears (see Figure 4.7), select one or more items from the list and then click **Move**, **Rename**, **Delete**, or **Open**, depending on what you need to do with the item(s). If you need to create a new folder, click the **Create New Folder** icon on the toolbar, type a name for the folder, and then press **Enter**.

Figure 4.7   Use the Organize Favorites dialog box to move, rename, or delete items.

4. When you finish moving, renaming, or deleting items or adding folders, click **Close**.

Using Windows Explorer is another way to organize your favorites. Right-click the Start button and choose **Explore** from the menu to open the Windows Explorer. Open Favorites under the Windows folder. Move, delete, and rename the items or add new folders in Windows Explorer.

Clearing the Document Menu

The documents you have opened recently appear on the Documents submenu of the Start menu. This gives you a quick way to start up a document that you worked on recently—choose Documents from the Start menu and click the name of the document.

This list may not reflect the files you have used over the last week or so, especially if you were opening and closing files looking for something. In that case, you'd probably like to clean up the list.

To clear the Documents list:

1. Choose **Settings, Taskbar & Start Menu** from the Start menu, or right-click the taskbar and choose **Properties** from the menu.

2. Select the **Start Menu Programs** tab (refer to Figure 4.1).

3. Under **Documents menu**, click **Clear**. This removes *all* the file names from the Documents list.

4. Click **OK**.

What if you only want to remove one or two items from the list? Do one of the following:

- Right-click the name you want to remove and select **Delete** from the menu (this only deletes the name from the list, not the file from your disk).

- Drag the name off the menu and then drag it into the Recycle Bin.

Adding Programs to the Startup Window

There may be some applications that you want to automatically start when Windows 98 opens, such as an anti-virus program or your word processor. To start programs automatically:

1. Open the Taskbar Properties dialog box and select the **Start Menu Programs** tab.
2. Click **Add**.
3. Click **Browse** and select the program. Click **Open**.
4. Click **Next**. Under **Select folder to place shortcut in**, click the **StartUp** folder.
5. Click **Next**. Enter a name for the program shortcut.
6. Click **Finish**.

When you boot up your system, the program you selected will automatically start up after Windows 98 opens.

During installation of some programs, you're asked to remove programs from the StartUp folder. Choose **Programs, StartUp** from the Start menu and then drag all the program entries off the menu and onto the desktop. Then reboot your computer before doing the installation. After you finish the installation process, drag the shortcuts back onto the Start menu.

In this lesson you learned how to add and remove programs from the Start menu, how to reorganize the entries on the Programs and Favorites submenus, how to clear the Documents list, and how to make programs start automatically after Windows 98 opens. In the next lesson you'll learn how to add and remove software and hardware.

Adding and Removing Software and Hardware

In this lesson you learn how to add and remove software programs and hardware devices. You also learn how to configure Windows 98 to work well with your hardware.

When You Buy Software

When you purchase software, you need to be certain that your new software will perform well in Windows 98. Consider the following:

- Make sure the software you purchase is designed to run under Windows 98. It should say that on the package, but if you're not certain, ask the salesperson at the store before you pay. If you're buying from a catalog, and it isn't clear that the software works with Windows 98, call the catalog company and ask them before you place the order.

- All software packages have system requirements that list the hardware, operating system (Windows 95 or Windows 98), memory, and disk space your system must have for the software to work on your computer. If your system does not meet these requirements, you can't use the software. Either plan to upgrade your system before you purchase the software, or find another version of the software that will work within your system's capabilities.

TIP   **How Do I Know If My Computer Meets System Requirements for Software?**   Choose **Settings, Control Panel** from the Start menu. Click the **System** icon to open the System Properties box. The General page (see Figure 5.1) will show the type of computer and the amount of RAM you have on your system.

To find how much room you have on your hard disk, open My Computer and select the icon for your hard disk. The status bar at the bottom of the window will tell you how much free space you have (it should be more than the software requires).

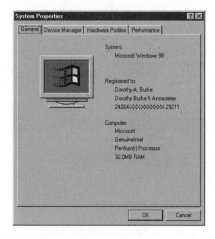

Figure 5.1   The System Properties box tells you the amount of RAM installed on your computer.

- Many software packages also have system recommendations. Although the system requirements list what your system *must* have for the software to run on it, the recommendations list the hardware and software specifications under which the software runs most smoothly. For example, you may have 8MB of RAM memory, which meets the minimum requirements of the software, but the recommendation is 16MB. This probably means that the software performance will slow if you have more than one window open or if you are performing a complicated procedure.

If you can live with the slower performance, then you don't need to worry. However, when speed is important or when you need to have more than one application open at a time, you might want to consider upgrading your system memory to have the software perform at its best.

- Check to see if the software comes on disks or CDs. You can't install software from a CD unless you have a CD-ROM drive. However, if you have both a 3^1/$_2$-inch disk drive and a CD-ROM drive, you should opt for the CD version of the software. Installation from a CD is much faster, you often get bonus files on a CD, and CDs are less likely to have faults or produce errors.

 TIP **RAM** The RAM (Random-Access Memory) is the working memory of your computer, as opposed to the hard disk or floppy disk, which are storage memory. RAM keeps track of your current operations, each character you type or delete, and each calculation you perform, until you save the file into your storage memory. RAM also keeps a copy of your current application open while you're working, plus any other applications or windows you may have open. The greater the memory (measured in megabytes) the more operations you can do or applications you can have open at the same time.

Preparing to Install

Once you remove the shrink wrap from your software package, you should do the following:

1. Find the installation instructions for the software and read them carefully before you install.

2. Locate the serial number of the software. You may need it during the installation process, and you should record it for later use. The serial number may be on the outside of the package, but more often it's on the CD case or on the envelope that holds the disks. Sometimes you'll find it on the inside front cover of the software manual.

3. Read through the software license agreement before you install. It automatically becomes effective once you open the software, so it helps to know what you're agreeing to. Software is copyrighted (unless it is shareware, the name for software that isn't copyrighted), and these agreements are to ensure that you don't install the software on more than one computer (unless you've purchased a software license that allows a specified number of users to be installed). Otherwise, you violate the agreement and the software company can prosecute you. Violation of this software license agreement is called "pirating."

4. Close all open programs or windows on your computer, leaving only Windows 98 running. If you don't, the installation program will request it later.

5. Any programs that start up when Windows starts may be running in RAM memory. Close down these programs before you start installation. If required by your installation instructions, you may have to temporarily remove these programs from your StartUp window. Refer to the instructions in Lesson Part III, 4, "Customizing the Start Menu," to learn how to do this.

 TIP   **Recording Serial Numbers**   Make sure you record your software serial number in a place where you can find it later. Should you have a problem after installation and need customer support, you'll probably have to tell the support person your serial number. Also, should your computer be permanently damaged or stolen or a fire destroy your copy of the software, you may be able to get another copy from the software company if you provide the serial number and proof of permanent loss. It may also help to record the date and place of purchase and the customer support number along with the serial number.

Installing Software

Follow the installation instructions that come with the software package. Place the first disk in the disk drive (this is usually referred to as the install disk) or the CD in the CD-ROM drive. From this point, the installation differs according to how the software company set it up.

There are generally three ways installation occurs:

- An installation or setup program starts running immediately on your screen when you insert the CD. Follow the on-screen instructions.
- The instructions ask you to click the **Start** button on the taskbar and choose **Run** from the menu. The Run dialog box appears (see Figure 5.2). Enter the path and name of the file that starts the installation or setup process. This should be in your instructions, but you can find it by clicking **Browse** and looking for the file (usually called Install.exe or Setup.exe). Click **OK** to start the installation and follow any on-screen instructions.

Figure 5.2 · The Run dialog box.

- The instructions ask you to choose **Settings, Control Panel** from the Start menu. When the Control Panel opens, click the **Add/Remove Programs** icon. The Add/Remove Programs Properties box appears (see Figure 5.3). Click **Install** to start the Installation Wizard. Insert the floppy disk or CD in the appropriate drive if you haven't already. Click **Next**. Windows 98 automatically detects the installation program or asks you for the command line (enter the command or click **Browse** to find it). Click **Finish** and the installation process begins. Follow the on-screen instructions.

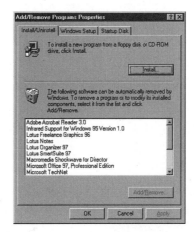

Figure 5.3   Click Install to install a new program from a CD or disk.

TIP   Quick Rebooting   You may be asked to reboot your computer after installing the software. Hold down the Shift key as you click Start, choose **Shut Down**, select **Restart the Computer**, and click **Yes**. Instead of starting the computer from scratch, this method only restarts Windows. That's all you really need to reset certain Windows 98 parameters to work with your new program, and it saves a considerable amount of time.

217

Removing Programs

Too often, users think that all they need to do to remove a program is delete the files in the program window. That may work with MS-DOS but it doesn't with any Windows program. When a Windows program installs it also adds hidden and system files in the Windows folder and entries are made into the Windows registry. If you just delete the program folder, these additional files will be left behind and may cause error messages.

To properly remove a program:

1. Choose **Settings, Control Panel** from the Start menu.

2. When the Control Panel opens, click the **Add/Remove Programs** icon. The Add/Remove Programs Properties box appears (refer to Figure 5.3).

3. From the list at the bottom of the dialog box, select the program you want to remove. Click **Add/Remove**.

4. A dialog box appears that asks for confirmation of your order to uninstall the program. Click **Yes**.

5. When Windows 98 alerts you that the software has been removed, click **OK**.

6. Click **OK** to close the Add/Remove Programs Properties dialog box.

The removal of some programs isn't as clean as it should be. Error messages may appear during the process because Windows 98 needs instruction from you about files that are needed for other programs, data files in the same folder, or unknown components. You may still have to remove some pieces of the program manually as a result.

 TIP **The Software Isn't Listed** Not all programs are eligible for Windows 98 Uninstall. The names of those programs won't appear on the list. You will have to manually delete the files for that software.

Adding New Hardware

Windows 98 has a component called *plug-and-play*, which identifies installed devices when Windows 98 is installed or booted up and automatically loads the device driver needed to work with the hardware. The necessary configuration changes are also made to the operating system.

This makes it sound as if there will never be a hardware installation problem again. However, there can be problems. The most significant problem is legacy hardware, that is, hardware that was made prior to Windows 95 and the advent of plug-and-play. Windows 98 probably does not have the device drivers for older hardware, although a current device driver may work. The device driver is a program file that makes it possible for Windows 98 to communicate and control the hardware.

A similar problem occurs if your new hardware was designed after the release of Windows 98. Your installation disk may not have the necessary device driver for your latest "widget." Sometimes the manufacturer of the device provides the driver on a disk with the equipment, or you can call the hardware manufacturer for it. Some of the newer device drivers may be available from Microsoft's Web site.

If Windows 98 doesn't automatically detect your newest hardware after you've put it into your system (assuming you did that correctly), reboot your system. With plug-and-play compatible hardware (it should say so on the box or in the instructions), you should turn off your system before installing and then start up your system again. Many people plug in the hardware without doing this, so rebooting gives Windows 98 a chance to detect the equipment. You should contact the manufacturer's technical support if you know the software is plug-and-play and Windows 98 can't find it. You may have installed it incorrectly, which means you need help anyway, or the device may not be working properly.

For hardware that you know is not plug-and-play or that you've installed correctly and is still not working (although you've confirmed that the device is in working order), you can run the Add New Hardware Wizard:

1. Close any open programs.
2. Choose **Settings, Control Panel** from the Start menu.
3. Click the **Add New Hardware** icon.
4. The Add New Hardware Wizard starts. Click **Next**.
5. The Wizard warns you that Windows 98 is going to search for any new plug-and-play devices. Click **Next** to continue.
6. Any new devices Windows 98 detects are listed in the dialog box. If the hardware you installed is listed, click **Yes**, select the item, and click **Next**. Click **Finish** when the installation is complete and ignore the remaining steps.

   If the device isn't listed, click **No**. Click **Next**.

219

7. The wizard recommends that you let Windows 98 search for hardware that isn't plug-and-play compatible. Click **Yes** and then click **Next**. Then click **Next** to initiate the search (if that search is unsuccessful, the wizard reports that and asks if you want to select the hardware—click **Next** and go to step 8). If the search is successful, click **Next**. Click **Finish** when the installation is complete and ignore the remaining steps.

   If you don't believe Windows 98 can detect the hardware, or if you've already tried the search and didn't find the hardware, click **No**. Then click **Next**.

8. Select the hardware device from the Hardware types list. Click **Next**.

9. Select the manufacturer and model (see Figure 5.4), or the next nearest compatible model, or a generic model if the one you have isn't listed. If you have a disk with the setup or device files for the hardware, or the drivers are on the Windows 98 installation disk, click **Have Disk**, insert the disk into its drive, and specify the location of the device driver. Click **Next**.

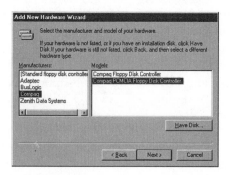

Figure 5.4   Select the manufacturer (or Standard) and then choose the model.

10. When Windows 98 informs you that it has installed the hardware, click **Finish**. If Windows 98 was still unable to install the hardware, contact the manufacturer's technical support for help.

Adding Windows 98 Components

Windows 98 has a number of components included on the installation disk but aren't automatically installed on your system. For example, some of the disk management tools, the desktop themes, the online service options, Web TV for Windows Viewer, QuickView, the Clipboard viewer, and more are optional components.

To install additional components on your system, have your installation disk handy and do the following:

1. Choose **Settings, Control Panel** from the **Start** menu.

2. When the Control Panel opens, click the **Add/Remove Programs** icon.

3. Select the **Windows Setup** tab (see Figure 5.5).

Figure 5.5 Check the components you want to add to your system.

4. In the Components box, a list of components appears. Each one has a check box in front of it. If the box is checked, the component is installed on your system. A gray check box means only some of the components in that group are installed. A description of the selected component appears at the bottom of the dialog box. To see what's included in a component, select it and click **Details**.

5. To add a component, click the box to check it.

To remove a component, click the box to deselect it.

To add only part of a component, click **Details**, select the parts you want on your system, click **OK** to return to the Add/Remove Programs Properties dialog box.

6. Insert the installation disk, click **Have Disk**, and then specify the location of the component files.

7. Click **OK** to close the Add/Remove Programs Properties dialog box.

In this lesson you learned about adding new software and hardware to your system, plus additional Windows 98 components. You also learned to remove software programs. In the next lesson you'll learn about how to set up your computer if there is more than one user and how to protect your system with passwords.

Sharing Workstations and Setting Passwords

In this lesson, you learn how to set a password for your computer and how to configure your computer for use by more than one person.

Why Use a Password?

If you're worried that an unauthorized person might attempt to use your computer in your absence, use a password. The password is the key to your system. Unless you enter the correct password, you cannot begin working in Windows.

When Windows boots up, a dialog box appears, requesting your password (see Figure 6.1). Enter your user name (if it isn't automatically entered) and then your password. When you type the password, Windows enters asterisks in the text box. Click **OK**. Windows may ask you to confirm the password by entering it again. If so, type it and click **OK**. Then your desktop appears.

Figure 6.1 Enter your password in order to gain access to your computer.

TIP   **Password Versus Login**   Don't confuse the Windows password with a network login password. If your office uses a network, the network administrator assigns a password to you that allows you to access the network. The Windows password doesn't give you access to the network. It only protects your own computer. You can use a Windows password even if you don't work with a network, and you can make your Windows and Network passwords the same if you like.

Setting Up a Password

To set up a Windows password:

1. Choose **Settings, Control Panel** from the Start menu.
2. When the Control Panel opens, click the **Passwords** icon. The Passwords Properties box appears (see Figure 6.2).

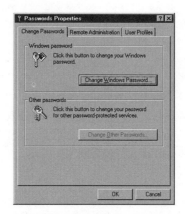

Figure 6.2   Click Change Windows Password.

3. Click **Change Windows Password**. The Change Windows Password dialog box appears (see Figure 6.3).

Figure 6.3   Enter the password you want to use in the New password text box.

4. Enter your password (up to 25 characters) in the **New password** box. Passwords are case-sensitive, so be sure to remember which words you capitalize, because "LETMEIN" is a different password than "LetMeIn." Be careful to spell the password correctly, because you will only be able to see asterisks as you type.

5. In the **Confirm new password** box, enter the password again, exactly as you did the first time.

6. Click **OK**.

7. A confirmation dialog box appears, saying that your password has been successfully changed. Click **OK**.

8. Click **Close** to exit the Passwords Properties dialog box.

Changing Your Password

You must be careful to protect your password so other people don't learn it. It helps to change your password periodically, just in case someone has been looking over your shoulder or might have guessed your password.

To change the password:

1. Choose **Settings, Control Panel** from the Start menu.

2. When the Control Panel opens, click the **Passwords** icon. The Passwords Properties box appears.

3. Click **Change Windows Password**. The Change Windows Password dialog box appears (refer to Figure 6.3).

4. Enter your previous password in the **Old password** box (this proves you're authorized to make the password change).

5. In the **New password** box, enter your new password.

6. In the **Confirm new password** box, enter the new password again, exactly as you did the first time.

7. Click **OK**.

8. A confirmation dialog box appears, saying that your password has been successfully changed. Click **OK**.

9. Click **Close** to exit the Passwords Properties dialog box.

TIP **Removing a Password** If you no longer need a password for your computer, you remove the password by changing it. Enter your current password in the **Old password** box, but enter nothing in the **New password** or **Confirm new password** boxes.

Configuring for Multiple Users

Because you set up your desktop the way it suits you, Windows 98 is personalized for your use. But what if you're not the only person who uses your computer? Maybe there are different shifts with different users on each shift, or perhaps two part-time workers share the same computer. At home, you may want different settings for each family member who uses the computer. Whatever the situation, it helps if each user has a different password so they can't see the others' personal files. Also, it would be nice for each person to be able to set up his or her own desktop.

Windows 98 is able to accommodate a setup that includes more than one user. Each user has his or her own unique user name, password, and user profile. The profile stores a person's unique settings. Then, when you log onto the computer with your name and password, your settings appear.

To set up a user profile:

1. Choose **Settings, Control Panel** from the Start menu.

2. When the Control Panel appears, click the **Users** icon.

3. When the Enable Multi-user Settings dialog box appears, click **Next** to continue.

4. In the **User name** box, enter the name of the first user. Click **Next**.

5. (Optional) If you don't already have a password, a dialog box appears, asking for one. Enter one in the **Password** box and then type it again in the **Confirm password** box. Leave the boxes blank if you don't want to use a password. Click **Next**.

6. Under **Items** (see Figure 6.4), check the items you want to be able to personalize—Desktop folder and Documents menu, Start menu, Favorites folder, downloaded Web pages, or My Documents folder.

Figure 6.4 Check the items you want to personalize.

7. Choose **Create copies of the current items and their content**, or, to save space, click **Create new items to save disk space**.

8. Click **Next**.

9. Click **Finish**, and Windows 98 restarts.

When Windows 98 reboots, select your name from the list of users and enter your password to continue.

When you set up additional people, follow steps 1 and 2 of the preceding procedure. The User Settings dialog box appears (see Figure 6.5). Click **New User**. Then follow the remaining procedures for setting up a user profile.

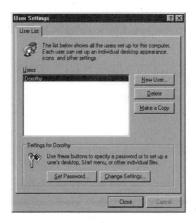

Figure 6.5 Open the User Settings dialog box to add or remove users, change users' passwords, or change users' settings.

To set your password (each user must do this), open the User Settings dialog box, select your name, and click **Set Password** to see the Change Windows Password dialog box (refer to "Changing Your Password" for the procedures to create or change your password).

To choose a different set of items you want to be able to personalize, click **Change Settings** and select the items you want. Click **OK**. Click **Close** to exit the User Settings dialog box.

Now that more than one person is using the computer, you must let Windows 98 know when you are finished using the computer and when another person starts. From the Start menu, choose **Log Off**. Click **Yes** to confirm it.

When you next use the computer, provided the last person logged off properly, you will see the Enter Password dialog box (see Figure 6.6). Select your name and enter your password. Then click **OK**.

Figure 6.6   Select your name from the Enter Password dialog box and enter your password.

Any changes to your desktop, such as the wallpaper, shortcuts, Start menu customization, and so forth, is now stored as part of your user profile. When another user works on the computer, these settings may be entirely different.

In this lesson you learned about passwords and how to set them, plus how to set up your computer so it can be used by different people. In the next lesson you'll learn about configuring your peripheral devices and sound options.

Configuring Peripheral Devices and Sound Options

In this lesson you learn to set the options that control your monitor resolution and color, make it possible to use multiple monitors, control sound on your computer, and configure your keyboard and mouse.

Configuring Video Options

Depending on the video adapter installed on your computer, you may be able to adjust the resolution and the number of colors displayed on your monitor. This is especially important with the newer, larger monitors.

A computer screen is made up of *pixels*, which are small units or "dots" that display individual colors on your screen. In a single picture on the screen, each pixel is assigned a color. When seen as a whole the dots come together visually to make the picture.

A standard VGA monitor has 640×480 pixels (640 pixels across each row and 480 rows). When a larger size monitor still uses 640×480 pixels, the size of the pixels increases and that makes the items on the screen larger but may also cause fonts or figures to look jagged or unfinished. Increasing the size of the pixels doesn't improve the *resolution*, so you should set a larger screen to display more pixels—800×600 or 1024×768. The more pixels used to create the picture, the higher the screen resolution. With a higher resolution, the monitor picture is crisper and easier to read (although the characters may seem smaller than in the 640×480 setting).

To control the screen resolution, or number of pixels displayed, do the following:

1. Choose **Settings, Control Panel** from the **Start** menu, and click the **Display** icon, or right-click the desktop and choose **Properties** from the pop-up menu.

2. When the Display Properties dialog box opens (see Figure 7.1), select the **Settings** tab. (Don't be disturbed if your Display Properties dialog box is not exactly like the one shown in Figure 7.1. Some video adapters change the appearance of the dialog box, and yours might be slightly different than the one shown.)

Figure 7.1   Under Screen area, drag the slider to select the number of pixels you want displayed.

3. Under the Screen area, drag the slider toward **More** (if the Screen area is grayed out, your video adapter is not capable of changing the screen resolution). The number of pixels to be displayed appears beneath the slider.

4. Click **Apply**.

5. A dialog box appears, telling you that Windows will resize your screen. Click **OK**. If the screen doesn't reappear correctly (don't worry if it flickers at first), wait about 15 seconds and Windows will restore the original setting. Windows may ask to restart your computer in order for the changes to take effect; let it.

If you don't like the new setting, follow the preceding steps and change the setting back.

Still not satisfied? Is the picture better but the font is too small? To fine-tune the resolution, calibrate your display to match the dimensions of your screen. At the same time, change the size of the screen fonts.

Grab a ruler and follow these steps:

1. Open the Display Properties dialog box and select the **Settings** tab.
2. Set the **Screen area** to higher than 640×480.
3. Click **Advanced**.
4. When the Properties dialog box for your video adapter appears (see Figure 7.2), select the **General** tab (your dialog box may differ from the one shown, as the features of each video adapter are different).

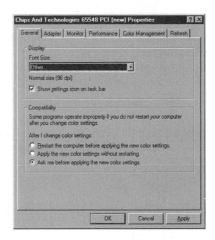

Figure 7.2 To be able to quickly set the resolution in the future, check **Show settings icon on task bar**.

5. Under **Display**, choose **Small Fonts** (the normal size), **Large Fonts** (about 120% of normal size), or **Other** from the **Font size** drop-down list.
6. (Optional) If you chose Other, the Custom Font Size dialog box opens (see Figure 7.3). Hold your ruler up to the ruler on the dialog box. Drag the ruler in the dialog box until it matches the one in your hand. Click **OK**.

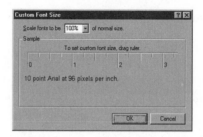

Figure 7.3   Match your ruler to the ruler on the screen to set the resolution to match your screen dimensions.

7. Windows 98 warns you that the settings won't take effect until you restart Windows. Click **OK**.

8. Click **OK** to close the video adapter Properties dialog box, and then click **OK** to close the Display Properties dialog box.

TIP   **Change Resolution from the Taskbar**   If you need to change your screen resolution frequently (some graphics programs require different resolutions), it would be easier to access it from the taskbar. To add a display settings icon to the taskbar, open the Display Properties dialog box, select the **Settings** tab, click **Advanced**, and check **Show settings icon on task bar**. Click **OK** to close each of the dialog boxes. Then to change the resolution, click the monitor icon and select the resolution you want from a pop-up list.

It's also possible to set the number of colors your monitor displays. Some color monitors only display 16 colors; others display as many as 4 billion (32-bit True Color). The more colors your monitor displays, the better your color pictures appear (especially photographs)—up to a point. At that point, adding more colors can't make the picture any better. Increasing the number of colors also has a down side: it takes more bits of data to display more colors, which may slow your computer processor.

Working with Graphics   Some graphics programs, especially photo **TIP**   editors, have requirements about the number of colors you display. Your application may not be compatible with higher color levels, so consult your manual before adjusting the color settings.

To set the number of colors displayed, follow these steps:

1. Open the Display Properties dialog box and select the **Settings** tab (refer to Figure 7.1).

2. Under **Colors**, select the color setting you want to use. Only the color settings available with your video adapter are listed.

3. Click **OK**.

4. Windows 98 warns that your new settings may not be compatible with some of your programs unless you restart the computer immediately. Choose whether you want to restart the computer now with the new settings or apply the new settings without restarting. Click **OK**.

Configuring for Multiple Monitors

Windows 98 allows you to have as many as nine monitors connected to your computer, all at one time. A different application can show on each monitor. This is particularly useful to Web page developers, who need to see how their creations appear in different Web browsers. For anyone developing applications for the graphical user interface (GUI), it may be useful to view the results on different quality monitors. Anyone else who constantly has to switch between applications while working will also appreciate this ability.

For each monitor you want to add to your system, you must install a PCI graphics adapter. Then connect the monitors and power up the system. Windows 98 detects the multiple monitors. The primary monitor is the one that displays your desktop items (if the monitor you want to use as primary isn't displaying these items, you need to turn off the computer and switch connections with the monitor that did display them and then restart the system).

CAUTION

Laptops are Exceptions Some laptops are already configured by the manufacturer to handle an additional monitor, so you can set up a full-size monitor when working at home or in the office.

With multiple monitors, you can move programs from one monitor to another, as well as specifying color and resolution settings for each monitor. Open the Display Properties dialog box, select the **Settings** tab, and do one of the following:

- **Arrange the monitors**   Drag the monitor icons so their positions reflect the actual physical arrangement of monitors around your computer. However, when you want to drag items from one monitor to another, rearrange the monitor icons so they are next to each other before you drag the application items.

- **Move items between monitors**   Click each icon to display its number in the corresponding monitor. Rearrange the monitor icons to place the ones you're dragging to or from either side by side or one over another. Click **OK** or **Apply**. Then drag the item to the appropriate monitor.

- **Setting screen resolution**   Click the monitor icon that represents the monitor you want to adjust. Check **I want to use this monitor** if you're working with a secondary monitor. Drag the slider under **Screen area** to set the resolution.

- **Setting number of colors (color depth)**   Click the monitor icon that represents the monitor you want to adjust. Check **I want to use this monitor** if you're working with a secondary monitor. Select the setting you want from the **Colors** drop-down list.

Color and resolution settings must be set for each separate monitor.

Click **OK** to exit the Display Properties dialog box and accept your settings.

Configuring Sound Options

A computer with a sound card and speakers can be a lot of fun, especially when you're playing games or if you like to listen to music CDs. There are also certain sounds associated with events on your computer, like beeping for an error message. That can be embarrassing in an open office.

To control the sounds made by your computer:

1. Choose **Settings, Control Panel** from the Start menu.
2. When the Control Panel appears, click the **Sounds** icon. The Sounds Properties dialog box appears (see Figure 7.4).
3. From the **Events** list, select the event for which you want to change the sound.

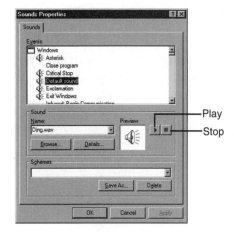

Figure 7.4 A list of sound events appears at the top of the Sounds Properties dialog box.

4. Select a sound from the **Name** drop-down box. These sounds files are stored in the Media subfolder of the Windows folder. If you have sounds in other locations, click **Browse** and select the sound file. Click **Details** to see the properties dialog box for the selected sound.

5. To hear the selected sound, click the **Play** button next to the Preview. To stop the playback, click the **Stop** button.

6. To change the sounds for a set of events, make a selection from the **Schemes** drop-down box (schemes are not automatically loaded during Windows 98 Setup, so you may have to load them from the installation disk). The sounds associated with the Events will change to reflect your selected scheme.

7. Click **OK**.

To change the volume of the sounds emanating from your computer, click the speaker icon on the taskbar and drag the slider up or down the Volume bar. Check **Mute** to turn off the sound.

Configuring Multimedia Devices

With a sound card installed on your computer, you have the ability to record sounds, play music CDs, and control other audio devices you've installed.

1. Choose **Settings, Control Panel** from the **Start** menu.
2. In the Control Panel, click the **Multimedia** icon.
3. The Multimedia Properties dialog box appears (see Figure 7.5). Each tab represents a different type of device:

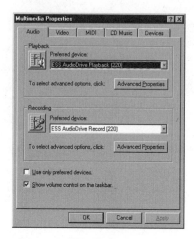

Figure 7.5 Your audio and visual settings are made in the Multimedia Properties box.

- **Audio**   Select your **Preferred device** for **Playback** and **Recording**. Click **Advanced Properties** to set the performance for each. The advanced properties for the playback also let you specify your speaker setup.
- **Video**   Choose the size of the video window when you play a video on your screen.
- **MIDI**   Change your sound synthesizer settings. Specify a single instrument, or choose a scheme to get a set of MIDI voices.
- **CD Music**   Specify the CD-ROM drive you want to use for playing music CDs and set the music volume. To have Windows use digital playback, check **Whenever possible, use digital playback on this device**.
- **Devices**   Change the properties for an individual multimedia device by selecting a device from the list and then clicking **Properties**.

4. Click **OK** to accept your settings and close the dialog box.

Some of your multimedia devices may have additional utilities for you to control their settings. Refer to the manual for each device when you want to use it.

To learn how to use the Windows 98 Multimedia features, see Part IV, Lesson 6, "Using Windows 98 Entertainment Features."

Configuring Your Keyboard and Mouse

Windows 98 lets you adjust the operation of your keyboard and mouse to suit your abilities and preferences.

To configure your keyboard:

1. Choose **Settings, Control Panel** from the **Start** menu.

2. In the Control Panel, click the **Keyboard** icon. The Keyboard Properties dialog box appears (see Figure 7.6).

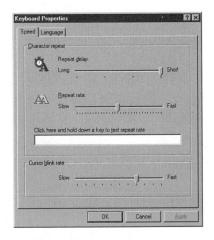

Figure 7.6 Set the character repeat options for the keyboard.

3. Under **Character repeat**, control what happens when you hold down a key on the keyboard.

   Repeat delay   Use the slider to set the amount of time between when you hold down a key and the time the character repeats. If you have trouble with your hands or fingers such as arthritis, or are just learning to type, you may have trouble removing your fingers from keys fast enough to prevent the typing of multiple letters. In that case, adjust the delay toward **Long**.

   Repeat rate   Use the slider to adjust the speed how fast the character repeats when you hold down the key.

4. To test your settings, click in the **Click here and hold down a key to test repeat rate** box. Then hold down a key to see what happens.

5. Click **OK**.

The Language tab of the Keyboard Properties box, lets you add another language to use with your keyboard (it doesn't translate for you). If you add languages, you may also select a keyboard shortcut to switch languages when using the computer or place an indicator on the taskbar.

TIP

Windows Button   Some of the newer keyboards have Windows and menu buttons that open the Start menu or act as if you right-clicked the screen.

Windows 98 lets you swap mouse buttons for left-handed users, adjust your double-click speed, choose different pointers for different events, adjust the speed of the mouse pointer, or create a trail to follow to help you locate the pointer. To adjust the mouse options:

1. Choose **Settings, Control Panel** from the Start menu.

2. In the Control Panel, click the **Mouse** icon. The Mouse Properties dialog box appears (see Figure 7.7).

Figure 7.7   Left-handed users can swap the mouse buttons for easier use.

3. On the **Buttons** tab, click **Left-handed** if you need to swap the functions of the left and right mouse buttons.

4. You may have difficulty making the double-click on the mouse because you can't click fast enough. Or, possibly you click so fast your double-click doesn't register. For either problem, you need to adjust the Double-click speed on the Buttons tab. Drag the slide and then double-click in the test area to see if it suits you.

5. On the Pointers tab, select a type of mouse pointer and choose a different picture (use **Browse** to find the file). Or, to change the settings for all the mouse pointers, choose a **Scheme**.

6. A frequent complaint is having trouble finding the mouse pointer on your screen. It either moves too fast or "disappears" before you can locate it. You need to change the Pointer speed on the Motion tab. You can also check Show pointer trails to have an "after-image" of the mouse pointer stay on the screen after the pointer moves. This trail shows where the mouse is going (slide for a shorter or longer trail).

7. Click **OK**.

For more information on adjusting the keyboard and mouse settings to handle disabilities, see Lesson 14, "Accessibility Options."

> **IntelliMouse and IntelliKeyboard** These Microsoft devices have extra features that give you added flexibility when working with Windows 98. The extra button on the IntelliMouse, for example, allows you to scroll the screen without clicking a scrollbar. When you add these devices, Windows 98 will automatically detect them when you restart your computer. For more information on these devices, refer to the literature that came with the device or open the Microsoft Web site.

In this lesson you learned to set options for your video adapter, multiple monitors, sound, multimedia devices, keyboards, and mice. In the next lesson, you'll learn how to configure a modem.

Configuring a Modem

In this lesson, you learn how to add a modem to your system, specify how it dials out, and change or refer to its properties.

What Is a Modem?

A modem is a device that allows you to send and receive data via the telephone lines. It translates your data (which is in a digital format) into a form that can be carried over the phone line (which normally carries analog, or voice, signals). The modem sends the translated data; it also translates analog data received through your phone line into the digital format your computer uses. If you have a fax/modem, your modem can receive and send faxes also.

It is a piece of hardware that is either internal (inside your computer case) or external (plugged into a port on your computer). In addition to being connected to your computer, it's connected to a telephone line.

Adding a Modem

Installing the modem is a two-part process. The first part involves the hardware, and those instructions are included with the hardware. The second part involves setting it up for your system so Windows 98 and your communications software know it's there. The second part is covered here.

To add a modem to your system:

1. Choose **Settings, Control Panel** from the **Start** menu.
2. When the Control Panel appears, click the **Modems** icon. The Modems Properties box appears (see Figure 8.1).

Figure 8.1 The Modem Properties box lists the modems installed on your computer.

3. Click **Add**.

4. If you have a laptop, the Install New Modem asks what type of modem you want to install: PCMCIA modem card or Other. Select one and click Next.

TIP **PCMCIA** PC Cards are a hardware innovation for use with portable computers. Different types of devices, such as modems and network adapters, are available on these PC Cards, which can be inserted in the computer when needed and removed when not needed or when another device needs to use the same slot. Windows 98 plug and play detects the presence of these cards and immediately loads the appropriate drivers.

5. Windows 98 will attempt to detect your modem unless you check **Don't Detect My Modem; I Will Select it From a List** (in that case, skip to step 7).

6. Click **Next**. The detection process begins. When Windows detects your modem and port, go to step 10. If Windows doesn't detect the new modem it will ask you to choose it from a list. Click **Next**.

7. The wizard shows you a list of modem manufacturers and modem models (see Figure 8.2). Select one each from **Manufacturers** (use Standard Modem Types if you don't know the manufacturer) and from **Models** (use a standard or generic type if you don't know the specific model, or the nearest model if yours isn't listed). Then click **Next** to go to the next step. (Have the disk with the driver software available in case Windows asks for it.)

241

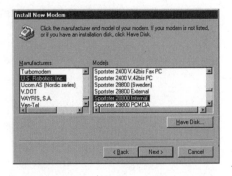

Figure 8.2   Select the manufacturer and model of your modem.

8. Select the port that the modem will be using.

 Port   Computers have several connectors into which you can plug cables or peripherals. These "plugs" are called ports. Each port has a name. The ports used for modems are called COM ports and are distinguished by number (COM1, COM2, COM3, and so forth). Only one peripheral may be assigned to one COM port, so if your modem is using COM2, no other peripheral is assigned to that COM port.

9. Click **Next**. Windows 98 sets up the modem.

10. Click **Finish**.

Modifying Dialing Properties

Before your modem can dial out by using HyperTerminal, Dial-Up Networking, or a communications software package, you need to specify what area code it's calling from and how it dials outside calls.

1. Open the Modem Properties dialog box.

2. Click **Dialing Properties**. The Dialing Properties dialog box opens (see Figure 8.3).

3. Found in the **I Am dialing from** box, the **Default Location** setting is the location you use most often when dialing out. If your computer is a desktop located in the office, the default location is the office; if it's located at home then the default location is your home. The location only becomes an issue when you have a portable computer, and you could be dialing from anywhere. In that case you have to decide on your default location.

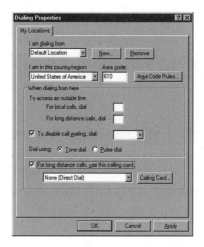

Figure 8.3 Enter the information needed to establish your current dialing location.

4. Select the name of the country for your default location from the **I am in this country/region** drop-down list.

5. Enter the area code for the location in the **Area code** box. If you need to dial your area code to reach other numbers in your own area code, click **Area Code Rules** and enter the numbers for which you must use an area code.

6. You may have to enter a prefix before dialing out, such as 8 for local calls and 9 for long distance. Enter the appropriate codes in the **For local calls, dial** and **For long distance calls, dial** boxes.

7. If the telephone line you use for your modem has call waiting service, check **To disable call waiting, dial** and select or enter the code needed to disable call waiting while your modem is on the line. If you don't disable call waiting, an incoming call will interrupt your modem session.

8. Click **Tone dial** or **Pulse dial**, depending on which service you have on the modem phone line.

9. If you plan to use a calling card when dialing out, check **For long distance calls, use this calling card**. Then select the type of calling card you use. If your calling card is not listed, or if you need to enter access numbers or a Personal ID Number (PIN), click **Calling Card**. Click **New** to enter a new calling card name, and then enter all the dialing information for that name and then click **OK**.

243

10. You should add other locations if you're using a portable computer. You may want one for home and another for office, or even a third for hotels. To add another location, click **New**. Enter a name for the new location and click **OK**. Then follow steps 4 through 10 to set up the new location.

11. Click **OK** to accept your choices and close the dialog box.

Changing Modem Properties

You would rarely change modem properties, except for specifying a different port, unless asked to do so by customer support. However, you may need to refer to these settings while installing communications software.

To access the modem properties:

1. Open the Modems Properties box.

2. Click **Properties**. The Properties dialog box appears for your modem (see Figure 8.4).

Figure 8.4 Select a different port from the drop-down list.

3. To change the communications port, select one from the **Port** drop-down list.

4. To set the Speaker Volume for the modem (if that choice is available), drag the triangular indicator between **Low** and **High**.

5. To change the **Maximum speed**, select the speed (in baud) from the drop-down list (consult the literature that came with your modem to find the maximum speed).

6. Select the **Connection** tab to refer to the connection settings (see Figure 8.5). Do not change these without consulting the specific settings for your modem or speaking to technical support at the modem manufacturer.

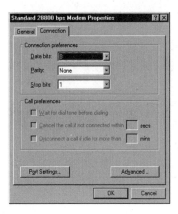

Figure 8.5 The Connection properties of your modem.

7. Click **OK** to return to the Modem Properties box and then click **Close**.

In this lesson, you learned how to configure your modem and set your dialing properties. In the next lesson, you'll look at the Device Manager.

Understanding and Using the Device Manager

In this lesson, you learn what the Device Manager is and how you can use it to configure your hardware.

What Is the Device Manager?

When you install a new device on your system you should rely on Windows 98 to detect the new device and configure it. You plug the device into the computer and turn the computer on. Windows 98 reads the device ID and then loads and initializes the device drivers. It also notifies applications that the new device is available. You, the user, only have to answer a few questions that appear on the screen. This automated installation process is called *plug-and-play*. Most newer peripheral devices are plug-and-play compliant, so you'll have no problem installing and configuring them.

When you install older hardware devices on your system (called "legacy" devices), use the Add Hardware Wizard in the Control Panel. It will walk you through getting Windows 98 to recognize the new hardware. If Windows 98 can't find the device, you'll have to enter the name and tell it where to find the device driver, so have your device disks handy. The wizard gives you step-by-step instructions and properly configures your device for you. For more information on adding new hardware, see Part III, Lesson 5, "Adding and Removing Software and Hardware."

So where does the Device Manager fit in? You use the Device Manager when you must manually change a device's configuration or when you need to look up information on the device's configuration. The Device Manager also tells you the status of the device, and whether it is working properly.

TIP **Changing Device Configurations Can Cause Problems** The Device Manager is a tool for advanced users who understand configuration parameters and the consequences of changing settings, so don't treat it lightly. Don't change settings without consulting the systems person in your office or your device manufacturer's technical support.

Finding Information on Your Hardware

When you need information on the device configuration of your hardware, look in the Device Manager:

1. Choose **Settings, Control Panel** from the Start menu.

2. When the Control Panel appears, click the **System** icon. The System Properties box appears.

3. Select the **Device Manager** tab (see Figure 9.1).

Figure 9.1 The System Properties box with the Device Manager tab selected.

4. The dialog box lists all the hardware devices on your computer, organized by category. Click the plus sign (+) next to the type of device about which you want more information to see the devices under that category. An X through the device icon means the device has been disabled; a circled exclamation point through the icon indicates that the device is experiencing a problem.

5. Double-click the icon for the hardware device you're researching. The
Properties box opens for that device (see Figure 9.2). The General page of
the dialog box tells you the name of the device, the manufacturer, the
version, and the device status. The other tabs in the dialog box change
depending on the device you select:

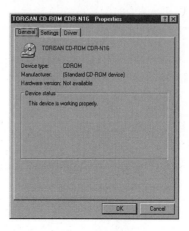

Figure 9.2 The Properties box for a CD-ROM drive.

General lists the device type, manufacturer, hardware version, and the
current status of the hardware. Hopefully, the latter is "This device is
working properly." If your computer has more than one hardware
profile (for laptops, there is usually a profile for docked and another for
undocked, because different devices are associated with each state),
check **Disable in this hardware profile** if you don't need that device
when using the current hardware profile.

Settings provides information on the current configuration settings for
the device. You can't change any of the gray information. For example,
on a disk drive you can't assign a new drive letter if that option is gray.

Driver tells you what device driver file is being used by your device
and may offer additional driver files so you can change the driver.

Resources specifies what system resources the device is using. As long
as there are no resource conflicts, you won't have to change these
settings. You can double-click the resource and change the setting
manually, but if you do, the resource setting becomes fixed and the

system loses its flexibility to adjust resources according to changing demands. Check **Use Automatic Settings** to have Windows 98 allocate resources for you.

6. Click **OK** to accept any changes you made; click **Cancel** to close the Device Manager without making changes.

The Device Manager also gives you the option of viewing the devices by connection. When you choose that view, the devices are listed under the hardware to which they are connected.

When you remove hardware from your system, you should also remove the device from the Device Manager (this isn't necessary if the equipment is plug-and-play). In the device list, select the item and click **Remove**.

Printing Device Information

You may find it helpful to have a printout of the information concerning a hardware device as part of your disaster control plan (in case you have to set up your system after a crash).

To print hardware information:

1. Open the Device Manager.
2. To print information about all your hardware devices, select **Computer** and then click **Print**.

   To print information about a specific device, click the icon for that device and then click **Print**.
3. When the Print dialog box appears (see Figure 9.3), choose **System summary** to print a report organized by resource type that lists which hardware is using each resource. Choose **Selected class or device** to print a report of the resources and device drivers used by the hardware device you selected. Choose **All devices and system summary** to print a complete report about the hardware that details each piece of hardware and lists all resources used by the hardware. If you want to store this information in a file instead of having a printout, check **Print to file**. Click **OK**.

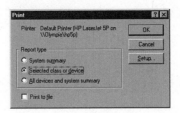

Figure 9.3   The Print dialog box.

4. Click **OK** to close the Device Manager.

In this lesson you learned how to find information about your hardware devices, how to check their settings, and how to print hardware information. In the next lesson you'll learn about managing your fonts.

Managing Fonts

In this lesson you'll learn about fonts—what they are, how to control which fonts are available on your system, how to add new fonts and delete fonts. You'll also learn how to add characters to your text that aren't on your keyboard.

What Are Fonts?

Fonts are typefaces. When you're using applications, such as Word, you apply fonts to your text to change the appearance of the characters.

Fonts are generally characterized as being *serif* or *sans serif*. A *serif* is a short stroke at the end of, or at an angle to, the letter form. Times New Roman is a serif type, but Arial is a sans serif type. Sans serif type is frequently used for larger-sized text, such as in headlines and presentations, while serif type is usually recommended for body type. These are not hard and fast rules.

There are also special fonts that can be decorative (such as Brush Script, Fraktur, or Posse) or that provide symbols (such as Symbol, Monotype Sorts, and Wingdings).

A font also has the following characteristics:

- **Size**. Type size is measured in points (there are 72 points in an inch), measuring from the top of the tallest letter in the font (such as h, t, l, or an uppercase letter) to the bottom of the letter that hangs lowest, such as g, y, or p.
- **Type style**. Styles include bold, italic, bold italic, underline, and strikethrough.
- **Effects**. Some fonts have effects, such as shadow, embossed, or engraved.

- **Case**. Case involves capitalization, such as uppercase and lowercase, but can include *small caps* (the lowercase letters are also capitals but smaller than the uppercase letters).

- **Width**. Width involves the horizontal size of the text. Wider than normal characters are *expanded*; narrower than normal are *condensed*.

Because you apply fonts in your application, you probably don't realize that the fonts in your system are controlled by Windows. That's why the same fonts are available to all your applications.

Fonts aren't just for printing nice-looking documents. Some of the fonts on your system control the appearance of text on your desktop, window titles, icons, menus, and so forth. Other fonts can do double-duty, as screen fonts and as printer fonts.

To view the fonts on your computer:

1. Choose **Settings, Control Panel** from the Start menu.

2. When the Control Panel opens, click the Fonts icon to open the Fonts folder (see Figure 10.1). There is an icon in the folder for each font on your computer. The symbol (such as TT) in the center of the icon indicates the name of the developer or manufacturer of the typeface or the type of typeface (TT is True Type).

3. Double-click a font icon to view the font in several sizes (see Figure 10.2). Click **Print** to print out a sample of the font to see how it looks on your printer. Click **Done** to close the font window.

4. Choose **File, Exit** from the menu or click the Close button to close the Fonts folder.

CAUTION

I Don't See My Font!   You may have fonts that appear in the font lists in your applications but don't appear in the Fonts folder. Those fonts are probably printer fonts, not software fonts, and they aren't installed on your computer.

They are "resident" on your printer and are only available when you are using that printer. In some applications, such as Microsoft Word, these printer fonts are indicated by a printer icon in front of the font name. Because there are no font files on your computer for the printer fonts, they don't appear in the Fonts folder.

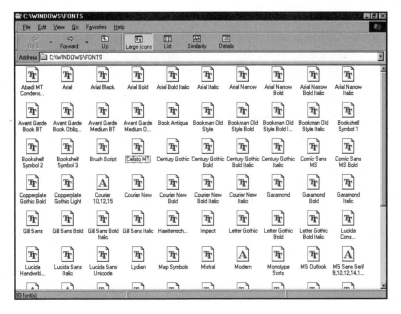

Figure 10.1 The Fonts folder has icons for every font on your computer.

Figure 10.2 Each font window provides the name of the designer, a full list of characters, and examples of the font in different sizes.

The Fonts window resembles My Computer, except that its toolbar has fewer icons. Large Icons, List, and Details produce the same results as those choices from the View icon in My Computer. One unique button on the Fonts toolbar is

Similarity. You use this button when you want to find any fonts that are similar to a designated font:

1. Open the **Fonts** folder.

2. Click **Similarity** on the Fonts toolbar (see Figure 10.3).

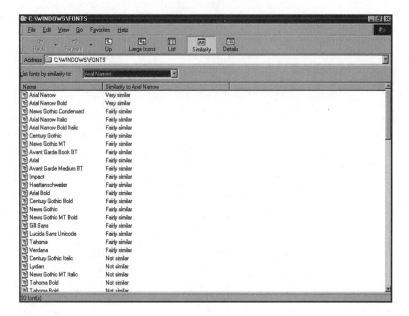

Figure 10.3   Click Similarity to help find fonts that look like the one in which you're interested.

3. From the **List fonts by similarity to** drop-down list, select the font that is the object of the search (you are looking for fonts similar to this font).

4. The order of the fonts is listed in the **Name** column and goes from most similar to least. The **Similarity** column indicates how similar the fonts are.

5. Click Large Icons, List, or Details to change the view.

6. Choose **File, Exit** from the menu or click the Close button to close the Fonts folder.

Adding Fonts

Only a few fonts are added to your computer when you install Windows 98 (Arial, Times New Roman, and Wingdings, for example). Other fonts are added by application programs to meet their specific needs. Any additional fonts must be added by you. Font files are fairly inexpensive, and some are given away, but you must install them in order to use them.

To add a font or fonts to your computer:

1. Open the **Fonts** folder.

2. Choose **File, Install New Font** from the menu.

3. From the **Drives** list, select the drive where your fonts are located (see Figure 10.4). Under **Folders**, select the folder where the font you want is stored.

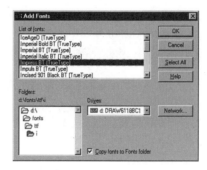

Figure 10.4 Select the Drive and Folder where your font is stored.

4. Select the font you want to add from the **List of fonts** box (click **Select All** to select all the fonts in that folder).

5. Make sure **Copy fonts to Fonts folder** is checked.

6. Click **OK**.

Removing Fonts

In a fit of passion, you added all those beautiful fonts and neat symbols. Now you need to make space on your hard disk or you need to clean up your fonts because you have too many listed when you try to apply fonts in your applications. You need to remove fonts from your Fonts folder:

1. Open the **Fonts** folder.

2. Select the font or fonts you want to delete.

3. Choose **File, Delete** from the menu.

4. When Windows asks if you're sure you want to delete these fonts, click **Yes**.

255

Using Character Map

There are many characters that aren't available from the keyboard, such as the copyright symbol, the registered mark, the pound or yen symbols, the cent symbol, and so forth. Many applications provide methods for incorporating these symbols into your documents, but there are some applications that do not.

When you need to use one of these "special" characters, you access it from the Character Map:

1. Choose **Programs, Accessories, System Tools, Character Map** from the **Start** menu.

2. The Character Map dialog box opens (see Figure 10.5). Select the font that contains the symbol you want from the **Font** drop-down list. All the characters in that font appear.

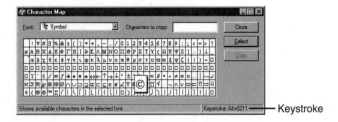

Figure 10.5   When you click on a symbol you see a magnification of it.

3. To view a symbol, use the arrow keys or click on the symbol to magnify it.

4. When you identify the symbol you want, click **Select**. The character appears in the **Characters to copy** box. You may add as many symbols as the box will hold.

5. Click **Copy** to copy the items in the **Characters to copy** box to the Clipboard.

6. Switch to the application and position your insertion point where you want to place the symbol(s). Choose **Edit, Paste** from the menu.

For many symbols, the Character Map displays a Keystroke at the bottom right of the dialog box. Instead of copying and pasting symbols, use the keystrokes. At the insertion point in your document, hold down the first key (usually Alt) and then type the numbers on the number pad on your keyboard. A symbol appears. If it isn't the symbol you expect, select it and change the font to match the font from the Character Map.

In this lesson you learned about typeface, font size and style, and how to add or remove fonts from your system. You also learned how to use the character map to access characters that don't appear on the keyboard. In the next lesson you'll learn about computer viruses.

Computer Viruses

In this lesson, you learn what a computer virus is and what steps you can take to prevent and cure viruses.

What Is a Computer Virus?

A computer virus is a lot like a virus in a human. It is an incomplete piece of programming that can do nothing on its own but, if attached to another program, can take over the other program and carry out its own mission instead of that of the host program. So, when you run the host program, it does something wholly unexpected and usually unwelcome. It may do something benign, like displaying a message on your screen. Or it may do something malicious, like deleting files or reformatting your hard disk.

Part of the programming built in to every virus is the ability to spread itself to other programs. When you run a program that is infected with a virus, the virus loads into your computer's memory and waits for opportunities to install copies of itself into other programs on your computer. Then, when you send a newly infected program to someone else, his programs become infected too. Because programs reside everywhere in modern computers, in the boot record of every disk, in .com, .exe, and .dll files, and even in data files, you can pass computer viruses around with ease, so you must take extraordinary measures to avoid passing them around.

There are, in general, three kinds of viruses:

- **Boot sector viruses** These infect the program that resides in the boot sector of every hard and floppy disk. They load themselves into your computer's memory when you boot up your computer (which is when the boot sector program runs). Your computer becomes infected when you receive an infected floppy disk, forget to remove it from your disk drive when you turn off your computer, then re-boot with it in the drive the next time you turn on your computer. This loads the virus into your computer's memory. From there, it infects your hard disk and every other floppy disk that you may put into the floppy disk drive.

- **Program file viruses** These infect executable program files, such as .exe and .com files, and the library (.dll) and overlay (.ovl) files that the executables call into memory from time to time. Your computer becomes infected when you run the infected program. Then the virus infects other programs on your computer.

- **Macro viruses** These infect specific kinds of data files. For example, Microsoft Word data files (.doc and .dot files) can store programming in the form of Word macros. A Word macro can be programmed to act like a virus, in the sense that, when you run Word and load the data file containing the macro into memory, the macro writes a copy of itself into your Normal template. From there it can write itself into every other Word file that you load into memory. And, sooner or later, you will send one of those files to a coworker.

The statistics on the number of new computer viruses being created every day are staggering—there are a lot of programmers out there with way too much time on their hands. While it's bad enough if your home computer gets infected (only you are inconvenienced), if a virus hits your computer at work, the ramifications can be much more far-reaching.

When a virus makes its way into an office computer, the chances of it "spreading" are good, as people in an office often share files. Just like spreading germs that make everyone get the flu, sharing infected disks spreads a virus through an entire company's computer system in very little time.

Curing and Preventing Computer Viruses

Obviously, prevention is better than a cure. Not downloading files or bringing disks from home will make it much less likely that your office PC will contract a virus. But there will be times that you have to accept a file from someone. What can you do? That's where virus protection software comes in.

Virus protection software reads files and disks, looking for viruses, and "cures" them by removing the virus or by alerting you that it doesn't have the "cure" for your virus. If the virus protection software can remove the virus, you can then safely open the file. If the virus protection software cannot remove the virus, it's best not to use the file, and you should consider deleting it.

Most virus protection software will run whenever your computer is running, and it will check all new programs as you install them. You can also run a check of a disk if someone gives you a file you must load on your PC.

It's a good idea to upgrade your virus protection software at least every six to eight months. There is a difference between upgrading and updating. Updating usually involves installing files that will virus-check against new viruses found or made since your virus protection software was released. Upgrading usually refers to installing a new version of the virus software itself, which typically includes new features, not just protection against newly discovered viruses. Typically, you purchase upgrades from your computer store or from the software manufacturer. And typically, you download updates from the software company's Web site. Virus protection software programs cost around $50. Since viruses have been known to completely incapacitate a computer, resulting in hours of work to rebuild the operating system and programs, virus protection is an inexpensive type of insurance. Better safe than sorry!

You can learn more about viruses on the Web. Search for "virus" or stop by the sites of virus protection software companies. Two of the largest (though hardly the only) companies that make virus protection software are McAfee Associates, Inc. and Symantec Corporation. McAfee makes a product called ViruScan; their Web site is www.McAfee.com. Symantec is the maker of Norton Antivirus products and can be found at www.symantec.com. See Part V, "Windows 98 and the Internet," for more information on using the Internet Explorer Web browser and downloading files from the Web.

In this lesson, you learned what a computer virus is and what you can do to help prevent viruses. In the next lesson, you'll learn who to call and how to prepare for the call when you need help with your computer hardware or software.

Rebooting, Restarting, and Disaster Planning

In this lesson, you learn what to do if a program stops responding or hangs up your system. You also learn what Windows Safe Mode is and how to prepare for operating system problems by creating a boot disk.

Using Ctrl+Alt+Del

If you have used previous versions of Windows, or are a tried-and-true DOS aficionado, you may find that Ctrl+Alt+Del is a hard habit to break. It is a habit you *should* break, however, because Microsoft does not recommend rebooting a Windows 98 machine in this way.

Ctrl+Alt+Del restarts the computer without regard to open programs. In previous versions of Windows and DOS, it was the recommended "catchall" action to take if your computer or program stopped responding. But Windows 98 needs to save information about programs and files before they shut down, and pressing Ctrl+Alt+Del prevents that from happening. In Windows 98, Ctrl+Alt+Del must be pressed twice before it reboots the PC. This keeps you from shutting down "illegally" and activates the Close Program dialog box, which will allow you to end a task legally.

If a program has stopped responding and you receive an error message in Windows 98 to that effect, you should:

1. Press **Ctrl+Alt+Del**.
2. The Close Program dialog box appears. If a program has stopped responding, the words "not responding" will appear next to the program name in this dialog box.
3. Select the program you want to close and click the **End Task** button.

This closes down the program. You can restart the program by selecting it from the Start menu, reinstalling the program if it continues to fail, or calling technical support for that software program. If you have continued problems, check your software documentation and visit the Web site of the software manufacturer. Many software companies keep lists of known "bugs," or problems, at their Web site and recommended fixes or workarounds.

Restarting Windows 98

Correctly restarting and shutting down Windows 98 is very important. If you need to restart the computer, doing so correctly ensures that people connected to shared resources such as printers or files do not lose data because you are restarting or shutting down Windows 98.

If you close a program using Ctrl+Alt+Del and then choose **End Task** in the Close Program dialog box, other programs that you have running at that time are not affected. But what happens if Windows 98 itself stops responding and you can't shut down legally? You might have to reboot the computer by pressing Ctrl+Alt+Del a second time.

Doing so will probably cause Windows 98 to run ScanDisk and then start in **Safe Mode**. (For more information on ScanDisk, see Part II, Lesson 11, "Disk Management.") Safe Mode is a sort of stripped-down mode of Windows 98. It is the operating system running in default mode, without loading network connections, CD-ROM drivers, or printer drivers. Only the default settings and minimum device drivers are used. Safe Mode is designed to help the Windows administrator or consultant in diagnosing operating system problems and is beyond the scope of this book. However, if you shut down Windows illegally by pressing Ctrl+Alt+Del twice, you may find yourself in Safe Mode when you restart.

You'll know you are in Safe Mode because it is written all over the Windows screen. To exit Safe Mode and start up Windows 98 in Standard mode:

1. Select **Start, Shut Down** from the taskbar.
2. The Shut Down Windows dialog box appears. Select **Restart the Computer**.
3. Click **Yes** to restart Windows.

Disaster Planning

The better prepared you are for a disaster, the less likely it is that the disaster will happen. Why? Well, if you are prepared for a disaster, your potential disasters are merely inconveniences!

Two very important steps you can take in disaster preparation are to back up your PC hard drive and create a system boot disk.

Backing Up the Entire Hard Drive

Throughout this book, we talk about the importance of backing up your data. But there is one more type of backup you might want to consider—backing up the entire hard drive.

There was a time, as computer professionals, when we would not have suggested that anyone back up an entire hard drive. After all, if your data was backed up and your hard drive failed, you could simply reinstall the operating system and software programs and then restore your data. Time-consuming, perhaps, but straightforward.

These days, you can't reinstall your operating system and programs because manufacturers don't always provide you with the CDs when you buy your computer. What would you do if your hard drive failed? Or what would you do if you decided to upgrade or change your operating system and your computer failed to run? Without the original software CDs, you could not reinstall software or your original operating system.

Therefore, it's a good idea to back up the entire drive of a new PC shortly after you bring it home. Do this once, and you don't really need to back it up again. Put the backup tape or disks in some secure place and, hopefully, you'll never have to use them again. For more information on backing up, see Part II, Lesson 10, "Using Task Scheduler and Backing Up."

 TIP **An Alternative to Backing Up the Hard Drive** Some computer manufacturers offer the CDs containing your operating system through their ordering department for an additional charge. You may want to purchase the CDs instead of using backup. Contact your computer manufacturer for more information.

Creating a Startup Disk

You should have a startup disk to start your computer if you are experiencing problems starting Windows. Create the startup disk and keep it in a safe place. Use it only when your computer hangs when it starts Windows. Place the startup disk in the floppy disk drive before you reboot or start the computer.

If you are experiencing problems that require you to use the startup disk, you might need the help of a professional or a very experienced Windows/DOS guru. These kinds of problems and their fixes are beyond the scope of this book, but creating a startup disk will assist the person helping you when he is trouble-shooting your PC.

To make a startup disk, you need a high-density $3^1/_2$-inch floppy disk. It should contain no other files, and we recommend you store this disk in a safe place label it "startup disk." Hopefully, you will never have to use it.

To create a startup disk:

1. Choose **Settings, Control Panel** from the Start menu.
2. In the Control Panel, select **Add/Remove Programs**.
3. The Add/Remove Programs Properties box appears. Click the **Startup Disk** tab.
4. Click **Create Disk** and follow the instructions for creating the startup disk. Store your startup disk in a safe place.

 TIP **Emergency Startup Disk** If you upgraded to Windows 98 and installed the program yourself, you may have been asked to create an Emergency Startup Disk at that time. This serves the same function as the startup disk.

Using Your Startup Disk

One of the biggest improvements in Window 98 is that the start-up disk you just created has drivers for most CD players on it. With past versions, the start-up disk did not have CD drivers on it. When you booted the system with the old start-up disk you could not see your Windows installation CD. Since your Windows installation CD is your probable destination if you are forced to use the start-up disk, you found yourself in a "Catch-22" situation—unable to see the files you need to fix your system.

You will need to use the start-up disk if Windows 98 stops booting correctly. For example, you have just accidentally erased all the files in your Windows directory and then turned the computer off. In this situation it is unlikely you will ever see your Windows Login Screen. If something like this happens:

- Insert your start-up disk in drive A.
- Turn your machine off and then back on. Your machine will come up in MS-DOS mode.
- Place your Windows 98 Disk in your CD.
- Type **cd D:** (assuming your CD is Drive D).
- Type **setup**. If the setup program is not on the root directory of your CD, use the dir (list directory) and cd (change directory) commands to get into the directory that contains setup.exe. Then type setup.
- Follow the Windows Setup menus. Depending on what kind of problem caused your inability to boot into Windows 98, you may get anywhere from none to all of your previous programs and data back. This is why you need to make a backup while your machine is running normally. If you haven't, you could lose all the information, settings, and programs you worked so hard to enter.

If you were farsighted enough to make a complete system backup, and create a recovery disk, you can restore everything just the way it was using the System Recovery Wizard.

- Boot your system with the startup disk. When asked, enable CD-ROM support.
- Format drive C. Remember, you will lose all the data on drive C: when you reformat it. The only way not to lose something is to back it up.
- Put in your Windows 98 CD-ROM.
- Create a folder named WIN98 on your hard disk using the command **md WIN98**.
- Copy all the files in the WIN98 folder of your Windows 98 CD-ROM into the WIN98 folder on your C Drive using the command **copy d:\WIN98*.* c:\WIN98**, assuming your CD-ROM is drive D.
- Copy the files PCRESTOR.BAT AND MSBATCH.INF from the the folder named \TOOLS\SYSREC to the root folder of your Drive C using the commands **copy D:\TOOLS\SESREC\PCRESTOR.BAT C:** and **copy D:\TOOLS\SESREC\MSBATCH.INF C:**. Again assuming your CD-ROM is drive D.

- Type **CD C:** and **PCRESTOR.BA**T to start the recovery process. Read the welcome message, then press any key.

- You will now be run through the system setup. Once Setup is complete, the System Recovery Wizard will load. Follow its screens to completion. This will require you to use the files you made during your complete system backup. Be sure, when asked, to restore your Registry, Hardware, and Software settings.

After the Recovery Wizard is complete, you should be fully restored to the point where you made your last complete system backup.

In this lesson, you learned about rebooting, restarting, and disaster planning. In the next lesson you'll learn about printing in Windows 98.

Printing in Windows 98

In this lesson, you learn to print from an application, control the print job, and connect to a network printer.

Installing a Printer

You can easily install a printer to work with all of your Windows applications. Windows includes many drivers for various manufacturers' computers. To install a printer, you need your Windows CD-ROM or a disk containing printer drivers that came with your printer.

 TIP **Printer Drivers** Software programs you install to your computer. The drivers make the printer work with Windows 98 and your Windows applications.

To install a printer, perform the following steps:

1. Choose **Settings, Printers** from the **Start** menu. The Printers window appears.
2. Click the **Add Printer** icon to display the Add Printer Wizard dialog box. Click **Next** to begin installing a new printer.
3. Choose whether to install a local printer or a network printer and then choose the **Next** button.

 TIP **Local or Network Printer?** A local printer is one connected directly to your computer; a network printer is one that may be connected to another computer on the network and is used by several workstations in addition to yours.

4. In the third Add Printer Wizard dialog box, choose the Manufacturer of your printer, such as HP (Hewlett-Packard), and then the model of the printer, such as DeskJet 550C as shown in Figure 13.1.

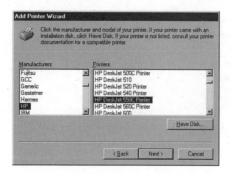

Figure 13.1   Choose the printer you want to install.

5. If you have a disk from the printer's manufacturer that contains Windows 98 drivers, insert the disk into the disk drive and click the Have Disk button; alternatively, insert your Windows 98 Setup CD-ROM and click the Next button. If you don't have the drivers, try visiting the printer manufacturer's Web site or the Microsoft Web site at www.microsoft.com to search for the printer driver you need.

6. Follow the directions onscreen. When Windows finishes setting up the printer, it returns to the Printers window.

Printing from an Application

The steps for printing from any Windows application are very similar. The biggest difference is that some dialog box options change from program to program. Most programs offer a Print icon on the toolbar that you can click to print one copy of the job; however, in some programs, the print icon displays the Print dialog box. To print from a Windows application, follow these steps:

1. Choose **File, Print**, and the Print dialog box appears. Figure 13.2 shows the Print dialog box in the WordPad accessory program.

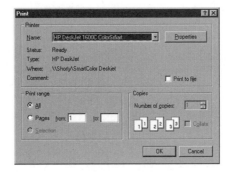

Figure 13.2 Use the Print dialog box to specify printing options.

2. Set any of the printing options described in the following list. Some applications will offer more specialized options; see a particular application's Help feature if you have questions:

Print Range Specify the pages you want to print. For example, you can print all pages, the current page, a range of pages, or a selection of text (which you select before opening the Print dialog box).

Copies Enter the number of copies you want to print. Often, you can choose a print order (front to back, for example) and whether to collate the copies.

Print to File Prints the document into a file, which you can use to print your document from a computer that doesn't have the program you used to create it. (You then print the file by typing **print filename** at the DOS prompt of any computer. All document formatting is preserved.)

Printer If you have several printers available, you can choose the printer to which you want to send the job.

Properties or Setup Usually leads to a dialog box in which you can set paper size, orientation, paper tray, graphics resolution, and other options specific to your computer.

Collate Copies Prints the copies (and multiple copies) of a multiple-page document in binding order from 1, to 2, to 3, and so on. If you are printing six copies of a six-page document, the job will print in sets.

3. When you're ready to print, choose **OK**. Windows sends the job to the printer.

CAUTION

Printing Errors If your job doesn't print and you receive an error message from Windows, check to see that the printer is turned on and there is paper in it. If the message indicates that you may have a paper jam, check the printer and clear the jam. If you still can't print, make sure the cable is not loose and try turning the printer off and on again. Try printing again. If you continue to have problems, click **Help** and search for printing. Open the Troubleshoot Printing document. This document will help you to identify potential problems with your printer setup.

TERM

Print Job A print job is a document you're printing. Each time you choose **OK** in the Print dialog box, you send a print job to the printer (whether that document contains one page or many).

Working with the Print Folder

When you print a document, the printer usually begins processing the job immediately. But what if the printer is working on another job that you (or someone else, if you're working on a network printer) sent? When that happens, there is a print queue that holds the job until the printer is ready for it.

TERM

Print Queue A holding area for jobs waiting to be printed. If you open the contents of the queue, the jobs appear in the order they were sent to the printer.

You can check the status of a print job you've sent by looking at the Print queue, found in the Printer's folder. Figure 13.3 shows three jobs in the Print Queue. The print queue window displays the information about the jobs.

Document Name	Status	Owner	Progress	Started At
Microsoft Word - Employee Han...	Printing	DOROTHY	0 bytes of 1...	2:05:58 PM 1/20/98
Microsoft Word - catdata.doc		DOROTHY	3.70KB	2:06:08 PM 1/20/98
Microsoft Word - Installing Wind...		DOROTHY	771KB	2:06:18 PM 1/20/98

3 jobs in queue

Figure 13.3 Use the Print queue to track your print jobs.

270

To display the Print queue, follow these steps:

1. Choose **Settings, Printers** from the **Start** menu.

2. In the Printers folder, click the icon of the printer you want to use.

Empty Print Queue? If no jobs appear in the Print queue, the job has already been sent to the printer.

CAUTION

Controlling the Print Job

It's hard to control just one or two print jobs because they usually are sent to the printer too quickly. However, if there are several jobs in the print queue, you can control them. For example, you can pause and resume print jobs, and you can delete a job before it prints.

Additionally, you can control the printer or just one particular document. You can, for example, cancel one document or all documents in the queue.

Pausing and Resuming the Queue

You may want to pause the queue and then resume printing later if, for example, the paper in the printer is misaligned or the printer is using the wrong color paper. Pausing the print queue gives you time to correct the problem. To pause the print queue, choose **Printer, Pause Printing**. You can also right-click the document and select **Pause**. To resume printing, choose **Printer, Pause Printing** a second time to remove the check mark beside the command. If you want to hold up the printing on only one document in the queue, select that document and choose **Document, Pause Printing**.

TIP **Printer Stalled** If your printer stalls while it's processing your print job, Windows displays the word "stalled" in the printer status line in the queue. Choose **Printer, Pause Printing** to remove the check mark from the command and start printing again. If the printer stalls again, see if there's a problem with the printer (it might be offline or out of paper, for example).

Deleting a Print Job

Sometimes you'll send a document to the printer and then change your mind. For example, you may think of additional text to add to a document or realize you forgot to check your spelling. In such a case, deleting the print job is easy, if you can catch it in time.

To delete a print job, follow these steps:

1. Open the Print queue by choosing **Settings, Printers** from the Start menu; click the Printer icon.

2. Select the job you want to delete.

3. Choose **Document, Cancel**.

 TIP   **Clear the Queue!**   To remove all files from the print queue, choose **Printer, Purge Print Jobs**.

Using Drag-and-Drop Printing

When you are able to see icons for both the printer and the document on your screen, take advantage of a quicker way to print documents. Drag the document file icon over the printer icon and release the mouse button. The document falls into the print queue and is printed. This is called *drag-and-drop printing*. You may want to make a printer shortcut on your desktop to facilitate this.

In this lesson, you learned to print from an application, control the print job, and connect to a network printer. In the next lesson you'll take a look at Accessibility Options.

Accessibility Options

*In this lesson, you will learn about some of the options
Windows 98 has to help make computers accessible for the
physically challenged.*

Using the Accessibility Wizard

Windows 98 has a number of features that help people who have difficulty
using keyboards and mice. The fastest way to set up these options is to use the
Accessibility Wizard:

1. Choose **Programs, Accessories, Accessibility, Accessibility Settings
   Wizard** from the **Start** menu.
2. The Windows Accessibility wizard opens (see Figure 14.1). In the first
   panel you are asked to choose a readable font.

Figure 14.1   Select the font size.

3. Click **Next**. On this screen you can select how to implement the selected font (see Figure 14.2). You can change the font size, change the screen resolution, or use the Microsoft Magnifier program.

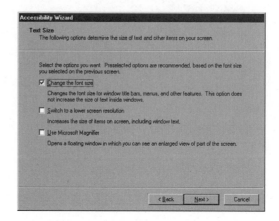

Figure 14.2 Font size options.

4. Once you have a font that is comfortable, click **Next**. This screen (see Figure 14.3) asks if the user:

- Is blind
- Is deaf
- Has difficulty using the keyboard or mouse
- Wants to set administrative options

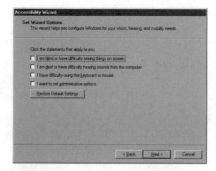

Figure 14.3 Accessibility Options.

5. Click **Next**. Screens appear relating to each item you checked. Adjust the settings on each screen and click **Next** to go to the next screen.

- **Scroll Bar and Window Border Sizes** There are four different Scroll Bar and Windows Border sizes to choose from. When you have a satisfactory setting, click **Next**. The setting takes effect.

- **Minimum Legible Text Size** A size scale appears next to a sample window. Move the slide up the scale to make the text larger, until the text in the sample is readable. When you click **Next**, the wizard displays settings to be made automatically to make the text larger for you: switch to a smaller screen resolution, change the font for windows, or use the Microsoft Magnifier. The selected options take effect immediately when you click **Next**.

- **Icon Size** Choose **Normal**, **Large**, or **Extra Large** as the icon size. A preview window shows the result of your choice. Click a suitable size and then click **Next** to have the setting applied.

- **Color Settings** A sample window appears with a set of color contrast settings beside it. Select a setting and then see how it affects the sample. When you find a setting that suits you, click **Next**. The setting takes effect immediately.

- **Sound Sentry and Show Sounds** To have Windows generate a visual warning when the system normally creates a sound, click **Use SoundSentry**. Then select a visual warning for windowed programs and another for full screen text programs. To see captions for speech and sounds made by Windows programs, select Yes on the **Show Sounds** panel. Click **Next**.

- **Sticky Keys** To be able to hold down one key at a time when using Shift, Ctrl, or Alt instead of having to push them all at once, select Yes on the Sticky Keys panel. Click **Next**.

- **Bounce Keys** If you want Windows to ignore brief or repeated keystrokes, answer Yes to the **Use Bounce Keys question**. Choose to ignore keystrokes that are faster than the time you specify, or to ignore quick keystrokes and keys must be held down for the specified time. Test your settings in the available text box. To hear a beep when you press keys, check **Beep when keys pressed or accepted**. Click **Next**.

- **Toggle Keys** Check **Use ToggleKeys** to play a sound when Caps Lock, Num Lock, or Scroll Lock is pressed.

- **Extra Keyboard Help**   For the nonmouse user, click **Show extra keyboard help in programs**. Click **Next**.

- **MouseKeys**   If you would rather use the numeric keypad to move the mouse pointer, click, double-click, or drag, check **Use MouseKeys**. Set the pointer's top speed and acceleration by using the slider. Make the choice of holding down Ctrl to speed up and Shift to slow down the mouse pointer. Select whether you want MouseKeys to work when NumLock is on or off. Click **Next**.

- **Set the Mouse Cursor**   Select the style and size of mouse pointer you want to use. Click **Next**.

- **Mouse Button Settings**   Choose **Right-handed** or **Left-handed** to set the function of the mouse buttons. Click **Next**.

- **Mouse Speed**   Here you can change the speed of your mouse pointer. Click **Next**.

- **Mouse Trails**   If you have difficulty tracking the mouse across the screen, you can cause the mouse to leave a more visible trail. Click **Next**.

- **Shortcut Keys**   Select the shortcut keys you want to use to turn off StickyKeys, FilterKeys, toggleKeys, and High Contrast. Click **Next**.

- **Set Automatic Timeouts**   Choose whether you want to turn off the accessibility features when the system is idle for a specified time. Click **Next**.

- **Default Accessibility Settings**   If you want these settings to also apply to all the new users of your workstation, answer Yes to the apply settings to all users question. Click **Next**.

- **Save Settings to File**   Click **Save Settings** to have your settings saved to a disk that you can use to configure other computers the same way as your workstation. Click **Next**.

6. Click **Finish**.

CAUTION

I Don't Have the Accessibility Wizard   The Accessibility Wizard is an optional component of Windows 98, as are many accessibility options such as Microsoft Magnifier. Refer to Part III, Lesson 5, "Adding and Removing Software and Hardware," for instructions on how to load these additional components.

Using Accessibility Properties

Even if you don't have the Accessibility Wizard, there are properties that you can set which aid or duplicate the options available in the wizard. Some can be found in the keyboard and mouse configurations in the Control Panel (see Part III, Lesson 7, "Configuring Peripheral Devices and Sound Options." Others are controlled by the Accessibility Properties.

To set the Accessibility Properties:

1. Choose **Settings, Control Panel** from the Start menu.
2. When the Control Panel opens, click the **Accessibility Options** icon. The Accessibility Properties dialog box opens (see Figure 14.4).

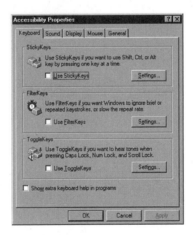

Figure 14.4   The Accessibility Properties dialog box offers keyboard, sound, display, mouse, and general settings.

3. Select the tab for the type of settings you want to make:
   - **Keyboard**   Turn on StickyKeys, FilterKeys, ToggleKeys, and extra keyboard help. Click the **Settings** buttons to specify options for these features.
   - **Sound**   Turn on SoundSentry and Show Sounds. Click **Settings** to specify options for SoundSentry.
   - **Display**   Turn on High Contrast. Click **Settings** to choose the level.

- **Mouse** Turn on MouseKeys. Click **Settings** to choose options.
- **General** Set an automatic reset after idle time, notification, or alternative device access (other devices that access keyboard and mouse features).

4. Click **OK** to exit from the dialog box.

In this lesson you got a quick overview of the Accessibility Options available in Windows 98. In the next lesson, you will learn how to start and exit Windows applications.

Working with Windows Applications

Starting and Exiting Windows Applications

In this lesson, you learn to start and exit an application running in Windows 98, as well as how to view the common elements of Windows application screens.

Opening a Windows Application

Windows provides a Start menu from which you can perform many tasks, including starting Windows programs. To display the Start menu, click the Start button on the Windows taskbar. You can open the Help feature from the Start menu; you also can open various applications from the Start menu by choosing the Programs command. The menus you see stemming from the Programs menu will vary depending on your system setup (see Figure 1.1).

To open an application, follow these steps:

1. Choose the **Start** button.
2. Select **Programs** to display the Programs menu.

3. Choose the application you want to open if it's listed on the Programs menu; alternatively, select the group containing the application you want to open and then choose the application from the submenu.

Most applications are listed on the Programs menu

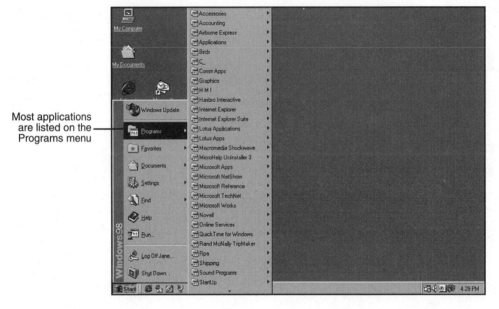

Figure 1.1 Access applications or other programs' menus from the Programs menu.

 TERM **Program Groups** The Programs menu displays various group names—such as Accessories, Online Services, Startup, and so on—that display a menu of related applications when selected. You can identify a program group by the Folder/Program icon in front of it and the right-arrow following the command. Accessories, Online Services, and StartUp are installed when you install Windows. You may also have program groups for Microsoft Office, Lotus SmartSuite, or other applications you've installed on your computer.

 TIP **Open Documents** If you've recently worked on a document, you can open it from the Windows Start menu. Click the Documents command on the Start menu to display a list of recently opened documents. Click the document you want to open. The source application opens with the document, ready for you to work on.

282

Viewing an Application's Window

Depending on the application you open—whether it's a word processor, database, spreadsheet, or other program—the application window includes elements particular to the tasks and procedures used for that application. For example, the cursor may appear as an I-beam (for typing), an arrow (for pointing), or a cross (for selecting cells in a spreadsheet program); the "document" area may appear as a blank sheet of paper or a table with many cells.

Most applications, however, display the following elements: title bar, menu bar, toolbars, ruler, scroll bars, a document area, and a status bar. Figure 1.2 shows the screen you see when you open the Windows accessory WordPad.

There's Always Help If you need help with any application, you can click the Help menu in that application and select a help topic. You can also press the F1 key in many applications to activate the Help screens.

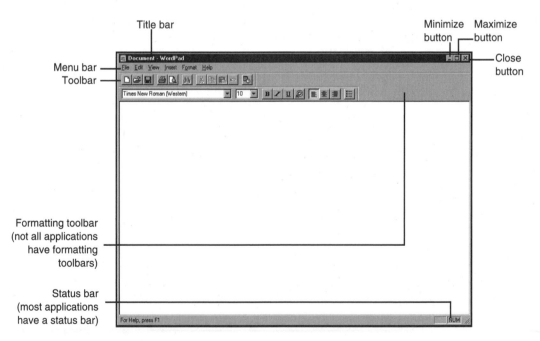

Figure 1.2 Most application screens contain similar elements.

Exiting an Application

You should always exit an application when you're done with it to ensure that your documents are saved before Windows shuts down. You can exit most Windows applications in one of the following ways:

- Choose the **File**, **Exit** command.
- Click the Close button (X).
- Choose **Close** from the **Control** menu.
- Double-click the application's Control menu icon.
- Press **Alt+F4**.

CAUTION

If You Get a Message Before Closing   If the application displays a message asking you to save the document before you close the program, choose **Yes** to save, **No** to close the application without saving the changes, or **Cancel** to return to the application. If you choose **Yes**, the application might display the Save As dialog box, in which you assign the document a name and location on your computer's drive.

In this lesson, you learned to start and exit a Windows 98 application as well as how to view the common elements of Windows applications' screens. In the next lesson, you'll learn how to work with multiple windows.

Working with Multiple Windows

In this lesson, you learn how to arrange windows, switch between windows in the same application, and switch between applications.

Arranging Windows on the Desktop

Windows 98 (as well as Windows 95 and Windows 3.1) is designed so that you can have more than one application or window open at a time. Some applications permit you to open several windows *within* the application itself. As you can imagine, opening multiple applications with multiple windows can make your desktop pretty cluttered. It is important to know how to manipulate and switch between windows. This lesson teaches you how to work with multiple windows.

When you have multiple windows open, some windows or parts of windows are inevitably hidden by others, which can make navigation confusing. Windows 98 provides several tools to help you arrange open windows. To view the available choices for arranging multiple windows, right-click in any gray area of the taskbar.

Cascading Windows

A good way to get control of a confusing desktop is to right-click a gray area of the taskbar and choose **Cascade Windows**. When you choose this command, Windows arranges all the open windows on top of each other so that the title bar of each is visible. Figure 2.1 shows a cascaded window arrangement using WordPad, Solitaire, and Microsoft Word. To access any window that's not on the top, simply click its title bar. That window then becomes the active window.

TIP   **Active Window**   The active window is the one in which you are working. You activate a window by clicking its title bar, clicking anywhere inside the window, or by clicking its button on the taskbar. The active window's title bar becomes highlighted, and the active window comes to the front.

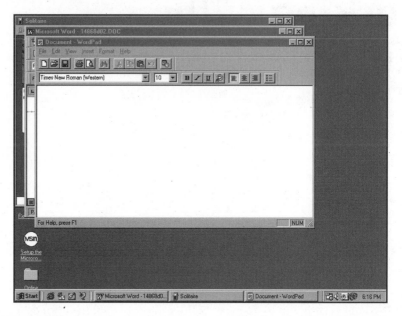

Figure 2.1   With cascaded windows, you can easily access opened applications.

You can click and drag the title bar of any window to another location on the desktop, and you can use the mouse to resize the window borders of any open window, even when it is cascaded with other windows.

Tiling Windows

If you need to see all open windows at the same time, right-click the taskbar and choose either Tile Windows Horizontally or Tile Windows Vertically. When you choose to tile, Windows resizes and moves each open window so that they all appear side by side (vertically) or one on top of the other (horizontally), as shown in Figure 2.2.

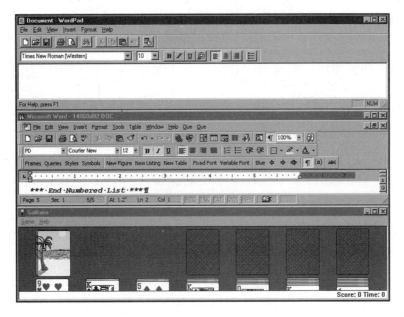

Figure 2.2 Tile windows so you can see a part of each window at the same time.

Minimizing All Windows

You can minimize Windows by clicking the Minimize button on each open window, or you can quickly minimize all open windows by using one of these two commands:

- Click the Show Desktop icon (see Figure 2.3).
- Right-click a gray area of the toolbar and choose Minimize All Windows.

Figure 2.3 Quickly minimize all open windows by clicking the Show Desktop icon on the Taskbar.

Moving Between Applications

When open applications are not maximized, you might be able to see all the open windows overlapped on-screen. In this case, you can click any window to bring it forward. Often, however, it's easier to work in a single application by maximizing the application's window. Switching between applications then requires a different procedure. You'll most likely use the taskbar to switch from application to application by clicking the minimized application button on the taskbar.

After opening several applications—such as WordPad, Paint, and Solitaire—use the taskbar by following these steps:

1. Click the button on the taskbar that represents the application you want to bring forward (see Figure 2.4).

Figure 2.4   All open and minimized application windows appear on the taskbar.

2. To switch to another open application, click its button on the taskbar. The open window minimizes back to the taskbar and is replaced by the next application you select.

Moving Between Windows in the Same Application

In addition to working in multiple applications in Windows, you also can open multiple windows within many applications. If you are using a mouse, you can move to a window by clicking any part of it. When you do, the title bar becomes highlighted, and that particular window comes to the front so you can work in it.

Figure 2.5 shows multiple document windows open in Microsoft Word. You can switch between the windows, arrange windows, and open and close windows within the application, just as you can manipulate windows within the Windows 98 program.

Use the Window
menu in your
application to
cycle between
maximized
windows

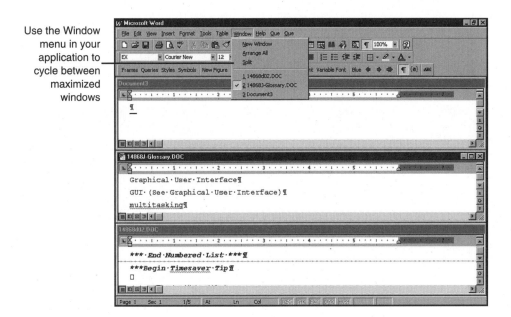

Figure 2.5 Three document windows are open within Microsoft Word.

Open multiple document windows by using **File**, **Open**. By default, each window is maximized within the document area. To switch between open, maximized windows, click the Window menu and select the document from the list at the bottom of the menu. Alternatively, you can press **Ctrl+F6** to cycle through open windows.

To view multiple document windows on-screen, follow these steps:

1. Restore the document window by clicking the document's **Restore** button. The open document windows cascade in the document area. The **Restore** button replaces the **Maximize** button.

TIP **No Window Menu?** If your open application does not have the word Window on its menu bar, that application does not support opening multiple files.

2. To activate an open document window, click in the window's title bar or press **Ctrl+F6**.

3. To tile the windows, choose **Window, Arrange All**. Windows reduces each open document window and tiles them (horizontally) in the document area.

TIP   **They're All Just Windows**   You can use the window frames to resize each window. Likewise, you can minimize, maximize, open, and close the windows as you would any window. See Part I, Lesson 3, "Working with a Window," for more information.

In this lesson, you learned how to arrange windows, switch between windows in the same application, and switch between applications. In the next lesson, you'll learn how to copy and move information between windows.

Copying and Moving Information Between Windows

In this lesson, you'll learn about the Clipboard and how to copy and move information between windows.

What Is the Clipboard?

One of the handiest features of the Windows environment is its capability to copy or move information (text, graphics, and files) from one location to another. This feature enables you to share information between document windows, applications, and other computers on your network.

When you cut or copy data from an application, Windows places the data on the Clipboard; it remains there until you cut or copy again. You can paste the data from the Clipboard to a document or application. Note, however, that you don't have to open the Clipboard to use it—and 99 percent of the time, you won't. You simply cut or copy your data, and then paste it to a new location.

 TIP **Copy, Cut, and Paste** When you copy information, the application copies it to the Clipboard without disturbing the original. When you cut information, the information is removed from its original location and placed in the Clipboard (don't confuse cutting with deleting, which removes the information but does not store it in the Clipboard for retrieval later). When you paste information, the application inserts the information that's on the Clipboard to the location you specify. (The copy on the Clipboard remains intact, so you can paste it again and again, if necessary.)

You can view the information on the Clipboard by choosing **Start**, **Programs**, **Accessories**, **System Tools**, and **Clipboard Viewer** (see Figure 3.1). In the Viewer, you can save the contents to a file name, add or remove text, edit the text, and open saved Clipboard files.

CAUTION

Where's the Clipboard Viewer?   The Clipboard viewer doesn't automatically load when Windows 98 is installed. You can install it by choosing **Settings**, **Control Panel** from the Start menu and then clicking the **Add/ Remove Programs** icon. Click the **Windows Setup** tab, select **System Tools** from the Components list, and then choose **Details**. Check **Clipboard Viewer** and then click **OK**. Click **OK** to close the dialog box (you may need to insert your Windows 98 CD or disk in its drive). For more information on adding programs, see Part III, Lesson 5, "Adding and Removing Software and Hardware."

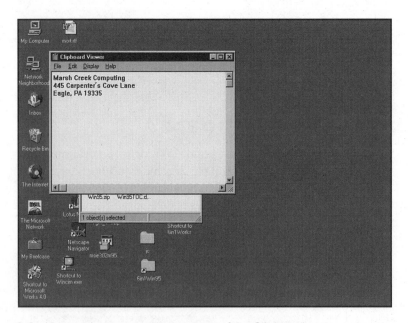

Figure 3.1   View and even save the contents of the Clipboard.

TIP   **Without a Trace**   When you turn off your computer or exit Windows, the contents of the Clipboard disappear. Be sure you save the contents of the Clipboard if you want to use the text or graphics later.

Selecting Text for Copying or Moving

Before you can copy or cut text, you must identify the text by selecting it. Selected text appears in reverse video (highlighted). Figure 3.2 shows selected text in a WordPad document.

To select text, follow these steps:

1. Position the mouse pointer just before the first character you want to select.

2. Press and hold the left mouse button, and drag the mouse pointer to the last character you want selected.

3. Release the mouse button, and the selected text appears highlighted.

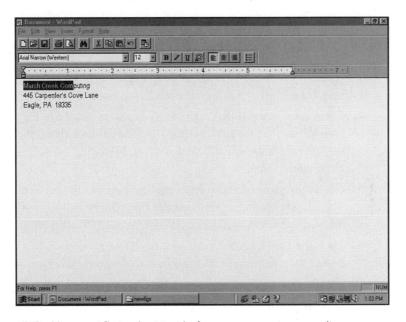

Figure 3.2 You must first select text before you can cut or copy it.

 TIP **Quick One-Word Selection** Quickly select one word of text by double-clicking the word.

Where's My Selected Text? If you press an alphanumeric key (a letter, number, or any other character) while text is highlighted, Windows deletes the selected text and replaces it with the character you typed. Choose **Edit**, **Undo** or press **Ctrl+Z** (in most applications) to reverse the action.

293

Selecting Graphics

The procedure for selecting graphics depends on the Windows application you use. In a word processing program such as WordPad or Microsoft Word, you select a graphic by clicking the object. In a program such as Paint, however, there are special tools for selecting shapes. Because the procedure may vary, you should refer to the instructions for each application. However, no matter how you select a graphic, small handles appear on the corners and sides of the graphic frame to indicate it is ready to copy or move.

Copying Information Between Windows

After you select text or graphics, the procedures for copying and pasting are the same in all Windows applications. To copy and paste information between windows of the same application, as well as between windows of different applications, follow these steps:

1. Select the text or graphic you want to copy.

2. Click the **Copy** button on the toolbar, or choose **Edit**, **Copy**. You can, alternatively, use a keyboard shortcut, such as **Ctrl+C** for copy. A copy of the selected material appears on the Clipboard; the original selection remains in place.

3. Click to position the insertion point where you want to insert the selection. You can switch between document windows or between applications as learned in Part IV, Lesson 2, "Working with Multiple Windows."

4. Click the **Paste** button, choose **Edit, Paste**, or press **Ctrl+V**. Windows copies the selection from the Clipboard to the insertion point.

 TIP **Multiple Copies** Because the selected item remains on the Clipboard until you copy or cut again, you can paste the same information from the Clipboard multiple times.

Moving Information Between Windows

In all Windows applications, you can use a similar procedure to move selected text or graphics with cut and paste. To cut and paste information between windows of the same application or windows of different applications, follow these steps:

1. Select the text or graphic.

2. Click the **Cut** button choose **Edit, Cut**, or press **Ctrl+X**. Windows removes the selection from its original location and places it on the Clipboard.

3. Place the insertion point where you want the selection to appear.

4. Click the **Paste** button, choose **Edit, Paste**, or press **Ctrl+V**. Windows copies the selection from the Clipboard to your document. (A copy remains on the Clipboard until you cut or copy something else.)

CAUTION

Memory Problems   If you copy or cut a large amount of text or a graphic to the Clipboard, it remains there until you copy or cut another item. This consumes a large amount of RAM, so it may slow down your operations or cause errors such as "Out of Memory." If you're able to open the Clipboard viewer, you can clear the Clipboard contents from there. The quick fix is to cut or copy a single character, so that item replaces the current contents of the Clipboard.

In this lesson, you learned about the Clipboard and how to copy and move information between windows. In the next lesson, you learn to use WordPad.

Using WordPad

In this lesson, you'll learn how to create, edit, format, and save a document in WordPad.

What Is WordPad?

WordPad is Window's word processing program. With WordPad, you can create documents such as letters, memos, reports, lists, and so on. Although WordPad is a word processor, it is very basic. For example, you cannot check your spelling or grammar in WordPad, and there are a limited number of toolbars and icons to help speed your work. However, you can create, edit, and format many simple documents with WordPad. Basically, it's fine to use if you don't have another word processor, such as Microsoft Word, Lotus Word Pro, or Corel WordPerfect.

To access WordPad, follow these steps:

1. From the Desktop, choose the **Start** button, select **Programs**, and then **Accessories**.

2. Click the **WordPad** option at the bottom of the **Accessories** menu. The program appears with a new, untitled document in the window for you to use, as shown in Figure 4.1. A blinking vertical bar, called the insertion point, appears in the upper-left corner of the document area.

TIP

Insertion Point The point at which the text you type will appear.

Like most word processing programs, WordPad has text-wrapping; you don't need to press **Enter** at the end of each line. Press **Enter** only to mark the end of a paragraph or to insert a blank line on the page.

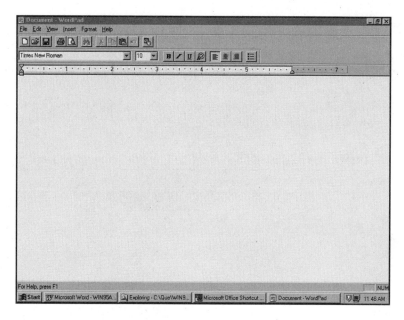

Figure 4.1 Use the WordPad program to create documents.

The WordPad screen contains the following elements:

- The application name (WordPad) and the document name (the generic name is "Document" until you assign a name by saving the document) in the title bar
- The menu bar containing WordPad menus
- Two toolbars containing shortcuts for saving and formatting your documents
- A ruler that enables you to set tabs and measure margins
- The text insertion point, which marks the location of the text you enter
- A status bar that offers helpful tips and information about the program

TIP **Windows Elements** Note that the WordPad window contains many of the same elements as other Windows programs: Minimize, Maximize, and Close buttons, a Control Menu button, a window border if the window is restored, and so on.

Need Help? The Help feature in WordPad works similarly to the Help feature in Windows. If you need help, access the Help menu or press F1.

Moving the Text Insertion Point

To move the insertion point with the mouse, just click the place in the text that you want to move to. To move the insertion point using the keyboard, see the options in Table 4.1. You can use these keys to move the insertion point around without disturbing existing text. You cannot move the insertion point beyond the last character in your document.

Table 4.1 Moving the Insertion Point with the Keyboard

Press	To Move
↓	Down one line
↑	Up one line
→	Right one character
←	Left one character
Page Up	Previous screen
Page Down	Next screen
Ctrl + ←	Next word
Ctrl + left arrow	Previous word
Ctrl + Page Up	Top of screen
Ctrl + Page Down	Bottom of screen
Home	Beginning of line
End	End of line
Ctrl + Home	Beginning of document
Ctrl + End	End of document

Inserting and Deleting Text

To insert text within existing text, simply place the insertion point in the appropriate location (using the mouse or the keyboard) and begin typing. The existing characters move to the right to make room for the new text as you type. When characters move to the right as you type, you are in Insert mode, which is the default mode of WordPad. If you press the **Insert** key, Insert will toggle off, putting you in overwrite mode. In Overwrite mode, new text that you type will replace old text.

To delete a single character to the left of the insertion point, press the **Backspace** key. To delete the character to the right of the insertion point, press the **Delete** key. To delete larger amounts of text, select the text and press the **Delete** key (see the next section to find out how to select text).

Selecting, Cutting, Copying, and Pasting Text

Before you can work with existing text, you must select it. To select text with the mouse, click at the beginning of the text and drag the I-beam pointer over the text so that it appears highlighted. To select text with the keyboard, place the insertion point at the beginning of the text, press and hold the **Shift** key, and use the techniques described in Table 4.1 to move to the end of the text you want to select. When you release the **Shift** key, the text you marked appears highlighted.

WordPad uses the Windows Clipboard to store any cut or copied text until you cut or copy again. To cut and copy text, select the text first and then use the **Edit** menu or the **Cut** and **Copy** buttons on the toolbar. To paste, move the insertion point to the location in which you want to paste the text and then choose **Edit**, **Paste**, or click the **Paste** button on the toolbar. For more information on cutting, copying, and pasting, see Part IV, Lesson 3, "Copying and Moving Information Between Windows."

Formatting a Document

You can affect the appearance of your document onscreen and on paper by changing the formatting. Formatting refers to the appearance of a document, including the font style and size, text alignment, and page layout.

You can format text before or after you type it. To format text before you type it, choose the formatting attributes and then enter the text; the formatting continues until you change it again. To format text after you type it, select the text you want to change and then apply the specific formatting changes.

Formatting Text

You can change the following text attributes to improve the appearance of your text or to set it apart from other text:

- **Font** Choose from Arial, Times New Roman, and so on, to change the look of the text.

- **Font Style** Apply Bold, Italic, Bold Italic, Underline, Superscript, or Subscript attributes to change the style of the text.

- **Font Size** Choose from 10-point, 12-point, 72-point, and everything in between (or even larger) to change the size of your type for headlines, fine print, and so on. (There are about 72 points in an inch.)

To change the font, font style, or font size, follow these steps:

1. Select the text to be formatted.

2. Choose **Format**, **Font** from the WordPad menu bar. The Font dialog box appears (see Figure 4.2).

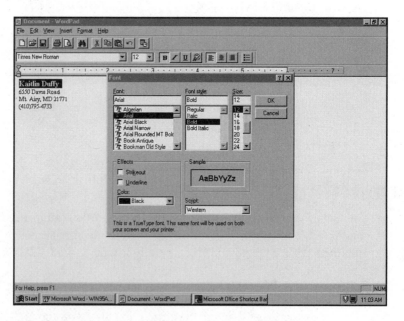

Figure 4.2 Change the look of the text on the page in WordPad.

3. Select the font, font style, and size options you want. The Sample Area shows sample text with options you selected.

4. Choose **OK** to apply the changes.

TIP **Quick Formatting** Use the Format bar above the ruler to apply a font, size, or attribute to selected text. Just click the down arrow beside the font or size drop-down list; or click the **Bold**, **Italic**, or **Underline** buttons on the Formatting tool bar to apply a style attribute. You will find Bold, Italic, and Underline buttons in many Windows programs.

Figure 4.3 shows a document with formatting applied to selected text. Note that you can use multiple fonts and font sizes to add interest and emphasis.

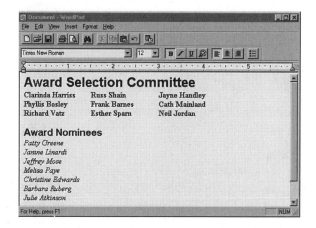

Figure 4.3 You can vary the font, size, and style of text within your document to add emphasis to important text.

TIP **Regular** A font that has no attribute applied (such as bold, italic, or underlining) is called *regular*.

Aligning Text

By default, text is aligned with the left margin. However, you can right-align text or center it between the margins.

TIP   **Alignment**   *Left-aligned* text is flush along the left margin of the page and ragged along the right edge; left-aligned text is the default alignment for most word processing programs. *Right-aligned* text is the opposite of left-aligned. *Centered* text is ragged on both the left and the right sides, but each line is centered between the two side margins. *Justified* text makes the text flush with both the left and right edges of the page and is available in many programs; however, WordPad doesn't support justified text.

To align text:

1. Select the text.

2. Use the formatting toolbar buttons to choose the alignment:

   - **Left**
   - **Center**
   - **Right**

Adjusting Page Margins

You can change the page margins using the Page Setup dialog box. You can also choose page size and orientation in this same dialog box.

CAUTION   **Page Settings**   Before you change your paper size, source, or the orientation of the page, check your printer documentation to verify that it can print to a special setting. Many printers, for example, cannot print to small paper envelopes and most printers have a required margin (usually at least .25 inch).

To change page margins:

1. Choose **File, Page Setup**. The Page Setup dialog box appears, as shown in Figure 4.4.

2. Choose **OK** to apply the margins to your document.

TIP   **Paper Size Changes**   Click the drop-down arrow beside **Size** in the **Paper** area to select another paper size, such as #10 commercial size envelope or 8$\frac{1}{2}$-by-14-inch paper. You can also choose the paper tray or envelope feeder, if applicable, from the **Source** drop-down list.

Figure 4.4 Change the margins in the Page Setup dialog box.

Saving a Document and Exiting WordPad

To avoid losing the changes you've made to your WordPad document file, you need to save your work often. The first time you save a document, you assign it a name and location on the disk. From that point forward, you save the document without naming it again. If you attempt to exit WordPad or close the file without saving the file, or without saving your most recent changes, WordPad will prompt you to save the document.

To save a WordPad document:

1. Choose **File**, **Save As**. The Save As dialog box (shown in Figure 4.5) appears.

2. In the **Save In** drop-down list, choose a drive to save the file to.

3. In the list box, double-click the folder in which you want to save the file.

4. In the **File Name** text box, enter a name for the file; you can take advantage of Windows long file names by entering letters, numbers, and spaces that exceed the previous DOS eight-letter limitations.

5. Choose **Save**. Windows saves the file, closes the dialog box, and returns to the document onscreen. The name in the title bar changes from "Untitled" to the name you assigned your document.

6. To exit WordPad, click the **Close** (X) button or choose **File**, **Exit**.

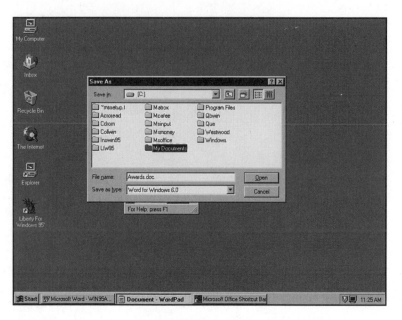

Figure 4.5   Give the file a name and choose a location on the disk.

 TIP   **Save As or Save?**   Choose **Save As** to assign a file name and location to your document the first time you save it or anytime you want to save a file under a new name or location. Use **Save As** when you need to save different version of a document. Choose **Save** to save any changes you make to a document that's already been named.

In this lesson, you learned how to create, edit, format, and save a document in WordPad. In the next lesson, you learn to use Paint, a Windows accessory.

Using Paint

In this lesson, you learn to open the Paint application, create a drawing with Paint, and save the drawing.

What Is Paint?

Paint is a Windows graphic program that allows you to create drawings you can use, either alone or in other Windows application such as Microsoft Word, Lotus Word Pro, or Corel WordPerfect.

To open the Paint program and begin a drawing, follow these steps:

1. From the Desktop, choose the **Start** button and then **Programs**, **Accessories**.
2. Click **Paint** from the Accessories menu. The Paint window opens as shown in Figure 5.1, ready for you to draw.

In addition to the standard application window parts, (title bar, control button, and so forth) the Paint window also has a set of drawing tools (called the toolbox) located on the left and a color palette at the bottom of the window. When drawing with Paint, you can use outline or fill colors.

 Outline and Fill Colors The overlapping boxes to the left of the color palette show the currently selected outline color (the box on top and to the left) and the fill color (the box underneath and to the right). The *outline color* is the color you use when you draw lines and outlines for objects, and the *fill color* is the color of the inside of any objects you draw.

The box below the toolbar identifies the width of a line and the options for the currently selected tool in the toolbox. Depending on which tool is selected, you use this box to determine how wide a line the line tool draws, how wide the eraser is, whether a shape is filled or transparent, and so on. Table 5.1 shows each of the tools in the toolbox.

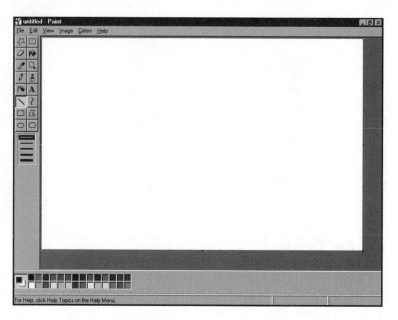

Figure 5.1   Use the Paint tools and menus to create a drawing.

Table 5.1   Tools in the Paint Toolbox

Tool	Name
	Free-Form Select
	Select
	Eraser/Color
	Pick Color
	Fill
	Magnifier
	Pencil
	Brush
	Airbrush

Tool	Name
A	Text
╲	Line
⌇	Curve
▢	Rectangle
◸	Polygon
⬭	Ellipse
▢	Rounded Rectangle

Drawing in Paint

Drawing with a mouse can be difficult at first, but practice always makes a difference. You use your mouse to draw lines, curves, and shapes, as well as to enter text in Paint.

The following list describes different ways to draw:

- To select the fill color, right-click any color in the palette.
- To select the line color, click any color in the palette.
- To select the size of the drawing, choose **Image**, **Attributes** and enter the width and height in the Attributes dialog box (see Figure 5.2). Click **OK**. The new size is defined by eight small black handles or boxes, outlining the specified area.
- To choose the type of object you're going to draw, click a drawing tool in the toolbox at the left of the screen.

CAUTION

Which Tool Should I Use First? Try starting with either the rectangle tool, the ellipse tool, or the straight line tool to experiment. Then branch out to the other tools as you learn more about the program.

Figure 5.2   Choose the size of the drawing before you begin drawing.

- To select a line width for any line, curve, rectangle, ellipse, and so on, click the line size you want in the line box in the lower-left corner of the screen.

- To draw an object, point at the area where you want the object to appear (within the boxed Image area), press and hold the left mouse button, and drag the mouse pointer until the object is the size you want.

CAUTION

Oops!   If you add to your graphic and then decide you don't like the addition, choose **Edit**, **Undo** (or press **Ctrl+Z**) to undo the change you made.

A Perfect Circle Every Time   To draw a perfect circle, select the **Ellipse** tool, hold down the **Shift** key, and click and drag the mouse pointer. You can also use this technique to draw a perfect square with **Rectangle** tool or a perfectly straight line with the **Line** tool. This method applies to many Windows drawing, graphics, and word processing programs.

Adding Text to a Graphic

Using the **Text** tool, you can add text to a graphic such as a logo or illustration. To add text to a graphic, follow these steps:

1. Select the **Text** tool.

2. Drag the **Text** tool to create a rectangle in which you will type the text. A rectangle that will hold the text and an insertion point appear.

3. Before you type, choose **View**, **Text Toolbar**. The Fonts toolbar appears, as shown in Figure 5.3. Choose the font, size, and attributes from the Fonts toolbar.

4. Click the insertion point within the rectangle and type your text, pressing **Enter** at the end of each line. When you finish typing the text, choose another tool from the toolbox or click the next place you want to insert a new line of text. If you want to make a change to the formatting of the text, select the text and use the Font toolbar.

5. Click outside of the text box anywhere to accept the text you just entered.

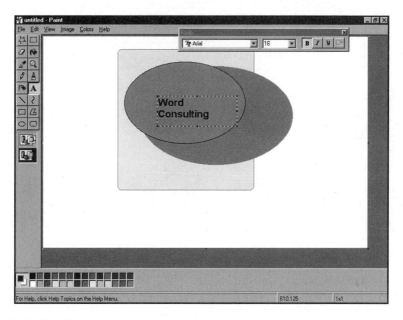

Figure 5.3 Use Paint's tools to create a company logo.

CAUTION **After You Leave, You Can Never Go Back** You can't edit or reformat text once you've accepted it; you can only erase it. To erase the text, click the **Select** tool, draw a frame around the text and choose **Edit**, **Cut**. (This also works for any lines or shapes you want to erase.) Be careful when cutting, however; you can cut out parts of shapes and text and leave other parts intact.

TIP **Move or Size Object** To move the text (or any other part of the drawing), select it with the **Select** tool and then drag it to a new position, To resize an object, select it and then position the mouse pointer over one of the handles around the selection rectangle. Drag the two-headed arrow to change the size of the text or object.

Figure 5.4 shows a logo using graphics and text created in Paint, with the text selected and ready to move.

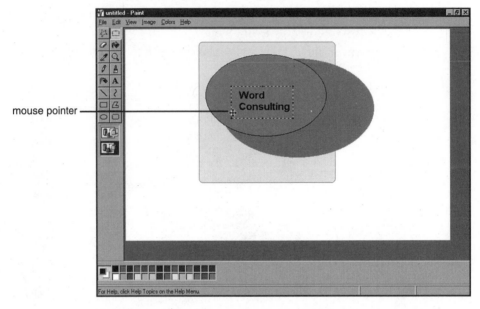

mouse pointer ——

Figure 5.4   The mouse pointer indicates the object is ready to be moved.

Saving a Drawing

To save a drawing, follow these steps:

1. Choose **File, Save As**. The Save As dialog box appears.
2. If you want to change the file type, choose a file type from the **Save As Type** drop-down list box.
3. In the **Save In** drop-down box, choose a drive in which to save the file.
4. In the list box, double-click the folder to which you want to save the file.
5. In the **File Name** box, enter a name for the file. Choose **Save**, and Paint saves the file.
6. To close **Paint**, click the **Close** button or choose **File, Exit**.

In this lesson, you learned to open the Paint program, create a simple drawing with Paint, and save the drawing. In the next lesson, you are introduced to the Multimedia capabilities of Windows 98.

Using Windows 98 Entertainment Features

In this lesson, you'll learn how to use some of the Multimedia tools included with Windows 98.

What Is Multimedia?

Multimedia, as the name implies, is a combination of two or more mediums. *Mediums* can include sound, fixed pictures, moving pictures, and animation. The main components of Windows 98 Multimedia are the Sound Recorder, CD Player, Media Player, the ActiveMovie Player, and (optionally installed) WebTV for Windows.

The ability to work with multimedia in Windows 98 is not automatic—you must have the correct hardware installed before you can achieve success using multimedia tools. You need to have a sound card, CD-ROM drive, speakers, and microphone connected to use most of the tools here. Fortunately, most PCs come with these components as standard these days. However, even if you don't have these components, they are pretty easy to obtain and install. For more information, refer to Part III, Lesson 7, "Configuring Peripheral Devices and Sound Options."

Windows 98 multimedia programs are found in the Entertainment section of the Accessories programs (see Figure 6.1). If you upgraded from Windows 95, you'll find these programs relocated from the Multimedia category to the Entertainment category. This, of course, may not be true if you have customized the Start Menu or added multimedia software in the Multimedia category.

If your PC came with Windows 98 installed, there is a good chance that many of the optional features of Windows 98 are installed. If you do not see some of the features described in this chapter, and you have the Windows 98 install CD, you can add these features by accessing the **Control Panel** and choosing **Add/ Remove** programs. Click on the Windows Setup tab and select the items you wish to install. For more details on Windows setup, see Part III, Lesson 5, "Adding and Removing Software and Hardware."

Figure 6.1 shows the **Start**, **Programs**, **Accessories**, and **Entertainment** menu selections. The DVD Player is an optional Windows install, and you use this only if you have a DVD player. WebTV for Windows is also an optional install, so you may not see that choice on your menu.

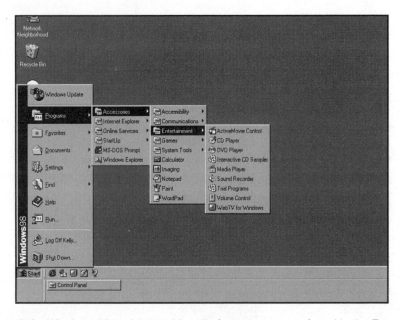

Figure 6.1   Windows 95 and 3.1 multimedia features are now found in the Entertainment category of Windows 98.

The following list briefly describes the purpose of the items and programs found in the Entertainment menu.

- CD Player Program, for playing audio CDs on your CD ROM drive.
- DVD Player(optional install) Software, which controls the activity of the DVD (Digital Video Disc) player. Functions of the DVD player are similar to those of the CD player.

- Interactive CD Sampler Program, which runs the CD sampler program from the Windows 98 install disk. Look here to learn about other Microsoft products.

- Media Player Program, which plays various types of multimedia sound files.

- Sound Recorder Program, which records sound using your computer.

- Trial Programs Program, which installs trial (partial programs, or programs with automatic expiration dates) from the Microsoft Windows 98 CD ROM. By installing the trial programs, you have an opportunity to "test drive" software programs such as Microsoft Money as well as some game programs.

- WebTV for Windows (optional install) Program, which controls viewing live TV programming on your PC. You must have a TV tuner card or video card with a TV tuner to use this option.

- Volume Control Program, which controls the computer's sound card volume.

Using the Sound Recorder

With a sound card installed, you can use the Sound Recorder to record, play back, and manipulate sound file characteristics including adding an echo, changing playback speed, and mixing with other files. To access the Sound Recorder choose **Start**, **Programs**, **Accessories**, **Entertainment**. From the Entertainment menu, choose **Sound Recorder**. The Sound Recorder appears (see Figure 6.2).

Figure 6.2   The Sound Recorder Program.

Recording Sounds

With the Sound Recorder open and an audio input device (microphone) connected to or built into your computer, you can record sounds by performing the following steps:

313

1. Select **File**, **New**.

2. To begin recording, click the **Record** button (the round circle).

3. To stop recording, click the **Stop** button (the rectangle).

4. To save your file choose **File**, **Save As**.

TIP   **Recording Your First CD?**   You can specify the default sound quality before you record a sound. On the **Edit** menu, click **Audio Properties**, and then click the quality that you want from the list (you must have a read/write CD drive to record on CDs).

Playing Sounds

With the Sound Recorder open and an audio input device connected to your computer, you can record sounds by performing the following steps:

1. Select **File**, **Open**.

2. Open the folder containing the sound file you want to play, and then click the **Play** button (the single triangle).

3. When the file is completed, the Sound Recorder player will stop, or to stop the sound playback in progress, click the **Stop** button (the rectangle).

TIP   **Instant Replay?**   Use the **Seek to Start** or **Seek to End** buttons (the double triangles) to quickly move to the beginning or end of your recording.

Editing and Working with Effects

Using the Sound Recorder, you can cut parts of sound files and mix them with other files. You can also increase and decrease speed, play in reverse, add echo, and even change the quality by converting the file format. Descriptions of how to perform these steps follow:

- Deleting Part of a Sound File Move the slider bar to the place in the file that you want to cut and, using the Edit menu, click **Delete Before Current Position** or **Delete After Current Position**.

- Change the Speed of a Sound File. From the Effects menu, click **Increase Speed** or **Decrease Speed**.

- Reverse Play. From the Effects menu, click **Reverse** and then click **Play**.

- Add Echo. From the Effects menu, click **Add Echo** and then click **Play**.

- Undo Changes. From the File menu, click **Revert**; click **Yes** to confirm the restoration.

- Change Sound File Quality. From the File menu, click **Properties**, and from the **Format Conversion** area, select a format from the list. Click the **Convert Now** button, specify the format and attributes you want for the sound file, and then click **OK**.

- Insert a Sound File into Another Sound File. From the File menu, click **Open**, and then double-click the file you want to insert. Move the slider bar to where you want to insert the other sound file. On the Edit menu, click **Insert File**. If you insert a sound into an existing sound file, the new sound replaces the original sound after the insertion point. Type or double-click the name of the file you want to insert.

CAUTION   **Compressed Files**   You can change the effects in and edit only uncompressed sound files. If you don't see the green line in Sound Recorder, the file is compressed and you cannot change it until it is uncompressed.

Operating the CD Player

You can use the CD-ROM drive on your computer to play music CDs. You must have a sound card installed, and a speaker system (either internal or external). With the CD Player, you can play CDs, switch the order in which you play tracks, and select specific tracks to play. If you have a multiple CD player, you can queue up more than one CD, shuffle through the stack, or continuously play multiple CDs.

To use the CD Player, follow these steps:

1. Choose **Start, Programs, Accessories, Entertainment**. From the **Entertainment** menu, choose **CD player**. The CD Player appears (see Figure 6.3); if you have a data CD or no CD in the CD-ROM Drive, you see the message Data or no disc loaded.

2. Insert the CD. Click the **Play** button to play, the **Pause** button to temporarily stop the CD, and the **Stop** button to stop the music.

3. To change the order of the tracks that play, as opposed to playing the tracks in the order they fall on the CD, choose **Options**, **Random Order**.

Figure 6.3 Use the CD Player to play music CDs from you computer.

CAUTION

Still Won't Recognize the CD? If you insert a CD and your CD player still does not recognize it, you need to make sure you have a sound card installed in your computer and that you have a Windows 98 driver for the sound card installed. Double-click the **System** icon in the Control Panel and select the **Device Manager** tab. Double-click the **Sound, Video, and Game Controllers** device type to see if there is an installed sound card. If you see a yellow circle with an exclamation point in it or no sound card listed, you have a problem.

TIP **Not Loud Enough?** To adjust the volume of the CD Player, choose **View**, **Volume Control**. The Volume Control application appears—use this to adjust the volume.

Using the Media Player

Use the Media Player to play audio, video, and animation files in Windows 98. You can play a multimedia file, rewind the file, and fast forward the file. You can also copy a multimedia file into a document that you or someone else can play back. Video for Windows files has an AVI extension.

To open and use the Media Player, perform the following steps:

1. Choose **Start**, **Programs**, **Accessories**, **Entertainment**, and then select **Media Player**. The Media Player window is now displayed

2. From the Device menu, select the device type you want to play: **ActiveMovie** (animation), **Video for Windows**, or **CD Audio**.

3. If you choose the **ActiveMovie** or **Video for Windows** option, an Open dialog box appears from which you can locate and choose the file you want to play. If you choose the **CD audio** option, then choose **File, Open** to select the file you want.

4. Choose the Play button to play the file.

Using the ActiveMovie Player

The ActiveMovie Player is similar to the Media Player; you can play animated clips or movies on both applications. Files you play using the ActiveMovie Control Box include the following types: MPEG, MPE, MPG, MPA, ENC, and DAT. These extensions represent various file types of movies or animations that have been compressed somewhat due to their very large size.

To use the ActiveMovie program, follow these steps:

1. Choose **Start**, **Programs**, **Accessories**, **Entertainment**, and then choose **ActiveMovie Control**. The Open dialog box appears.

2. Choose the file you want to play and then click the **Open** button.

3. As the file plays, you can control the movie from the ActiveMovie Control box.

Placing a Multimedia File in a Document

You can place any multimedia file in a document so you or someone else can play the file at any time from within the document. You can copy the multimedia file and then paste it into the document.

To use a multimedia file in a document:

1. In the Media Player, open the **File** menu and choose **Open**.

2. Double-click the file you want to copy.

3. Choose **Edit, Options** and specify the options you want.

4. Open the document to which you want to paste the file and position the insertion point.

5. Choose **Edit, Paste**.

To play back a multimedia file from within a document, double-click the icon representing the file.

Using WebTV for Windows

You can use WebTV for Windows even if you don't have all of the necessary hardware to watch TV programs on your PC. Here, we show you how to use WebTV for Windows to download TV programming information (times and dates of TV shows).

To actually watch TV programs on your PC, you need a video adapter that is compatible with the viewer. You also need a digital satellite connection, or a digital cable connection. With these tools or a high speed Internet connection, you can receive TV programs.

WebTV for Windows is an optional install component of Windows 98. You can run Windows setup to install the viewer if it is not installed on your PC. To learn how to run Windows setup, see Part III, Lesson 5, "Adding and Removing Software and Hardware."

After WebTV for Windows is installed, you can use it to download local programming and view the TV schedule for your area (and your cable carrier) if you have an Internet connection. For example, you could download five days of program information and then update that information every couple of days from G-Guide at http://broadcast.microsoft.com.

To download local programming, you must be connected to the Internet (with a constant connection, or through your ISP using dial-up networking) before following these steps:

1. Click **Start, Accessories, Entertainment, WebTV for Windows**.
2. Double click **Channel 96 (TV Config)**. This is your configuration page. Click the **Go To** button and choose **Get TV Listings**.
3. Click the **G-Guide** hyperlink.
4. Your web browser will open on the programming page of the **G-Guide** site. Follow the instructions for downloading programming information. You will be required to enter your ZIP code and to select from a group of cable providers.
5. When the download is complete, (you see a message indicating so), close your web browser and disconnect (optional) your Internet connection.
6. Your programming will look similar to the programming guide shown in Figure 6.4.

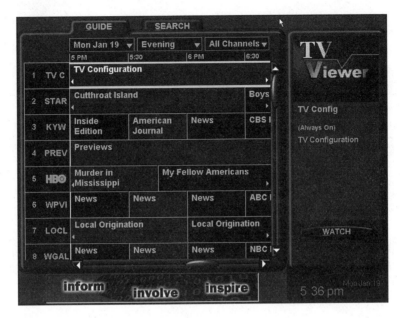

Figure 6.4 After you have downloaded the programming guide, you can search for your favorite programs, topics, or actors, and set alarms for your favorite TV programs.

To get help using WebTV for Windows, press **F1**. To exit WebTV for Windows, press **F10** and click the **Close** button.

In this lesson, you learned how to use the Media Player, the ActiveMovie Player, CD Player, and TV Viewer. In the next lesson, you learn more about the Windows 98 Control Panel.

OLE: Linking Data to Different Applications

In this lesson, you'll explore two concepts: linking and embedding. You'll learn how these concepts help you work with more than one application.

Sharing Information Between Applications

You can incorporate data that was created in one application into another application, such as a spreadsheet, word processing document, graph, drawing, or scanned image. Rather than keying in the information from the other application, you can "capture" it from its original application and place it in the document you're creating at the moment.

For example, you're writing a report. Data you need to incorporate in that report is contained in a spreadsheet. You want to capture that spreadsheet data and put it into your report document.

You can share information between applications using several methods:

- **Importing** converts data from its "native" program so you can include it in your current document. Generally, users import data when they can't open the source document. For instance, if you need a picture in your document, you import the picture from a clip art library into your document. Once you place the picture, you can't open the clip art file and change that picture, and if someone updates the original picture file, those updates do not automatically appear in your document. Your picture remains the same as it was when you imported it.

- **Edit, Cut** and **Edit, Copy** commands allow you to store data temporarily in the Clipboard (a memory holding area created by Windows) and then place it into your document with the Edit, Paste command. To learn more about cutting and pasting, see Part IV, Lesson 3, "Copying and Moving Information Between Windows."

- **Linking** utilizes the Clipboard (via the Cut and Copy commands) to bring data from a source document and place it into your document. Any updates to the source information will also appear in your document. All users of the document must have access to the source file, and the location of that source file cannot change or the link will fail.

- **Embedding** places an "object" created by another program directly into your document. You can edit the object's contents by activating the source application directly from your document (all you have to do is double-click on the object). Changing an embedded object does not change the source document.

 TIP **Object** An object is a single piece of data such as text, graphics, sound, or animation created by an OLE-supported application.

Programs that let you share data use one of two methods to share that information:

> **Dynamic Data Exchange (DDE)** is a communications protocol that lets you share data between two open applications. DDE is an older technology, so most programs in Windows support it.

> **Object Linking and Embedding (OLE)** extends your ability to dynamically share information between programs and program files. Because of OLE, you can embed or link files from another application into a document; or you can embed a new object and use the object's application to enter data into your document. Not all applications support OLE (especially older ones), so you may not be able to embed files from all your applications.

As a user, you don't have to know if an application supports DDE or OLE. Your application will automatically employ OLE if the originating application supports it and DDE if it doesn't. If a program supports neither DDE nor OLE, its menu simply won't offer you the option of linking or embedding pasted data.

Understanding Linking

When you link data from an application to your document, the linked object maintains a reference or pointer back to the originating file. Then, when the original file changes, the modifications also appear in your document.

For example; you copy data from a spreadsheet file containing your yearly budget into a word processing document and link the data to its source spreadsheet. Any new data you add to the spreadsheet file at the end of the first quarter will show up in your word processing document. Likewise, anyone else who linked the spreadsheet data to their own documents will also receive the updates to the spreadsheet.

As a user, you can't edit or update linked data without using the source application program. You would also need access to the source file and find the file at the same drive and directory or folder as listed in the reference pointer to the source file. In other words, if the file the data came from was on the server's drive F in the Import directory, you need to specify F:\Import as the source location to access the file from your computer.

What are the advantages of linking files?

- You can link files between older Windows programs that don't support embedding.
- You can change the source file and automatically update any documents you linked to it.
- Linked files require less memory than embedded objects.

What are the disadvantages?

- You can't change the location of the source file or delete it entirely because you'll break the link between documents.
- The linked document must be in a shared location.
- Lines that update automatically may slow down operations.

Creating Links

To create a link from a source document to the document you have open:

1. Start the application that created the source file.
2. Open the source file.
3. Select the data you want to copy. Choose **Edit, Copy**.

4. Switch to the document to which you want to add the linked data.

5. Position your cursor (insertion point) where you want to place the data or item.

6. Choose **Edit, Paste Special**. The Paste Special dialog box appears (see Figure 7.1).

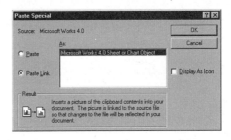

Figure 7.1 The Paste Special dialog box.

7. Select **Paste Link**.

8. Choose a display format in the As box.

9. If you'd rather see an icon in your document instead of the linked data, select **Display as Icon**. Figure 7.2 shows an example of an icon in a document.

Figure 7.2 The data displayed as an icon.

323

10. Click **OK**. If you didn't choose Display as Icon in step 9, the linked object appears in your document, similar to Figure 7.3.

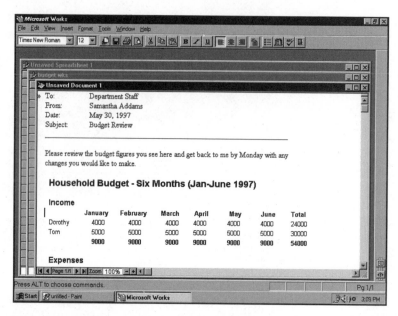

Figure 7.3   The linked data shown in the document.

Some applications support the newer OLE technology that lets you link data by using drag-and-drop. To do this:

1. Start up both applications—the application where you want to put the data (the destination application) and the application that created the data (the source application).

2. In the source application, open the file that contains the data you want to copy. In the destination application, open the document where you want to put the data.

3. Point to an empty space on the taskbar and click your right mouse button.

4. Choose **Tile Vertically** or **Tile Horizontally** from the pop-up menu to make both windows show at the same time.

5. Starting in the source application window, select the data you want to link.

6. Hold down the **Control** and **Shift** keys, and drag the selected data to your destination document.

7. Release the mouse button to drop the data where you want it to appear in the document.

Once your linked data appears in a document, your application tries to update that information each time you open that document. A dialog box appears asking if you want to refresh the information. Answer **Yes**.

Understanding Embedding

When you embed a file or object, a copy appears in your document. An embedded file maintains no connection to the source application file, so updates to the source file don't change your document.

What are the advantages of embedding?

- Since the document and the data are stored together in the same file, you don't need to maintain links, path names, and source files.
- You don't even have to keep the source data because it becomes part of the document.
- To update the embedded object, you can stay right in your document. You don't have to go out to the source application.

What are the disadvantages?

- The documents that contain embedded objects are larger than other documents, so they may take longer to open and they take up more storage space.
- If you update an embedded graphic, you may end up with a file that prints at a lower resolution than the original (not as clear a copy).
- The embedded document has no relationship to the original document. You have to update each document individually, instead of updating only the source document.

Embedding Objects

To embed a file:

1. Open the document where you want to store the embedded file.

2. Position your cursor where you want the object to appear.

3. Depending on the application you're using, the menu command may be Insert, Object or Insert, Picture.

4. A dialog box appears asking what type of object or what object file you want to embed. Figure 7.4 shows an Insert Object dialog box. Choose **Create New** to embed an empty object that you can complete from within your document.

Choose **Create from File** from the Insert Object dialog box (as shown in Figure 7.5) to select a file that you want to incorporate in your document.

5. Select the type of object or the name of the file and then click **OK**.

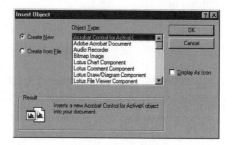

Figure 7.4   An Insert Object dialog box with Create New selected.

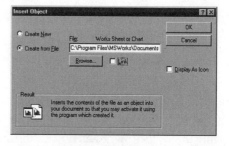

Figure 7.5   An Insert Object dialog box with Create From File selected.

To edit the data in an embedded object, double-click it to open the file in the source application, as shown in Figure 7.6. Make your changes and click the document outside the embedded object selection border.

You can also paste data to embed it in your document:

1. In the source application, select the data you want.

2. Choose **Edit, Copy** to copy it to the Clipboard.

3. Switch to the destination application and open the document where you want to place the embedded object.

4. Position your cursor in the document where you want the embedded object to appear.

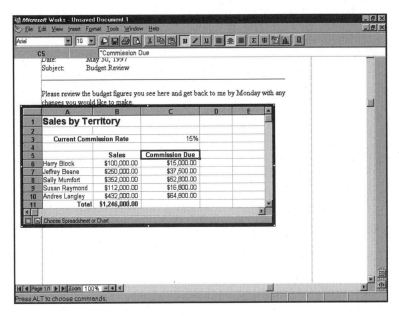

Figure 7.6 Editing the embedded object.

5. Choose **Edit, Paste Special**. The Paste Special dialog box appears (see Figure 7.7).

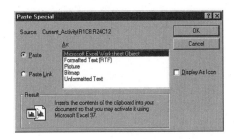

Figure 7.7 The Paste Special dialog box with Paste selected.

   6. Select **Paste**.

   7. From the As box, pick the source from which you copied the data.

   8. If you want to display an icon instead of showing the embedded data, check **Display as Icon**.

   9. Click **OK**.

 TIP   **Drag-and-Drop**   In Windows 98 you can drag-and-drop a file to embed it in a document. Open the application and the document where you want to put the data. Then click the **Start** button on the taskbar and choose **Programs**, **Windows Explorer**. In the Explorer, locate the file you want to embed. Drag that file icon onto your open document window and drop it where you want the embedded file to appear.

In this lesson, you learned about linking and embedding and how to place linked data and embedded objects into your application documents. In the next section you learn about the Internet and Windows 98, starting with an introduction to Internet Explorer 4.0.

Windows 98 and the Internet

Understanding the Internet and the Web

In this lesson, you learn basic Internet and Web concepts and terminology, including protocols, hypertext, and Web browsers.

What Are the Internet and the World Wide Web?

The World Wide Web is *part* of the Internet—they are not the same thing. Hopefully, a little background on each will clear this up.

The *Internet* is a worldwide conglomeration of computer networks, including networks located in government offices, universities, businesses, and so on. Thus, the Internet offers access to a vast collection of world knowledge. The Internet is a public place, and it is not owned and operated by any one company.

The *Web* is a collection of documents accessible through the Internet. These documents (or Web pages) contain a special technology called *hypertext*. When you click on hypertext, you are taken to a different document—maybe even to a different computer. This works much like the green text you see in Windows' Help files.

Clients and Servers

From this point on, you will be seeing the terms *client* and *server* quite often. While there indeed do exist massive volumes of technical material that define the role of client and server in a network or the Internet, there is a much simpler distinction that always applies, without exception:

All Internet transactions take place between one server and at least one client. A client makes a request for information. The server's job is merely to respond with either the information that was requested or some form of "No."

The software you use to communicate on the Internet consists of programs that perform the roles of clients. Your email program (Outlook Express Mail or Windows Messaging) is an email client. Your Web browser (Internet Explorer) is an HTTP client. Outlook Express News is a newsgroup client. You have more clients on your computer than a stockbroker on a bullish Friday.

But since you can *send* email to someone else, doesn't that make you a mail server? Not in the way the Internet works. Your email client program still initiates contact with the email server, by telling the server that it has something to send. The server acknowledges that request and begins the sending process. So the distinction between client and server often has more to do with the social standing between the two, rather than the content they exchange with one another.

Grasping Protocols

In order for computers to communicate over the Internet, they must follow sets of agreed-upon rules that are called *protocols*. The people who devised these rules were not only clever, they came up with cute names for their protocols, such as "gopher" and "World Wide Web." Other long, and often cumbersome, descriptive names were shortened to acronyms, such as Hypertext Transfer Protocol (HTTP) and Transmission Control Protocol/Internet Protocol (TCP/IP).

It's a good idea to understand some of these protocols as you "surf" the Web. You don't need to memorize or even fully understand all of these terms. However, as you learn to use Internet Explorer, you'll recognize the various protocols being used, since they appear at the beginning of the addresses you use, such as http://www.microsoft.com.

Surfing the Web   We're not sure who said it first, or when the phrase caught on, but it means to browse the Internet, just like the phrase "channel surfing" means to browse the channels on your TV.

- **Internet Protocol (IP)**   This is one of the most basic protocols. IP is the system that defines the "location," or IP address, of the networks that comprise the Internet. In a sense, IP forms the "map" of the Internet, and each network may be contacted at a point located on this map.

- **Transmission Control Protocol (TCP)**   TCP is the protocol that defines the structure of the data that's sent between IP networks (or "IP hosts"), as well as how that data should be sent from point to point in the IP internetwork. Following TCP protocol, data is broken into packets that are flushed through the Internet in the general direction of their recipient. There, they are collected and reorganized into their original sequence. Because TCP and IP work hand-in-hand, people refer to them together as TCP/IP.

- **File Transfer Protocol (FTP)**   FTP is a protocol designed for transferring large messages (whether or not you think of them as files) between two points. Using FTP, packets being sent between IP hosts can be checked for errors and resent without the entire message (file) having to be received first.

- **Hypertext Markup Language and Hypertext Transfer Protocol (HTML and HTTP)**   Together, they drive the World Wide Web. HTML defines a method of adding formatting to text files, so that when you view them with an HTML viewer (a Web browser), you see things like headlines, emphasized words, centered paragraphs, and embedded pictures. HTTP defines how HTML files are to be sent and received.

- **Telnet**   A protocol that defines how one computer can act like a terminal on another. Using a telnet program, you can log onto another computer and run programs on it, just as though you were sitting at its own console.

- **Gopher**   Servers that use gopher protocol present their content in the form of submenus. You pick items from menus; each menu item can be another menu, a program, or a file of some kind. The special strength of gopher is that any menu item may actually be on a gopher server that is different from the one that presented the menu to you in the first place. So by picking items from gopher menus, you can actually jump from one gopher server to another.

- **NNTP (Network News Transfer Protocol)**   UseNet servers store messages and forward them to each other using NNTP protocol. Multiple individuals can then read and post messages on these servers using a news reader program such as Outlook Express News.

Hypertext: The Heart of the Web

Documents on the World Wide Web (Web pages) often contain hypertext. Hypertext is special (typically blue and underlined) text that, when clicked on, takes you to a related Web page (see Figure 1.1). Thus, hypertext is like computerized footnotes. If you have ever read through a footnoted book or magazine article, you have encountered an asterisk or a little number following a word in the text. If you look at the bottom of the page, or maybe at the end of the article, you'll find that little number or asterisk followed by a reference. That reference might be another book or magazine article that provides additional information about the topic being discussed. Well, not only can computers provide you with that reference, they can also take you directly to that reference, even if it is located on another computer. By clicking a hypertext link, you leap instantly from one Web page to another, even if the other Web page is located on a computer (another Web site) halfway around the world.

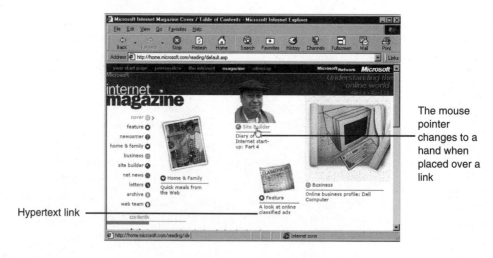

Figure 1.1   Hypertext links related Web pages.

Hypertext usually starts out as blue, underlined text. When you click on this text, you move to another Web page. If you later return to the original Web page, the link you clicked on has changed color, usually to purple. Some Web pages use colors other than blue and purple to designate hypertext links, but in any case, the color change lets you see which links on the current page you have already visited. (If you're not sure whether a bit of text is a hypertext link, move the mouse pointer over it. If the pointer changes to a hand, the text is a link.)

Hypertext is a part of HTML (Hypertext Markup Language). HTML is a set of standard notations that are embedded within a string of ordinary text. When you view the text with an HTML reader, it interprets the HTML notations as formatting commands. Plain text then becomes formatted text, complete with headlines, italics, centered paragraphs, and, best of all, pictures. Recently, HTML has been enhanced even further so that a Web page can include audio clips, video clips, and embedded programs.

You'll learn more about hypertext and the various forms that links take in Part V, Lesson 4, "Visiting a Web Site."

What's an Intranet?

An intranet is an internal Internet. Access to it is commonly restricted to company employees. Because an intranet can span the globe, many organizations find that it is cost-effective to share company information in this way. The protocols and rules are the same as the Internet—the difference is that it's a closed network available only to employees connected to the network inside of the company. The information available on the intranet is company information, usually proprietary in nature.

A company establishes an intranet by installing the TCP/IP protocol, a Web server, and Web browsers. Company documents and other information are converted to HTML format and placed on the intranet Web server(s). People in the company then use their Web browsers to view these documents—they simply type the local address of the document they wish to view, in a manner similar to entering an Internet address.

Being part of an intranet does not necessarily preclude having access to the Internet. You may have both.

TIP   Internet or Intranet?   Browser skills you learn here will apply to both a company intranet as well as the Internet.

Extranet A group of interconnected intranets. Companies doing business with each other may form extranets in order to share certain types of information.

In this lesson, you learned basic Internet and Web concepts and terminology. In the next lesson, you will learn to prepare your system for Internet access.

Configuring for Internet Access

In this lesson, you'll learn to set up your Internet connection by using the Connection Wizard. You'll also learn about Internet Service Providers.

What Is an Internet Service Provider?

The Internet is a network of computers, one talking to another, then another. In order to "jump on" the Internet, you must do so through a direct connection, or host computer. The Internet Service Provider (ISP) acts as that host computer. It is a company that provides the gateway for you to access the Internet.

ISPs come in different flavors, offering different levels of service:

- Indirect access
- Dial-up access
- Persistent connection

Indirect Access

You can get indirect access to the Internet through an online service, such as MSN, CompuServe, or America Online. You must be a member of an online service to use its features. Online services offer features above and beyond Internet access and e-mail handling. For example, MSN offers services such as travel assistance, games, an online library, automobile research, and shopping and special interest chat groups. Each online service offers different features, and belonging to an online service is rather like belonging to an information "club."

The benefit of using an online service is that it makes it very easy to navigate the Internet, providing customized search engines and links that lead you to popular places on the Web. On the downside, going through an online service to access the Internet is slower than if you take a more direct route.

If you want to see what an online service has to offer, it's easy, because they all offer a free trial period. Software for America Online, CompuServe, and MSN (among others) comes with Windows 98, so you can easily use the trial memberships to see which of them best suits your interests.

Dial-Up Connection

Another way to access the Internet is through a dial-up (modem) connection. The ISP acts as your gateway to the Internet, but does not provide any services beyond Internet email and Internet access. With such an ISP, you dial into their server, start your Web browser and surf the net. You can visit the same Web sites that you can through an online service, but the surfing, the searching, and the gathering of information require a little more effort on your part. You also don't get those extra club benefits such as travel services, games, and member chat groups.

Persistent Connection

The third way to connect to the Internet is through a persistent connection, such as your company's network. In such a case, the network is connected directly to the Internet through the network's gateway. You don't dial into your connection; instead, after you log on to the network, you are able to access the Internet.

 TIP   **Check with Your System Administrator First!**   If you plan on connecting to the Internet through your company's network, the necessary setup has probably already been configured by your system administrator. Do not set up an Internet connection without consulting your system administrator.

You must pay for ISP services. An online service tends to be more expensive than other ISPs because they have many more services to offer. Reliability is key in selecting a service provider. Check your local newspaper and with your friends to find ISPs, and call for pricing. The Connection Wizard, described next, also offers a listing of ISPs.

Using Connection Wizard

When you first start Internet Explorer, it displays the Connection Wizard. You can use the Connection Wizard to help you select an ISP, or to connect to an ISP with which you already have an account. If you already have an Internet connection set up on your computer, you can easily bypass the Connection Wizard by selecting the last option on its opening screen.

The next two sections explain how to use the first and second options that appear on that same screen.

TIP   I Want an Indirect Connection   If you plan on using an online service to access the Internet, you'll need to install and set up the service's software. To do that, use the appropriate icon, which you'll find in the Online Services folder (located on your desktop). Then select the third option on the opening screen to bypass the Connection Wizard.

Choosing an ISP

Before you choose an Internet Service Provider call up a few of the local computer stores and ask about ISPs. Most computer stores either have their own service or sell ISP connections for local companies. Better yet, ask your co-workers about their Internet Service Providers. Another option may be your regional telephone company. Many regional telephone companies such as Pacific Bell, have gone into the ISP business.

Typically, you should pay no more than $20 a month for normal service, which should include unlimited access. Unlimited access enables you to call in any time, but most systems will kick you out if you have been idle for 15 minutes. You should also get at least one mail box, although most ISPs will give you several. Finally, the ISP should provide some web space (This is for private use only; ISPs have different rates if you need a commercial web site.)

If you can't find a local service you can use the Connection Wizard to help you locate a service provider and open a new Internet account. To do this:

1. When you start Internet Explorer the first time, the Connection Wizard appears. To start it again at a later time, click **Start**, **Programs**, **Internet Explorer, Connection Wizard**.

2. A dialog box describing setup options appears (see Figure 2.1). Click **Next**.

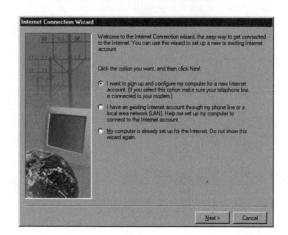

Figure 2.1   Enter Setup Options for Internet connection.

3. From here your computer will call a 1-800 number to get a list of service providers in your area. Follow the onscreen prompts to sign up for the service and complete installation.

Connecting to an Existing Internet Account

If you have an existing Internet account or did the research suggested in the last section and found an ISP, you can use the Connection Wizard to set up a dial-up (modem) connection to your ISP or an Internet connection through your LAN.

TIP   **Before You Begin!**   You'll need to know the following information before you connect to your ISP. Your ISP can provide you with all of the information you will need to connect to it. This may include, but is not limited to, the following:

ISP phone number	Username and password
ISP server name	Gateway address
IP address	Email address
Email server name and type	DNS address
SMTP server name	NNTP server name

If you are on a LAN, you should not use the Connection Wizard without first checking with your system administrator. If, however, you want to create a connection to a dial-up account, then follow these steps:

1. Click the **Start** button, **Programs, Internet Explorer, Connection Wizard.**

TIP   **This Takes Time!**   Configuring the Connection Wizard for the first time is a long process. At any time during the Wizard, you can click the **Back** button to return to previous screens, or click **Cancel** to end the configuration process. If you choose to **Cancel**, you can run the Wizard again at any time.

2. The Setup Options dialog box appears (refer to Figure 2.1). Choose **I have an existing Internet account through my phone line or a local area network (LAN)...** and click **Next.**

3. In the Set Up Your Internet Connection dialog box, select **Connect using my phone line** (see Figure 2.2). Click **Next.**

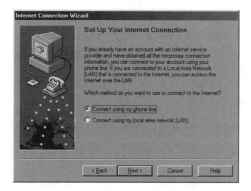

Figure 2.2   Connecting by using a phone line.

4. The Dial-Up Connection dialog box appears. Choose between an existing dial-up connection or a new connection. If you have used dial-up networking, you may see an existing connection available. If you select it, you can make changes to the connection. For a new connection, click **Create a new dial-up connection** and then click **Next.**

5. The Phone Number dialog box appears. Fill in the **Area code** and **Telephone number** fields, providing the access number for your ISP. Confirm that the **Country name and code** are correct; if not, change them. Do not select **Dial using area code and country code** unless it's a long-distance call to your ISP. Click **Next.**

6. The User Name and Password dialog box appears. Fill in the User Name field with your username as provided by your ISP, and your Password for accessing your ISP. For security purposes (in case someone is looking over your shoulder) the password appears in asterisks. Click **Next**.

7. The Advanced Setting dialog box appears. Choose whether or not you wish to change the advanced dial-up settings. These include using a SLIP connection, logging on manually, or using a login script, and/or entering a specific IP and DNS address to connect to. Your service provider will tell you if you need to set up any of these options. If you do, click **Yes**, and follow the prompts. Otherwise, select **No** and click **Next** to continue.

8. The Dial-Up Connection Name dialog box appears. Fill in a **Connection Name**, such as the name of your Internet Service Provider. Click **Next**.

9. The Set Up Your Internet Mail Account dialog box appears. In order to use Internet mail, you must have an Internet Mail account with your ISP. If you want to set up email, click **Yes**; otherwise, click **No** and skip to step 16. Click **Next**.

10. The Internet Mail Account dialog box appears. Select **Use an existing Internet mail account** and skip to step 16 if you already have one. Otherwise, choose **Create a new Internet mail account.** Click **Next**.

11. In the Your Name dialog box, enter your name as you want it to appear in the "From" field of outgoing messages. Click **Next**.

12. In the Internet Email Address dialog box, enter the address assigned to you by your Internet Service Provider, such as JFulton@aol.com. Click **Next**.

13. In the Email Server Names dialog box shown in Figure 2.3, select the type of mail server used by your ISP—the default is POP3. If you are unsure, accept the default. In the **Incoming mail server** and **Outgoing mail server** boxes, enter the name of your POP3 or IMAP server and SMTP server. Click **Next**.

14. The Internet Mail Logon dialog box appears. Select **Log on using** and enter your account name and password. If your ISP requires you to use Secure Password Authentication to access your email account, then select **Log on using Secure Password Authentication**. Click **Next**.

15. In the Friendly Name dialog box, enter a name for your Internet mail account. This can be the name of your ISP, or any descriptive name you would like it to be such as "Jennifer's Mail." Click **Next**.

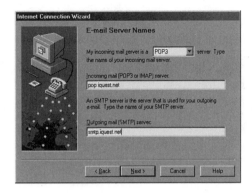

Figure 2.3 / Set up an email account.

16. The Set Up Your Internet News Account dialog box appears. A news service provides access to Internet newsgroups, as described in Part V, Lesson 12. To set up a news account, click **Yes**. Otherwise, click **No** and skip to step 22. Click **Next**.

17. To create a new account, click **Create a new Internet news account**. You can also make changes to an existing account, if needed, by selecting that option instead. Click **Next.**

18. Enter the name you wish to appear on your newsgroup postings. Click **Next**.

19. Enter the email address to which you wish people to reply to your newsgroup postings. Click **Next**.

20. Enter the address of your newsgroup server. Click **Next >**.

21. Enter a name for the newsgroup connection file, such as IQuest News. Click **Next >**.

22. In the Setup Your Internet Directory Service dialog box, Click **Yes** and follow the onscreen prompts to set up a new directory service. You may need to do this if your company's intranet provides an address book/ directory service for your use. However, in most cases, you *will not* need to do this, since Windows already provides access to the major directory services, such as InfoSpace, Bigfoot, and Four11. In that case, click **No**. Click **Next**.

23. The Complete Configuration dialog box appears indicating that you have successfully completed the configuration process. Click **Finish**.

In this lesson, you learned to set up your Internet connection to work with Internet Explorer 4, and how to sign up with an ISP or online service. In the next lesson, you'll learn to navigate the Internet Explorer window.

Understanding the Internet Explorer 4 Window

In this lesson, you'll learn about how to use the new Web browsing features of Internet Explorer 4, and how to move around within the window.

Starting Internet Explorer 4

Start Internet Explorer 4 by following these steps:

1. Click the **Internet Explorer** icon located on your desktop, or click the **Launch Internet Explorer Browser** icon located on the Quick Launch toolbar.

2. When you start IE4, the program looks to see if you are connected to the Internet so it can display the Microsoft home page (or the Web page you've chosen as your home page) and if you are not, it displays the Dial-Up Connection dialog box, shown in Figure 3.1. If needed, enter your **User name** and **Password** (your password is displayed as asterisks).

Figure 3.1 Filling in Connect information.

3. If you want, Windows can remember your password for you; select the **Save password** option.

4. You can also have Internet Explorer dial the connection for you automatically every time if you select the **Connect automatically** option.

5. Click **Connect**.

TIP **Working While Disconnected** If you want to work offline (disconnected from the Internet), click the **Work Offline** button. When you work offline, you can display any document that has been saved to your hard disk (or to your company's network). If you request to view a document that can not be located, then Internet Explorer will attempt to connect to the Internet again.

6. Depending upon your ISP, you may see a Post Dial Terminal window as shown in Figure 3.2. Type your user name and press **Enter**, then type your password and press **Enter** again. Click on **Continue** or press **F7**.

Figure 3.2 Post dial terminal window.

After your name and password have been verified by your ISP server, the Connected To dialog box disappears and is replaced by an icon on the taskbar, as shown in Figure 3.3. Internet Explorer then opens your start page—Microsoft's Start Page, your company's home page, your ISP home page, or a start page you designate as described in Part V, Lesson 7, "Customizing Internet Explorer 4." (See Figure 3.3.)

TERM **Start Page** The first page you see when you open IE4 is your Start page. From here, you can visit other pages on the Web. To return to this page at any time, click the **Home** button on the toolbar.

Home Page The "cover page" at an Internet or intranet site is called the site's home page. This is the first page that displays when you visit a site. The home page of a site usually contains a company logo and list of information available at the site.

TIP **Don't Forget to Hang Up!** When you are finished exploring the Internet, double-click on the Connected icon (see Figure 3.3.) and click **Disconnect** to hang up. Or, you can exit from IE4, and click **Disconnect** in the dialog box that appears.

Navigating the Internet Explorer 4 Window

The Internet Explorer Window, like all Microsoft windows, contains a title bar, minimize button, maximize/restore button, close button, a menu bar, several toolbars, and a status bar as shown in Figure 3.3.

Figure 3.3 Your Start page displays when you are connected to the Internet.

You operate the Internet Explorer window and its menus as you would any other Windows program. For example, to minimize the window, click the

Minimize button. To open a menu, click on it. If you need a refresher on Windows basics, see Lesson 3, "Working with a Window," and Lesson 4, "Using Menus," in Part I, "Navigating Windows 98."

The Internet Explorer 4 Toolbars

Internet Explorer has three toolbars, as shown in Figure 3.4:

Standard Buttons   This toolbar contains buttons for the most common commands, such as returning to your start (home) page. To use a button, click it.

Address   Here you enter the address of the Web page or Internet resource you wish to view. You can choose a previously viewed page by clicking on the arrow and selecting it from the list that appears. To learn more about addresses, see Part V, Lesson 4, "Visiting a Web Site."

Links   This toolbar contains buttons that jump you to useful pages on the Web, such as Microsoft's home page. You can add your favorite pages to this toolbar; see Part V, Lesson 7, "Customizing Internet Explorer 4," for help.

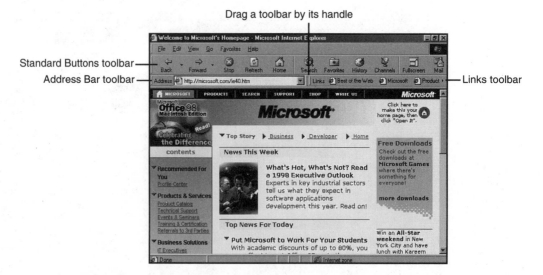

Figure 3.4   Internet Explorer has three toolbars.

Displaying a toolbar is an option. If a toolbar is not displayed, choose **View**, **Toolbars**, and select the toolbar you wish to display. A checkmark appears next to a displayed toolbar. Repeat these same steps to remove the checkmark and hide the toolbar.

TIP   **Hidden Links**   Initially, the Links toolbar is partially hidden. To display it, double-click on the word, **Links**. The toolbar slides over, partially covering the Address toolbar. To display both toolbars completely, drag the Links toolbar *to the right* by its handle (see Figure 3.4). You can also drag the Links toolbar below the Address toolbar using the handle.

As you point with your mouse to each icon on the toolbar, the icon is displayed in color and a frame appears around the icon, giving it a 3-D effect.

Table 3.1 lists each icon found on the Standard Buttons toolbar and gives a brief explanation of each icon.

Table 3.1   Standard Buttons Toolbar Icons

Tool	Name	Description	Keyboard shortcut (Hotkeys)
Back	Back	Returns you to a previously visited Web page.	Backspace
Forward	Forward	Moves forward to a Web page(only if you have gone back to a previous page).	Shift+Backspace
Stop	Stop	Stops action in progress. Stops a Web page from loading.	ESC

continues

349

Table 3.1   Continued

Tool	Name	Description	Keyboard shortcut (Hotkeys)
Refresh	Refresh	Reloads the current document.	F5
Home	Home	Returns you to your start page.	None available
Search	Search	Displays the Search Bar with tools for searching the Web.	None available
Favorites	Favorites	Displays a list of Web pages that you have marked as favorites.	Alt+A
History	History	Displays a list of pages you have recently visited.	None available
Channels	Channels	Displays buttons for accessing premium Web sites.	None available
Fullscreen	Fullscreen	Maximizes the viewing window.	F11
Mail	Mail	Displays the Mail menu for sending and reading messages.	Alt+G, M
Print	Print	Prints the current page.	Ctrl+P
Edit	Edit	Starts FrontPage Express so you can edit a Web page.	None Available

TIP   **Hidden Print, Edit Buttons**   If you don't see the Print or Edit buttons, select **View**, **Toolbar**, **Text Labels**. This turns off the button names, providing more room for displaying buttons.

To learn how to customize your toolbar, see Part V, Lesson 7, "Customizing Internet Explorer 4."

Navigating a Web Page

Although you may not yet know much about visiting Web sites (see Part V, Lesson 4, "Visiting a Web Site") you can still move around the Web page (document) displayed in the IE4 window. Use the scrollbar to move up and down a page displayed in IE4, or use the shortcut keystrokes described in Table 3.2.

Table 3.2   Keyboard Shortcuts for Moving Around a Web Page

Press	*To*
↑	Scroll up a document
↓	Scroll down a document
Page Up	Move one screen up the document
Page Down	Move one screen down the document
Home	Move to beginning of document
End	Move to end of a document
Tab	Move one cell or field to the right in a form or table.

In this lesson, you learned how to start IE4 and navigate in IE4. You also learn about the IE4 toolbars. In the next lesson, you'll visit some Web sites.

Visiting a Web Site

4

*In this lesson, you'll visit some Web sites. You'll also learn
about reading URLs and entering Web page addresses.*

Reading URLs

Every file on every computer on the Internet has an address at which it can be
located. Internet computers use something called Uniform Resource Locators, or
URLs, to specify the locations of these files. A URL looks something like this:

```
http://www.mcp.com/que/sample.html
```

The first part of the URL, the part that precedes the colon (:), indicates the type
of resource being accessed, or more appropriately, its *protocol*. You remember
protocols from Lesson 1: a set of rules that govern the transfer of data over the
Internet.

In the example, the resource type, or protocol, http, tells you the document is a
Web page, and that the computers will use the HyperText Transfer Protocol to
transfer the file to your computer. You might encounter other protocols as well,
such as ftp (file transfer protocol), gopher, nntp (network news transfer protocol), and so on. A colon and a double slash follow the protocol name.

 TIP **Visiting Newsgroups** Newsgroups are electronic bulletin boards in which
you can read and post messages to people who share a similar interest. See
Part V, Lesson 12, "Using Outlook Express News," for help in visiting a
newsgroup.

Next comes the domain name of the server that contains the resource being addressed. The domain name may consist of several parts. The WWW in this case is short for World Wide Web, and mcp is short for Macmillan Computer Publishing. The .com part at the end tells you that this site is a commercial enterprise. Other extensions you may encounter include .gov (government), .edu (education), .org (non-profit organization), .mil (military), and .net (Internet Service Provider.), and .int (international). These three letter extensions are used mostly in the United States. Two-letter extensions are used outside the United States, to designate a country. Table 4.1 lists some common two-letter extensions.

Table 4.1   Partial Listing of Two-Letter Extensions

Zone	Meaning
au	Australia
ca	Canada
fr	France
ie	Ireland
il	Israel
jp	Japan
nl	Netherlands
tw	Taiwan
uk	United Kingdom
us	United States

After the computer name is the location and name of the file on the computer. It is separated from the computer name by a single slash. The file may be located in the root directory or a subdirectory. The names of the directories precede the file name and are separated from each other and the file name by single forward slashes. In the example, the file, sample.html, is located in the que directory.

Here is the URL address again:

```
http://www.mcp.com/que/sample.html
```

and here are its parts:

```
protocol//domain_name/directory/filename
```

Visiting a Web Site

Now that you understand URLs, you're ready to take your first visit to a Web site other than your start page. For this lesson, you'll step through some basic and easy steps. In later lessons, you'll learn how to locate Web sites on your own. The objective here is for you to start.

You need to have IE4 open, and you need to be connected to the Internet to visit a Web site. Then:

1. Place your cursor in the Address field on the toolbar. Click once, and the current address (which is probably your start page) will be highlighted. Type the URL for the site you wish to visit, such as:

www.mcp.com

You don't need to type HTTP—because it's the default protocol, IE4 will fill that in for you. This is the URL for the Macmillan Publishing Company. Your new text will replace the existing text.

TIP   Address Correctly!   When typing addresses, it's important to use the *exact* space, periods, symbols and capitalization you see in the examples. Typing the address incorrectly could result in failure to locate the Web site you are seeking.

3. Press the **Enter** key. The Status bar will indicate the status of your search. It may say Finding site: www.mcp.com, then Opening page: www.mcp.com/index, then Done. When the status bar shows Done, the Web page at your requested site is finished loading.

4. You should now see the home page for Macmillan, if you used the URL in step 2. It's a big home page, and doesn't fit within your screen, so use the scroll bars or Page Up or Page Down to examine this page. (See Figure 4.1.)

Notice the highlighted text (such as Resource Centers) on this page? This is an example of hypertext that was discussed in Lesson 1. When you place your mouse on hypertext, you'll see your cursor change from a pointer to a hand and the address of the page to which the link refers will display on the status bar. A pop-up menu will also appear, displaying additional information about the link. Try it! Hold your mouse over hypertext. Remember: to activate a link and to jump to the associated page, you click on the hypertext.

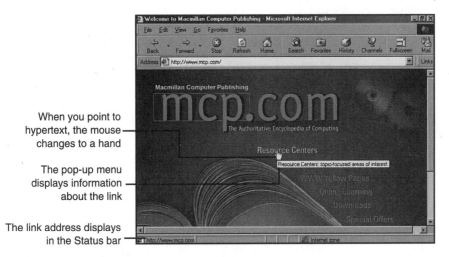

When you point to
hypertext, the mouse
changes to a hand

The pop-up menu
displays information
about the link

The link address displays
in the Status bar

Figure 4.1 Macmillan's home page at www.mcp.com.

After you've moved around a few pages, leave this Web site and go to another.
To do that, type the address of the site you wish to visit in the Address box and
press **Enter**. Here's an address to try:

```
nssdc.gsfc.nasa.gov/imgcat/html/mission_page/ST_Voyager_1_page1.html
```

There you can see photos of Saturn as found in Figure 4.2. Actually, it's very
likely that the page you are seeing will differ slightly from the one you see in
Figure 4.2. Web pages change all the time. New information is added and
designs are updated; the links, text, and information may also change. But you
can continue this little surf on your own. Click the underlined text to move
around the site.

CAUTION

It's Not There! If the page whose address is given here turns up missing,
don't despair; this happens all the time on the fast-changing Web. Try deleting
part of the address (starting from the right) and trying again. For example, try
just

```
nssdc.gsfc.nasa.gov/imgcat/html/mission_page/
```

or

```
nssdc.gsfc.nasa.gov/imgcat/html/
```

and so on, until you back into something. Then take the links on the page you
find to try to relocate the page you originally wanted. You can also try searching
for the page using a search engine, as described in Part V Lesson 5, "Web,
Site, and Document Searching." In fact, you can set up Internet Explorer to
automatically do the searching for you. (See Lesson 5.)

355

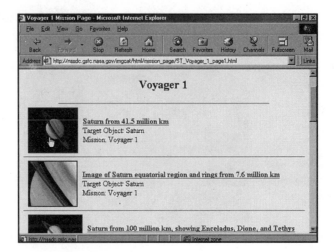

Figure 4.2   Learning about Saturn.

You'll also notice that if you hold your mouse over the graphics on this page, your cursor will change from a pointer to a hand, and the linked URL address will appear. These graphics are acting as hyperlinks, even though they are not text. When you click on one of them, you'll be taken to the associated page.

After you've roamed around Saturn a little, you might want to stop by NASA's Spacelink site for educators, which includes the shuttle launch schedule at:

`spacelink.nasa.gov`

Figure 4.3 shows Spacelink's home page and also displays how your cursor will appear when you hold the pointer over a link.

In the above examples, you visited one commercial and two government Web sites, identified as such by their three-letter extensions: .com and .gov.

Understanding Caching

A cache is a storage area for often-used information. The idea of a cache is that, by storing the data you use often in a convenient place, it takes less time for your computer to retrieve that information when you need it.

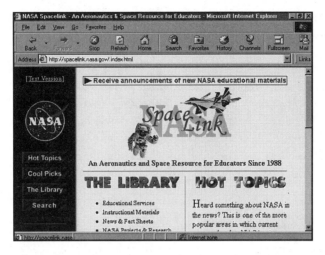

Figure 4.3   Visiting Spacelink at spacelink.nasa.gov.

It works like this: When you use IE4, pages that you visit are cached and stored in the C:\Windows\Temporary Internet Files folder. Then, when you use the back and forward buttons on the toolbar, the pages you previously visited load more quickly. This is especially noticeable with a page that contains a lot of graphics. When you re-visit a Web page with lots of graphics, you won't have to wait for all of the graphics to load again. Instead, IE4 finds the graphics files stored in your Internet Temporary Files folder and simply loads them from there, without attempting to download the graphics from the Internet.

Caching also enables you to view pages offline when you are not connected to the Internet. You just view the pages stored on your hard disk. When working offline, you can tell if a page is available by moving the mouse pointer over its link. If the link changes to a hand with a "do not" symbol (a red circle with a diagonal slash), then the associated page is not available on your system. If you click the link, Internet Explorer will attempt to connect you to the Internet so it can retrieve the page you want.

There are limits to the size of the cache, however. And when the cache becomes full, the oldest data in the cache is replaced by newer data. IE4 has settings with which you can determine how much of your total hard drive space should be allocated for storing temporary, or cached, files. See Part V, Lesson 7, "Customizing Internet Explorer 4," for more information on controlling cache settings.

Also, be aware that caching can be a problem when you are visiting sites that use real-time images. Real-time means that the images are changing constantly and frequently, to give you the most current image. If you have a stored image in your cache directory, you'll be viewing an out-of-date image. To see the most current information and override what is cached, click the **Refresh** button on the toolbar. In fact, you can click the Refresh button any time you suspect that you are seeing a cached version of a page, and not a currently downloaded one. For example, if you visit a weather forecast page with a graphic image of the current Doppler radar, and you visit that page again later on, you'll probably be looking at yesterday's weather.

Understanding Links

Links are embedded pointers to other Web pages. They appear within a Web page as colored text, pictures, or buttons. When you click a link, you jump to the page the link points to.

Several kinds of links are used on the Web, and they act as pointers to help you reach your destination. It would be impossible for you to know the URL (address) of every Web page you want to visit. So, Web page designers create links that contain URLs. Point and click, point and click…. That's all you really need to do when you're moving around a Web site. The different types of links you might see include: hypertext, graphics, gopher, ftp, and image maps.

TIP   **How Can I Tell if it's a Link?**   It's not as important to know what kind of link you're using, as long as you know it's a link. If you hold your pointer over something, and it changes from a pointer to a hand, then it's a link!

Graphic Links

A graphic link is simply a picture with an embedded address (see Figure 4.4). When you double-click the picture, your computer sends out a request for the page or object named in the address.

Gopher Links

A Gopher link is a link to a Gopher menu. In Part V Lesson 1, I talked about Gopher servers. Gopher servers use Gopher menus, and gopher links point to those menus. You can recognize a gopher link because its URL begins with "gopher:". (See Figure 4.5.)

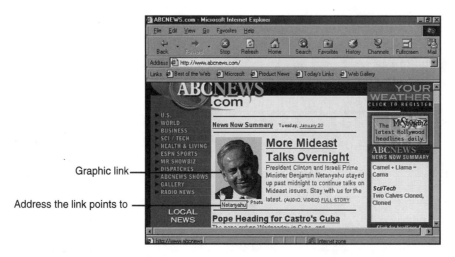

Graphic link

Address the link points to

Figure 4.4 A graphics link is a picture with an embedded address.

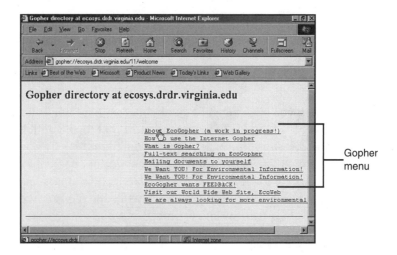

Gopher menu

Figure 4.5 A gopher link always starts with gopher://.

When you click on a Gopher link, you're taken either to another Gopher menu, a search page, or a document for viewing. Gopher systems are slowly being replaced with Web systems, which offer the same features (the ability to link documents together). So you will probably not find a lot of gopher links in your Internet travels, unless you visit a lot of university sites.

FTP Links

A File Transfer Protocol (FTP) link is a link to a file located on an FTP server. You can recognize an FTP link because its URL begins with "ftp:" (see Figure 4.6).

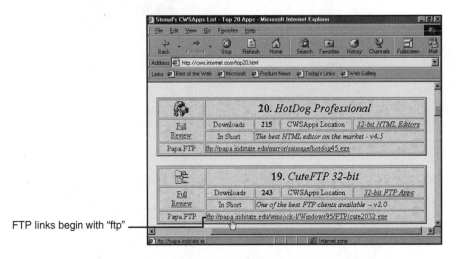

FTP links begin with "ftp"

Figure 4.6 File Transfer Protocol links begin with FTP.

When you click on an FTP link, Internet Explorer will typically attempt to download the file to your system. At that time, you'll be able to select the drive and directory in which you want the file stored. The length of time it takes to download a file to your system depends on the speed of your connection and the size of the file. Some files are large and can take quite a while, so be prepared. You can continue to work while the file is downloading, although you'll notice that your system is slower.

If Internet Explorer recognizes the type of file the FTP link points to, it will attempt to open that file (run it or display it) instead of downloading it to your system. For example, if you click on a link to a sound file, Internet Explorer will play it. To download the file instead, press and hold the **Shift** key as you click on the link.

Mailto Links

A mailto link provides a simple way for you to send an e-mail message to someone associated with the Web page (see Figure 4.7). Mailto links begin with "mailto:." When you click a mailto link, a mail form opens. The To: field is automatically filled in the Internet address that was contained in the mailto link. Pretty handy stuff. It's very helpful and ensures that you won't make any errors when typing the address.

mailto link

Click the link, and a pre-addressed email form appears

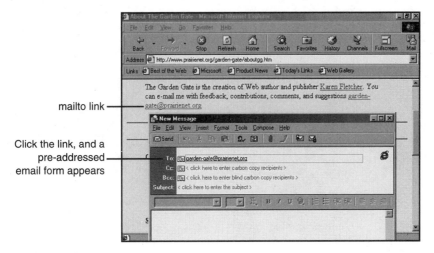

Figure 4.7   A Mailto: link brings up an email form.

Hypertext Links

Earlier in this lesson, you learned how hypertext looks and what it does. You've seen that hypertext is usually underlined, and often in a different color. This makes the hypertext stand out so that it is clear that clicking on that text will take you to a different page or site. When you return or go back to the original page after you have visited a linked page, the hypertext will appear in a different color on your screen. This allows you to easily see which links you've visited.

Image Maps

An image map is a single (usually large) picture that has different portions of it mapped to different addresses. That is, one part of the picture will point to Web page x, another part will point to Web page y, and a third will point to Web page z. You jump to different pages depending on what part of the picture you click. It's different than a graphic link, which points to only one Web page.

Figure 4.8 shows an image map. The image map is a single graphic, but it contains many embedded links.

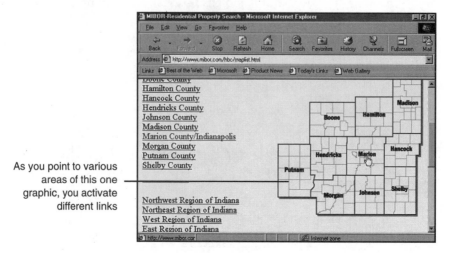

As you point to various areas of this one graphic, you activate different links

Figure 4.8   An image map contains many embedded links.

In this lesson, you learned how to enter URL addresses, and you learned about caching. You visited some Web sites, and you learned about various types of links, including image maps and mailto: links. In the next lesson, you learn how to search the Internet.

Web, Site, and Document Searching

In this lesson, you learn the types of searches you can perform with Internet Explorer 4. You also learn about search engines and how you can search the Web, search a document, or search a Web site.

Understanding Searches

There are several kinds of searches you can perform in Internet Explorer 4. You can search for information anywhere: on the Web, within a Web site, and in text on a Web page.

Searching the Web

You search the Web when you want to find public information on, for example, "Elvis." You search the Web with the aid of a search tool (also referred to as a search engine). A search tool or engine is a program that searches the Web continually for documents, recording their contents in a complex database. You provide a keyword or phrase to the search engine, and it searches its database for matches to your query. The results of your search are returned to you in a Web page, as a list of links pointing to those sites with the most hits at the top of the list.

Internet Explorer makes it easy to use a search tool by providing a list of some of the more popular search engines, such as Yahoo!, Infoseek, and Lycos. Although this is pretty convenient, you'll find that a search engine's advanced query features are available only if you visit the engine's actual Web site; for instance, visit www.excite.com for the Excite search engine's Web site.

TERM   **Hit**   A match between your search parameters and information found on a home page on the Internet. The more specific your search parameters, the smaller number of "hits" you will find.

If you searched for Elvis you might see an awfully long list of links—perhaps thousands more than you need. When you search for information, create a search string that will return the links you really want. For example, if you search for the phrase, "Elvis Presley," you won't find Elvis Costello in your search results. And searching for Elvis AND Sands AND "Las Vegas" AND "October 1973" is bound to return even fewer hits!

As you can see in the previous examples, most search engines support the use of quotations for enclosing phrases—words that belong together. In the first example, I suggested that you use the phrase, "Elvis Presley" instead of searching for just the word, Elvis. When you place words in quotations (as in "Elvis Presley," they are treated as a search unit, or phrase. Using quotations properly can help you achieve the search results you want. For example, the query, "Indy racing" will return fewer hits than the query Indy racing, because in the first query ("Indy racing"), the engine is looking for the words *together as a phrase*, and in the second query (Indy racing, without the quotes), it's looking for any documents that contain the words, "Indy" and "racing," but not necessarily together, or in that order.

Also, most search engines support the use of Boolean arguments, such as AND, OR, and NOT. In the earlier example, Elvis AND Sands AND "Las Vegas" AND "October 1973," the engine will search for documents that contain all of the following: Elvis, Sands, Las Vegas, and October 1973.

 TIP   **Dates in Queries**   Searching for a date is tricky, because the search engine tries to find an exact match for whatever you enter. So in the previous example, you'd only find a match if the date appeared in text as October 1973. If it appeared as October 10, 1973 or October, 1973, or anything else, you wouldn't have a match. AltaVista allows you to use the operator, NEAR, to solve this problem. If you enter October NEAR 1973, then it will search for the word "October" near the word 1973. So you'll get a match with October, 1973 and October 1973 and October 10, 1973 and the phrase, "In October of the year 1973,..."

You'll learn the steps involved in performing a search a little later in this lesson.

TIP **Automatic Search**   When you type a Web address into the Address box and Internet Explorer can not find the Web page, you'll see an error message. You can tell Internet Explorer to automatically attempt to locate the missing page for you by opening the **View** menu and selecting **Internet Options**. Click the **Advanced** tab, and select the option you prefer under **Search when URL fails**. Click **OK**.

Searching a Web Site

Many Web sites use search engine programs that index their own information, allowing you to search within the site itself. You can well imagine the amount of information that can be found at the Microsoft site, for example. When you visit the Microsoft site (www.microsoft.com) you can search the site to find information on Internet Explorer, or Microsoft Word, or any of their other products. Not all Web sites are indexed, or searchable, but you will find that larger sites typically provide search capabilities. Search engines within a Web site work much like search engines that search the Web. You create a query, click a **Search** button, and the results are returned to you as a list of hypertext links to the areas at the site that match your query. Although Web sites and search engines vary, searching a Web site is very similar to searching the Web, as described later in this lesson.

Searching a Web Page

Web pages can be as long as several printed pages. Therefore, in addition to searching the Web for information, you can search the contents of a Web page for text. Searching within a Web page does not, however, return a list of links. Rather, this type of search works just like using a Find command in a word processing program. So when you search for a word or string of words, IE4 will take you to the first occurrence it finds on that page. You can then search for the next occurrence.

Creating a Web Search

There are many search engines available on the Web. Search engines maintain their own databases of the contents of Web pages. Different search engines look for different Web site information and it's possible that your search results using Yahoo may be different than your search results using Excite. As you work with search engines, you may find that you prefer one over another.

To create a Web search:

1. Click the **Search** icon on the toolbar.

2. The IE4 screen will split into frames. The left frame displays the Search Bar.

TIP **Bigger Search Frame** Some search engines provide options that may not appear clearly within the Search frame. You can use the scrollbars to view them, or, to increase the size of the Search frame, simply drag its edge to the right. You can also open the search page in its own window by right-clicking on the word **Search** at the top of the frame, and selecting **Open in Window** from the shortcut menu that appears.

3. Open the **Choose provider** drop-down list, and select the search engine you want to use. The Search Bar displays a search text box to enter your search string (see Figure 5.1).

4. Enter your search criteria and click the **Search, Seek,** or **Submit** button to begin your search. You may see a warning telling you that you are about to send information over the Internet, which is not secure. Click **Yes.**

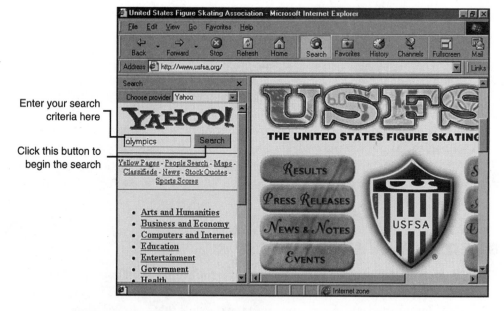

Figure 5.1 Entering search criteria.

5. Your search results appear in the left frame below your search criteria as shown in Figure 5.2. Search results are in hypertext. Scroll through the results until you find a document you would like to view and click the hypertext.

6. To search for something else, enter the new search criteria and click the **Search** or **Submit** button you'll find at the bottom of the left frame when using most of the search engines. When you are finished with your search, click the **Search** button *on the toolbar* to close the search frame.

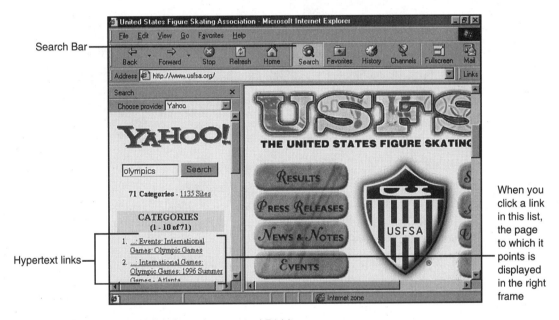

Figure 5.2   Yahoo! results returned 71 hits.

Depending upon the search tool you select, search results will vary. Some search tools return categories, as Yahoo! shows in Figure 5.2, as well as sites. Clicking a category reveals more sites. The search results will also tell you how many "hits" or Web sites it found that contain your search string. Remember, search results will vary from search tool to search tool. Figure 5.3 shows the results of the same search used in Figure 5.2 (olympics). This time I searched by using AOL NetFind.

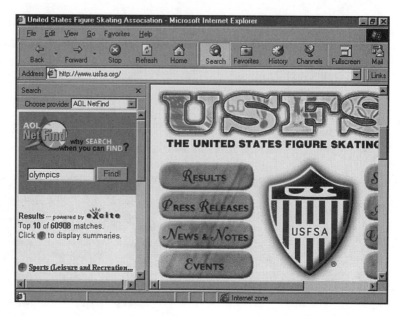

Figure 5.3   Same search, different results by using a different search tool.

When you select **Go, Search the Web,** a search page like the one shown in Figure 5.4 appears. Here, you'll find links to other search engines, some of which provide specialized searches, such as searching through newsgroup messages, or searching for people.

 TIP   **Start, Find**   The Start, Find menu contain additional search options, including **On the Internet** and **People**. On the Internet displays the search page shown in Figure 5.4. People displays a list of tools for tracking down people on the Internet.

Following Search Results

Once you have completed a search and see the search results listed on your screen, click the hypertext links (see Figure 5.2) to explore Web pages that contain your search string. When you click a link in the Search Bar, the right frame displays the contents of the selected page. The contents of the Search bar remain the same.

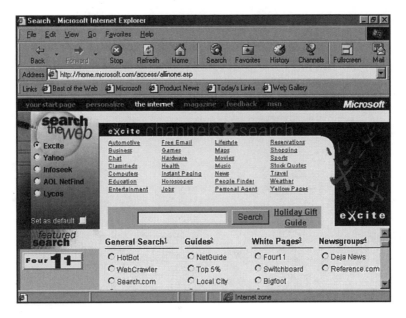

Figure 5.4 Microsoft's search page provides access to other search engines.

TIP **I Want to See More!** After searching for a Web page, it's frustrating if you can't see it clearly. To close the Search frame (and increase the viewing area), click the **Search** button in the toolbar.

When you select a link in the Search frame, some search engines will display another page of links. For example, when I search for "olympics," Yahoo! displays a page containing links within its Events: International Games; Olympic Games category. I selected the one that was listed as "The Official Olympics Home Page," and finally, the page appeared in the right frame, as shown in Figure 5.5.

Visiting a Search Engine Site

Another way to conduct a search is to visit a search engine site directly. For example, enter www.yahoo.com in the **Address** box on your toolbar, and you will find yourself at the Yahoo! site. Here's a list of the Web sites of the more popular search engines:

- **Yahoo!** www.yahoo.com
- **Excite** www.excite.com

- **AltaVista** altavista.digital.com
- **Infoseek** www.infoseek.com
- **Lycos** www.lycos.com
- **AOL NetFind** www.aol.com/netfind/home.html

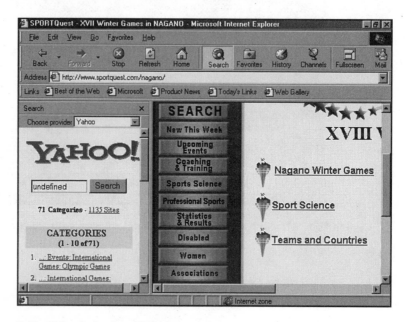

Figure 5.5 Yahoo! displays URLs in search results.

  TIP **Bigger Search** To perform an advanced search, you'll have better luck if you try the search engine's actual Web site. To display the Web site, you can usually click the logo at the top of the Search frame. You can also enter the site's address in the Address box, as in www.excite.com.

Searching for Text on a Web Page

To search the contents of a Web page, first open the page you want to search, and then:

1. Select **Edit, Find (On This Page)** or press **Ctrl+F**.
2. The Find dialog box appears (see Figure 5.6). Type the text you want to find in the Find What box.

3. For exact matches only, check the **Match whole word only** box. Selecting this option, IE4 would not return occurrences of your word when found within a larger word. For example, "Nesting" will not be found if the search word is "Nest."

4. To find and match the uppercase and lowercase of your word, check the **Match case** box.

5. Select **Direction Up** or **Down** to search toward the beginning or the end of the document.

6. Click **Find Next**. IE4 will move to the first occurrence of the word in your document. The Find dialog box remains open. To see the next occurrence, click **Find Next** again. If no match was found for your search, a message box appears indicating that IE4 has finished searching the document.

7. When you are finished searching, click **Cancel** to close the dialog box.

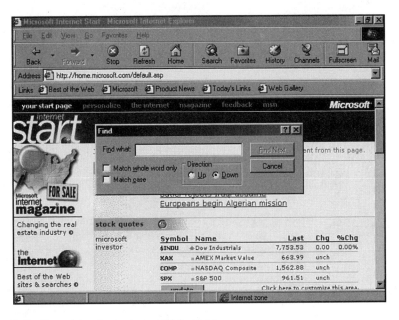

Figure 5.6 Searching for text on a Web page.

In this lesson, you learned the types of searches you can perform with Internet Explorer 4. You also learned the various methods of performing those searches. In the next lesson, you learn more about working with Web pages.

Working with Web Pages

6

In this lesson, you learn how to use History to view Web pages you have visited. You also learn how to change the display of Web pages and use the Favorites folder. In addition, you learn how to download files.

Returning to a Previously Viewed Page

IE4 keeps a history of the Web pages you visit. You can return to a Web page you have previously viewed in this session by clicking the **Back** button. This will display Web pages in the reverse order that you viewed them. To move back several pages, click the arrow to the right of the **Back** button, and select the desired page. To return to the original page, click the **Forward** button, or select a page from its list by clicking the arrow to the right of the **Forward** button.

CAUTION

History Rewrites Itself   When you move back through History, it is reset to the page you select. This means that the history of any pages between the current page and the one you select is lost—at least as far as the **Back** button is concerned. To return to a page you skipped in the list, click the **Forward** button or use the History window (which is discussed a little later in this section).

You can also view pages you have already visited by selecting them from the File menu:

1. Open the **File** menu.
2. In the History list of documents found at the bottom of the File menu, select the document you want to view, as shown in Figure 6.1.

The File menu list is emptied when you quit Internet Explorer.

TIP **Frequent Visitor** If you visit a page frequently, add it to your Favorites folder, as described later in this lesson. Adding pages to Favorites makes it easier to return to them whenever you want to.

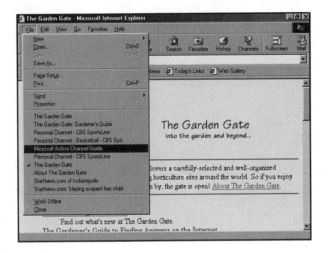

Figure 6.1 History list of documents found on the File menu.

TIP **Don't Forget the Address List** You can also visit pages from your current Internet session by clicking the drop-down Address list on the toolbar. (The pages you'll find here are the ones whose addresses you've actually typed into the Address box.)

Although the History list is emptied from the File menu after each Internet session, an entire history of links to all Web pages you have viewed in all sessions is kept in a folder called History, located in your C:\Windows directory.

To view the contents of your history folder:

1. Click the **History** button on the toolbar. The History bar appears in the left frame, as shown in Figure 6.2.

2. Click the link for the day or the week in which you visited the page. A list of folders for all the sites you visited appears. Each folder contains a list of pages you visited at that Web site.

3. Click the folder for the desired Web site.

4. Click the page you want to view. The contents of the selected page appear in the right frame.

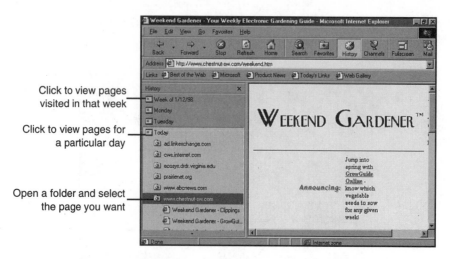

Click to view pages visited in that week

Click to view pages for a particular day

Open a folder and select the page you want

Figure 6.2   The History bar lets you quickly return to pages.

You can determine how many days files will stay in your History folder (the default setting is 20 days), and/or you can clear your History folder at any time.

To set number of days or clear the history:

1. Select **View, Internet Options** from the menu. The Internet Options dialog box appears with the General tab selected.

2. In the History section, click **Clear History** to empty the History folder.

3. To set the number of days that links stay in your History folder, change the value in the **Number of days to keep pages in history** field.

4. Click **OK** to save your changes and close the dialog box.

Changing How Text Is Displayed

You can change the way Web pages display in your browser by selecting a different font size and hypertext color. You can also turn off some multimedia settings, which will allow pages to load faster.

But This Doesn't Work!   Although you can change the font, size, and color of text using Internet Explorer's menus, note that some Web pages may override your choice.

CAUTION

To change the size of text:

1. Choose **View**, **Fonts** from the menu.

2. Select the font size you want (largest, larger, medium, smaller, smallest) from the cascading menu that appears.

You can also display text in a different font. Keep in mind that changes you make to the font may be overridden by Web pages.

To select a font:

1. Choose **View**, **Internet Options**. The Internet Options dialog box appears with the General tab selected.

2. Click the **Fonts** button. The Fonts dialog box appears.

3. Select the fonts you want in the **Proportional font** and **Fixed-Width font** lists.

Fixed-Width Font   A font (typeface) whose characters are all of equal width. For example, "W" takes up the same amount of space as "I."

Proportional Font   A font whose characters are of different widths. For example, "W" takes up more space than "I."

4. Click **OK** to close the Font dialog box.

5. Click **OK** to close the Options dialog box and save your changes.

You can also change the default text and background colors. The default setting tells Internet Explorer to use your Windows color settings for text and background color.

To change the default text and background colors:

1. Choose **View**, **Internet Options** from the menu. The Internet Options dialog box appears with the General tab selected.

2. Click the **Colors** button. The Colors dialog box appears (see Figure 6.3).

3. In the **Colors** section, remove the check next to the **Use Windows colors** option. Once this check is removed, you can select a text and background color by clicking the **Text** and **Background** buttons and choosing from the color palette (see Figure 6.3).

Figure 6.3 Changing the text or background colors.

4. Change link colors in the **Links** section by clicking the **Visited** and **Unvis-ited** buttons and choosing from the color palette. The **Use hover color** option lets you set the color of the link when the mouse pointer is resting on it.

5. When you have finished with your selections, click **OK** to close the dialog box and save your changes.

IE4 has the ability to display Web pages in their native languages. For example, if a Web page is written in French, there is typically an alternate English version. IE4 displays the English version by default. If you select French as a language, however, the French version is displayed if available, and if not, the English version is displayed. So keep in mind that adding or changing a language in your options does not *translate text*.

To select a language for viewing Web pages:

1. Choose **View, Internet Options** from the menu. The Internet Options dialog box appears.

2. Click the **Languages** button.

3. Click **Add**. Select a language from the list and click **OK**.

4. You're returned to the Language Preference dialog box. You can change the priority in which IE4 chooses the language to use by selecting a language from your master list and clicking the **Move Up** or **Move Down** buttons to change its order in the listing.

5. Click **OK**.

Using the Favorites Folder

IE4 gives you the ability to save Web pages in a folder called Favorites. By saving pages in Favorites, you can give them a descriptive name (or accept the default) or organize them into folders. You can also subscribe to the page in order to receive automatic updates to it. (See Part V, Lessons 8 and 9, for more information about subscriptions.)

Adding a Page to Favorites

To add a page to the Favorites folder:

1. Go to the Web page you want to add.

2. Open the **Favorites** menu and select **Add to Favorites**.

3. The Add Favorite dialog box appears (see Figure 6.4). Select the option you desire:

No, just add the page to my favorites   This option adds the page to the Favorites bar.

Yes, but only tell me when this page is updated   This option allows you to control when you want a copy of this Web page updated to your system. When a change occurs to the Web page, you'll be notified. You can then choose to download the page to your system (for offline viewing) or to wait. You may want to choose this option if you connect to the Internet via a modem.

Yes, notify me of updates and download the page for offline viewing This option automatically updates the Web page to your system when needed and then tells you that the page has been updated. This option is good if you have a persistent (network) Internet connection.

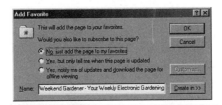

Figure 6.4   The Add Favorite dialog box.

4. Type a name in the **Name** box or accept the default name (which is the descriptive information provided by the Web page designer).

5. To store your favorites in a different folder, click **Create in>>**.

6. The Favorites folder structure appears, as shown in Figure 6.5. To create a new folder, click **New Folder**.

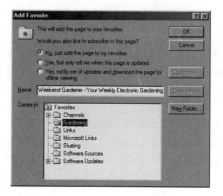

Figure 6.5   Creating a new folder.

7. The **Create New Folder** dialog box appears. Type a name for your new folder in the **Folder name** box and click **OK**.

8. Your new folder will now appear highlighted in the Favorites folder structure. Click **OK** to save your Web page in this folder. If the folder is not highlighted, click once on the folder, and then click **OK**.

TIP   Use Your Right Mouse Button   You can add favorites by right-clicking anywhere on your Web page. From the pop-up menu, select Add To Favorites. To add a link, right-click the link and select Add to Favorites.

Displaying a Favorite Page

To open a page stored in your Favorites folder:

1. Click the **Favorites** button on the toolbar. The Favorites bar appears, as shown in Figure 6.6, displaying a list of Favorites and folders.

2. If the page you want to open is in a folder, click the folder's icon in the Favorites bar.

Click here to close the Favorites bar

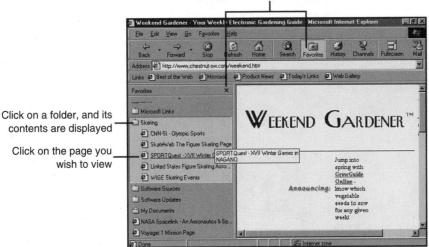

Click on a folder, and its
contents are displayed

Click on the page you
wish to view

Figure 6.6   Folders appear on the Favorites menu.

3. Select the page you want to view by clicking on it. The contents of the page appear in the right frame.

4. To remove the Favorites bar so you can see more of the Web page, click its **Close** button or click the **Favorites** button on the toolbar.

Managing Your Favorites

You may decide that you want to delete, move, or rename pages in your Favorites folders. To reorganize your Favorites pages:

1. Open the **Favorites** menu and select **Organize Favorites**. The Organize Favorites dialog box appears, as shown in Figure 6.7.

2. Highlight the folder or document you wish to move, rename, or delete. To open a folder and view its contents, double-click the folder.

3. Once you have highlighted a document or folder, click **Move**, **Rename**, or **Delete**.

- Selecting **Move** opens a Browse dialog box so you can highlight the folder you want to move your document to. Do so, and then click **OK**.

- Selecting **Rename** allows you to edit the folder or document name. Type the new name and press **Enter**.

- Selecting **Delete** activates a Confirm Delete dialog box asking if you are sure you want to delete this item. Click **Yes**.

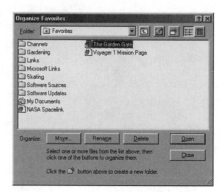

Figure 6.7   The Organize Favorites dialog box.

4. When you are finished organizing your Favorites pages, click **Close** to close the Organize Favorites dialog box.

Downloading Files from a Web Page

Web pages often contain links to files that you can download to your system, such as utility programs, browser enhancements, and bug fixes. Follow these steps to save the file:

Check Out That File   You should always run a virus scanner on any file you download from the Internet prior to using it. As an added precaution, you may wish to download files to a removable disk so they can be checked out without running any risk that they might infect your hard disk.

CAUTION

1. Click the link to the file you wish to download.
2. The Save As dialog box appears. Select the folder in which you want to save the file, rename the file if needed, and then click **OK**. The file is downloaded to your system. Note that some files are large and can take quite a while to download. However, you can continue to work while the file is downloading, although your system will act slower.

CAUTION

It Didn't Download!   If Internet Explorer recognizes the type of file the FTP link points to, it will attempt to open that file—that is, it will try to run it or display it instead of downloading it. To override this and to download the file instead, press and hold the **Shift** key as you click on the link to the file.

You don't always need a link to a file in order to be able to copy that file to your system. For example, if you wish to download an element of a Web page, such as an embedded graphic, you can. Follow these steps:

1. Right-click the element you wish to download, and select **Save Target As** or **Save Picture As** from the shortcut menu that appears.

2. In the Save dialog box, specify the drive and folder in which you want the file saved. Rename the file if needed.

3. Click **OK** to begin downloading the file.

In this lesson, you learned how to change your viewing preferences and how to use and organize Favorites. You also learned how to download files from the Internet. In the next lesson, you'll learn how to customize Internet Explorer 4.

Customizing Internet Explorer 4

In this lesson, you learn how to customize Internet Explorer. You also learn how to create a desktop shortcut to a Web page and use a Web image as wallpaper.

Customizing the Start Page

When you initially start Internet Explorer 4, it displays the Microsoft Home page, located at **www.microsoft.com**. You can change this page to some other Web page if you like, such as your favorite news page, or a page on your company's intranet. In addition, Microsoft offers a special page it calls the "Start Page," which you can customize and make your new starting page.

To change your starting page (known to Internet Explorer as *your* "home page") to something other than the Microsoft Home page, follow these steps:

1. Open the **View** menu and select **Internet Options**. The Internet Options dialog box appears.
2. Type the address of the page you wish to use in the **Address** text box. To use the currently displayed Web page as your home page, click **Current** instead. To return the home page setting to the Microsoft home page, click **Use Default**. To display a blank page as your home page, click **Use Blank** (this option gets IE4 up and running as quickly as possible, since there isn't anything to load).
3. Click **OK**.

The Microsoft Start page, shown in Figure 7.1, is located at **www.microsoft.com/default.asp**. You can easily customize this page and use it as your new home page.

Click these icons to change
a section you don't like

Open a drop-down list and
select the option you wish

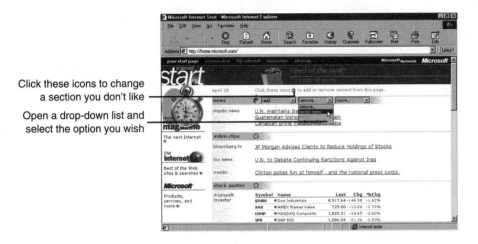

Figure 7.1 The Microsoft Start page.

1. Jump to the Microsoft Start page by typing the address **www.microsoft.com/default.asp** into the **Address** bar and pressing **Enter**. You're now ready to customize this page to suit your needs.

2. Click the happy face icons to change any of the existing sections of the Start page. For example, click the happy face icon in the Stock Quotes section.

3. Click the down arrow of the option you prefer (add, remove, or move), and select the option you want from the drop-down list that appears. For example, open the **Remove** drop-down list and select the **entire section** option.

4. To add new sections to the page, scroll down to the **Personalize this page** link, and click it. The Personalize page appears, as shown in Figure 7.2.

5. To add a new section, click its checkbox. For example, to add a search section to the Start page, click the **show on Start page** checkbox in the **Search** section.

6. You can add your own links to the Start page by turning on the **Your Links** section and entering the URLs for the links you wish to appear.

Click here to save your changes

Click this checkbox to add this section

Select a section and use the arrows to change its position on the page

Figure 7.2   You can add new sections to the Start page.

7. Make changes to existing sections by scrolling down to that section and selecting (or deselecting) the options you want. For example, scroll to the **News** section and select the **Time** option.

8. To change the order in which a section appears, select it from the **your page** list and use the up or down arrows to change its order in the list. (See Figure 7.2.)

9. When you're done making changes, click **update**.

10. You're returned to the Start page. To make it your home page, click the **Click here to make this your home page** link.

Adding Buttons to the Links Toolbar

Five preselected links (called Quick Links) appear on the default Link toolbar. You can insert additional Quick Links for your favorite and most-visited sites.

To insert a Quick Link, simply drag a link to the page you wish to add to the Links toolbar. A vertical line shows where the link will be inserted. (See Figure 7.3.) Release the mouse button, and the link is added.

To move, delete, or rename a Quick Link, open the **Favorites** menu and select **Organize Favorites**. Double-click the **Links** folder to open it. Then select the item you wish to move, delete, or rename, and click the appropriate button.

Figure 7.3 Drag a link to the Links bar.

Changing the Size of the Toolbar Buttons

You can make the toolbar buttons smaller so that they take up less room, giving you a larger viewing space. Follow these steps:

1. Open the **View** menu and select **Internet Options**. The Internet Options dialog box appears.

2. Click the **Advanced** tab.

3. In the **Toolbar** section, select the **Small Icons** option.

4. Click **OK**.

Creating a Desktop Shortcut

You can create a desktop shortcut to a Web page or to a hyperlink found on a Web page. Then, when you click (or double-click) the shortcut, IE4 will automatically start and load the page.

> **To create a shortcut to the current Web page**, right-click the page and select **Create Shortcut** from the shortcut menu. A message appears telling you that the shortcut will be added to the desktop. Click **OK**.

> **To create a shortcut to a link**, right-click the link and select **Copy Shortcut** from the shortcut menu that appears. Then right-click on the desktop and select **Paste Shortcut**.

Using a Graphical Image as Wallpaper

Images that you see on Web pages can be used as desktop wallpaper. When you see an image you would like to use as your wallpaper, right-click the image and select **Set As Wallpaper** from the pop-up menu.

Fast Loading Your Web Pages

Although graphics liven up Web pages, they also increase the time it takes your Web browser to download pages and display their content. To speed up the process, you can tell Internet Explorer to load only text, not graphics. If you later visit a page that has graphics you want to view, you can click the graphic's placeholder to view that image.

In addition, you can tell Internet Explorer to not play any sounds, videos, or animations, which also slow down the loading process. Follow these steps:

1. Open the **View** menu and select **Internet Options**. The Internet Options dialog box appears.
2. Click the **Advanced** tab.
3. Under **Multimedia**, click the options you do not want IE4 to load. This removes the checkmark in front of the option and turns it off. For example, click the **Show pictures** option to turn it off.
4. Click the **OK** button to save your settings.

Adjusting the Cache

To increase the speed at which Internet Explorer loads the pages you've previously visited, you can change the cache settings. The cache is a temporary storage area on disk for recently visited Web pages. If you later revisit the same Web page, IE4 loads that page from disk, rather than taking the time to download it from the Interent. To change your cache, take the following steps:

1. Open the **View** menu and select **Internet Options**. The Internet Options dialog box appears.
2. Click the **Settings** button under Temporary Internet files. The Settings dialog box appears.

3. Drag the slider below **Amount of disk space to use** to the right to increase the amount of disk space reserved for the disk cache. The more space you use for the cache, the more pages Internet Explorer can store on disk. These pages can then be quickly redisplayed when needed. To reduce the size of the cache, drag the slider to the left.

4. Under **Check for newer versions of stored pages**, specify how often you want Internet Explorer to check a cached page against the latest page on the Web:

Every visit to the page is a little excessive and will slow you down.

Every time you start Internet Explorer (the default setting) checks the page the first time you revisit it in a session.

Never is a little risky, because you might miss page updates, but it does make for speedy revisits.

 TIP **Latest and Greatest** You can click the **Refresh** button to override this option and download the current version of the page from the Internet.

5. Click the **OK** button to save your cache settings and return to the Internet Options dialog box. Click **OK**.

In the Options dialog box, the General Settings tab also has a button called **Delete Files**, which you can click to remove all cached files from your hard drive. If you're running low on disk space, this is the button to use to free up a few megabytes.

Setting Up Security Zones

As you send data and receive active content on the Web, Internet Explorer supervises your actions and the actions of the remote server and warns you of any risky activity. If you receive a warning dialog box, you can usually prevent similar warnings from appearing in the future by selecting the **In the Future, Do Not Show This Warning** option before giving your okay.

You can change the security level of any of the four different zones: the Internet zone (all sites not belonging to any of the other zones), the local intranet zone (your company's intranet), trusted sites zone (a list of sites whose security you trust), and the restricted sites zone (a list of sites to which you want to restrict access for others who might use your PC, such as your children).

To change your security settings, follow these steps:

1. Open the **View** menu, select **Options,** and click the **Security** tab.

2. Open the Zone drop-down list and select one of the four available security zones, as shown in Figure 7.4.

Select the zone whose
settings you wish to change

Select the security
level you wish

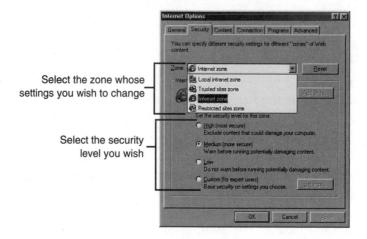

Figure 7.4   You can select a different security level for each zone.

3. Select the desired security level for that zone:

- **High** prevents you from submitting any information by way of a form, even a search form. In addition, Internet Explorer won't play Java applets, download ActiveX controls, or transfer any other potentially harmful programs or scripts to your computer. The High setting is useful for sites you place on the Restricted sites list.

- **Medium** turns on prompts, so Internet Explorer displays dialog boxes whenever you attempt to send data or download scripts or other active content. The Medium setting is useful for the Internet zone, where you may want to be prompted before doing anything risky.

- **Low** turns off the prompts, allowing you to submit information using a form, and allowing sites to send you active content. The Low setting is good for trusted sites, where you are fairly certain that nothing bad is going to happen.

- **Custom** allows you to enter specific security settings. For example, you may wish to prevent active content from being automatically downloaded to your computer, but you don't want a dialog box popping up on your screen every time you fill out a form.

 TIP **Is It Safe?** You can usually tell if a site is secure by looking at its address. If the address starts with https instead of http, the site is secure. Also, Internet Explorer displays a lock icon in the Status bar when you are at a secure site.

You can add and remove sites from the Trusted Sites and Restricted Sites zone. When you add sites to a zone, the security settings for that zone apply *to all the sites in that zone*. To add a site, follow these steps:

1. In the Internet Options dialog box, on the Security tab, click the **Add Sites** button. The resulting dialog box shows a list of sites in the selected zone, which should be empty, because you haven't specified any sites.
2. Click in the **Add this Web site to the zone** text box, type the site's address, and click the **Add** button. Repeat this step to add more sites to the zone.
3. To remove a site from the zone, click its address in the **Web sites** list, and click the **Remove** button.
4. If you want to connect to only secure Web servers (servers whose address starts with https:// rather than http://), select **Require server verification (https) for all sites in this zone.**
5. Click the **OK** button to save your list of sites.

To define the sites that make up the Local Intranet zone, follow these steps:

1. In the Internet Options dialog box, on the Security tab, click the **Add Sites** button.
2. Select the options you want:

    Include all local (intranet) sites not listed in other zones By selecting this option, you can exclude sites that are already listed under Trusted Sites or Restricted Sites.

    Include all sites that bypass the proxy server A *proxy server* is a computer that acts as a client in the server/client connection. Data is then scanned for viruses and other potentially damaging material, and filtered through to you, the true client. By bypassing sites that do not use the proxy server, you can hopefully prevent dangerous material from reaching your PC.

389

Include all network paths (UNCs)   UNC is short for Uniform Naming Convention, and it's the standard used when naming network file paths. By including all paths in the intranet zone, IE4 can access all files on the network (which your password allows).

3. To add sites to the Local Intranet zone, click **Advanced**, and follow the steps given earlier.

4. Click **OK** to return to the Internet Options dialog box. Click **OK** again.

 TIP   **Network Security**   Check with your Network Administrator before attempting to make changes to the security levels within the Local Intranet zone.

Censoring Internet Sites

If you have kids, you may want to prevent them from accessing sites not suitable for children. Some Web sites use ratings to define their content. The use of these ratings is voluntary; however, you can block access to any site that does not use a rating.

To block access to sites, follow these steps:

1. Display the **Internet Options** dialog box.

2. Click the **Content** tab, and click **Enable**. A dialog box appears, prompting you to enter a password.

3. Enter the password you want to use for changing the content settings, type it again to confirm, and click **OK**.

4. Change the settings you desire:

On the **Ratings** tab, you can set the level of language, nudity, sex, and violence you will tolerate by dragging a slider bar.

On the **General** tab, you can prevent access to sites that do not follow the ratings system. You can also change the password you entered in step 3 if you like.

On the **Advanced** tab, you can add new rating systems to Internet Explorer. You can also select a Ratings Bureau to use.

5. Click **OK**.

If someone tries to access a site that contains prohibited material, Internet Explorer blocks access to the site and displays a dialog box that allows you to enter a password to override the censor. If the user does not know the password, he or she cannot view the page.

 TIP **More Help** Security within IE4 is good, but if you want more control over the things your kids can access, be it a Web site, file download, email, newsgroups, and so on, you may want to check out programs specifically designed for this purpose, such as Net Nanny, Cyberpatrol, Cybersitter, and Kinder Guard.

The Content tab contains additional options for managing personal and site certificates. Internet Explorer uses these certificates to assure you that you are dealing with certified companies on the Web and to assure those companies that you are who you claim to be. You can obtain a certificate for yourself from a certificate authority, such as VeriSign. You receive certificates from sites as you visit them.

Selecting Default Programs

Internet Explorer is currently set up to use Outlook Express as your default email and newsreader and NetMeeting for placing Internet phone calls. If you then click a link for mail, a newsgroup, or a NetMeeting session, Internet Explorer automatically runs Outlook Express or NetMeeting. However, you can change this setting to use another program instead. In addition, you can select the program you wish to use for your Internet calendar and your contact list.

To select your default programs, display the Internet Options dialog box, click the **Programs** tab, and select the desired program for each category. Click **OK**.

In this lesson, you learned how to customize Internet Explorer. In the next lesson, you will learn how to subscribe to a Web site, a channel, or an Active Desktop Item.

Subscribing to a Channel, a Web Site, or an Active Desktop Item

In this lesson, you learn what a subscription is and how to subscribe to a channel, a Web site, or an Active Desktop Item.

What Is a Subscription?

Internet Explorer 4 allows you to update your favorite Web pages automatically by downloading the current copies of the pages you select right to your computer. Since Web content changes often, this can be a great time saver for you (you don't have to start IE4, enter an address, and skim through a page to see if there are any changes). To select the Web pages you wish to have automatically updated, you set up a *subscription*.

When you establish a subscription, you can schedule Internet Explorer to update your Web pages whenever you like, such as during off-hours or while you are asleep—assuming of course, that you leave your connection to the Internet active, or that you instruct Internet Explorer to connect to the Internet automatically when needed). Then in the morning, you can view the most current information available without having to log on to the Internet and find it.

You can subscribe to one of three things:

- **A channel** A *channel* is a special Web page that can update itself with a constantly changing display. A channel uses *push technology*. The idea here is that a business can then *push* its information to you, instead of relying on you to visit its Web site and *pull* the data down. Internet Explorer provides a listing of the channels to which you can subscribe, such as The Science Channel and MSNBC. Although many of these companies have Web sites on the Internet, they typically provide specialized content to subscribers.

- **A conventional Web site** Although a conventional Web site does not have the capability to push its data to you, you can subscribe to any site you wish and have its page downloaded to your computer at regular intervals. However, unlike a channel, once the page has been downloaded, its content does not change until the next time it is updated by you.

- **An Active Desktop Item** Information that is displayed on the desktop in a special window. Microsoft offers a selection of these items in its Gallery, such as a stock ticker and a current weather display. Some channels offer their own Active Desktop Items, which are also available through the Gallery, or through the channel's subscription page.

Using the Channel Bar

The Channel bar is a vertical listing of available channels to which you may or may not have subscribed. The Channel bar, shown in Figure 8.1, appears on the Active Desktop, as well as within Internet Explorer. In this lesson, I'll describe its use within the Web browser, but using the Channel bar from the desktop works the same way.

To display the Channel bar in Internet Explorer, click the **Channels** button. To hide it, click the **Channels** button again, or click the **X** at the top of the bar.

The Channel bar contains buttons for each of the channel categories, such as News and Technology. When you click one of these categories, a listing of channels in that category appears. You can then subscribe to the channel you wish (see the next section for details). At the bottom of the Channel bar, you'll find buttons for certain premium channels, such as Msnbc. You can even add channels to the Channel bar if you like.

After subscribing to a few channels, you can "channel surf" by simply clicking a channel's button on the Channel bar. The channel's contents are then displayed within the Internet Explorer window.

Channels button —

Channel bar —

Click this button to view the
most current channel listing

Click this arrow to view
more channels

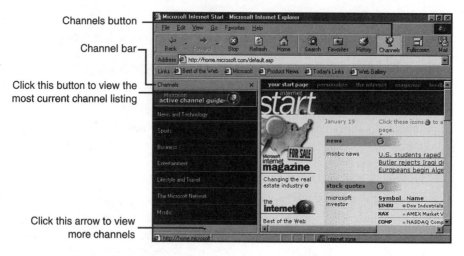

Figure 8.1 The Channel bar as it appears within IE4.

Subscribing to a Channel

To subscribe to a channel, follow these steps:

1. In Internet Explorer, click the **Channels** button to display the Channel bar.

2. Click on the **Active Channel Guide** button (see Figure 8.1). Internet Explorer downloads the complete listing of channels.

3. Click on a category such as **News and Technology**. A listing of channels in that category appears. (To see the Guide more completely, you may wish to click the **Channels** button again to remove the Channel bar.)

4. If needed, display the next set of channels by selecting the numbers **8-14** and so on.

5. Select the channel you want to add by clicking its logo. (If you point to a logo with the mouse, you can see a brief description of that channel.)

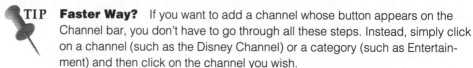

TIP Faster Way? If you want to add a channel whose button appears on the Channel bar, you don't have to go through all these steps. Instead, simply click on a channel (such as the Disney Channel) or a category (such as Entertainment) and then click on the channel you wish.

6. A preview of the channel appears. Each channel is set up a bit differently, so follow the on-screen instructions to subscribe to the channel you selected. Typically, you simply need to click on a button called **Add Active Channel** or **Subscribe**.

7. The Add Active Channel Content dialog box, shown in Figure 8.2, appears. Select an option:

No, add it to my Channel Bar   This option adds the channel to the Channel bar as a button. You can then use this button to quickly display the channel's contents whenever you wish, since the channel *will not* be updated on your system automatically.

Yes, but only tell me when updates occur   This option allows you to control when a channel is updated on your system. When a change occurs, you'll be notified. You can then choose to update the channel or to wait. You may want to choose this option if you connect to the Internet via modem.

Yes, notify me of updates and download the channel for offline viewing   This option automatically updates your channel when needed and then tells you that the channel has been updated. This option is good if you have a persistent (network) Internet connection.

Customize   Use this option to control exactly when and how the channel is updated. For example, you can instruct IE4 to make the Internet connection when needed. See Part V, Lesson 9, "Managing Subscriptions and Working Offline," for details.

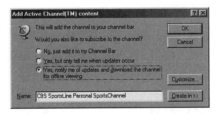

Figure 8.2   You choose how or if you want the channel to be updated.

After you've subscribed to a channel, it appears in the right-hand pane. If you'd like to maximize the viewing area, click the **Full Screen** button on the toolbar. To return the viewing area to its original size (and redisplay the Address and Links toolbars, along with the menu), click the **Full Screen** button again.

Some channels offer an option for adding a desktop item as well. See the later section "Subscribing to an Active Desktop Item" for help.

If you selected the option **Yes, but only tell me when updates occur** in step 7, when it's time for the channel to be updated, Internet Explorer will check the page to see if there's been a change (assuming you're connected to the Internet). If the page has been changed, Internet Explorer will notify you by placing a red asterisk on the channel's logo, as shown in Figure 8.3. To update the page (download it to your system for viewing), click on the logo.

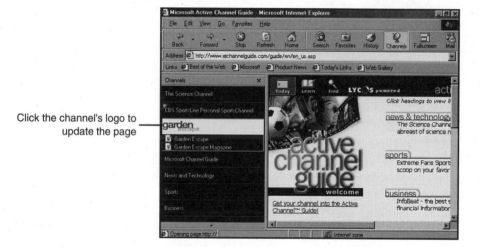

Click the channel's logo to update the page

Figure 8.3   IE4 will let you know when a channel needs updating.

Subscribing to a Web Site

You can set up a site subscription for an existing Favorite, for a new Favorite, or for the currently displayed page. Follow these steps to set up a site subscription:

1. Open the page you want to subscribe to, and then choose **Favorites, Add to Favorites**.

   Or, right-click the shortcut that points to the page you want to subscribe to and select **Add to Favorites.** The shortcut may be within a Web page, on the Windows desktop, in the Quick Launch toolbar on the taskbar, or in the Organize Favorites window (select **Favorites, Organize Favorites**). The Add Favorite dialog box appears, which is similar to the one shown in Figure 8.2.

2. Select the option you want:

   No, just add the page to my favorites   This option adds the page to the Favorites bar. When you're connected to the Internet, to jump to this Web page, click on its name on the Favorites bar.

Yes, but only tell me when this page is updated This option allows you to control when you want a copy of this Web page updated to your system. When a change occurs on the Web page, you'll be notified. You can then choose to update the page to your system (for offline viewing) or to wait. You may want to choose this option if you connect to the Internet via modem.

Yes, notify me of updates and download the channel for offline viewing This option automatically updates the Web page to your system when needed and then tells you that the page has been updated. This option is good if you have a persistent (network) Internet connection.

Customize Use this option to control exactly when and how the Web page is updated to your PC. See Part V, Lesson 9, "Managing Subscriptions and Working Offline," for details.

3. Click **OK**.

Subscribing to an Active Desktop Item

Some channels provide an Active Desktop Item for display on the desktop, such as a stock ticker, sports update, weather update, and so on. Several Active Desktop Items are shown in Figure 8.4. Active Desktop Items appear on the desktop in their own windows. Follow these steps to add an item:

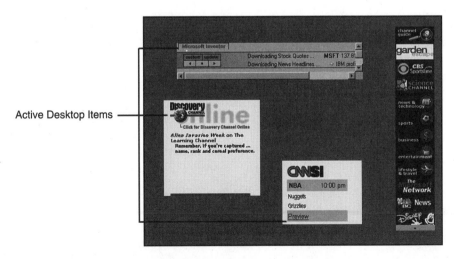

Active Desktop Items

Figure 8.4 Push technology comes to the desktop.

1. Follow the steps in the section "Subscribing to a Channel" to display a channel you like. When you see the option to add a desktop item, click on **Add to Active Desktop.**

2. You'll see a message asking if this is okay. Click **Yes.**

3. A verification dialog box confirming your selection appears. Click **Yes.** To change the frequency at which the desktop item is updated, click **Customize Subscription** and then follow the steps in Part V, Lesson 9, "Managing Subscriptions and Working Offline."

 TIP   **More Items!**   Microsoft maintains a Gallery of Active Desktop Items that you can use to quickly add several items to your desktop. Just type the address **www.microsoft.com/ie/ie40/gallery** into the **Address** text box and press **Enter**. Select a category from the list on the left, such as **Entertainment**. Then click on an item to add it to your desktop.

You can move Active Desktop items; simply place the mouse pointer on top of the item's window, and a title bar appears. Click on this title bar, press and hold the mouse button, and drag the window wherever you like.

To remove the item from your desktop temporarily, click on its close button. See Part V, Lesson 9, "Managing Subscriptions and Working Offline," for steps on how to remove your subscription permanently.

To make room for more items on your Active Desktop, remove your icons, as shown in Figure 8.4. Right-click on the desktop and select **Properties.** Click the **Effects** tab, and select the **Hide icons when the desktop is viewed as a Web page** option. Click **OK.**

In this lesson, you learned how to subscribe to channels, Web pages, and Active Desktop Items. In the next lesson, you'll learn how to make changes to your subscriptions and work offline.

Managing Subscriptions and Working Offline

9

In this lesson, you learn how to make changes to your subscriptions. You also learn how to work offline.

Managing Subscriptions

Once you've established a subscription to a channel, a Web page, or an Active Desktop item, they are pretty much carefree. (If you need help in establishing a subscription for the first time, see Part V, Lesson 8, "Subscribing to a Channel, a Web Site, or an Active Desktop Item," for help.) However, you may still wish to make changes from time to time, such as changing the option of whether or not you wish to be notified when updates occur. In this section, you'll learn how to modify your subscriptions and even delete them when needed.

Modifying Subscriptions

You manage your subscriptions with the Scheduled Tasks accessory, whose Subscriptions area is accessible through Internet Explorer. Follow these steps:

1. Open the **Favorites** menu and select **Manage Subscriptions**. The Subscriptions window, shown in Figure 9.1, appears.
2. Select the subscription you wish to change, and click the **Properties** button.

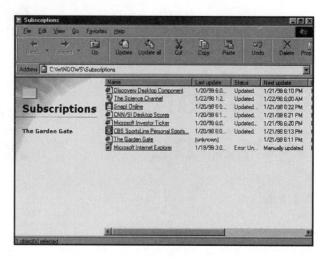

Figure 9.1   You manage your subscriptions with the Subscriptions window.

3. To change how you are notified when a subscription is updated, click the **Receiving** tab and select the options you desire:

Only notify me when updates occur   Internet Explorer will notify you of updates, but it will not download the updated page. (Internet Explorer notifies you of updates by displaying a red asterisk on the channel's button or the Web site's icon.)

Notify me when updates occur, and download for offline viewing   Internet Explorer automatically downloads the page at the scheduled time.

Send an email message to the following address   When a page is updated, Internet Explorer will notify you via email. Click the **Change Address** button to change the email address where you want updated notices sent.

4. If you chose **Notify me when updates occur, and download for offline viewing** in step 3, Internet Explorer automatically downloads the site's home page and all related graphics at the scheduled time. To have additional related pages downloaded, and to automatically download sounds, videos, and other items on the page, click the Advanced button and select any of the following options, as shown in Figure 9.2:

Figure 9.2 Advanced options.

Download channel's Home Page and Table of Contents if available   This option is on by default.

Download all content specified by the channel's publisher   Internet Explorer downloads not just the Home page, but any pages the publisher wants to include. You may not want to turn this option on, because some Web sites contain many pages, and as a result, the publisher might pack your drive with a bunch of pages you may never look at.

Images   Internet Explorer downloads images contained in the page. This is enabled by default.

Sound and video   Internet Explorer downloads any background sounds and video clips on the page.

CAUTION

Large Files Take Time   Sound and video files can be quite large, so you may not want to automatically download them.

ActiveX Controls and Java applets   Internet Explorer downloads any ActiveX controls or Java applets on the page. However, you may not want to select this option, because it is possible for programmers to develop destructive ActiveX Controls and Java applets and place them on Web pages. If such controls and applets are downloaded automatically to your system, they could do a lot of damage.

Never download more than *xx* Kb per update   This option allows you to limit the size of the download to prevent Internet Explorer from cluttering your disk with a lot of junk you'll never have time to look at.

5. To change when a subscription is updated, click the **Schedule** tab. Then select the options you desire:

To set a regular schedule for your updates, click the **Scheduled** option. Then select a schedule from the drop-down list. You can make changes to this schedule by clicking the **Edit** button. To create a new schedule, click **New**.

After choosing the Scheduled option to set a regular schedule, you may want to select the **Dial as needed if connected through a modem** option as well. This allows IE4 to automatically connect to the Internet as needed in order to update the subscription.

If you prefer to update the subscription manually, select the **Manually** option. Then, when you want to update the subscription, open the **Favorites** menu and select **Update All Subscriptions**. (To update this subscription only, return to the **Schedule** tab and click the **Update Now**.)

To prevent your work from being interrupted by a scheduled update, select the **Don't update this subscription when I'm using my computer** option.

6. When you're through, click **OK**.

Canceling Subscriptions

To cancel a subscription, you first must display the Subscriptions window. Follow these steps:

1. Open the **Favorites** menu and select **Manage Subscriptions**. The Subscriptions window appears.

2. Click on the subscription you wish to change, and select **Properties**.

3. On the **Subscription** tab, click the **Unsubscribe** button to remove this subscription permanently.

4. A confirmation dialog box appears. Click **Yes**.

5. Click **OK**.

 TIP **Keep That Item!** Rather than unsubscribing to an Active Desktop item, you can temporarily hide it. Just point to the item and click its **Close** button.

You can also cancel a subscription in the Subscriptions window by selecting it and pressing **Delete**.

Updating Subscriptions

Most of your subscriptions are updated periodically without your help. However, you can update a subscription early if you like. In addition, if you've set up a subscription to update manually, it will not be updated until you follow these steps:

1. Open the **Favorites** menu and select **Manage Subscriptions**. The Subscriptions window appears.

2. Select the subscription you wish to update, then click the **Update** button. If you want to update all your subscriptions, click **Update all**.

 TIP **Please Notify Me** If you set up a subscription to have Internet Explorer only notify you of updates, when the page has changed, a red asterisk appears next to the page's logo to indicate that it is new. If the page is a channel, click the channel's button on the Channel bar to update the page.

Working Offline

If you connect to the Internet through a modem, chances are pretty high that you will not be connected at all times. Whenever you're not connected to the Internet, you're considered to be working *offline*. You can choose to work offline when you first start Internet Explorer by clicking the **Work Offline** button in the Connected To dialog box when it appears (which it will, as soon as you enter an address).

If you're connected to the Internet and would like to work offline for awhile, open the **File** menu and select **Work Offline**. A network icon appears on the status bar, as shown in Figure 9.3. If you attempt to select a link that points to a page that has not been downloaded to your system, the mouse pointer changes to a handle with a "don't" symbol next to it. (See Figure 9.3.)

If you select a channel or perform any other Web-related task while you're offline, Internet Explorer will ask if you wish to connect. To continue to work offline, simply click the **Stay Offline** or the **Work Offline** button. To connect to the Internet, click **Connect** instead. You can also return to work by opening the **File** menu and selecting **Work Offline** to remove its check mark.

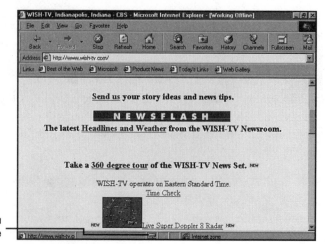

This icon tells you that you
are offline

Figure 9.3 Working offline.

As silly as it may sound, if you've been working online, and then you attempt to disconnect from the Internet by using the Work Offline command on the File menu, you're not really taken "offline." True, Internet Explorer is taken "offline," meaning that it will no longer request information from Internet servers, *but your connection is still on.* So if you connect to the Internet via modem, you'll want to double-click the **Connection** icon on the taskbar and select Disconnect to actually break the connection.

> **TIP** **Automatic Shutdown** If you connect to the Internet through a modem, and Internet Explorer detects 20 minutes of inactivity, it automatically disconnects you from the Internet. You can then continue to work offline, or reconnect when needed.

In this lesson, you learned how to change your subscriptions, and even delete them when needed. You also learned how to work offline. In the next lesson, you'll learn how to configure Outlook Express for email and news.

Configuring Outlook Express

In this lesson, you'll learn about Outlook Express and how to set it up for email and news.

What Is Outlook Express?

With Outlook Express, you can send and receive email messages and read and post newsgroup messages, as shown in Figure 10.1.

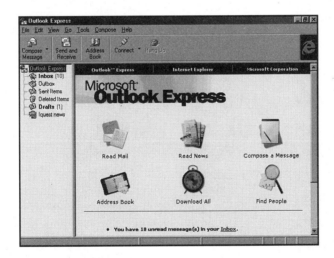

Figure 10.1   Outlook Express handles both email and newsgroup messages.

Email (short for electronic mail) is messages that are sent electronically from one computer to another. To send a message, you enter an address, type your message, and then instruct Outlook Express to send it. In addition to text, you can include file attachments with your messages, such as a sales worksheet or a company profile.

An email address usually consists of a person's name and email provider, such as jfulton@indy.net. The address tells your email server where the message is supposed to go. To receive messages, connect to your email server and request your incoming mail. Your mail is copied to your system and then (typically) removed from the server.

Outlook Express also handles newsgroup messages. *Newsgroups* are public discussion groups where messages are posted to the group in general, where they can be read and responded to. There are lots of Internet newsgroups, covering every topic imaginable. You'll learn more about newsgroups in Lesson 12, "Using Outlook Express News."

Outlook Express's features are accessible through Internet Explorer, although you can run it as a separate program if you like. However, before you can use Outlook Express, you must first configure it.

Using the Connection Wizard to Configure Email and News

The first step in using Outlook Express is configuring it. In order to do that, you will need the following information from your Internet Service Provider:

- User name and password that you use to log in and get mail.
- Email address, which is usually your name (although it can be a nickname, a title, or anything), followed by @, followed by the name of your ISP (Internet Service Provider), as in bfrank@speed.net.
- Name of the incoming and outgoing mail server. Typically, your incoming mail is handled by a POP (Post Office Protocol) or IMAP (Internet Message Access Protocol) server, while your outgoing mail is handled by an SMTP (Simple Mail Transfer Protocol) server. A server name might look something like smtp.speed.net.

- Name of the newsgroup server. Newsgroup messages are handled by an NNTP (Network News Transport Protocol) server. A typical news server's address will probably look something like news.speed.net.

To setup Outlook Express, you use the Connection Wizard. If you completed the necessary screens when you set up Internet Explorer back in Lesson 2, you can skip these steps.

To set up Outlook Express for email, follow these steps:

1. Start Outlook Express by clicking the **Launch Outlook Express** button on the Quick Launch toolbar, or by clicking (or double-clicking) the **Outlook Express** icon on the desktop.

2. The Outlook Express dialog box appears, asking if you'd like to connect to the Internet. Because you don't need to be connected to the Internet to complete this task, select **Don't dial a connection** from the drop-down list and click OK.

3. Open the **Tools** menu and select **Accounts**. The Internet Accounts dialog box appears. (See Figure 10.2.)

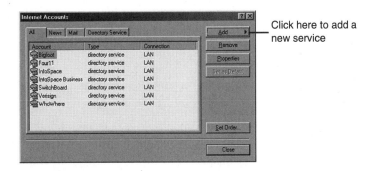

Click here to add a new service

Figure 10.2 Enter your email information first.

4. Click **Add**. Select **Mail** from the shortcut menu that appears.

5. In the **Display name** text box, enter your name as you want it to appear in the From field of outgoing messages. Click **Next**.

6. In the **E-mail address** text box, enter the address assigned to you by your Internet Service Provider, such as JFulton@indy.net. Click **Next**.

7. Select the type of mail server used by your ISP—the default is POP3. If you are unsure, accept the default. In the **Incoming mail (POP3 or IMAP) server** text box, enter the name of your POP3 or IMAP server. In the **Outgoing mail (SMTP) server box**, enter the name of your SMTP server. See Figure 10.3. Click **Next**.

Figure 10.3   Enter the names of your email servers.

8. Select **Log on using** and enter your account name and password. If your ISP requires you to use Secure Password Authentication to access your email account, then select **Log on using Secure Password Authentication** instead. Click **Next**.

9. Enter a name for your Internet mail account. This can be any name, such as the name of your ISP, as in "Indy Net Mail." Click **Next**.

10. Select the connection type you use with Internet Explorer. For example, select **Connect using my phone line**. Click **Next**.

11. If you selected the **Connect using my phone line** option in step 10, then select the Internet connection you created for Internet Explorer and click **Next**. Otherwise, skip this step.

12. Click **Finish**. You're returned to the Internet Accounts dialog box.

To set up Outlook Express for use as a newsgroup reader, follow these steps:

1. From the Internet Accounts dialog box (shown in Figure 10.2), click **Add** and select **News** from the shortcut menu that appears.

2. Enter the name you wish to appear on your newsgroup postings. Because newsgroup postings are public, you may wish to use a pseudonym, although your email address can still be traced. Click **Next**.

3. Enter the email address to which you wish people to reply to your newsgroup postings. Click **Next**.

4. Enter the address of your newsgroup (NNTP) server, as shown in Figure 10.4. If you must log on to your newsgroup server, select the **My news server requires me to log on** option. Click **Next**.

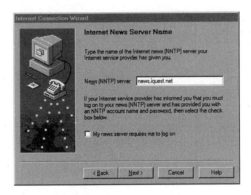

Figure 10.4 Setting up Outlook Express for news.

5. Enter a name for the newsgroup connection file, such as Indy Net News. Click **Next**.

6. Select the connection type you use with Internet Explorer. For example, select **Connect using my phone line**. Click **Next**.

7. If you selected the **Connect using my phone line** option in step 6, then select the Internet connection you created for Internet Explorer and click **Next**. Otherwise, skip this step.

8. Click **Finish**. You're returned to the Internet Accounts dialog box. Click **Close**.

9. You'll be asked if you wish to download a list of newsgroups now. Connect to the Internet and click **Yes** if you would like to do that now. Otherwise, click **No**.

> **TIP** **Which Should I Choose?** You may want to select **No**, because downloading this list will take a while, and you may wish to learn more about email at this time. If you select **Yes**, skip to Lesson 12 to learn more about newsgroups.

In this lesson, you learned how to set up Outlook Express for email and news. In the next lesson, you'll learn how to use Outlook Express to send and receive email messages.

Using Outlook Express Mail

In this lesson, you'll learn how to open and close the Outlook Express program, read and reply to mail, create mail, and use the Outlook Express News Reader.

Opening and Closing Outlook Express Mail

You can start Outlook Express Mail in various ways:

- Click the **Launch Outlook Express** button on the Quick Launch toolbar.
- Double-click the **Outlook Express** icon on the desktop.
- Open the Go menu in Internet Explorer and select **Mail**.
- Select **Start, Programs, Internet Explorer, Outlook Express**.

As you'll see in upcoming sections, you can perform certain tasks from within Internet Explorer without actually starting Outlook Express. For example, you can create and send an email message.

TIP **Importing Your Addresses** The first time you start Outlook Express, it asks if you want to import your addresses from Windows Messaging. If you've been using Windows Messaging, it's probably a good idea to import your old addresses into Outlook Express. You may or may not want to import old messages as well. Just follow the steps in the Import Wizard that appears.

To exit from Outlook Express Mail, choose **File, Exit** or click the **Close** button.

The Outlook Express Mail Window

Outlook Express provides a communications hub from which you can access both email messages and newsgroups. Whenever you start Outlook Express, it displays the opening window, shown in Figure 11.1. This communications hub displays icons for reading mail and newsgroup messages, composing messages, accessing the address book, downloading your messages, and finding people on the Internet.

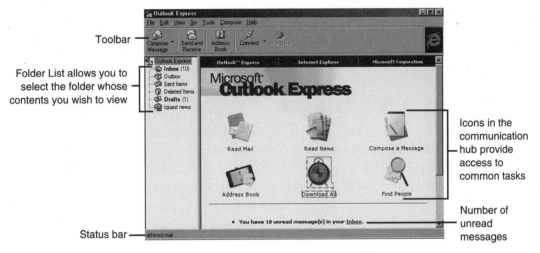

Figure 11.1   Outlook Express provides a communications hub for all your messaging needs.

From the Folder List (in the left pane), you can access your Inbox (incoming mail), Outbox (outgoing mail), Sent Items, Deleted Items, and Drafts, along with any news servers you set up in Outlook Express News, and any new folders you might create.

The opening screen also displays the number of unread messages in your Inbox, along with the number of messages in your Outbox and the Drafts folders.

TIP   **Incoming!**   If you want, you can bypass the communications hub and display the contents of the Inbox (your incoming mail) when you start Outlook Express. Just scroll down to the **When starting, go directly to my "Inbox" folder** option and select it.

Using the **View, Layout** command, you can customize the layout of Outlook Express, displaying either of these optional elements:

Outlook Bar   A vertical bar of icons representing each Outlook folder: Inbox, Outbox, and so on. You can use this bar to change from one folder to another.

Folder Bar   This bar, which appears just above the main viewing area, provides a drop-down list from which you can select the folder (Inbox, Outbox, and so on) that you wish to view.

You can also change the location of the toolbar and the characteristics of the *Preview pane* (the window in which you view messages) with the *View, Layout* command.

Sending a Message

To send an email message to someone, you will need to know her address. A typical email address looks something like this:

```
jfulton@indy.net
```

The first part is the user name (usually some abbreviation of the person's name), followed by @, and the name of that person's service provider. To send a message to someone who uses an on-line service, such as America Online, use an address something like this:

```
jfulton@aol.com

71234.9244@compuserve.com

jfulton@msn.com
```

To help you locate a person's address, you can use one of the many "white pages" on the Internet—just open the Edit menu and select **Find People**. Once you have the address of the person to whom you wish to send a message, follow these steps:

TIP   **Using Internet Explorer**   To create a message from within Internet Explorer, click the **Mail** icon on the toolbar and select **New Message**. If you want to send a copy of the current Web page in a message, select **Send Page** instead. To send a link to the Web page, click **Send a Link**.

1. Click the **Compose Message** icon in the communications hub. Or, if you'd like to select a stationary for your message, you can click the arrow next to the Compose Message icon in the toolbar, and select the stationary you'd like to use. A New Message window appears (see Figure 11.2.).

Address Book icon

Type the recipient's address here

Enter a subject

Use the Formatting toolbar to format your text

Type your message here

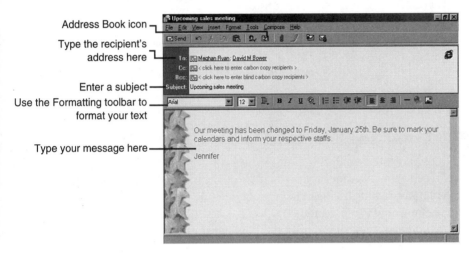

Figure 11.2 Creating an email message.

2. Enter the address of the recipient in the **To** field. To enter a second address, type a semicolon (;) first. Or you can click the **Address Book** icon next to the To field to add an address. This displays the Select Recipients dialog box, in which you can choose the recipient's name from a list, (assuming you added the recipient to the Address Book—you'll learn how to use the Address Book later in this lesson).

CAUTION

Be Careful About Upper and Lower Case Be sure to use proper case (upper and lower) when entering an email address. For example, JFulton@speed.net is not the same as jfulton@speed.net or Jfulton@speed.net.

3. To send a copy of the message to someone, enter their address in the **Cc** (carbon copy) or **Bcc** (blind carbon copy) fields. When you use **Cc** or **Bcc**, a copy of the message is sent to the person you indicate, except that with **Bcc**, no one else who receives the message is aware that a copy was sent to that person.

4. Add a topic for the message in the **Subject** field.

5. Type your message in the Message field. This area of the screen is like a word processor. Your lines of text will wrap automatically when you reach the right margin. You only have to press **Enter** at the end of each paragraph.

6. If you like, use the Formatting toolbar to format your message text. For example, select some text and click the **Bold** button to make it bold. You can change the font, size, style, color, and alignment of text, among other things.

CAUTION

Forget Formatting? Recipients who do not use an HTML-compatible email program such as Outlook Express or Netscape Mail will not see your fancy stationary or any formatting (such as bold or underline) that you use. They will, however, still be able to read the text of your message just the same.

7. To send the message when you are done, click the **Send** button. If you wish to send the message later, open the File menu and select **Send Later**. The message is placed in your Outbox. If you would like to finish the message at a later time, open the File menu and select **Save**. The message is placed in your Drafts folder.

TIP

Save That Message! If you dial in to your Internet Service Provider by modem, you may prefer to create your outgoing messages while offline, save them temporarily in your Outbox, then send them all at once the next time you dial in.

When you're ready to send messages saved to your Outbox, open the Tools menu and select **Send**. To complete any draft messages you may have created, click the Drafts folder in the Folder List, and double-click your message to open it. Make your changes and click **Send**.

If your message is improperly addressed, the message will be sent back to you by an automated mail server, informing you that the message was undeliverable.

Setting Priorities, Attaching Files, and Other Options

Prior to sending a message, you can spell check it for errors, attach files such as sales reports and budget revisions, and set priority options, among other things:

- To spell check the message, open the Tools menu and select **Spelling**, or press **F7**. You can set up Outlook Express to spell check your mail automatically. Open the Tools menu and select **Options**. Click the **Spelling** tab and select the **Always check spelling before sending** option.

- To set a high priority for the message, choose **Tools, Set Priority, High**.

- To attach a file, click the **Insert File** button (the paperclip) in the toolbar. Select the file you want to attach, then click the **Attach** button. Outlook Express Mail adds the file, represented by an icon, to your message.

- To insert a graphic in your message, click the **Insert Picture** button on the Formatting toolbar (the last one on the right). Select the graphic you want to use, choose an alignment and border option, and add additional spacing around the image if you like. Then click **OK** to add the graphic to your message.

- To check the names you've typed against those in your Address book, click the **Check Names** button (the face).

- If you have a signature file (a text file with a common closing), you can insert it by clicking the **Insert Signature** button (the pen).

- To send someone your public key (public certificate or digital ID) so he can encrypt a message and send it to you, click the **Digitally sign message** button (the red envelope). If you wish to send an encrypted message to someone, he must digitally sign a message that *he sends to you*. The public key that's attached to the message you receive is automatically placed in your certificate file. After receiving someone's public key, to send that person an encrypted message, you create the message and click the **Encrypt message** button (the blue envelope).

Using the Windows Address Book

If you know someone to whom you often send email messages, you should save his email address in your Address Book. Saving the addresses you use often prevents you from making a mistake when addressing messages. In addition, you can save other information about your contact, including his postal address and phone number. To enter an address into the Address Book, follow these steps:

1. Click the **Address Book** button on the toolbar.

2. Click the **New Contact** button. The Properties dialog box appears, as shown in Figure 11.3.

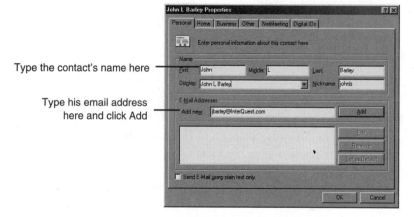

Type the contact's name here ⎯

Type his email address here and click Add ⎯

Figure 11.3   Adding someone to the Address Book.

3. Enter the contact's name in the **First**, **Middle**, and **Last** text boxes.

4. Type a **Nickname**. If you later type this nickname in the To field of a message, Outlook Express automatically fills in the correct address for that person.

5. Select how you want the contact to be displayed from the **Display** list. You'll probably want to display your contacts by their name, company name, or a nickname, although you can type anything you want in this field.

6. Type the contact's email address in the **Add new** text box and click **Add**. If the person has more than one email address, you can repeat this step as needed.

7. If you know for sure that this person uses an email program that *does not* support the use of HTML formatting, select **Send E-Mail using plain text only**.

8. You can enter additional personal and business information for this contact using the other tabs. When you're finished, click **OK**.

TIP **Quick Address** When someone sends you an email message, you can easily add that person's information to the Address Book. First, you must open the message in a window (as explained later in this lesson). Then open the **Tools** menu, select **Add to Address Book,** and select **Sender**.

If you have large groups of people to whom you typically send the same message, such as everyone in your department, you can place several addresses in a group, and use the group to send email messages to everyone. To create a group, click the **New Group** button in the Address Book window. Enter a name for the group and select the addresses you wish to add.

Addressing a Message with the Address Book

Now that you have addresses in your Address Book, you can use them to send email messages. Just follow these steps:

1. In the New Message window, click the **Address Book** icon in front of the **To** field. The Select Recipients dialog box appears, as shown in Figure 11.4.

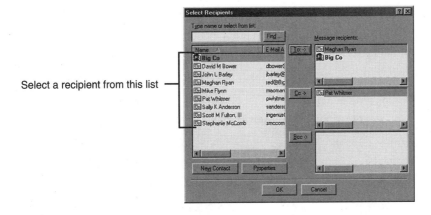

Select a recipient from this list

Figure 11.4 Choose a recipient from the Address Book.

2. Select a name or a group from the list on the left.

3. Click the appropriate button: **To**, **Cc**, or **Bcc**.

4. Repeat steps 2 and 3 to add more names. When you're finished, click **OK**.

417

TIP   **A Quicker Way**   Remember that if you've entered a nickname for a contact, you can use it to enter an address by simply typing the nickname in the **To**, **Cc**, or **Bcc** field of the new message.

Retrieving and Reading Your Messages

When someone sends mail to you via the Internet, it arrives at your Internet mail server. To read the mail, you have to retrieve it from the server. You can do this manually or set up Outlook Express Mail to do it for you at timed intervals. (Even if you use a dial-up modem connection, you can have Outlook Express check for mail periodically and dial in if necessary.)

To retrieve your messages, log on to the Internet and click the **Send and Receive** button. Your incoming messages are placed in the Inbox. To view a list of messages, click the **Read Mail** icon in the communications hub (the opening screen), or select the **Inbox** folder in the Folder List.

Unread messages appear in bold. To read a message, do any of the following:

* Select a message in the upper-right pane. Read its contents in the lower-right pane, as shown in Figure 11.5. To view the next unread message, press **Ctrl+U**.

* Double-click a message in the upper-right pane to open the message in a separate window. After viewing the message, press **Esc** to close the window.

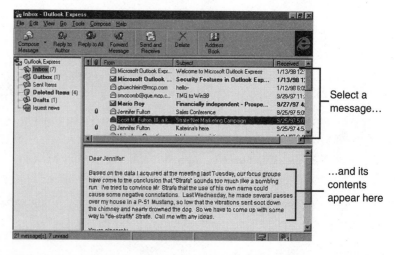

Figure 11.5   Outlook Express displays a Preview pane showing the contents of the selected message.

To set up Outlook Express so that it checks for email messages at particular intervals, open the Tools menu and select **Options**. On the **General** tab, select the **Check for new messages every XX minutes** option, and set the interval you desire (the default is every five minutes). To allow Outlook Express to dial into the Internet automatically, click the **Dial Up** tab and select the **Automatically dial when checking for new messages** option.

Saving a File Attached to a Message

A message that has a file attached to it appears with a paperclip icon. In order to use the file, you must save it to disk. Follow these steps:

1. Double-click on the message that contains the file attachment to open the message in its own window.

2. The file appears below the message text as an icon. To save the file to disk, open the File menu and select **Save Attachments**.

3. Select the name of the file you wish to save from the cascading menu that appears.

4. Change to the drive and folder in which you want to save the attachment, then click **Save**. You can rename the file if you want to by typing a new name in the **File name** text box.

Replying to a Message

When you reply to a message you receive, Outlook Express automatically copies the text of the original message into your reply. Each line of this text is marked with a > symbol in front of it so it is easily identified as the original text. You can delete this copied text if you don't want it in your reply.

Also, when you create a reply, it is automatically addressed to the sender of the original message. In addition, the subject of the original message becomes the subject of the reply, but with the word RE: preceding it.

To reply to a message, follow these steps:

1. Click either the **Reply to Author** (to reply to the sender of the message only) or the **Reply to All** (to reply to the sender and anyone who received a copy of the original message) button on the toolbar.

2. If you opened the message in a separate window, open the Compose menu and select either **Reply to Author** or **Reply to All.** A Reply message window opens.

3. Type your text above the text of the original message. If you want to delete any of the original text, select it and press **Delete**.

4. Click **Send**, or if you wish to send the message later, open the File menu and select **Send Later.**

 TIP   **Forward, Please**   To forward a message instead, select the message and click the **Forward Message** button. You can then type a message of explanation; the original message is sent as a file attachment.

Deleting Old Messages

After you begin sending and receiving messages, you'll soon accumulate quite a few. To delete old messages, follow these steps:

1. Select the messages you want to delete. To select more than one message, press and hold the **Ctrl** key as you click each message header.

2. Click the **Delete** button on the toolbar.

Deleted messages are moved to the Deleted Items folder. If you need to retrieve a message deleted by accident, display the contents of the folder by selecting it from the Folder List. Then select the message you wish to save. Drag the message to the folder in which you want to keep it. For example, drag the message to the Inbox folder in the Folder List.

To empty the Deleted Items folder, right-click on it in the Folder List, and select **Empty Folder** from the shortcut menu that appears.

 TIP   **Empty the Trash**   To set up Outlook Express so that it empties the Deleted Items folder whenever you exit the program, open the **Tools** menu and select **Options**. Select the **Empty messages from the "Deleted Items" folder on exit** option and click **OK**.

In this lesson, you learned how to send and receive messages with Outlook Express. In the next lesson, you'll learn how to read and post newsgroup messages with Outlook Express.

Using Outlook Express News

In this lesson, you'll learn how to use the Outlook Express News Reader to read and post newsgroup messages.

What Is Outlook Express News?

As you learned in the previous lesson, Outlook Express contains an email program. It also includes a newsgroup reader. A *newsgroup* is a discussion forum on the Internet. The "discussion" takes place through email messages. You participate in a newsgroup by subscribing to it, then reading the messages (also called *articles*) that others have posted in the newsgroup and, optionally, posting your replies to those messages.

There are over 20,000 newsgroups on the Internet. Each one specializes in a particular discussion topic. Internet Service Providers and Internet-based special interest groups maintain newsgroup discussions on computers known as News servers.

You will probably not have access to every newsgroup—there are simply too many of them, and they come and go so quickly. Instead, your service provider will offer a selection of popular newsgroups to which you can subscribe.

Anything Goes Newsgroups are public forums, and as such, you can
never be quite sure what you'll find there—including pornography, rude
CAUTION language, and discrimination. So be careful of the newsgroups you select, and
of the messages you post.

Opening and Closing Outlook Express News

You can start Outlook Express News in several ways:

- To start Outlook Express News from within Microsoft Internet Explorer, click the **Mail** button and select **Read News**.
- In the communications hub of Outlook Express, click **Read News**.
- To switch from Outlook Express Mail to Outlook Express News, either choose **Go, News,** or simply select your **News** icon in the **Folder List**.

Retrieving a List of Newsgroups

Before you can begin to participate in newsgroup discussions, you must first dial in to your News server and retrieve a list of available newsgroups. The first time you do this, it may take some time, because this can be a lengthy list. However, after the first time, retrieving the list should go quickly because all you have to do is update the list.

To retrieve a list of newsgroups from your News server, follow these steps:

- Click the icon for your news server in the Outlook bar. The first time you do this, Outlook Express will ask if you'd like to view a list of newsgroups. Click **Yes,** and Outlook Express begins downloading a list of available newsgroups from your Internet Service Provider.
- To update the newsgroup list, click the **News groups** button or select **Tools, Newsgroups** from the menu.

You'll see a dialog box showing the progress of the download. When Outlook Express is finished, the Newsgroups dialog box, shown in Figure 12.1, displays the list of available newsgroups.

Subscribing to and Unsubscribing from Newsgroups

To subscribe to a newsgroup, follow these steps:

1. When the download process described in the previous section of this lesson completes, scroll through the list of available newsgroups.

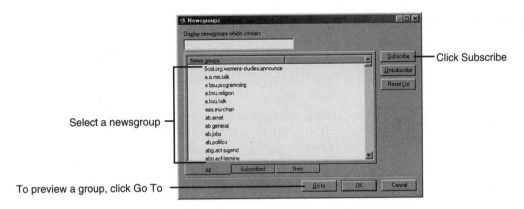

Click Subscribe

Select a newsgroup

To preview a group, click Go To

Figure 12.1 The Newsgroups dialog box.

2. When you see a newsgroup that you would like to preview, select it. Then click **Go To**. This closes the dialog box, creates a subfolder for that newsgroup under the news server's folder, and fills the folder with the current set of articles in that newsgroup. This folder is removed when you close Outlook Express.

TIP **Preview's Over** If, after previewing the messages in a newsgroup, you decide to subscribe to it, select it in the **Folder List**, open the **Tools** menu and choose **Subscribe to this newsgroup**.

3. If you want to retrieve future articles posted in a newsgroup, select the newsgroup in the Newsgroups dialog box and click **Subscribe**, then click **OK** (refer to Figure 12.1). This closes the dialog box, creates a subfolder for that newsgroup under the news server's folder, fills the folder with the current set of articles, and in the future, retrieves new articles from the news server.

4. If you don't want to scroll through a long list of available newsgroups, you can enter a word in the **Display newsgroups which contain** field at the top of the Newsgroups dialog box. As you enter words, the list of newsgroups is automatically narrowed down to just the newsgroups that contain the words you type.

If you want to unsubscribe from a newsgroup, select it in the Newsgroup dialog box and click the **Unsubscribe** button. Click **OK** to close the dialog box. You can also unsubscribe from a newsgroup in the Folder List by selecting the group, opening the Tools menu and choosing **Unsubscribe from this newsgroup**.

Reading Messages

After Outlook Express News has retrieved messages from a news server, you can read them. Follow these steps:

1. Click the icon for your news server in the Folder List. A list of subscribed newsgroups appears in the upper right pane, as shown in Figure 12.2.

List of messages —

News server's icon —

List of subscribed — newsgroups

Message contents — appears here

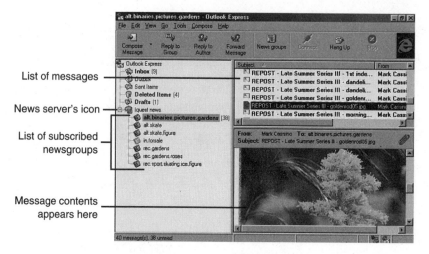

Figure 12.2 Viewing newsgroup messages.

2. Double-click the newsgroup name.

3. A list of messages in the selected newsgroup appears. Unread messages appear in bold. Take one of the following steps:

- Select a message in the message (upper right) pane. Its contents appear in the preview (lower right) pane.

- Double-click a message in the message pane. The message opens in its own window.

4. To view the next unread message, press **Ctrl+U**.

Thread Newsgroup messages and their replies form a thread, which, when read, form a discussion.

Threaded messages are grouped under the original message. To see the messages in a thread, click the **plus sign** that appears in front of the original message.

TIP **Next, Please** When you open a newsgroup with a lot of postings, only some of the messages in that group are downloaded to your computer. After reviewing these messages, you can download more by opening the **Tools** menu and selecting **Get Next 300 Headers**.

Posting Your Own Messages

After reading a message, you may post a reply to the newsgroup, or reply privately to the author of the message, or reply to both:

- To post a reply to the newsgroup, either click the **Reply to Group** button in the toolbar or choose **Compose, Reply to Newsgroup**.
- To reply privately to the author, either click the **Reply to Author** button in the toolbar or choose **Compose, Reply to Author** in the menu.
- To reply to both, choose **Compose, Reply to Newsgroup and Author** in the menu.

Enter the text of your reply just as you would in a mail reply. When you are finished, click the **Post** or **Send** button.

CAUTION

Take That Back! If you decide to cancel your posting after you've sent it, select the message, open the **Compose** menu, and select **Cancel Message**. (If someone has already viewed your message, this command will not delete it from his computer.)

If you would like to begin a new thread by posting a message on a different topic, follow these steps:

1. Select the newsgroup you wish to post a message to.

2. Click the **Compose Message** button.

3. Type a subject.

4. Type your message in the large text box.

5. Click the **Post** button.

TIP   **Posting the Same Message to Several Newsgroups**   To post copies of your message to other newsgroups, open the **Tools** menu, and choose **Select Newsgroups**. Select the newsgroups you wish to add, and click **Add**. Click **OK**.

In this lesson, you learned how to use Outlook Express News. You learned how to retrieve and post newsgroup messages. In the next lesson you learn to create web pages in FrontPage Express.

Understanding FrontPage Express

In this lesson, you'll learn how to create your own Web pages with FrontPage Express.

What Is FrontPage Express?

FrontPage Express is a web page creator and editor. With it, you can create and edit your own web pages, and then put those pages out on the Internet (or your company's intranet) for all to see. FrontPage Express is a trimmed-down version of Microsoft FrontPage Editor, so when you're ready for a more feature-rich web editor, you won't have to learn a new software package from scratch. You can transfer the skills you learn in FrontPage Express to FrontPage Editor.

To start the FrontPage Express program:

1. Click **Start**.
2. Choose **Programs**.
3. Choose **Internet Explorer, FrontPage Express**. The FrontPage Express window opens. Figure 13.1 shows FrontPage displaying a web page. Your window will be blank.

Format toolbar ──
Standard toolbar ──
Forms toolbar ──

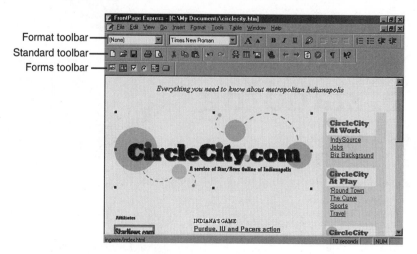

Figure 13.1   The FrontPage Express window.

The FrontPage Express Tools

There are three toolbars in FrontPage Express—the Format toolbar, the Standard toolbar, and the Forms toolbar (refer to Figure 13.1). If you want to know what a button does, point to the button with your mouse. A small yellow box called a *ToolTip* appears beneath the button telling you the name of the tool. The Status Bar at the bottom of the screen displays a short explanation of what the tool does.

The Format toolbar contains the buttons you need to change the appearance of the text on your Web page. If you use other Microsoft products, many of the formatting tools are familiar to you. Table 13.1 will help you identify the tools and how to use them. (You'll learn more about formatting your web page text later in this lesson.)

Table 13.1   The Format Toolbar

Button	Description	Purpose
Normal	Change style	Select a paragraph style
Times New Roman	Change font	Change text style
A˙	Increase Text Size	Make text bigger

Button	Description	Purpose
	Decrease Text Size	Make text smaller
	Bold	Bold text
	Italic	Italicize text
	Underline	Underline text
	Text Color	Change text color
	Align Left	Align paragraph to left
	Center	Center paragraph
	Align Right	Align paragraph to right
	Numbered List	Create a numbered list
	Bulleted List	Create a bulleted list
	Decrease Indent	Outdent both margins of paragraph
	Increase Indent	Indent both margins of paragraph

The Standard toolbar contains tools that allow you to navigate the pages, open and save, cut, copy, and paste, and more. See a description of the tools in Table 13.2.

Table 13.2 The Standard Toolbar

Button	Description	Purpose
	New	Create new Web page
	Open	Open existing Web page

continues

Table 13.2 Continued

Button	Description	Purpose
	Save	Save current page
	Print	Print page
	Print Preview	Preview page prior to printing
	Cut	Move text to Clipboard
	Copy	Copy text to Clipboard
	Paste	Paste text from Clipboard
	Undo	Undo last action
	Redo	Undo the undo
	Insert WetBot Component	Insert an Include, Search, or Timestamp component
	Insert Table	Add a table
	Insert Image	Add a graphic
	Create or Edit Hyperlink	Add a link to another page
	Back	Display previous open page
	Forward	Move forward to next open page
	Refresh	Reload the page
	Stop	Stop the current action
	Show/Hide ¶	Show or hide paragraph marks
	Help	Get help

With the Forms toolbar, you can add special elements to your web page that allow the viewer to make choices, such as drop-down lists, option buttons, checkboxes, and more. Table 13.3 lists the tools on the Forms toolbar and their purposes.

Table 13.3 The Forms Toolbar

Button	Description	Purpose
	One-Line Text Box	Insert text box
	Scrolling Text Box	Insert scrolling (marquee) text box
	Check Box	Insert check box
	Radio Button	Insert option button
	Drop-Down Menu	Insert drop-down list
	Push Button	Insert command button

Creating a Web Page

Although FrontPage Express creates and formats web pages in HTML (Hypertext Markup Language), you don't have to worry about learning HTML. *HTML*, by the way, is code that is inserted into a text document so that a web browser (such as IE4) can display that text with formatting, such as bold, italics, and so on. You'll find that creating a web page in FrontPage Express is similar to making a document in a word processor—if you select some text and click the bold button, FrontPage inserts the proper HTML coding for you.

 TERM **Hypertext Markup Language (HTML)** The standard language (or codes) used to describe the contents and layout of a web page. When HTML codes are added to a text document, they tell the web browser how to format and display the contents of the web page.

To start a new web page in FrontPage Express, follow these steps:

1. Open the File menu and select **New**. The New Page dialog box opens (see Figure 13.2).

Figure 13.2   The New Page dialog box.

2. Select one of the available templates or wizards to help you design the type of web page you want. Select **Normal Page** to start with a blank page.

 TIP   Fast Page   You can also click the **New** button to create a new, blank, page.

3. Click **OK**. If you've selected a wizard, follow the instructions on the dialog boxes to build your page; if you chose a template, replace the sample text with your own text and pictures. On a Normal Page, you start with a blank page and can add text and pictures as you wish.

When you save the file by clicking the **Save** button, FrontPage Express saves your work directly to the web (if you installed Microsoft Web Publishing Wizard) or to a file.

Editing an Existing Web Page

You can open existing web pages from the Web and edit them if you have the Microsoft Web Publishing Wizard installed. Otherwise, you can open an HTML file from your hard disk or network.

To open an existing web page, follow these steps:

1. Click **Open**. The Open File dialog box appears.

2. If you want to open an HTML file from your computer or network, select **From File** and enter the path and file name of the file (click **Browse** to find the file if you don't know the path or name). If you want to open a page from the Web, select **From Location** and enter the address.

3. Click **OK**.

After the file opens, edit it as you would a word processing document and then save it.

Formatting Text

As with a word processor, you can select text and apply the formatting, or you can turn on the formatting before entering the text, type the text, and then turn off the formatting.

You can apply formatting using the tools on the Format toolbar (refer to Table 13.1), or choose **Format, Font** to set the appearance of characters (see Figure 13.3) or **Format, Paragraph** to specify paragraph styles.

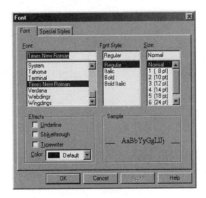

Figure 13.3 The Font dialog box.

If you're comfortable with formatting word processing pages, you won't have any difficulty applying new formatting attributes—simply make your selections in the dialog box and click **OK**. However, you may be surprised that text size is listed as 1, 2, 3—these are simply the settings you must use for HTML. To apply special HTML format codes (such as blinking text) to text on your web page, click the **Special Styles** tab and select the style you want.

Changing the Page Properties

Set margins, choose a page background or background sounds, or title your page using the Page Properties box. Choose **File, Page Properties**, and the Properties dialog box is displayed. Here is an explanation of each of the four tab selections in the Page Properties dialog box:

- **General**   On this page (see Figure 13.4) you can specify a title for your web page, a default target frame, base location (default web directory), and a background sound (click **Browse** to find the sound file).

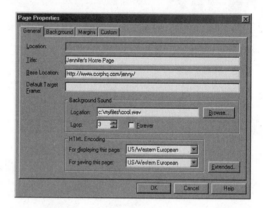

Figure 13.4   The Page Properties box with the General tab selected.

- **Background**   Select this tab (see Figure 13.5) to set a background color for your page or to choose a background image you want to appear behind your text (click **Browse** to select the file). You can make the background image a watermark (faded picture). You can also pick the colors you want to use for your hypertext.

- **Margins**   If you want to specify a top or left margin, select the **Margins** tab.

- **Custom**   You can specify system and user variables for your page by selecting the **Custom** tab. These options are only for experienced HTML users.

Click **OK** to accept your selections.

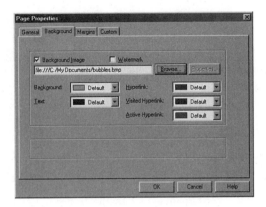

Figure 13.5 The Page Properties box with the Background tab selected.

Adding Hypertext, Images, and WebBot Components

A good web page contains hypertext links to lead you to related web pages and pictures to illustrate your topic. At the very least, you'll want to create text links to the other pages in your web site.

CAUTION

Links to Other Sites Keep in mind that some web sites require you to obtain their permission before including a link to their site from your web page. At the very least, be sure that your link is to the main web page—*the home page*—of any site you include.

Creating Links

To create a hypertext link, follow these steps:

1. Select the text you want to use as the hypertext link.
2. Click the **Create or Edit Hyperlink** button on the Standard toolbar. The Create Hyperlink dialog box appears (see Figure 13.6).

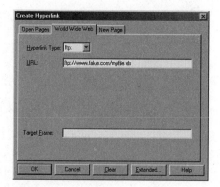

Figure 13.6   The Create Hyperlink dialog box.

3. Perform one of the following:

- To link to a page you've been editing, click the **Open Pages** tab, and select the page from those listed. You can link to a bookmark on the page, or a frame.
- To link to something on the WWW, click the **World Wide Web** tab, select the type of object you wish to link to from the **Hyperlink Type** list, and enter its URL.
- To create a new page and link to it, click the **New Page** tab, enter a title and filename (URL).

Bookmark   A mark set within the text of a page, enabling you to link to some point other than the top of that page.

Frame   Frames divide a browser window so that several web pages can be viewed at the same time (refer to Figure 13.1).

4. Click **OK**.

Adding Graphics

To add images to your page, follow these steps:

1. Position your insertion point where you want to place the graphic image.
2. Click the **Insert Image** button on the Standard toolbar.
3. When the Image dialog box appears, enter the location of the image file or click **Browse** to select the file.

4. Click **OK**. The image is inserted, and selection handles appear around it. To move the image, drag it. To resize the image, drag a handle.

Handle When you click on an object, (such as a graphic image), handles (small boxes) appear around its edges. You can resize an object by dragging one of these handles. See Part IV, Lesson 5, "Using Paint," for help in sizing and moving graphics.

Inserting WebBots

You can insert WebBots into your web page in order to automate certain tasks, such as updating the date that appears on a page to the current date every time you make changes to the page. There are three WebBots included with FrontPage Express, although there are many more in the standard version of FrontPage:

- **Include** Allows you to include a web page within this page. For example, you could create a web page with several text links, each pointing to a different page within your web site. After saving this "link toolbar," you could use this bot to include the toolbar at the bottom or top of each web page.
- **Timestamp** Adds the current date to the page, and updates that date automatically each time you change the page.
- **Search** Puts a search bar on your page. This enables the user to search the pages of your web site for particular text (that is, if your web site provider supports FrontPage extensions).

To add one of these features to your page:

1. Position your insertion point where you want to put the WebBot.

2. Click the **Insert WebBot Component** button on the Standard toolbar.

3. When the Insert WebBot Component dialog box opens, select the WebBot component you want to insert and click **OK**.

4. A dialog box opens specific to the component you selected. Enter the information requested and select the desired options. Click **OK**.

5. The WebBot Component appears on your page (see Figure 13.7).

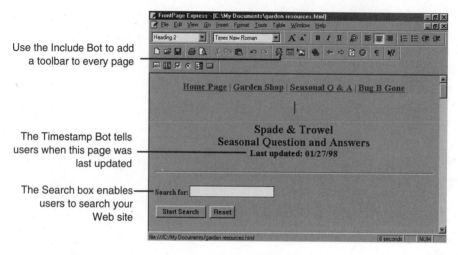

Use the Include Bot to add a toolbar to every page

The Timestamp Bot tells users when this page was last updated

The Search box enables users to search your Web site

Figure 13.7   WebBots perform special tasks.

CAUTION

FrontPage Extensions   Some FrontPage Express features, such as WebBots, are not supported over the Internet as a whole, and they require that you publish your web page on a server that is running the FrontPage Extensions.

In this lesson, you learned the basics of creating or editing a web page using FrontPage Express. In the next lesson, you will learn about HyperTerminal.

Using HyperTerminal

In this lesson, you learn about HyperTerminal, a communication tool that comes with Windows 98. You will also learn how to create a HyperTerminal connection and dial into another computer.

What Is HyperTerminal?

HyperTerminal allows you to remotely connect to another computer. You use HyperTerminal to connect to bulletin boards (the ones that haven't already switched to the Internet, that is) or to other computers (including your friend's). For example, you might use HyperTerminal to connect to your Internet Service Provider the first time, in order to download your startup files. Or you might connect to your local bank (with the proper passwords, of course), or to your local computer group's computer. You might even be able to use HyperTerminal to connect to your company's computer from the comfort of your living room.

If the computer you wish to connect to is running Windows, Microsoft recommends that you use Dial-Up Networking rather than HyperTerminal, but you will find HyperTerminal useful when connecting to bulletin boards, government agencies, and colleges.

 Bulletin Boards Small online services that act as meeting places for people with common interests. Many government agencies and schools uses bulletin boards to allow people access to information regarding their services or schools. Software companies provide bulletin boards for downloading files, or bug fixes. Bulletin boards are fairly easy to set up and maintain, and require a computer, a modem, and bulletin board software. You'll find lots of bulletin boards run by individuals out of their homes.

Creating a Connection

To connect to another computer using HyperTerminal, you need to create a reusable connection file for each computer you want to communicate with. (HyperTerminal comes with connection files already set up for communicating with AT&T Mail, CompuServe, and MCI Mail.)

 TIP **Make it Easy on Yourself** If you plan to use your modem often (and you don't want to tie up your voice line), contact your local phone company to inquire about adding a second line just for your modem—it's more than worth it. You might also want to look into faster telecommunications options such as ISDN and T1 lines, although they are a bit pricey for the home user.

To create a HyperTerminal connection, follow these steps:

1. Click **Start,** select **Programs, Accessories, Communications, HyperTerminal**.

2. The HyperTerminal folder opens as shown in Figure 14.1.

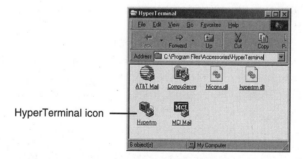

HyperTerminal icon —

Figure 14.1 The HyperTerminal Folder contents.

3. Click or double-click the **HyperTerminal** icon.

4. The Connection Description dialog box opens (see Figure 14.2). Type a name for your connection in the **Name** box and select an icon. Click **OK**.

5. The Connect To dialog box appears. Type the **Phone number** for your new connection. Check the **Country code, Area code** and modem type (in **Connect using**) to be certain they are correct. Click **OK**. (See Part III, Lesson 8, "Configuring a Modem," for more information.)

Select the icon
you wish to use

Figure 14.2 Choose an icon for your new connection.

6. The Connect dialog box appears. **Default Location** is selected in the **Your location** box. If you are using a laptop and want to create a different location name, type the new name; otherwise accept **Default Location** as your location. Click **Dialing Properties**. The Dialing Properties dialog box appears (see Figure 14.3).

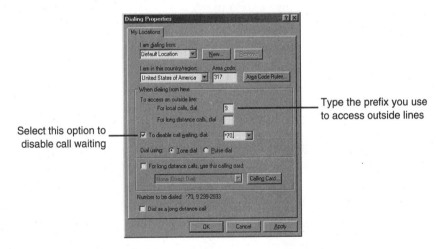

Select this option to
disable call waiting

Type the prefix you use
to access outside lines

Figure 14.3 Disable call waiting in the Dialing Properties dialog box.

7. If you need to dial a prefix for an outside line, supply this information in the **When dialing from here** section of the Dialing Properties box. If your phone has call waiting, disable it by placing a check mark in the **To disable call waiting, dial:** box. Select the prefix to disable call waiting from the drop-down list or type the numbers and characters yourself. Click **OK**.

CAUTION

Disable Call Waiting!   Be sure to disable call waiting before you connect to another computer, dial into the Internet, or use Dial Up Networking. (Of course, if you get a second phone line for your modem in order to avoid this problem, simply don't add calling features such as call waiting.) The signal you hear on your phone, indicating that another call is coming in, can interfere with data transfer. In many areas of the country, dialing the prefix *70 will disable call waiting. When you hang up from your call, call waiting is reactivated automatically. If you aren't sure which prefix you should use, check the front pages of your local phone book.

8. The Connect dialog box appears. You can now dial to another computer by clicking **Dial**. If you do not want to dial out now, click **Cancel** to close the dialog box. When prompted to save your file, click **Yes**.

Your new connection icon now appears in the HyperTerminal folder. You can close this window, dial into another computer (see the following section), or if you need to change or edit this connection, right-click the icon and choose **Properties**.

Dialing Into a Computer

Once you've created a connection file, follow these steps to dial into another computer or bulletin board:

1. If you do not have the HypterTerminal folder open, click **Start**, select **Programs**, **Accessories**, **Communications**, and **HyperTerminal**.
2. Click (or double-click) your new connection icon.
3. The HyperTerminal window opens and the Connect dialog box appears. Click **Dial**.
4. The Connect dialog box closes and the HyperTerminal window becomes active. You are now connected to the other computer.

Connecting to a Bulletin Board

To connect to a bulletin board (a private online service), establish a connection with HyperTerminal and dial into the bulletin board as described previously. Different bulletin boards run different software, but after you use one bulletin board, you'll get the hang of it. All bulletin boards require you to log on and often ask you to assign yourself a password if this is your first visit (see Figure 14.4). Some bulletin board services are free; others charge a membership fee.

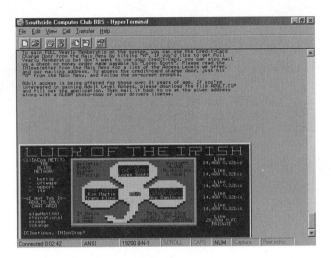

Figure 14.4 Bulletin Board log on.

After you log on you will see a menu of services available at the site. After you have finished exploring the site, leave the bulletin board by signing out. A common method for signing out is to type **G** (for good-bye) at the prompt.

To download a file from a bulletin board, select from a menu of files that can be downloaded from that server. This list is usually accessed from a menu on the first page of the bulletin board. After you have located the file you want to download, you will need to select a File Transfer Protocol. Instructions for downloading are usually given to you by the bulletin board service.

In this lesson, you learned how to set a HyperTerminal connection and dial into another computer. In the next lesson, you'll learn how to use My Computer and Explorer to browse the Internet.

Web Integration and My Computer/ Windows Explorer

In this lesson, you learn how Web functionality is integrated with My Computer and Windows Explorer, in the form of single-clicking, HTML display of folder contents, and Web browsing.

How the Single-Click (Web Style) Option Affects Windows

As you learned earlier, Windows 98 includes the Active Desktop, an option that allows you to download current Web content to your desktop. As discussed in Part II, Lesson 2, "Using My Computer," often associated with, and yet separate from, the Active Desktop is another option: *single-click*. This option (known as Web style) allows you to select items simply by pointing at them, and to open objects by single-clicking, rather than double-clicking on them.

Web style affects not only how My Computer and Windows Explorer work, but other parts of Windows as well, such as the desktop. For example, with Web style on, you can click on the Outlook Express icon on the desktop to start the program.

The Web style option also affects how objects appear. For example, with Web style, the icons on the desktop appear with underlined titles. Also, when you point at them with the mouse, the pointer changes to a hand, as shown in Figure 15.1.

In My Computer or Windows Explorer, Web style allows the contents of folders to display like Web pages. Web pages give you the flexibility to annotate your files and organize them the way you like. (See Figure 15.1.) If you don't want to use Web pages to display the contents of your folders, you don't have to—you can turn Web page view on (or off) for individual folders as needed, and still use the single-click (Web style) option.

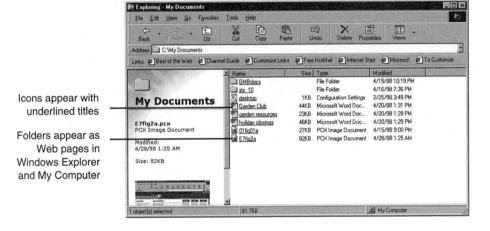

Icons appear with underlined titles

Folders appear as Web pages in Windows Explorer and My Computer

Figure 15.1 The single-click option affects the desktop as well as Windows Explorer and My Computer.

 TIP **Very Versatile** Remember, you can use the Web style option with either the Classic or the Active Desktop.

To turn on Web style, follow these steps:

1. Click **Start**, select **Settings**, and select **Folder Options.**
2. On the **General** tab, select **Web Style**.
3. Click **OK**.

 Change of View Turning on Web style does not immediately affect how files are displayed in My Computer or Windows Explorer. As you'll learn later in CAUTION this lesson, you control whether folders are viewed as Web pages.

Customizing the Single-Click (Web Style) Option

The single-click, or Web style, option can be easily customized to meet your exact needs:

1. Click Start, select **Settings**, and select **Folder Options**.

2. On the **General** tab, select **Custom, based on settings you choose**. Then click **Settings**.

3. The Custom Settings dialog box, shown in Figure 15.2, appears.

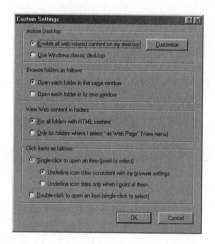

Figure 15.2   Customize your own style.

4. Select the options you desire and click **OK**:

    Active Desktop   Here, you can switch between the Classic and the Active Desktop.

    Browse folders as follows   Select what you want to happen when you open a folder in My Computer or Windows Explorer. By default, both My Computer and Windows Explorer display the contents of each folder you select in the same window.

    View Web content in folders   This option applies only to Windows Explorer. Here, you can control whether all your folders or only those you specifically choose (with the **View, As a Web Page** command) are viewed as Web pages.

Click items as follows Here, you can switch between single and double-clicking. You can also select when (and if) icon titles are underlined. If you select to go by your browser settings, you can choose to have underlining appear all the time, none of the time, or only when you point at an icon (something IE4 calls "hovering").

Displaying the Contents of a Folder Using HTML

As you learned earlier, when you turn Web style on, it does not immediately affect how the contents of a folder are viewed in My Computer or Windows Explorer. To display your folders as Web pages, follow these steps:

1. First, make sure that Web style (the single-click option) is turned on: Click **Start**, select **Settings**, and select **Folder Options.** Then, on the **General** tab, select **Web Style**. Or, from within My Computer or Windows Explorer, open the **View** menu, select **Folder Options**, and select **Web Style**.

 TIP **Some Style** You do not have to turn Web style on for everything; you can turn it on for particular folders only, if you wish. You'll learn how later in this lesson.

2. In Windows Explorer or My Computer, select the Web page view: click the arrow on the **Views** button and select **As Web Page**. The contents of your folders are displayed as shown in Figure 15.3.

Folder contents appear as Web pages

This panel displays file information

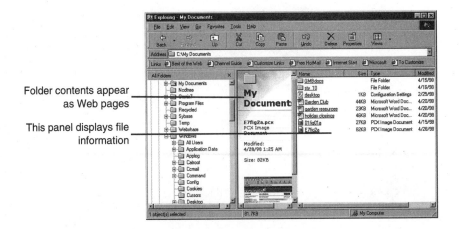

Figure 15.3 Folders can be seen as Web pages.

When you use Web style, you can display file information however you like, within the context of the Web page. For example, in Figure 15.3, files are listed using the Details view; in Figure 15.1, they are listed using the Large Icons view. Select the view you wish with the **Views** button.

Turning on Web Style for a Single Folder

You don't have to display the contents of all your folders as Web pages. Instead, you can modify the Web style option as needed.

For example, if you wish to use single-clicking, but you don't want to view your folders as Web pages, turn Web style on, but *do not select* the **As Web Page** from the **Views** button in My Computer or Windows Explorer.

If you like double-clicking, but wish to view your folders as Web pages, follow these steps:

1. From within My Computer or Windows Explorer, open the **View** menu, select **Folder Options**, and select **Custom**.

2. Click **Settings**. The Custom Settings dialog box, shown in Figure 15.4, appears.

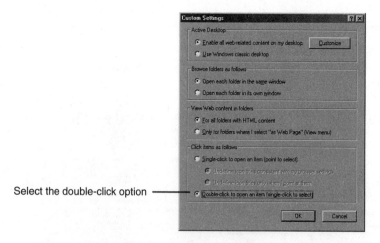

Select the double-click option

Figure 15.4   Customize how you wish to view and select files.

3. Under **Click items as follows**, select **Double-click to open an item**. Click **OK**.

4. Click **Close**.

5. Make sure Web view is turned on: click the **Views** button and select **As Web Page**.

If you want to use single-clicking but you only want to view some folders as Web pages, follow these steps:

1. Turn on Web style: From within My Computer or Windows Explorer, open the **View** menu, select **Folder Options**, and select **Web Style**. Click **OK**.

2. Make sure that Web page view is turned off: click the **Views** button and select **As Web Page** if needed, to remove the checkmark.

3. Create an HTML folder page for each folder you wish to view as a Web page. See the next section for help.

Creating an HTML Folder Page

Windows 98 has a standard Web page view, as shown in Figure 15.3. You can customize this view by creating an HTML folder page for select folders (see Figure 15.5). To do this, you will use an HTML editor (or a simple text editor such as Notepad), and edit a file called folder.htt (HyperText template).

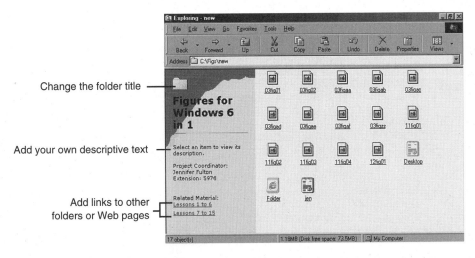

Figure 15.5 You can create your own HTML folder page

To create an HTML folder file, follow these steps:

1. In My Computer or Windows Explorer, change to the folder you wish to customize.

2. Open the **View** menu and select **Customize this Folder**. The Customize this Folder dialog box appears.

3. Select **Create or edit an HTML document** and click **Next**.

4. Click **Next** again, and Notepad starts.

5. Make whatever changes to the HTML document you like. Then save the file and exit Notepad. You're returned to the Customize this Folder dialog box.

6. Click **Finish**.

The folder.htt file is a text file that contains HTML codes. If you know HTML, making modifications to this file will not be difficult. For those of you with only limited knowledge of HTML, here are some changes you might wish to try:

CAUTION

What Happened? If you make a mistake while changing the folder.htt file, your file list display may be difficult, if not impossible to read. To restore your file list, remove the customization to the folder, as explained in the section, "Removing Folder Customization."

To change the folder title, replace these lines:

```
<p class=Title>
<!--webbot bot="HTMLMarkup" startspan alt="&lt;B&gt;&lt;I&gt;Web View
Folder Title&lt;/I&gt;&lt;/B&gt; " -->
%THISDIRNAME%
<!--webbot bot="HTMLMarkup" endspan -->
```

with these:

```
<p class=Title>
<!--webbot bot="HTMLMarkup" startspan alt="&lt;B&gt;&lt;I&gt;Web View
Folder Title&lt;/I&gt;&lt;/B&gt; " -->
Figures for Windows 6 in 1
<!--webbot bot="HTMLMarkup" endspan -->
```

To add descriptive text for the folder, change these lines:

```
<!-- HERE'S A GOOD PLACE TO ADD A FEW LINKS OF YOUR OWN -->
<!-- (examples commented out)
        <p>
<br>
```

to these:

```
<br>
<br>Project Coordinator: Jennifer Fulton
<br>Extension: 5978
<br>
<p>
<br>
```

You could create some links to a few other folders by changing these lines:

```
<a href="http://www.mylink1.com/">Custom Link 1</a>
<p class=Links>
<a href="http://www.mylink2.com/">Custom Link 2</a>
-->
```

to this:

```
Related Material:
<br>
<a href="file://c:/lessons">Lessons 1 to 6</a>
<p class=Links>
<a href="file://c:/morelessons">Lessons 7 to 15</a>
-->
```

Of course, you could create links to Web pages instead of folders if you like. You could also make one more adjustment—adding a bitmap behind the text in the left panel. Change these lines:

```
<html>
    <link rel=stylesheet href="%TEMPLATEDIR%\webview.css"
title="Win98">
    <head>
```

to this:

```
<html>
    <link rel=stylesheet href=c:\figs\jen.css title="Win98">
    <head>
```

The file, jen.css is a HyperText Style Sheet. To create one like it, use Notepad to open the file, c:\windows\web\webview.css. Then use the **File, Save As** command to save the file in the figs folder as some filename you can remember, such as jen.css. Do not change the original webview.css file, or you'll affect all of your folders. After saving the file under its new name, change this line:

```
#Panel    {position: absolute; width: 30%; height: 100%; background:
white URL(res://webvw.dll/w98left.bmp) no-repeat; overflow: auto}
```

to this:

```
#Panel    {position: absolute; width: 30%; height: 100%; background:
white URL(file://c:/My Documents/jen.bmp) no-repeat; overflow: auto}
```

After you're done, the Figs folder's appearance changes to that shown in Figure 15.5. (By the way, you'll learn how to add a graphic behind the filenames in the right panel in the next section.) If you have more than a passing interest in programming web pages you might want to look at Teach Yourself Web Publishing with HTML 3.0 or one of the many books on Microsoft FrontPage 98.

Adding a Graphic Background to a Folder

In the previous section, you learned how to create an HTML Folder page to make many adjustments in the appearance of a folder. If you don't want to go to all that trouble, but you would like to add some pizzazz, a simple thing to try is adding a graphic image behind the file list in the right-hand panel of the Web page display. (See Figure 15.6.) You can also add a graphic to your file list display even if you're not using Web page view.

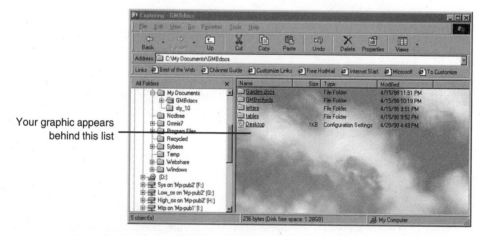

Your graphic appears
behind this list

Figure 15.6   Add a graphic behind the file list.

When selecting your graphic, choose something that is not too detailed, so text that appears on it will be easy to read. Follow these steps:

1. In My Computer or Windows Explorer, change to the folder you wish to customize.

2. Open the **View** menu and select **Customize this Folder**. The Customize this Folder dialog box appears.

3. Select **Choose a background picture** and click **Next>**.

4. Select a graphic from the list, or click **Browse** to search for one.

5. If you like, select a different **Text** color to use. Click **Next**.

6. Click **Finish**.

Removing Folder Customization

Whether you decide to customize a folder view by creating an HTML Folder page, or by adding a graphic background, you can easily restore your folder to the standard view:

1. In My Computer or Windows Explorer, change to the folder you wish to customize.

2. Open the **View** menu and select **Customize this Folder**. The Customize this Folder dialog box appears.

3. Select **Remove customization**. Click **Next >**.

4. You'll see a message asking you if this is all right. Click **Next**.

5. Click **Finish**.

Browsing the Web with My Computer/ Windows Explorer

With the help of the Links and Address toolbars, My Computer and Windows Explorer can be used to browse the Web as easily as you browse the Internet. The process is similar to using Internet Explorer:

1. Type the address of the Internet (or intranet) resource you wish to view in the Address toolbar and press **Enter**.

2. If you're not currently connected to the Internet, you'll see a dialog box asking if you wish to connect. Click **Connect**.

453

The page whose address you typed appears in the right-hand frame, as shown in Figure 15.7.

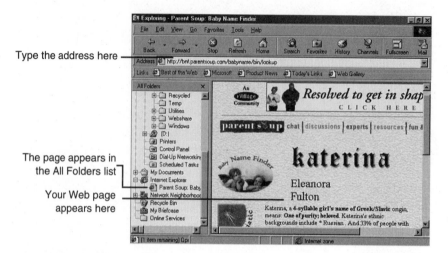

Type the address here

The page appears in the All Folders list

Your Web page appears here

Figure 15.7 You can browse the Web as easily as you browse your files.

Just as folders you've visited appear on the File menu, so do the Web pages you've visited in that session. So to visit a previously viewed Web page, simply open the **File** menu and select it from the list. You can also use the **Back** and **Forward** buttons as you would within Internet Explorer. (See Part V, Lesson 4, "Visiting a Web Site," for help.

TIP Browsing Folders You can also use the Address bar to browse folders on your desktop, or out on the network. Simply enter the path to the folder, such as F:\sales\jan\ and press **Enter**.

In this lesson, you learned how to use the Web style (single-click) option, and how to customize it for your use. You learned how Web style affects My Computer and Windows Explorer. You also learned how to use My Computer and Windows Explorer as a Web browser.

Networking and Mobile Computing with Windows 98

Using Network Neighborhood

In this lesson, you learn about network basics and how to use Network Neighborhood. You also learn the basic components of Network Neighborhood and how to change your network password.

What Is a Network?

Network is a generic term that refers to things or people that are connected. In the specific context of the work environment, a network is a group of PCs that are connected (typically by cable or phone lines) and can share information and resources. The Internet is a network, but typically we call it the Internet, Web, or World Wide Web. An intranet is a network, but typically we call it an intranet.

Two factors determine which term we use to define networks: how the computers are connected (cables, telephone wires, infrared devices) and how they communicate (the protocol they use). The *Internet* is a global conglomerate of computers that typically communicate over telephone lines using a protocol called TCP/IP (Transfer Control Protocol/Internet Protocol).

A *network* typically describes a closed environment of PCs with limited access (usually within a company or department) connected by cables, using a client/server protocol such as Microsoft or Novell NetWare.

An *intranet* is a closed environment (usually within a company or department) with limited access, in which computers connected by cables use Internet protocol (TCP/IP) to communicate. It is possible to have connections to the Internet, an intranet, and a network when you are working in a large corporation. It is also possible to dial into a closed network or intranet, depending on how your corporate networking is configured.

TERM **Protocol** A set of rules that allows communication between computers, such as HTML (Hypertext Markup Language) and TCP/IP (Transmission Control Protocol/Internet Protocol).

Here we discuss communication and sharing resources over an installed corporate network. For information on the Internet, and on dialing into a network, see Part V, "Windows 98 and the Internet."

About Clients and Servers

Most corporate networks consist of servers and clients, although some consist solely of workstations (called "peer-to-peer" networks). Peer-to-peer networks are networks that you can install at home to share computers and printers. At work, your PC is likely a Windows 98 client attached to one or more servers running Windows NT, Novell NetWare, or Microsoft LAN Manager (see Figure 1.1). At work, you might attach (log on to) more than one server: a file server on which you are storing files, a server running messaging software through which you send and receive mail, or a server that runs a specific software program such as Lotus Notes.

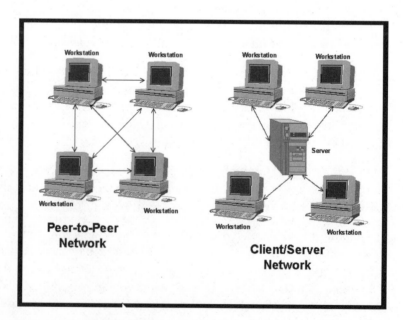

Figure 1.1 A peer-to-peer network connects workstations; a client/server network connects workstations to one or more servers.

Workstation   Any computer that is attached to a network for the purposes of using the network resources. A workstation computer can run Windows 98, DOS, Windows 3.1, Windows NT, and other operating systems.

Client   A computer running software that allows it to communicate with a server. A client is also a workstation.

Server   A computer whose purpose it is to store files or programs and provide file and program access to clients.

When you connect to a network, you gain certain advantages:

- Access to shared resources, such as modems and printers
- Access to shared data, such as files and directories
- The capability to send and receive electronic mail messages with others on the network using a mail program
- Access to shared software programs, such as Microsoft Word or Excel
- The capability to back up your files to the server (see your system administrator for more information)

If you are new to workstations, you may need a little time to become accustomed to choosing resources you need—such as printers and drives. But, for the most part you'll find working on a network is the same as working on a standalone PC.

What Is Network Neighborhood?

Network Neighborhood is your control center for network resources. Its existence on your desktop indicates that you have a network connection (although it doesn't mean you are necessarily connected at all times).

Access to Network Neighborhood requires that you be logged into the network; the login process usually occurs when you start up your PC. Some of these resources may require an additional login at the time you access the resource by clicking its icon. In Figure 1.2, Network Neighborhood displays links to computers in a workgroup and on a network.

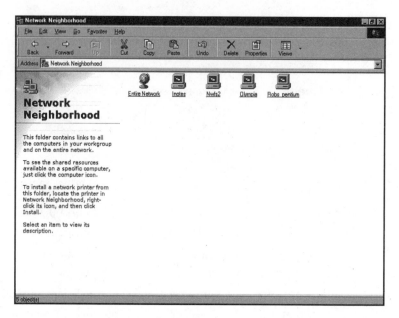

Figure 1.2 Network Neighborhood displays computers on the network. Double-clicking a computer will display its shared resources.

Workgroup A group of computers that share resources. They are also likely to be within close physical location to yours (such as in the same office or on the same floor in a building).

As shown in Figure 1.2, icons contain descriptive names to help you identify computers or servers by their names. Icons do not help you differentiate between a workstation and a client or server, so you need to know the names of the workstations and servers in your organization.

Windows 98 allows you to share your computer, local printer, and so forth, and these devices may appear in the Network Neighborhood when others access it. The Network Administrator determines what is to be shared in a corporate environment, however, and you should not attempt to share resources without consulting him first.

Network Administrator The Network, or System, Administrator is the person who oversees and manages the network. The administrator can grant a user permission to access certain files and resources, troubleshoot problems with the network, and control each computer on the network. The administrator has the ability to track each user's activities on the network.

If you have two computers running Windows 98 at home and one printer, you can create a peer-to-peer network and share the printer between the two computers. You can also share the drives on the computers, allowing access to each other's data. To share resources in this way, you need network cards and wiring in addition to Windows 98. To learn more about configuring networks at home, see *Windows 98 Unleashed* (Sams Publishing, 1998).

Logging on to a Network

To gain access to your network and identify your computer to other computers on your network, you are required to log on. You remain logged on until you are finished using the network. Then you log off. When you shut down Windows 98, it will automatically log you off the network, and your computer will not appear to other users in Network Neighborhood. You are also logged off automatically when you turn off your computer.

To log on, you usually need to type your user name and password. The user name that appears when you log on to Windows and the password you enter are those that you or the system administrator created. The devices provide security not only for your work, but for the entire network. Therefore, someone who does not know his or her user name and password cannot log on to the network. Your log-on screen will look the same as, or very similar to, Figure 1.3.

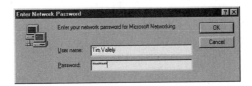

Figure 1.3   You must log on before you can access the network.

TIP   **Log On**   Provide a user name and password recognizable by network software (originally provided by your network administrator, although you may have changed the password). When you log on, you're essentially telling the network that you're ready to share its resources. The network uses your log-on as a key, of sorts, to identify which resources you may use.

Your Network Administrator has configured your setup to allow for access to software, servers, printers, and other computers. Your desktop may be part of that configuration, and if you log on under someone else's name and password, your individual customization will not appear.

Accessing Network Neighborhood

When you connect to a network drive, you add a whole new set of folders and files—not to mention other resources—to your working environment. After connecting, you can remain connected to that network while you work and can even access other servers and resources if required.

To open Network Neighborhood, click the Network Neighborhood icon on your desktop (see Figure 1.4). If the Network Neighborhood icon does not appear, your computer is not configured for networking. You should contact your Network Administrator.

Figure 1.4   If the Network Neighborhood icon does not appear on your desktop, your PC is not configured for the network.

If you click Network Neighborhood and do not see your network in the Network Neighborhood window, double-click the Entire Network icon. The Entire Network window opens, displaying the networks and domains available to you.

 Domain   A group of computers that share the same security system so that a user has to use only one ID and one password to be able to access resources within the domain.

Understanding the Network Neighborhood Window

Figure 1.5 shows the Network Neighborhood window displaying several computers as well as the Entire Network icon. Your display will differ from the one shown in this figure; it may show more or fewer computers, as well as their names. But the features of Network Neighborhood and the practice of using it are the same as we describe here.

The Network Neighborhood window contains only one Contents pane, unlike the Windows Explorer window, which is divided into two parts—drives and folders on the left, and the content of the selected drive or folder on the right.

If your Toolbar is not showing, choose **View**, **Toolbar** from the menu.

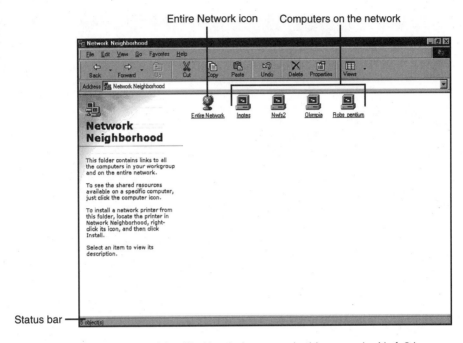

Figure 1.5 Computers are identified by their names. In this example, Nwfs2 is a file server; its name stands for NetWare File Server 2, named so by the Network Administrator.

If you don't see the status bar on your window, choose **View, Status Bar** from the menu. The status bar displays the number of objects (files and folders) in the window and the number of bytes they take up in memory space when an object is selected. If you select one or more files, the Status Bar changes to display the number of selected files and how many bytes of memory they total.

To open any server, computer, or folder, simply click the icon representing the resource. Items that appear in Network Neighborhood are items that you have permission to access. Figure 1.6 displays the resulting window when a computer icon representing computer Olympia is clicked. This computer has a shared local printer attached, as well as four shared drives, A:, C:, D:, and E:. Drive E is a CD-ROM drive. Its descriptive name, given by the user, helps others to know that it is a CD-ROM drive. Drive A: is a floppy drive. To learn more about sharing your drives, see Part VI, Lesson 3, "Sharing Your Folders, Files, and Printers."

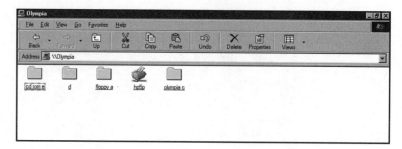

Figure 1.6 Drives are represented by file folder icons, printers by printer icons.

You'll learn more about moving around and selecting items in Network Neighborhood in Part VI, Lesson 2, "Navigating Network Neighborhood."

CAUTION

Can't Find Your Network? If you cannot access a network drive, don't panic. The server might be down for repair, a cable might have come loose, you might not have permission to view other computers, or some other problem might have occurred. These problems can easily be solved by contacting your network administrator or help desk.

Creating Shortcuts to Network Resources

You can create shortcuts to computers found in Network Neighborhood on your desktop, saving you from opening Network Neighborhood. You might want to do this if you access a computer or file server frequently. We don't recommend that you create shortcuts for everything in Network Neighborhood, or your desktop can become quite cluttered.

To create a shortcut, open Network Neighborhood, locate the resource you want to create a shortcut to, and right-click it with the mouse. Next, drag (with the right mouse button) and drop the resource onto your desktop, and select Create Shortcut(s) Here from the context menu that is displayed. Click the shortcut to access the resource. Remember, though, if you log off, or if the computer that contains the resource is disconnected from the network, the shortcut will not work.

Closing Network Neighborhood

You close Network Neighborhood just as you close any other window in Windows 98—by selecting **File**, **Close** from the menu or by clicking the Close button (X) in the upper-right corner of the Network Neighborhood window. Closing Network Neighborhood does not log you off the network.

Logging off a Network

There may be occasions when you want to log off the network but not shut down your PC. To log off the network, choose **Start**, **Log Off** (your name). (See Figure 1.7.) When the dialog box asks you if you are sure, click **Yes**. A new dialog box will appear, allowing you to log back on. Click **Cancel** when this box appears. Using this method, Windows will restart without logging you on to the network.

Figure 1.7 Use the Start menu to log off and on the network.

To reconnect to the network, choose **Start**, **Log Off**. Click **Yes** and supply your user name and network password. The log on dialog box will appear, where you can type a name and password.

Changing Your Password

For security reasons, you should change your network password—and any other passwords you use—on a regular basis. In fact, most networks can force users to change their passwords on a periodic or predefined basis by setting a

465

certain age limit for passwords used. Administrators can sometimes specify that passwords cannot ever be reused, forcing users to come up with creative ways to pick and, more importantly, remember passwords.

You may or may not have a Windows password. Your network password and your Windows password can be the same, if you wish. Changing either password requires that you open the Password dialog box. Here, we show you how to change your network password. In Part III, Lesson 6, "Sharing Workstations and Setting Passwords," we discuss setting and maintaining Windows passwords.

To change your network password:

1. From the Windows desktop, choose **Start**, **Settings**, **Control Panel**.
2. The Windows Control Panel opens. Click the Password icon, shown in Figure 1.8.

Figure 1.8   The Control Panel provides access to changing network and Windows passwords.

3. On the Change Passwords properties sheet (see Figure 1.9), click Change Other Passwords.

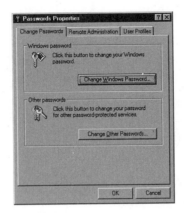

Figure 1.9 The Change Other Passwords button provides access to your network password.

4. In the Select Password dialog box (see Figure 1.10), select the network for which you want to change your password. Once you have selected the network, click the **Change** button.

Figure 1.10 You may see more than one network listed in the Change Password dialog box. Select the one for which you want to change your password.

5. Type your old password, and then type your new password in the next dialog box. You will be prompted to type your new password twice. Click **OK** when you are finished.

6. Your new password will take effect the next time you log on to the network.

In this lesson, you learned some network basics and the components of Network Neighborhood. You also learned how to change your network password. In the next lesson, you'll learn more about navigating Network Neighborhood.

Navigating Network Neighborhood

In this lesson, you'll learn how to change the way files are viewed in Network Neighborhood by changing settings found on the toolbar and menus. You'll also learn how to search for a file in Network Neighborhood or for a computer on the network.

Changing Displays

You can view the icons in the Contents pane in several ways. These choices are found on the View menu or by clicking the Views drop-down list on the toolbar:

- **Large Icons** This view shows the icons scattered in the window. Only the names of the files or folders appear below the icons (see Figure 2.1).
- **Small Icons** Shows the icons in reduced size, lined up in rows alphabetically (see Figure 2.2).

Views menu ⎯

Views drop tool on toolbar ⎯

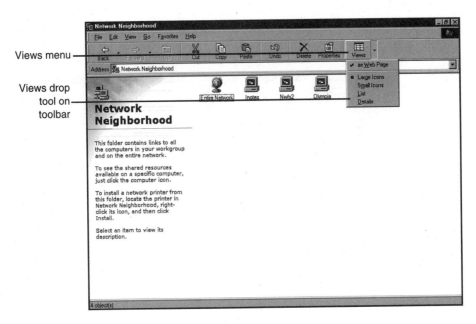

Figure 2.1 Network Neighborhood showing large icons.

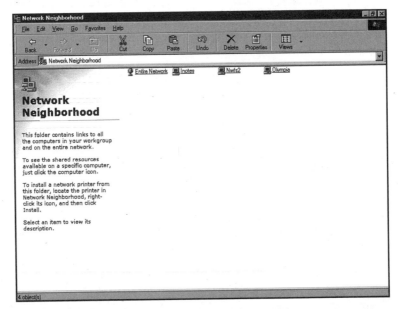

Figure 2.2 Network Neighborhood displaying small icons.

- **List**   Looks similar to small icons, except that it is organized vertically (see Figure 2.3).

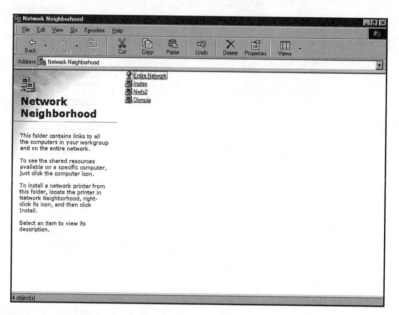

Figure 2.3   Network Neighborhood in List view.

- **Details**   Small icons are listed vertically, providing comments associated with the resource (see Figure 2.4). You can click the column headers to sort the resources by the information in that column. Click once for ascending order (A–Z) and again for descending order (Z–A).

The icons are generally shown in alphabetical order, but you can change the order by choosing **View, Arrange Icons**, and then selecting the order you want by selecting Comment, or select Auto Arrange to let Windows 98 arrange them for you.

If you've accidentally moved the icons around and you want them put in straight lines again, choose **View, Line Up Icons**. This option is available only for the Large and Small Icons views.

If you've made changes to the folder you're currently viewing and they haven't appeared yet, choose **View, Refresh** from the menu to bring the window up to date.

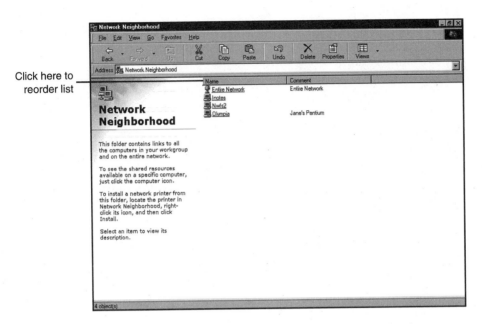

Click here to
reorder list

Figure 2.4 List view can be sorted in ascending or descending order.

Using the Network Neighborhood Toolbar

To see the toolbar (see Figure 2.5), choose **View, Toolbar** from the menu. Table 2.1 lists the buttons and what they do.

Figure 2.5 The Windows Network Neighborhood toolbar.

Table 2.1 The Toolbar Buttons

Button	Name	Use
Back	Back	Once you have clicked an icon in Network Neighborhood, this tool returns you to the previous view.
Forward	Forward	Once you have used the Back tool, this tool goes forward one view at a time.

Button	Name	Use
Up	Up One Level	If the window you are in is a folder on a drive or a folder within another folder, click this button to move up one level to the drive or folder that is the "parent" of the one you have open.
Cut	Cut	Click to remove a selected file or folder from the window and store it in the Clipboard.
Copy	Copy	Click to duplicate a selected file or folder from the window and store the copy in the Clipboard.
Paste	Paste	Click to insert the contents of the Clipboard into the active window.
Undo	Undo	Click to undo the last action you performed.
Delete	Delete	Click to delete a selected file or folder.
Properties	Properties	Click to bring up the Properties window for the selected drive, folder, or file.
Views	Views	Click the down arrow to reveal a list of views and select a different view.

Using the Menu

The menu bar on the Network Neighborhood window offers six choices.

- The **File** menu is context-sensitive and changes depending on which items you have selected in the Network Neighborhood window. Opening new folders, mapping network drives, creating shortcuts, deleting and renaming files or folders, checking file and folder properties, and closing the window are all commands found on the File menu. Use Work Offline when you want to view Web pages without connecting to the Internet. This works only if the Web pages are stored in a folder.

- The **Edit** menu includes the Undo command (to undo your last action), as well as Cut, Copy, and Paste. Use Select All to select all of the files and folders in the window and Invert Selection to select all the files and folders not selected while deselecting the currently selected files.

- Under the **View** menu is a series of options for looking at the files and folders with differently sized icons or in a different order.

- Use the **Go** menu to move forward or back or up one level. If you have an Internet or intranet connection, you can also use the **Go** menu to open a home page, visit a Web site, or open the Channel guide. Depending on your mail system and Internet connections, you can also access your email by choosing **Mail, access Internet news services**, and using News. To switch from Network Neighborhood to My Computer, choose **My Computer**. To open your address book, choose **Address Book**, and to use NetMeeting, choose **Internet Call**.

- Use the **Favorites** folder to access, manage, and organize your Favorites folder. For more information on the Favorites folder, see Part V, Lesson 6, "Working with Web Pages," or Part III, Lesson 4, "Customizing the Start Menu."

- The **Help** menu offers a way to open the Help Topics window as well as the About Windows dialog box. About Windows tells you which version of Windows you're using, its copyright date, the name of the licensee, the amount of memory available to Windows 98, and the percentage of system resources available.

As you can see from these menu choices, you can access the Web directly from Network Neighborhood. New features of Windows 98 include built-in browsing capabilities in Network Neighborhood, My Computer, and Windows Explorer. Of course, you can always launch your Web browser, such as Internet Explorer, to browse the Web, but by expanding Network Neighborhood, My Computer, and Windows Explorer, Microsoft has made it easier and faster for you to work the Web.

Because Network Neighborhood, My Computer, and Internet Explorer share similar Web capabilities, information on using these Web options can be found in one lesson in this book. To learn about these Web capabilities, see Part V, Lesson 15, "Web Integration and My Computer/Explorer," for more information.

Exploring Network Neighborhood

You may prefer to "explore" Network Neighborhood—that is, view it using a two-pane view, as shown in Figure 2.6. To activate this view, right-click the Network Neighborhood icon on your desktop and choose Explore from the pop-up menu.

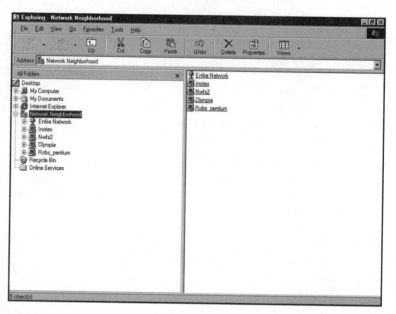

Figure 2.6 When you explore Network Neighborhood, it takes on the look and feel of Windows Explorer.

Not all files are displayed when you open a folder. Some system files are hidden. Also, if you are accustomed to DOS, you've probably noticed that no file extensions appear in Windows 98. For more information on DOS, see Appendix B, "DOS and Legacy Applications."

To change how and what files the Network Neighborhood displays, choose **View, Options** from the menu. Select the folder options you prefer. If you are not familiar with folder options, see Part II, Lesson 2, "Using My Computer." Folder options that you select in Network Neighborhood will apply to My Computer and Windows Explorer.

Finding a Computer or File on the Network

In addition to viewing folders and files in Network Neighborhood, you can locate computers or files on the network using the Start menu.

This is particularly useful if you know the name of a file but aren't sure in which folder it is stored on a file server—or, if you want to access another networked computer by name without having to open the Network Neighborhood window.

To use the Start menu to locate a computer:

1. Click the **Start** menu. Point to **Find** (see Figure 2.7), and then to **Computer**.

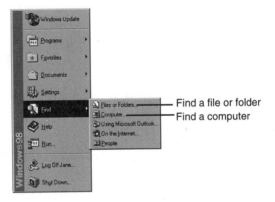

Figure 2.7 Use the Start menu to quickly locate computers, files, or folders in lieu of opening Network Neighborhood.

The Find: Computer dialog box opens, as shown in Figure 2.8. Enter the name of the computer you wish to find, and click **Find Now**.

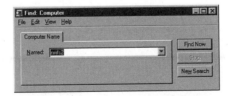

Figure 2.8 Enter the name of the computer you wish to access.

The Find: Computer dialog box expands (see Figure 2.9). When the computer is located, its name will appear in the Name field. To access the computer, click the computer icon.

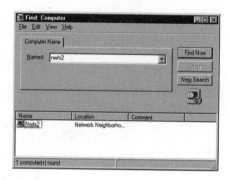

Figure 2.9   Access a computer's shared resources by clicking the computer icon in the Find dialog box.

A new window appears, showing you the shared resources of the computer.

To locate a file or folder using the Start menu:

1. Click the **Start** button and point to **Find**, then to **Files** or **Folders**.
2. The Find: All Files dialog box appears (see Figure 2.10). Enter the name of the file you wish to locate in the Named field.
3. Use the drop-down menu of the Look in: field to indicate which computer you wish to search (refer to Figure 2.10).

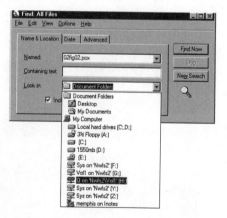

Figure 2.10   Available shared computers and folders appear in the drop-down list when you search for a file or folder.

4. Click **Find Now**. The dialog box expands, and the folder or file appears in the bottom half of the dialog box, as shown in Figure 2.11.

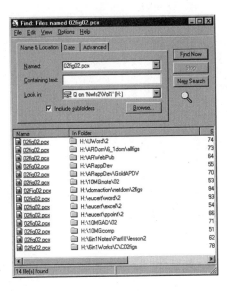

Figure 2.11 If multiple copies of a file exist within subfolders of the folder you have specified, multiple copies will appear in the Find dialog box.

5. To access the file or folder, click its icon in the dialog box. If you searched for and found a folder, clicking on it will open a new window displaying its contents. If you searched for and found a file, clicking the file will open the program that the file was created in and will open the file in that program. Of course, the file will open in its program only if you have the software program needed to run the file and if the file type is properly associated with the program. After you've located a file or folder, you can select it and then delete, rename, copy, or cut the file or folder.

To learn more about file association, see Part II, Lesson 9, "Registering Files."

In this lesson, you learned how to use Network Neighborhood to look at the files and folders on your computer or other computers, how to change the views, and how to use the toolbar and menus. In the next lesson, you will learn how to share folders, files, and printers.

Sharing Your Folders, Files, and Printers

In this lesson, you learn to share your folders, files, and printers with others on your network. You also learn how to map network drives.

Sharing Folders on Your Computer

It's a good idea to check with your Network Administrator before you share your folders, files, and printers on your network. He may have suggestions for you regarding shared information. For example, he may suggest that you put shared files on the file server instead of sharing the folders on your computer. Storing on the file server will save disk space on your computer. If you share a printer, your PC must be turned on and connected to the network in order for others to use the printer. Your Network Administrator might want to implement methods that would allow printer sharing using network resources, such as a printer server.

You can designate any folder, file, or hard drive disk on your computer as shared. When you share these resources you can assign them a share name to help others easily identify the item. This is helpful if everyone in the company uses similar naming conventions for folders, such as "My Documents" or for printers, such as "HP5." Using a share name, you can identify your folder as "Jones's Clients" or "Jones's printer." You can also assign a password to restrict access to the folder.

Once you have shared a resource, other users have access to it through Network Neighborhood. They must, of course, be logged on to the network in order to access the shared item.

Configuring Your PC to Share Resources

To set up sharing on your computer, follow these steps:

1. Choose **Start**, and select **Settings**, **Control Panel**.

2. Click the Network icon in the Control Panel. The Network dialog box appears.

3. In the Configuration page, choose the File and Print Sharing button. The File and Print Sharing dialog box appears.

4. Select the option **I Want to be Able to Give Others Access to My Files**.

5. Choose **OK** to close the dialog box, and Windows returns to the Network dialog box.

6. Choose **OK** to close the Network dialog box.

7. Restart your computer for the change to take effect.

After choosing to share your files and printers with others on the network, you can choose who can have access to them. Depending on the type of access control you have chosen, you may be able to specify individual people or groups who will have access to each shared resource.

To set access control, open the Network dialog box and choose the Access Control tab as shown in Figure 3.1. Select either Share-level access control to set a password, or User-level access control to provide a list of people. If you choose Share-level access control, you can assign a password to each shared file. If you choose User-level access control, you must specify a NetWare file server or Windows NT Server file server in the Obtain List of Users and Groups From box. For a small, home-based network or a peer-to-peer network, select the Share-level access control option. The User-level access control option is for client/server networks and may require assistance from a system administrator to set up.

Sharing a File, Folder, or Drive

Once you have configured file sharing properties, you can share a folder, drive, or file by following these steps:

1. In My Computer, right-click the file, folder, or disk drive and choose **Sharing** to display the Sharing page on the Properties sheet (see Figure 3.2).

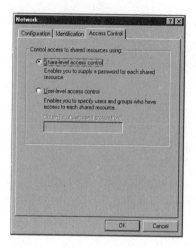

Figure 3.1 Access Control Tab where you can specify who has access to shared resources.

CAUTION

No Sharing Tab? If the Sharing tab is not visible when you open the Properties sheet, you must enable file and printer sharing services. To learn how to do this, see the "Configuring Your PC to Share Resources" section of this lesson.

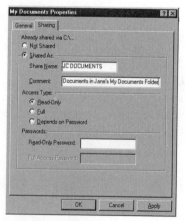

Figure 3.2 Share files, folders, drives, or printers.

2. Select the **Shared As** option.

CAUTION

Think About Sharing Your Entire Drive Before You Do! If you really want to share your entire hard drive, go ahead. But think first about the implications. Do you want people to have access to *all* of your files? Should you accidentally share your hard drive, remove sharing as described in this section.

3. You can accept the default share name for the file, folder, or drive—or type a new name in the Share Name text box.

4. Enter a comment text box, if you wish.

The comment appears in the *Details* view of your computer when other users select it in Windows Explorer or Network Neighborhood. (See Figure 3.3.) Comments can help users locate shared information.

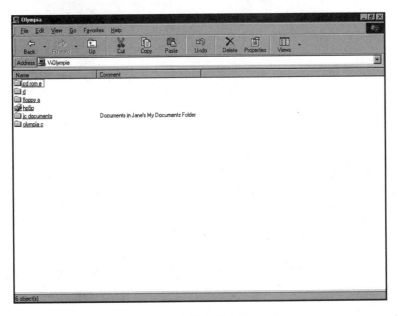

Figure 3.3 The Details view in Network Neighborhood displays comments you have added in the Sharing Properties box.

5. Select one of the Access Type options to specify the access for the shared resource.

6. You can grant users two levels of access to a shared file, folder, or drive. If you want users to be able only to read files and run programs in a folder, select the **Read-Only** option. If you want to be able to read, modify, rename, move, delete, or create files and run your programs, select the **Full** option.

481

If you want to limit access to the shared resource to certain users, assign a password to the resource and give the password to only those users. If you select the Depends on Password option, you need to enter two passwords—one for users who have read-only access to your files and one for users with full access. If you want all users to have access to your resources, don't assign a password.

7. Click **OK**.

You can quickly tell if you have designated a resource as shared by looking for a hand beneath its icon in Windows Explorer or My Computer as shown in Figure 3.4.

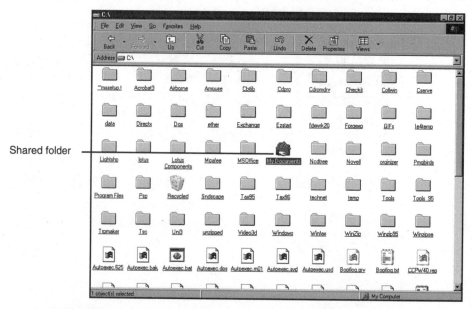

Figure 3.4 A shared folder displays with a shared icon.

To change the properties of a shared resource, click the resource icon with the right mouse button and change the share name, comment, access privileges, or password.

To remove sharing from a folder, follow these steps:

1. In My Computer, right-click the folder and choose **Sharing**.

2. Select **the Not Shared** option and click **OK**.

Sharing Your Printer

Peer-to-peer networks also enable printer-sharing. To set printer-sharing on your computer, follow these steps:

1. Choose **Start**, and select **Settings, Control Panel**.

2. Double-click the Network icon in the Control Panel. The Network dialog box appears.

3. In the Configuration page, select **Client for Microsoft Network**s from the list of installed network components.

4. Choose the **File and Print Sharing** button. The File and Print Sharing dialog box appears.

5. Select the option **I Want to be Able to Allow Others to Print to My Printer**.

6. Choose **OK** to close the dialog box, and Windows returns to the Network dialog box.

7. Choose **OK** to close the Network dialog box.

After choosing to share your printer with others on the network, you can choose who will have access to your printer by following the steps described in "Sharing a File, Folder, or Drive" found earlier in this lesson.

Mapping Drives

Windows enables you to use drive mapping when connecting to a disk or folder on another computer. Drive mapping is a method of assigning a drive letter to represent a path that includes the volume, directory, and any subdirectories leading to a folder. The drive mapping you create follows the path for you, thereby saving you time; instead of opening folder after folder, you can use the drive map to quickly go to the directory or resource. Mapping is especially handy when you're constantly using a file or resource on another workstation.

To map a drive, follow these steps:

1. Right-click My Computer or Network Neighborhood.

2. Choose **Map Network Drive**.

3. The Map Network Drive dialog box appears, as shown in Figure 3.5. Click the Path down arrow. If you have recently connected to the drive, the path appears in the list box. It the path is not in the list box, enter the path in the following format: \\computername\sharename.

Figure 3.5   The Map Network Drive dialog box.

4. If a password is required, you will be prompted to supply the password.

5. To reconnect the drive every time you restart your computer, select **Reconnect at logon**.

6. Click **OK**.

To break the connection to the mapped drive, follow these steps:

1. Right-click the My Computer or Network Neighborhood icon on your desktop and click the Disconnect Network Drive icon.

2. The Disconnect Network Drive dialog box appears (see Figure 3.6); choose the drive you wish to disconnect and click **OK**. The connection and the icon are now removed.

Figure 3.6   Disconnecting network drive mapping.

In this lesson, you learned to share your folders, files, drives, and printers with others and to disable sharing. You also learned how to map and disconnect a network drive. In the next lesson, you learn to share a fax modem.

Attaching to Network Printers

In this lesson, you learn to attach to printers within your network.

Working with Network Printers

You have already learned the basics of installing, sharing, and working with local printers. In this chapter we address how to connect to printers set up on the network by your Network Administrator.

Network printers can change location and are controlled by other users or a Network Administrator. If problems arise when you are using a network printer, troubleshooting is much easier if you understand how to attach to a relocated or new printer on the network.

Printing from Applications

Printing to network printers from within an application requires the same commands and menu items that you use to print locally. Windows handles the network communications and creates a Printer Driver for each attached network printer. As with local printers, you can access network printer configuration information in the Printer Properties sheet. In this sheet, you can change the network printer's properties for default or specific printing tasks. For example, you can specify the default paper size, number of copies, color options, and output quality.

When you select to print a document within an application, a print file is created by the application and sent to the printer over the network. A *print file* contains the spooled printer data and commands that are being temporarily stored prior to printing. The Network Redirector, which is part of the Windows 98 core network architecture, determines whether the print file destination is a local or network printer. The print file contains the data that is being sent to a printer containing both printable and unprintable characters. Unprintable characters are used to control the printer and, ultimately, the output of your file.

Drag-and-Drop Printing

To perform drag-and-drop printing over the network, you use the same procedure as you do for local printing. For more information on printing in Windows 98, see Part III, Lesson 13, "Printing in Windows 98." However, items printed using drag-and-drop printing are sent to the computer's default printer. Windows asks you to make it the default printer prior to printing the file. When initially connecting your PC to a network, this printer might not be available. Ensure that you are logged in to the network and verify your printer connection before setting it as the default printer.

You may want to create multiple shortcut icons to the same printer, each icon with different settings (like portrait or landscape). Copy the current printer shortcut to the Clipboard and paste it to the desktop. Click on it and then choose **Printer**, **Properties** from the menu. Set the properties you want for the icon. Then click OK and close the window. Right-click the icon and choose **Rename**. Enter an appropriate name and press **Enter**.

Adding a Network Printer

Adding a network printer is quite similar to adding a local printer and the same Windows Wizard walks you through the process. Connecting to a network printer requires that you know the printer name. If you are not sure of the correct address for the network printer, you can choose to browse the network. Browsing enables you to check which network printers are currently available. Some servers require passwords to view what network resources they have available. If you desire access to a server, but do not know the password, contact your Network Administrator for help.

You must also know the printer make and model. Again, if you don't have this information, contact your Network Administrator.

To add a network printer using the Add Printer Wizard, perform the following steps:

1. Choose **Start, Settings, Printers,** and then double-click the **Add Printer** folder.

2. From the first Add Printer Wizard screen, shown in Figure 4.1, click the **Next** button. Windows 98 then displays the next Wizard screen, which asks you to decide if you are adding a Network or a Local Printer.

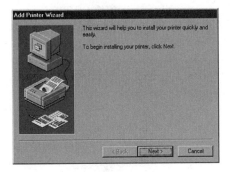

Figure 4.1   The first screen of the Add Printer Wizard.

3. Choose the **Network Printer** option to connect your PC to a network printer. Click the **Next** button located at the bottom of the window.

4. Next, identify the network path to the printer. Select the **Browse** button to view Network Neighborhood (see Figure 4.2).

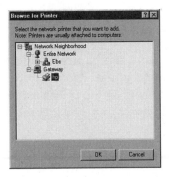

Figure 4.2   Use the Browse option to see printers on your network.

5. Network Neighborhood displays a list of all the servers and workstations connected to your network. Find the appropriate printer and select it. Then click the **Next** button.

   The Wizard accesses the selected printer and determines whether the computer that controls it can download an appropriate printer driver. If a driver is available, the Wizard automatically loads the driver and sets a default configuration for the printer. If a driver is not available, the Wizard asks you to specify the printer's make and model.

6. Select the manufacturer and printer model by scrolling the Wizard screen lists; then click **Next**. The screen now offers a default name for your printer. The name should adequately describe the printer for later identification.

7. The Wizard asks whether you want this printer to be your default printer; select **Yes** or **No**. Follow this decision by selecting the next control, as shown in Figure 4.3.

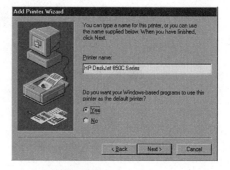

Figure 4.3 Enter a name for your printer and set its default status.

8. The final Wizard screen provides the controls to print a test page on the printer you just added. You can print the test page by selecting **Yes**; select **No** if you do not want to print the test page. As a general rule, you should always print a test page to verify the successful completion of the Add Printer Wizard.

9. Click **Finish**.

In this lesson, you learned to attach to and use a network printer. In the next lesson you learn about running Windows 98 on a Laptop computer.

Working on a Laptop Computer

In this lesson you'll learn some of the unique things about Windows 98 that apply only to working on a laptop or notebook computer. You'll also learn about traveling with a laptop or notebook computer.

Undocking Your PC

Because laptop (or notebook) computers are portable, they have some features not generally found on desktop computers. The Windows 98 operating system senses these differences, so you may find a few features on your laptop version of the operating system that you won't see on a desktop.

Many laptops today are equipped with docking stations. You remove the laptop from the docking station when you leave your office and take it home or on the road. The docking station usually has your network connection, if you have one, so you can access the office network when your laptop is docked at the office. It may also contain your floppy disk drive or your CD-ROM drive, although these may be removable so you can carry them with you.

Computers with docking stations maintain two configurations—one for when they're docked and one for when they're not. You may see **Eject PC** on your laptop's Start menu (see Figure 5.1). This appears when your computer is docked. When you select this option, Windows 98 tells the computer to undock. Then you can physically remove the computer from its docking station if it doesn't eject automatically.

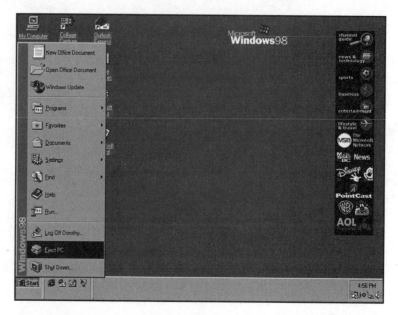

Figure 5.1 Eject PC appears when your laptop is in its docking station.

CAUTION

Switching Configurations The first time you switch docking configurations after you install Windows 98, the operating system will reconfigure your computer immediately after you boot up the system again. This will create a short delay before you can use the system.

Managing Power Consumption

Because laptops rely on battery power at least part of the time, managing the use of power can be important. You need to know how much charge is left on your battery. Normally, a power meter appears on the taskbar (see Figure 5.2). When you point to it, pop-up text displays the amount of battery power remaining (see Figure 5.3).

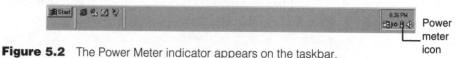

Power meter icon

Figure 5.2 The Power Meter indicator appears on the taskbar.

When your computer is running on the battery, the meter looks like a battery, as in Figure 5.2. The meter looks like a plug with a lightning bolt over it when your computer is plugged in and the battery is charging.

Figure 5.3   When you point to the Power Meter, pop-up text displays the current charge on the battery.

You may also have a Start menu entry called **Suspend**. Not all laptops display this option, but it is displayed for computers capable of a *standby*, or hibernation, mode. The standby mode allows you keep your computer available for use but conserves power consumption, which is important if you are running on battery power. During standby, your monitor and hard disk are turned off. When you start the computer again, the desktop is returned to the same state that it was in before you went into standby. If the **Suspend** option is not displayed on the Start menu, you may be able to choose **Stand by** as an option when you choose **Shutdown**.

CAUTION

Save Your Files   Before you put your computer on standby mode, save your work. The content of your computer's memory isn't saved on your hard disk while the computer is on standby. Standby maintains your laptop in its current state (where you left off), using only battery power to retain the RAM memory. That saves you from having to boot up open applications and files you were working on, and find your place in the file you had open. Saving your work is a safety precaution in case something happens while you are in suspend mode.

Setting Power Management Options

If your computer has built-in power management features, you have control over the settings for the low battery alarm, for different power schemes for the way you're using the computer, and whether the power meter appears on the taskbar. You control this from the Power Management Properties box.

To change the Power Management settings, do the following:

1. Choose **Settings, Control Panel** from the Start menu.

2. Click the **Power Management** icon to open the Power Management Properties dialog box (see Figure 5.4).

491

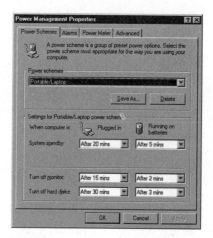

Figure 5.4   You set the standby timing on the **Power Schemes** tab of the Power Management Properties box.

3. On the **Power Schemes** tab, the **Portable/Laptop** power scheme should be selected. The other options are **Home/Office Desk** or **Always On**.

4. Set the amount of time that will elapse without activity before the computer goes into its standby mode. In the **System standby** drop-down boxes, set the amount of time to elapse when the computer is plugged in and when it's running on batteries.

5. In the **Turn off hard disks** drop-down boxes, set the amount of time to elapse without activity before the hard disk turns off when the computer is plugged in and when the computer is running on batteries.

6. Click **Apply** to apply the settings without closing the dialog box; click **OK** to apply the settings and close the dialog box.

To set the low-battery alarm:

1. Open the Power Management Properties dialog box and select the **Alarms** tab (see Figure 5.5).

2. Under Low battery alarm, check **Set off low battery alarm when power level reaches**. Slide the indicator to set the level of battery power at which you want the alarm to activate.

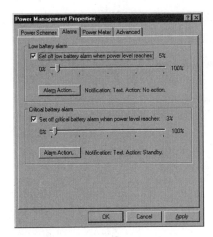

Figure 5.5 Set the options for the low battery and critical battery alarms.

3. Click **Alarm Action** to select the type of alarm—**Sound alarm** or **Display message** (see Figure 5.6). Under **Power level**, set the action to occur when the alarm goes off. Enable **When the alarm goes off, the computer will** to have an action taken and then select the action from the drop-down list— **Standby** or **Shutdown**. Enable **Force standby or shutdown even if a program stops responding** to force the action. Click **OK** to return to the Properties box.

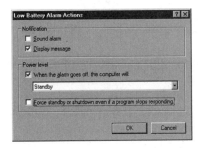

Figure 5.6 Select the type of notification and the action the computer takes when the alarm is activated.

4. Under **Critical battery alarm** (refer to Figure 5.5), check **Set off low battery alarm when power level reaches**. Slide the indicator to set the level of battery power at which you want the alarm to activate. To select the type of alarm or action, follow the instructions in step 3.

5. Click **Apply** to apply the settings without closing the dialog box; click **OK** to apply the settings and close the dialog box.

The Power Management Properties box also has settings for the Power Meter. Click the **Power Meter** tab and enable **Show details for each battery** if you want to see information for more than one battery in your computer. On the **Advanced tab**, check **Show power meter on taskbar** to see the meter. If you want to prevent someone else from accessing your computer by taking it off standby, check **Prompt for password when computer goes off standby**. Click **OK** to accept your changes.

Receiving Calls While on Standby

What if you need to receive faxes or email while your computer is on standby? If you have a PC Card modem, Windows 98 automatically turns it off when the computer goes on standby.

There is, however, an option to make it possible for your computer to receive calls (such as fax messages) even while it's on standby. On the **Advanced** tab of the Power Management Properties dialog box, select **Turn on computer to receive phone calls over the modem.** Then make sure you turn on the program that answers your phone before you put the computer on standby. If you have an external modem, make sure you turn that on.

When the call comes in, the computer becomes active for the duration of the call and then returns to standby at the end of the call.

Direct Cable Connection

You don't have to be part of a network to access shared folders on other computers. Windows 98 can help you set up a serial or parallel cable connection to another computer. If that computer has access to the network, so will your laptop.

To add a Direct Cable Connection, follow these steps:

1. Choose **Programs, Accessories, Direct Cable Connection** from the Start menu.

2. When the Direct Cable Connection Wizard appears, select **Host if** the computer you are sitting at is the one that has the resources you want to

access or **Guest** if you want to access the resources of another computer from this computer. Most of the time, if you are setting this up from your laptop computer, you should select **Guest**. Click **Next**.

3. Select the port you want to use. You must use the same type of port on both computers (serial to serial or parallel to parallel port).

4. Plug in the cable. Click **Next**.

5. On the other computer, set it up as the **Host** if your laptop is the **Guest**, or vice versa.

6. Click **Finish** on both machines.

CAUTION

I Don't Have Direct Cable Connection   Direct Cable Connection is a component of Windows 98, and it's possible that it wasn't loaded on your computer when you installed Windows 98. You must add the component from your installation disk. Follow the instructions in Help for adding a Windows component.

Traveling with Laptops and Notebooks

If you've never traveled with your computer, you'll find some basic and essential information here on how to do so with as little pain as possible. If you're a seasoned computer traveler, you might still find a few tips to make traveling with your computer safe and comfortable.

Obtain Local Access Numbers

Obtain local access numbers for your ISP or commercial online service provider and plug them into your program before you leave home. Hotels can charge as much as $1.00 for local phone calls. Why not save the cost for the call to obtain the local access number by obtaining it before you leave home?

Buy the Right Case

The number-one priority for traveling with a laptop (or notebook) computer is a good case. "Good" should take into consideration size (not too big, not too heavy), padding (to protect your computer) and straps (good, strong straps). The next consideration is the manner in which you will carry this case; on the shoulder, like a briefcase, or on your back. Laptop cases can be expensive ($40 to $200), and you should consider all of these factors before you buy.

Generally, cases with shoulder straps seem to be extremely popular. Be warned, however, that if you also own and carry a shoulder strap briefcase and a shoulder strap purse, adding a shoulder strap laptop leaves you one shoulder short!

If your travel involves extensive flying and running through airports, you might want to use a backpack computer case. This leaves your hands and shoulders free for your briefcase or other items.

Whatever you do, don't even think about packing the computer inside a suitcase or checking it as baggage. Packing it inside a suitcase, even nested among lots of clothes for padding, is a guarantee for breakage.

If your travel takes you by automobile, you might want to consider a short-handled or shoulder strap case that can fit on the passenger seat of the car. This way, when you're tied up in traffic, you can read your email.

Charge the Batteries

It may sound silly to remind you to charge the computer battery. But it's no sillier than admitting how many times we've left home without doing so. If you travel extensively, consider buying a second or long life battery for your computer.

If your computer uses PC cards, be aware that some PC cards (such as modems) stored in their slots while the computer is in a power down state may suck the battery dry in as little as two hours. Consider removing the cards when the computer is turned off and storing them in your case.

Remember the Supplies and Peripherals

We're not suggesting that you take the kitchen sink, but we do suggest that you think about how you will be using your computer before you leave for a trip. For example, if you plan to log on to your client's network, do you need to take a network cable? Here's a list of a few items you might want to pack in your computer case:

- **Phone cord**   You'll need to dial out to pick up your mail. Don't assume that the hotel will have a phone cord for you.
- **Extension cord**   Don't leave home without an extension cord! It's not unusual to find that the bathroom has the only available outlet in a hotel room. Beyond the obvious, working in the bathroom can make it difficult to reach the telephone jack.

- **Network cable**   This, of course, is necessary only if you have networking capabilities.

- **Map software**   If you have map software, why not take it with you? Many people plan a trip using their map software and then leave the CD at home when they are on the road.

- **Extra floppy disks**   You can save extra copies of your data files on floppy disks if your laptop has a floppy drive when it's portable.

Don't forget to copy all the files you need from your desktop computer or network. Use My Briefcase to help you (see Lesson 6, "Using My Briefcase").

Protect Yourself from Theft

Laptop computers are very, very popular with thieves. We've read statistics that claim one in every 14 laptops were stolen in 1997. We didn't witness these thefts and can't promise you that this figure is correct, but the figure represents an increase of 20 percent over 1996. Laptops are being stolen from airport security conveyor belts, parked cars, locked office buildings at night, and hotel rooms.

Here are safety measures you should consider:

- Never check your laptop as luggage at the airport. If you do and it's not stolen, it's still likely to end up damaged.

- If you decide to place it on the security conveyor belt, don't do so until you are the next in line to pass through the metal detector. Better yet: hand it to the security guard.

- Carry it in a nondescript case. Don't use a carrying case that has the manufacturer's name plastered all over it.

- Lock up the PC when you are away. If the hotel has a safe in the room and the PC fits in the safe, use it. Don't leave it in a drawer or, worse yet, on the desk in your hotel room, and don't check it with the bellhop.

- When you must walk away from the PC in a public place such as your client's office, remove the PC cards and secure the PC with a cable lock.

- Encrypt sensitive data stored on your laptop.

- Protect valuable data by using removable hard drives, if possible.

- Buy theft insurance.

Understand and Respect Airport Security and FAA Regulations

Although some of the newer x-ray equipment at airports has been designed not to damage your PC, check with the security guard before you place your computer on the belt. In most airports, expect that you will be asked to remove your PC from its case and boot it up at airport security. This is another reason for leaving home with a charged battery. Security will look to see that you are actually carrying a working PC, not some type of plastic explosive or something like that. It may seem an inconvenience to have to do this, but it is for your safety and the safety of others. Remove your PC and place the case on the belt for the X-ray machine.

There will be periods just before takeoff and landing when the pilot or crew will request that all electronic devices be shut down. There are some people who might advise you that this practice by the airlines is unnecessary—that your computer could not possibly interfere with signals and transmissions used for takeoff and landing. Despite what others say, it is our understanding that it is an FAA requirement to turn your equipment off when asked. So please do shut down.

In this lesson, you learned how to prepare for traveling with your laptop. You also learned some precautions you can take to reduce the chance your laptop will be stolen while you are traveling. In the next lesson, you learn about using My Briefcase.

Using My Briefcase

In this lesson you will learn how to use My Briefcase to transfer files back and forth between your laptop and your desktop computer.

What Is My Briefcase?

Laptop users who also have desktop computers often transfer files back and forth between computers as they work on the files, first in the office and then out on the road. But the problem is—which version of a file is most current?

My Briefcase is a special type of folder that helps you move files back and forth between the two computers and synchronize the file versions so both of your computers are up to date. The advantage of using My Briefcase is that you put all the files to be transferred in one place, which reduces the copying time, and the ability to see which files were changed so you can update the originals.

To open My Briefcase, click the icon on your desktop (see Figure 6.1). You can also open the folder from My Computer or Windows Explorer by clicking the folder icon there.

Figure 6.1   Click My Briefcase to open the folder.

The My Briefcase folder window resembles My Computer and shares many of the same features (see Part II, Lesson 2, "Using My Computer," to learn more about these features). Two obvious differences are the added buttons on the toolbar (Update All and Update Selection) and the Briefcase menu (see Figure 6.2).

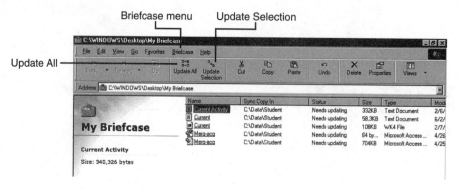

Figure 6.2   The My Briefcase folder in Details view.

Creating a Briefcase Folder

What if you don't have an icon for My Briefcase? Then you have to create a Briefcase folder. Follow these steps:

1. Right-click on an open space on your desktop.

2. Choose **New, Briefcase** from the pop-up menu. A briefcase icon appears on the desktop.

3. If you want to give the briefcase another name, right-click the icon, choose **Rename** from the pop-up menu, type the new name, and press **Enter**.

Adding Files to the Briefcase

Adding files to My Briefcase is only a little different from adding folders to any other folder. Follow these instructions:

1. Open the folder where the files you need are stored.

2. Make sure you can see the icon for My Briefcase or have the My Briefcase folder open.

3. Select the files you want to transfer to My Briefcase.

4. Drag the files onto the icon for My Briefcase or into the My Briefcase window.

Because My Briefcase is located on the same drive as the files you transferred, you might think that this action would move the files. However, when working with My Briefcase, the files you drag are only copied, so the originals remain in the folder from which you dragged them.

Refer to Part II, Lesson 3, "Managing Files with My Computer," or Part II, Lesson 7, "Managing Files with Explorer," to learn more about copying and moving files.

 TIP   **Send To**   Select a file or folder you want to put in My Briefcase, right-click it, and select **Send To, My Briefcase** from the menu.

Moving My Briefcase to a Floppy Disk

For two computers that are connected, either over a network or by direct connection, using My Briefcase is relatively simple. Just copy the files from shared folders on your desktop computer or network computer into My Briefcase on your laptop. Then you can work on the files in My Briefcase without the two computers being connected. When you reconnect the computers, you update the files (see "Updating Files" later in this lesson).

What's different about working with a floppy disk? Without a network or direct connection, you must resort to floppy disks to transfer the data from one computer to another. My Briefcase can make it easier for you.

1. At the first computer (for example, your desktop PC at work), insert an empty floppy disk into the disk drive.

2. Use My Computer or Windows Explorer to open the drive, making sure you're also able to see My Briefcase on the desktop.

3. Drag My Briefcase into the disk window. The files are copied to the floppy disk.

4. Remove the floppy disk and insert it in the other computer (such as your laptop).

5. Open My Computer or Windows Explorer so you can see both the floppy disk and the folder where you want to store My Briefcase, and then drag My Briefcase from the floppy to the new folder.

When you're ready to transfer My Briefcase back to the original computer, view both its current folder and the floppy disk. Drag My Briefcase back to the floppy disk. Insert it into the other computer. Then drag My Briefcase from the floppy disk back to the original folder or the desktop.

Checking File Status

Although My Briefcase makes it easy to copy all the files at once over the network or onto a floppy, it also lets you know which files have been modified.

To check the status of a file or folder in My Briefcase, do the following:

1. Open the My Briefcase folder.

2. Select the file or folder you want to check.

3. Choose **File, Properties** from the menu or click the **Properties** button on the toolbar, or right-click the file or folder icon and choose **Properties** from the pop-up menu.

4. When the File Properties dialog box appears, select the **Update Status** tab (see Figure 6.3).

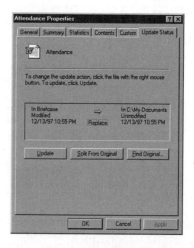

Figure 6.3 Check the status on the Update Status tab of the File Properties dialog box.

5. If the file in My Briefcase is the same as the original file from which it was copied, the words "The sync copy outside the Briefcase is up-to-date with the one in the Briefcase" appear near the top of the dialog box. "Up-to-date" shows in the center of the dialog box.

   If the file in My Briefcase has been modified and saved more recently than the original file, instructions appear on how to update the file. The word "Replace" appears in the middle of the dialog box. The arrow points toward the original file.

If the original file has been modified, so it was saved more recently than the file in My Briefcase, instructions appear on how to update the file. The word "Replace" appears in the middle of the dialog box. The arrow points toward My Briefcase.

6. Click **OK** or **Cancel** to close the dialog box.

CAUTION

It Says Delete! When your original file has been moved or deleted, the word "Delete" appears in the middle of the File Properties dialog box. If you know you didn't delete the file, click **Find Original**. If that doesn't locate the file, use **Find** on the Start menu. Once located, move the file back to its original location or rename it to the original name.

A quick way to see which files need updating is to view the files and folders in My Briefcase in Details view. One column in the Details view is **Status**. It shows whether a file needs updating or is up-to-date (see Figure 6.4).

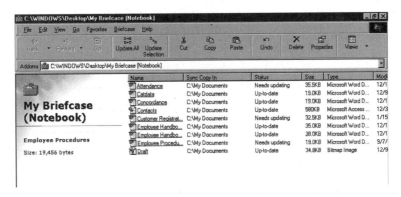

Figure 6.4 Check the Status column in the Details view to see if a file is up-to-date.

Updating Files

When you add a file to My Briefcase, a link is established between the original file and its copy in My Briefcase. My Briefcase synchronizes the two copies of the file.

In the Details view of My Briefcase (refer to Figure 6.4), the **Sync Copy In** column displays the path of the original file. It also appears on the **Update Status** tab of the File Properties dialog box (refer to Figure 6.3), where the modified or unmodified status of the individual files is displayed in addition to the last modified date and time.

To update the file that is out-of-sync with the other copy, do one of the following:

- Select the file in My Briefcase, open the File Properties dialog box, and click **Update**. Then click **Close** to close the dialog box.
- Select the file(s) in My Briefcase and then click **Update Selection** on the toolbar or choose **Briefcase, Update Selection** from the menu.
- Click **Update All** on the toolbar to update all the files in My Briefcase or choose **Briefcase, Update All** from the menu.
- Select the file(s) in My Briefcase and then choose **File, Update** from the menu.
- Select the file(s) in My Briefcase and then right-click on one. Choose **Update** from the pop-up menu.

Removing Sync Links

There may be times when you don't want changes to the file in My Briefcase to modify the original file, and vice versa. To break the link between the original file and the copy in My Briefcase, do the following:

1. Open My Briefcase.
2. Select the file.
3. Choose **Briefcase, Split from Original**.
4. A dialog box appears requesting confirmation that you want to prevent any future updates of the file. Click **Yes**. The file in My Briefcase becomes an "orphan" and cannot be updated.

The File Properties box also has a Split from Original button on the Update Status tab.

In this lesson you learned how to use My Briefcase to transfer files between computers and synchronize their updates. In the next lesson you'll learn how to connect to a network from a remote location by using Dial-Up Network.

Connecting to a Network from a Remote Location

In this lesson, you'll learn to attach to your office network using Dial-Up Networking.

Dial-Up Networking Basics

Remote access with Windows 98 is easier and more powerful than in any previous version of Windows. If you are connecting to an Internet service provider, using remote mail from home, or simply connecting to a server-based LAN, Dial-Up Networking can make the connection for you. Dial-Up Networking allows you to use the resources on the network as if you were physically connected to the LAN rather than remotely connected through a modem.

Remote access is accomplished with new Windows 98 networking components and a dial-up adapter, so you can easily use remote networking. Because remote networking is built in at the core of Windows 98, programs that require networking automatically start the Dial-Up Networking component when they run in order to establish a connection. A good example is Internet Explorer. When you attempt to connect to a resource that requires a network connection, Internet Explorer automatically opens the Dial-Up Networking dialog box to attempt a connection to the network.

Remote access with Windows 98 requires only the addition of a modem, installation of Dial-Up Networking components, and the phone number for the remote connection. This connection can be an Internet service account, a Windows 98 or Windows NT dial-up server, a NetWare Connect server, or other third-party servers. This section covers connecting to a Windows NT or Windows 98 dial-up server.

Preparing Your Computer

With Dial-Up networking, you can connect to a network and access shared information even if your computer is not a part of that network. Of course, you must have rights to access the other network and will undoubtedly have to provide a user name and password (supplied by your network administrator).

To prepare your computer for dial-up services, follow these steps:

1. Choose **Start**, **Settings**, and select the **Control Panel** folder. Choose the **Network** icon, and the Network dialog box appears.

2. Click the Identification tab of the Network dialog box, as shown in Figure 7.1.

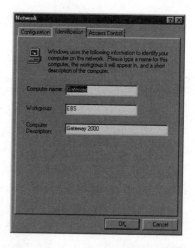

Figure 7.1   The Identification tab of the Network Dialog box.

3. Enter the name of your computer, in the Computer name text box. This name must match the name given to you by the network administrator.

4. Enter the Workgroup name. *Workgroup* refers to a Windows NT, Window 98, or Windows for Workgroups workgroup, the logical grouping of peer machines in a Windows network. This information should also be supplied to you by your network administrator.

5. Click **OK**.

6. Windows 98 states that you must restart your computer before the new settings take effect and asks if you want to restart the computer. Choose **Yes** to restart with the new settings.

Now that you have tackled the installation and configuration of your dial-up connection, you can proceed with configuring a dial-up connection.

Making a Dial-Up Connection

Windows provides a Dial-Up Connection Wizard that makes it easy to create connections for Dial-Up Networking. After the wizard leads you through the process, you're ready to make your call. To run the Wizard, follow these steps:

1. Open the **Start** menu and choose **Programs, Communications Accessories, Dial-Up Networking**. The Dial-Up Networking window appears.

2. Click **Make New Connection**. The first box of the Make New Connection Wizard appears, as shown in Figure 7.2.

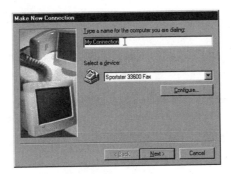

Figure 7.2 The Make New Connection Wizard.

3. Enter the name to identify the remote computer to which you will attach.

4. Select your modem.

5. Choose the **Configure** button if you need to set any specific options. The modem's Properties sheet will appear, containing such information as port, speaker volume, baud rate, data bits, parity, and so on. Choose **OK** to return to the Wizard.

6. Choose **Next**. The second wizard dialog box appears, as shown in Figure 7.3.

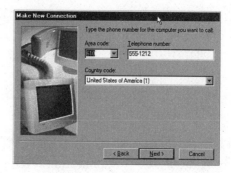

Figure 7.3   Type in the telephone number and country code for your new connection in this dialog box.

7. Enter the remote (host) computer's modem telephone number and your country code.

8. Click **Next**. Another wizard box appears, telling you the connection was successfully created.

9. Click **Finish**. The new connection is added to the Dial-Up networking window.

Modifying a Connection

You can change a phone number, modem configuration, and even the server type for a Dial-Up connection. First, you must open the Dial-Up Networking window. Then follow these steps:

1. Right-click the Dial-Up Connection icon you want to modify.

2. Select the **Properties** command. The connection's general properties sheet appears, as shown in Figure 7.4.

3. To reconfigure the modem, choose the **Configure** button. The Modem Properties sheet appears and offers options such as port, speaker volume, speed, parity, and so on.

4. To set the server, click the Server Type tab (see Figure 7.5).

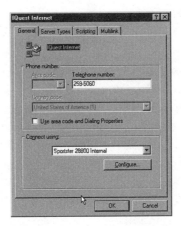

Figure 7.4   The Properties sheet.

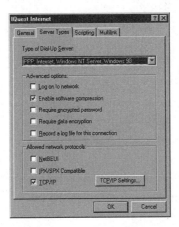

Figure 7.5   Select the server type you want to access.

5. In the Type of Dial-Up Server drop-down list, choose the type of server to which you want to connect. The drop-down list may include any of the following:

- CISPPP PPP Connection Using CompuServe Networks. You will have this only if CompuServe client software has been installed on your computer.

- CSLIP UNIX Connection with IP Header Compression. Use this to connect to the Internet, but only if your Internet Service Provider tells you to do so.

- NRN NetWare Connect. Use this to connect directly to a NetWare file server that runs NetWare Connect.

- PPP Windows 98, Windows NT 3.5, Internet. Use this to connect to a Windows NT computer that runs Remote Access Service (RAS), to connect to a Windows 98 computer running Dial-Up Networking Server software, or to connect to the Internet (but only if your Internet Service Provider tells you to do so).

- SLIP UNIX Connection. Use this to connect to a UNIX network or to the Internet (but only if your Internet Service Provider tells you to do so).

- Windows for Workgroups and Windows NT 3.1. Use this to connect to a Windows NT 3.1 or Windows for Workgroups computer running Remote Access Service (RAS).

Other choices may appear in the list if you have installed client software for third-party remote network access products. For example, if you connect to a LAN using Shiva LANRover or Shiva NetModem products, your Shiva client software may appear in this list.

6. In the Advanced options area, choose from the following options:

   - **Log on to Network**   Dial-Up Networking logs on to the network using the name and password you use to log on to Windows.

   - **Enable Software Compression**   Specifies whether data is compressed before it is sent. Speeds up the transfer, but both computers must be using compatible compression.

   - **Require Encrypted Password**   Specifies that only encrypted passwords can be sent to or accepted by your computer.

7. In the Allowed Network Protocols area, choose **NetBEUI** to connect to the peer-to-peer network.

8. Choose **OK** to close the dialog box. Choose **OK** again to close the connections properties dialog box.

Connecting to the Dial-Up Network

You can add further connections to your Dial-Up Networking window at any time. When you're ready to connect to the network, open the Dial-Up Networking window, turn on your modem, and follow these steps:

1. Double-click the **Connection** icon in the Dial-Up Networking window. The Connect To dialog box appears.

2. Enter your **Password**. You can choose Dial Properties if you have any last minute changes to make to the information.

3. Choose the **Connect** button. The Connecting To dialog box shows your progress. When the connection is made, Dial-Up verifies your user name and password with the remote computer.

4. When your logon is complete, Windows 98 shows the connection status dialog box that monitors the connection. You're connected to the remote network and can use any resources to which you have been given access.

CAUTION

The Remote Computer Hangs Up Unexpectedly There might be noise over the phone lines that is interrupting the connection. You could try calling again and hope for a better connection. Also, you might have gone too long without typing anything and have timed out.

In this lesson, you learned how to attach to a network using Dial-Up Networking and create and modify connections.

Appendixes

Installing Windows 98

In this appendix you will learn how to install Windows 98 on your system if you're upgrading from Windows 95 or Windows 3.1. Installation can take up to 60 minutes.

Before You Start

Before you load Windows 98 on your computer, check these system requirements. You may have to clear space on your hard disk, get a new hard disk, upgrade your memory, or upgrade your processor.

Your system must meet these requirements to successfully install Windows 98:

- A 486SX, 66 MHz or higher microprocessor.
- A minimum of 110MB of free space on your hard disk.
- 16MB of RAM.
- VGA or higher-resolution monitor.
- Windows 95 or Window 3.1 operating system, or access to a command prompt.
- Microsoft Mouse or compatible pointing device.

These are the minimum requirements. You probably will want more than the minimum of hard disk space available, and you may want to consider more RAM. Also, if you have a 486 computer you should be aware that Windows 98 may be sluggish.

You should also have a high-density, 3.5-inch floppy disk available to create an Emergency Startup Disk. You also need a CD-ROM drive or access to one through a network because installing from a CD is faster than a disk install and installation from disks may not be readily available.

It is possible to check if your hardware is compatible with Windows 98, if you have access to the World Wide Web. There is a Hardware Compatibility List available at http://www.microsoft.com/hwtest/.

Upgrading from Windows 95

As part of the Setup process, Windows 98 reads the information in your current operating system.

Follow these instructions:

1. Back up all important data files and close all open windows before you begin installation. This includes any programs from the StartUp window (see Part III, Lesson 4, "Customizing the Start Menu" to learn how to remove programs from StartUp).

2. Insert the Windows 98 installation CD in your CD-ROM drive or Setup Disk 1 into your floppy disk drive.

   The Windows 98 Setup window may appear automatically if you're using the CD. If so, skip steps 3 to 6.

3. Click the **Start** button.

4. Choose **Run** from the Start menu.

5. When the Run dialog box appears, click **Browse**. Select the drive where you disk is and the Setup file. Click **Open**.

   Or, enter the drive letter and file name in the **Open** box, such as d:\setup.

6. Click **OK**. The Windows 98 Setup wizard opens.

7. Click **Continue**.

8. Setup begins collecting information about your hardware and software setup. When the License Agreement appears, read it and then click **I Accept the Agreement** and then click **Next**.

9. Setup checks your hard disk(s) for problems and initializes the system's registry database, prepares the Windows directory (folder), and checks the hard disk for enough space to install Windows 98. Then the Internet Channels dialog box appears. Select the name of the country that you would prefer to use as the "channel set" for information of interest available on the Internet. Click **Next**.

10. To start copying the Windows 98 files to your computer, click **Next**. Once the copying process is complete, Setup restarts your computer.

11. Windows 98 sets up any plug-and-play hardware you have on your system and finalizes settings. It then sets up the system configuration, the Control Panel, the Start menu programs, Windows Help, and the MS-DOS program settings. Setup then restarts your computer.

12. The Welcome to Windows 98 dialog box appears. Click **Register Now** to register your software online (if you have an Internet connection). Click **Begin** to close the Welcome to Windows 98 dialog box.

Upgrading from Windows 3.1

As part of the Setup process, Windows 98 reads the information in your current operating system.

Follow these instructions:

1. Start Windows 3.1.

2. Back up all important data files and close all open windows before you begin installation.

3. Insert the Windows 98 CD into your CD-ROM drive or Setup Disk 1 into your floppy disk drive.

4. Choose **File, Run** from the Program Manager menu.

5. When the Run dialog box appears, click **Browse**. Select the drive where you disk is and the Setup file. Click **Open**.

Or, enter the drive letter and file name in the **Open** box, such as d:\setup.

6. Click **OK**. The Windows 98 Setup wizard opens.

7. Click **Continue**. Follow the onscreen instructions (see "Upgrading from Windows 98," steps 8 through 12).

Installing from MS-DOS

Before you start installing Windows 98 on an MS-DOS system that does not have Windows 3.1 or Windows 95 installed, you need to be aware that once Windows 98 is installed you may not be able to use some of your current software. That includes MS-DOS! Windows 98 becomes your operating system. To learn how to run MS-DOS programs from Windows 98, see Appendix B, "DOS and Legacy Applications."

Because of this, you would be well advised to back up your system before installing Windows 98.

You may also have to reinstall some of your applications after you install Windows 98, and you'll probably have to upgrade some applications to versions compatible with Windows 98. It's probably advisable to upgrade even your older software that appears to work on Windows 98, especially if it was designed for Windows 3.1 or DOS. The newer software is better designed to work on Windows 95 or Windows 98.

Windows 98 usually installs in the C:\Windows directory. If you want it to install in another location, allow the Setup program to create the directory for you. All you have to do is enter the drive and new directory name.

If you are using a network, have your computer name, workgroup name, and computer description available to supply to the Setup program.

Follow these instructions to install Windows 98:

1. Close all open applications and return to the command prompt (C:>).
2. Insert the Windows 98 CD into your CD-ROM drive or Setup Disk 1 into your floppy disk drive.
3. At the command prompt, type the drive letter for the disk drive holding your installation disk followed by a colon, backslash, and setup (such as, d:\setup).
4. Press Enter.
5. Once setup reviews your system for your current setup, software applications, hardware, and device drivers, the Setup wizard opens.
6. Follow the onscreen instructions to complete the installation.

Setup Options

The Setup wizard presents four options to you which let you choose what parts of the Windows 98 program to install. These options include:

- **Typical** installs all the components of Windows 98. Most users should choose this option.
- **Portable** installs the options that laptops or notebooks require, such as My Briefcase. It may not install all the other components of Windows 98.

- **Compact** should be your choice if you have limited space on your hard disk and you want the smallest possible installation. You won't get any of the components using this installation, so you will have to install any needed ones later (see Part III, Lesson 5, "Adding and Removing Software and Hardware").

- **Custom** lets you select the individual components to install with Windows 98.

In this appendix you saw the basic steps involved in installing Windows 98 as an upgrade. In the next appendix, you'll learn how MS-DOS fits into the Windows 98 picture and how to run your MS-DOS programs within Windows 98.

DOS and Legacy Applications

What Is DOS?

DOS, also known as MS-DOS and PC-DOS, is the original operating system of the PC. It provides a command-line interface, meaning that you see a plain screen with a prompt that looks something like C:\>. You enter a command at the prompt, and DOS carries it out, then presents you with a new prompt. If you run a program, for example, a word processor, the prompt is replaced by the word processor's interface until you exit from the word processor; then the command prompt reappears.

Windows is an extension of DOS. Among other things, Windows replaces the DOS interface with the Windows graphical interface. It also provides memory management so we can run multiple programs simultaneously (that is, we can multi-task). The earliest versions of Windows (through version 3.11) were obvious overlays of DOS—you booted your computer to DOS, then loaded Windows into memory by typing WIN at the command prompt. When you wanted to shut off your computer, you were supposed to exit Windows first.

Starting with Windows 95 (Windows version 4.0), and continuing with Windows 98 (Windows version 4.1), DOS sort of disappeared from view. The computer boots directly into the Windows interface and, when you shut off the computer, you don't have to return to a command prompt. But DOS is still there, lurking in the background, providing services to Windows.

You may be able to see DOS activity as your computer starts up. Perhaps a DOS screen will appear momentarily showing you that a DOS-based device driver started up. Or, if your computer did not shut down properly, at the next startup you might be prompted to run SCANDISK, a DOS-based program that will check the integrity of your hard disk drive.

And if you need to, you can boot your computer to a DOS prompt, instead of the Windows interface. Press Shift+F5 at startup to boot to a DOS prompt. Or press F8 to boot up to a menu of startup options (two of which are to boot to a DOS prompt).

Why is DOS important to you? Some of us still run programs that were designed to run from a DOS prompt. If you have to run such a program, you might have to configure Windows to run it properly. Some Windows-based programs will, when you add them to your computer, ask you to change a setting in one of the DOS configuration files, CONFIG.SYS or AUTOEXEC.BAT, which DOS reads and executes when you first start your computer. Yet other programs were designed to run under early versions of Windows. These programs won't be able to accommodate the long file names that Windows 95 and 98 permit you to use, and you will have to understand DOS file naming rules to use them. Finally, sometimes it is just easier to complete a task by entering a DOS command, if you understand DOS, than it is by a Windows method.

Understanding DOS File Naming Rules

Windows 95 and 98 permit you to name files and folders by using long, descriptive names. You can use up to 255 characters in a Windows 98 file or folder name. You can use uppercase or lowercase letters, numbers, spaces, commas, periods, and most of the non-alpha characters on your keyboard. You cannot use the following symbols: \ / : * ? " < > |. These symbols have special meanings to the DOS/Windows file system, and so don't work in file names.

DOS, on the other hand, and versions of Windows earlier than Windows 95, have very restrictive file naming rules. A name can have up to 11 characters, divided into two parts. The first part, the file name, can have up to eight characters. An optional extension, separated from the file name by a period, can have up to three characters. You can use letters, numbers, and most of the nonalpha characters on your keyboard. DOS automatically converts all letters to uppercase. You cannot use the following characters: \ / : ; , . * ? " ' = < > |. DOS file names cannot include spaces. Depending on the version of DOS, you may not be able to use the plus (+) or minus (-) characters.

> **Rule of thumb for naming files**   Rather than try to remember the arcane details of file naming rules, just remember this: Use letters and numbers. This way you'll never risk going afoul of the naming rules.

Programs that were designed to run under these earlier operating systems cannot read file names if they don't conform to the old rules. Windows 98 attempts to maintain backward compatibility with DOS by generating a second, DOS-compliant name for every file that you create with a DOS-illegal name. To create the second file name, Windows uses the first six legal characters of your file name, plus a tilde (~) and a number for the file name portion, and the first three characters following the last period (.) in your name for the extension portion. So a file that you name New Document.html would be called NEWDOC~1.HTM. If a file by that name exists, Windows will call the new file NEWDOC~2.HTM. If files exist with names through NEWDOC~9.HTM, Windows will create NEWDO~10.HTM, and so on.

The same rules apply when you create a folder (which, by the way, was known as a directory or subdirectory under DOS). So if you store New Document.html in the folder called My Documents on drive C:, the fully DOS-compliant name of your file would by C:\MYDOCU~1\NEWDOC~1.HTM.

If you use a file name at a DOS prompt in a version of DOS older than Windows 95, you have to use the DOS-compliant name. If you use a file name at a DOS prompt in Windows 95 or 98, you can refer to files by either name. But if you use a long file name and it has spaces in it, you have to enclose the whole name in double quotation marks ("file name"). Otherwise DOS interprets the spaces as delimiters between parts of the DOS command.

Using the DOS Prompt

If you ever need (or want) to use the DOS prompt you can display one in any of the following ways:

- In the **Start** menu, choose **Programs**, **MS-DOS Prompt**.
- In the **Start** menu, choose **Run**, then type *command* and press Enter.
- In the **Start** menu, choose **Shut Down**, then choose **Restart the computer in MS-DOS mode?**, then choose **Yes**.
- Create a customized shortcut that can act like either the first and second methods or the third method listed above, but tailored to your specific needs.
- As the computer starts up (when the words "Starting Windows 98..." appear on your screen), press Shift+F5.

- As the computer starts up (when the words "Starting Windows 98..." appear on your screen), press F8, then choose **Command prompt only** from the menu.
- As the computer starts up (when the words "Starting Windows 98..." appear on your screen), press F8, then choose **Safe mode command prompt only** from the menu.

Exactly which method above you use depends on your needs at the time. Each method loads DOS in a slightly different way than the others. Some DOS programs won't work properly if you use the wrong method to invoke DOS. Some features of Windows may not be available, depending on which method you use.

Windows DOS Sessions

The first two methods above open a Windows DOS session, that is, a window with a DOS screen in it, by running the DOS command processor, COMMAND.COM. When you want to close the Windows DOS session, you enter the **EXIT** command at the DOS prompt. When using DOS in this mode, Windows is still in your computer's memory, so you have access to your computer's hardware resources (things like CD-ROM drives) via Windows's drivers. But some DOS programs won't run in this DOS mode. By default, Windows will let you know when this is the case and suggest you switch to DOS mode, meaning that you should use the third or last method listed above to invoke a DOS session that does not make use of Windows drivers and features.

You can switch a Windows DOS session to full screen mode either by pressing the **Full screen** icon in the DOS window toolbar or by pressing Alt+Enter. You can revert to a DOS window by pressing Alt+Enter again. You can change the default so that a Windows DOS session always opens in Full Screen mode by opening the Properties dialog box and choosing **Full-screen** in the Screen panel.

When you are in a Windows DOS session, you can use the Select icon to enter Select mode, then use your mouse or the arrow keys to select a rectangular area in the DOS window. Then you can use the Copy icon to copy the contents of the selected area to the Windows Clipboard. You can also use the Paste icon to paste text from the Windows Clipboard into the DOS window at the cursor position. If you turn on Select mode by mistake, click the Select icon again to turn Select mode.

MS-DOS Mode

The third method listed above unloads Windows from your computer's memory entirely (except for a small stub), then loads COMMAND.COM. To end your DOS session, type **EXIT** at the DOS prompt or press Ctrl+Alt+Delete. The first "warm boots" your computer to reload Windows into memory; that is, it reloads both DOS and Windows. The second "cold boots" your computer; that is, it forces your computer to run its Power-on self test, after which DOS and Windows will reload. When using DOS in this mode, you only have access to your computer's hardware resources if you loaded DOS-based drivers into memory (via DEVICE statements in CONFIG.SYS) at computer startup.

 TERM **Warm Boot** A warm boot restarts the system without turning off the computer.

Cold Boot When you restart your computer by turning it off and then turning it on again, that's a cold boot.

You can also create a shortcut that will start an MS-DOS mode session but load DOS device drivers in memory as well. The easiest way to do this is to make a copy of the MS-DOS Prompt shortcut, then change its properties (the preceding fourth method). Right-click the shortcut icon and choose Properties to open the Properties dialog box. On the panel titled Program, choose the **Advanced** button to open the Advanced Program Settings dialog box. There choose **MS-DOS mode** and **Specify a new MS-DOS configuration**. Add DEVICE statements to the CONFIG.SYS file and any statements you want to the AUTOEXEC.BAT file. Instead of manually adding certain lines to these fields, you can press the Configure button and choose options from a list. The options you choose will become lines in the CONFIG.SYS and AUTOEXEC.BAT files.

When you use this shortcut to open an MS-DOS Mode session, Windows will force a cold boot of the computer to load a DOS session having the characteristics you set in your shortcut file. It will substitute the CONFIG.SYS and AUTOEXEC.BAT files in the shortcut's Properties dialog for the standard ones. When you exit the DOS session, the computer will cold boot again, this time back to Windows, using the standard CONFIG.SYS and AUTOEXEC.Bat files.

Booting Directly to DOS

The fifth, sixth, and seventh methods in the preceding bulleted list never load Windows into memory at all, but just load COMMAND.COM. You can't type

EXIT to end the DOS session with these three methods. Turn off your computer or press Ctrl+Alt+Delete to restart your computer when you want to end the DOS session.

When using DOS by the fourth or sixth method above, the statement "Windows is bypassing your startup files" will appear on your screen. That means that your system does not run any programs listed in CONFIG.SYS or AUTOEXEC.BAT, so hardware resources, such as CD-ROM drives, that get loaded via DEVICE statements in CONFIG.SYS, never get loaded and you don't have access to those resources.

The fifth method previously mentioned does run CONFIG.SYS and AUTOEXEC.BAT, so you do gain access to your CD-ROM drive if CONFIG.SYS has a DEVICE statement that loads a driver for it.

Running DOS Applications

DOS programs generally work on the assumption that no other program is running on the computer. They either manipulate the computer's hardware resources directly or they ask DOS to do so for them. When you run a DOS program from within Windows, Windows either sets up a *DOS virtual machine* for the program or actually unloads Windows so the program can run in a true DOS environment. A DOS virtual machine is a window environment that simulates a standard DOS computer environment. Most DOS programs can run in a virtual DOS machine, but some can't.

Just as with Windows applications, you start a DOS application by running its executable file. Windows 98 provides six different ways for you to do this:

- Choose the application's name in the menu. This runs the program on the basis of the shortcut file represented in the menu.
- Click a shortcut icon for the application on the desktop.
- Choose the application's executable file in Windows Explorer. If a shortcut file does not exist for the program, either in the folder where the program resides or in the Windows\PIF folder, Windows will create a shortcut in the program folder. If a shortcut file does exist in one of these two folders, Windows will set up the program's DOS environment according to the settings in the shortcut.

TERM   **PIF**   The settings for an application are stored in an application information file (PIF). This file has a .PIF extension to identify it. When you right-click a program's executable file and make changes to the properties, those modifications are recorded in the PIF file. When Windows starts a program it searches for this file to see how to configure the application.

- Enter the name of the application's executable file in the **Run** dialog box (which you can open by choosing Run in the Start menu). As with the method in the third bullet point, Windows will use a shortcut for the program if one exists in the program's folder or the Windows\PIF folder; otherwise it will create a shortcut.

- Enter the name of the application's executable file at a DOS prompt in an open DOS session (this is the old-fashioned way). The program starts in the DOS environment defined by the DOS session in which you enter the file name. Windows does not use or create a shortcut for a program when you start it this way.

- Use the START command in an open DOS session. The syntax is START *FILENAME [switches]*, where *FILENAME* is the name of the program's executable file and *[switches]* are optional switches defining how the program will start (enter START /? at a DOS prompt to see what switches are available). This starts the program in a new DOS session, different from the one in which the START command was entered. Windows uses an existing shortcut file, if it can find one, to define the settings of the new DOS session, or creates a new shortcut file for it.

You can recognize the executable file of a DOS program because its extension will be either .COM (for "command") or .EXE (for "executable"). Typically, small, simple programs will have a .COM extension and larger, more complex programs will have a .EXE extension. (By the way, all Windows executables have the .EXE extension.)

A third kind of executable file under DOS is a batch file. Batch files are text files that consist of one or more DOS commands, each on its own line. The file has a .BAT extension. If you type its name at a DOS prompt, the DOS command processor (COMMAND.COM) will read the file and execute each command in turn.

Windows (but not DOS) recognizes two other kinds of executable file, both of them shortcut files. Shortcut files pointing to DOS programs have the extension

.PIF (which stands for Program Information File). Shortcut files pointing to Windows programs have the extension .LNK (which stands for Link). When you click a shortcut, Windows runs the program to which it points.

Installing DOS Applications

DOS applications don't typically set themselves up to run in Windows 98. That is to be expected, because they weren't designed to run in Windows at all. Some DOS applications will come with an icon file and maybe a PIF file that you can use if you want to set them up under Windows. But beyond that, you are almost always on your own when setting up DOS applications to run under Windows 98.

To install a DOS application onto your computer you should follow the directions that came with it. If there aren't any printed directions, look for a *readme* file on the disk(s) that hold(s) the program. *Readme* files usually have the word *read* in their file names. If there is no such file, look for any file on the disk with a .TXT or .DOC extension.

Some programs you install simply by copying them to a folder/directory on your hard disk. Others may arrive in the form of a compressed file, and you will need to extract the program files from it. Still others may have an installation program, which will do the dirty work for you when you run it.

An installation program will typically have the word *setup* or *install* in its file name. If there is more than one file that looks like it could be an installation program, try running them. Installation programs almost always let you end them before they actually make any changes in your system.

Once you have installed your DOS application on the computer you will probably want to set up Windows 98 to run it. Whether you can do that or not and how you do it depends on the characteristics of the DOS application. They come in three general flavors:

- Programs that can run in a Windows-defined memory space and will let Windows dole out computer resources to them (that is, programs that can run in a DOS virtual machine).
- Programs that might put up with Windows but require exclusive use of your computer's resources (they *won't* run in a DOS virtual machine).
- Programs that won't tolerate the presence of Windows or DOS memory managers in memory at all.

Programs That Will Run in a DOS Virtual Machine

Most DOS programs will run in a DOS virtual machine defined by Windows. An occasional program might require that you tweak its shortcut's settings. But Windows 95 is very good at appearing to a program like a DOS environment. To set up a shortcut for these programs all you usually have to do is run them from the Run dialog box or by selecting them in a Windows Explorer window.

If the program comes with a PIF file, Windows will turn it into a DOS Shortcut for the program, using the PIF file's DOS settings. If no PIF file exists for the program, Windows will create one. It will look for the program in a file called APPS.INF, located in the Windows\INF folder. APPS.INF includes DOS settings for over 300 DOS applications. If the program isn't listed in APPS.INF, Windows will create a shortcut based on a default DOS environment.

Chances are your program will end up running fine in the DOS environment Windows chooses for it. In the rare instance that a program does *not* run well, or if it seems to be grabbing so much memory that there is none left over for other programs, then you can change the DOS environment by editing the shortcut file's Properties sheets. Do this by right-clicking the shortcut file (or the program file) and choosing Properties. This opens the Properties dialog box, where you can set all sorts of parameters for the program.

To determine what changes to make in the Properties dialog box, you should first run the MS-DOS Program Troubleshooter by choosing **Help** in the Start menu, then choosing **Contents**, **Troubleshooting**, **If you have trouble running MS-DOS programs**. This presents a help window that walks you through a list of possible symptoms then presents the solutions to you. Alternately, you can use the What's This? help (icon) to find out what each field in the dialog box means and experiment with settings to see if they improve the program's performance. If all else fails to make the program run acceptably, you should contact the author of the program to find out what Windows settings are best.

Programs That Won't Run in a DOS Virtual Machine

Some DOS programs require that you give them *exclusive* use of the your computer's resources. They cannot share resources with other programs. To run such programs from within Windows you have to revert to MS-DOS Mode, which is to say you have to unload Windows from memory to run them at all. That means that you can't run any other programs while such programs are running. You have to quit the program and restart Windows to run any other program.

To set up Windows to run this kind of program you have to create a shortcut that puts the computer in MS-DOS Mode. This is pretty easy to do, since DOS can detect when a program needs exclusive use of the computer's resources and will set up the shortcut for you. All you have to do is tell Windows to run the program, either by clicking the program in an Explorer window or by entering its file name in the Run dialog box.

What Windows does if it sets up an MS-DOS mode shortcut is turn on the MS-DOS mode option in the shortcut's properties sheet. You could do the same thing manually by choosing **Advanced** in the Program panel of the shortcut's Properties dialog, then choosing **MS-DOS mode**. In fact, you may have to choose **Advanced** to fine-tune the settings. For example, you might want to define CONFIG.SYS and AUTOEXEC.BAT files just for use by the program in question.

Programs That Won't Tolerate Windows or DOS Memory Management

Some programs simply won't run under Windows 98. Typically those are games that set up their own graphics environments and tax your computer's resources to its limits. Or they are programs that don't want to share the computer even with DOS; in effect they provide their own operating systems (or they *are* operating systems). Such programs require that you start the computer up to a DOS prompt instead of Windows. That means you must do one of two things:

- Set up your computer to display the boot menu at startup, so you could choose either Normal to start Windows or **Command Prompt Only** to load DOS but not Windows. Later you could start Windows manually by entering *win* at the command prompt. (This is how you loaded Windows in versions before Windows 95.)
- Set up your computer so it boots directly to a DOS prompt. From there you could run your DOS program or type *win* to start Windows. Optionally, you could also set up your computer so that CONFIG.SYS displays a menu from which you could choose to start Windows or your program.

Making the Boot Menu Appear When Your Computer Starts Up

You can make the boot menu appear either manually, by pressing F8 when the words *Starting Windows 98* appear on your screen, or automatically (so you don't have to hover over the computer as it starts up, ready to press F8 at the right moment). You can set a default choice in the boot menu, so it will make that choice after some number of seconds if you don't make another choice.

You can get the boot menu to appear automatically by editing the [Options] section of a file called MSDOS.SYS, located in the root directory of drive C:. Although the name implies otherwise, MSDOS.SYS is a text file. It is set by default as a read-only, hidden, system file, so to edit it you will have to turn off those attributes. Do that by entering the following command at a DOS prompt:

```
ATTRIB -R -H -S C:\MSDOS.SYS
```

After you finish editing the file, you should turn those attributes back on, either in the MSDOS.SYS Properties screen or by entering the following command at a DOS prompt:

```
ATTRIB +R +H +S C:\MSDOS.SYS
```

To set the startup menu to appear automatically when you start your computer, add the following variable to the [Options] section of MSDOS.SYS:

```
Bootmenu=1
```

If this variable does not appear at all or is set to 0, the boot menu does not appear except if you press F8 at startup.

To set the startup menu to default to a particular choice, add the following variable to the [Options] section of MSDOS.SYS:

```
BootMenuDefault=n
```

Where n is the number of the menu choice that should be the default. If this variable does not appear at all, the default is 1 (Normal) or 3 (Safe Mode), depending on whether Windows was properly shut down before the current restart.

To change the delay time before the boot menu automatically proceeds with the default choice, add the following variable to the [Options] section of MSDOS.SYS:

```
BootMenuDelay=n
```

Where *n* is the number of seconds before the system boots according to the default menu choice. If this variable does not appear at all, the delay is 30 seconds. Set *n* equal to zero if you want the system to wait forever for you to make a menu choice.

Booting Directly to DOS

To boot directly to a DOS prompt without the appearance of the boot menu, edit the MSDOS.SYS file (see previously), and add the following variable to the [Options] section:

```
BootGUI=0
```

If this variable does not appear at all or is set to 1, the system automatically boots to the Windows 95 graphical user interface. If the variable BootMenu appears and is set equal to 1, it will override the BootGUI variable; the boot menu will appear in spite of the BootGUI setting.

You can further automate the running of a DOS program at startup by entering a command in AUTOEXEC.BAT to start the program. If you want to have a choice at startup between starting a particular DOS program or starting Windows, then in addition to setting the BootGUI variable you can set up CONFIG.SYS to display a menu with the two choices. This is *not* the Windows 95 boot menu (which appears before DOS loads into memory) but rather a boot menu generated by DOS.

If, in the menu, you choose the DOS program, DOS reads the sections of CONFIG.SYS and AUTOEXEC.BAT that are necessary to set up the computer for the DOS program. If you choose Windows, DOS reads the sections of CONFIG.SYS and AUTOEXEC.BAT that are necessary to set up the computer for Windows.

To set up this menu, set up your CONFIG.SYS file as follows:

```
[menu]
menuitem=Windows
menuitem=programname
menudefault=programname,10

[common]
variables common to both programs

[Windows]
variables needed by Windows
```

```
[program name]
variables need by programname
programname pathname

[common]
more variables common to both programs
```

Set up your AUTOEXEC.BAT file as follows:

```
Commands common to both programs
goto %config%

:Windows
Commands needed by Windows
goto end

:programname
Commands needed by programname
C:\windows\win.com

:end
Commands common to both programs
```

In both listings above, *programname* is the name of the DOS program you want to run. The section titled [menu] in CONFIG.SYS contains the menu. The *menuitem* commands contain the menu choices. The *menudefault* command is optional. As written it sets *programname* as the default menu choice and 10 seconds as the amount of time that will pass before the system chooses the default choice itself and executes it. If it weren't there, Windows would default to the first *menuitem* choice and a 30-second timeout.

The *[common]* sections of CONFIG.SYS contain variables that DOS will read whichever choice you make in the menu. The *[Windows]* section contains variables that DOS will read only if you choose Windows in the menu. The *[programname]* section contains variables that DOS will read only if you choose *programname* in the menu.

Whichever choice you make in the CONFIG.SYS menu, DOS sets an environment variable called *config* equal to that choice (either *config=Windows* or *config=programname*). Then, in the AUTOEXEC.BAT file, *%config%* in the *goto %config%* statement is replaced by the contents of the environment variable, so that it becomes either *goto Windows* or *goto programname*.

:Windows, :programname, and *:end* are labels that the *goto* statements point to. DOS skips over every statement between a *goto* statement and the label it points to. So, whichever choice you make in the CONFIG.SYS menu, DOS executes the commands at the beginning of the Autoexec.Bat file, in the section preceded by the label of your menu choice, and in the section preceded by the *:end* statement.

Sharing and Using a Fax Modem

In this appendix, you learn to use Microsoft Fax.

Microsoft Fax Basics

Users who upgraded to Windows 98 from Windows 95 may have Microsoft Fax available to them if it was already installed under Windows 95. This program was included with Windows 95, but it doesn't ship with Windows 98. If you do have Microsoft Fax on your computer and you have a fax modem, you can send faxes directly from your computer.

In order for Microsoft Fax to work on your computer, you must also have Microsoft Exchange or Microsoft Outlook Express installed (see Part V, Lesson 10, "Configuring Outlook Express").

Microsoft Fax is compatible with Group 3 faxes worldwide, yet it also offers secure fax transmission as well as binary file transfer to another Microsoft Fax recipient. Microsoft Fax uses MAPI (Mail Application Programming Interface) so you can easily send a fax using an application's File, Send command or File, Print command, enabling fax in all users' applications.

Using Microsoft Fax

Unless you're sending your fax directly from an application—such as Microsoft Word—where you would follow the specific faxing instructions for that application, you compose and send a fax by doing the following:

1. From the **Start** menu, select **Programs, Accessories, Fax**.
2. Select **Compose New Fax** from the submenu.

3. The Compose New Fax wizard appears. Follow the instructions in the wizard to set up your fax message. Click **Next** to go to the next step or Back to return to the previous step.

4. The first screen of the Compose New Fax wizard asks you from what location you are dialing. Select that location from the drop-down list or click Dialing Properties and modify the settings (for more information on setting dialing properties, see Part VI, Lesson 7, "Connecting to a Network from a Remote Location"). Click **Next**.

5. You need to enter the name(s) of the recipients of the fax. Click Address Book to pick the names from your Outlook Address Book or enter a name and the related information in the fields provided. After you specify each recipient, click Add to List. When the list is complete, click **Next**.

6. Choose whether or not you want to include a cover sheet with the fax. If you click **Yes**, select the cover sheet you want to use (there is a separate Fax Cover Page Editor available to create your own cover sheets). Click **Options** to set a time to send the fax. Click **Next**.

7. Enter a subject for the fax and any comments you want included on the cover page. Click **Next**.

8. To attach files to the fax, click **Add File** and locate the file(s). Click **Next**.

9. To send the fax, click **Finish**.

To create your own fax cover sheet format, choose **Programs, Accessories, Fax, Cover Page Editor** from the **Start** menu. Click **Insert** and then select the item you want to place on the cover sheet. Move the item to place it where you want it on the page. Save the file when you're finished. The cover page will then be available when using the Compose New Fax wizard.

In this appendix, you learned how to send a fax in Windows 98 if you had Microsoft Fax installed before you upgraded from Windows 95.

Glossary of Terms

Accelerator Key   The one letter in each menu command that is underlined. Use this letter in combination with the Alt key as a keyboard shortcut to a menu selection.

Active Desktop Item   A special window whose contents is updated automatically on your system by its source computer (a Web site). See *subscription*.

ActiveX control   Element of a Web page created using ActiveX technology, a standard that Web developers use to create interactive objects and multimedia effects. With ActiveX, a programmer can create controls that react to user input and activity.

Address bar   The area of a window that shows the current file path or Web page address (URL). New file or address requests are entered here.

Application   A task-oriented software program, such as a word processor or graphics program. This term is also used to define programs within programs, such as a customer list within a database.

Backup   A specialized copy of folders and files that is stored as a file on a floppy disk, tape, or another network drive. Backup files can be restored in the case of damage or loss of original data files. Backup also defines the name of the Windows utility that backs up the files.

Bookmark   A mark set within the text of a Web page, enabling a link to some point other than the top of that page. In a word processing program, a bookmark is a placeholder that references a selection of text or a location of a document.

Boot   A term used to describe a computer's starting-up process, during which the operating system and configuration files are loaded into the computer's memory. A soft boot involves restarting the computer without powering the computer down; a hard boot involves restarting the computer by turning it off and then on again.

Browser   See *Web browser*.

Byte   A unit of measure—approximately the size of one character. A thousand bytes is a kilobyte (abbreviated K or KB), a million bytes is a megabyte (abbreviated MB, called "Meg"), and a billion bytes is a gigabyte (abbreviated GB, called "Gig").

Cache   A cache is a storage area for often-used information. Web browser cache folders are used to store frequently visited Web site addresses.

Cascade   The arrangement of multiple windows on the desktop in which each window is laid on top of another with only their title bars showing.

CD-ROM   A high capacity storage media. CD-ROM is an abbreviation for Compact Disc-Read Only Memory.

CD-ROM Drive   A drive that uses laser optics to read CD-ROMs.

Certificate   A file that verifies the identity of a computer when two computers communicate. Certificates are used to verify the identify of an email sender and to exchange and authenticate identities with an Internet server.

Channel   Web site to which one can subscribe to receive information from the Internet that uses Web pages that can update themselves, using *push technology*.

Channel Bar   A special toolbar that contains buttons for various channels. The Channel Bar appears on the Active Desktop, and also within Internet Explorer.

Client   In a network environment, a computer that uses programs or files located on a server and can make requests of that server. Also called a client computer or a workstation.

Client/Server   The relationship between the server computer, which controls the network and stores files and programs, and the workstation or client computers that are part of the network and access files and programs on the server.

Clipboard   See *Windows Clipboard*.

Compressed Volume File (CVF)   The single file in which the entire contents of a compressed drive are stored when you are using DriveSpace.

Compression   Reduction of the size of files.

Context sensitive   Software in which menus and help screens change depending upon the task or function being performed in the program.

Contiguous   Two items that are adjacent to each other.

Control Panel   A Windows utility that allows one to configure and customize a Windows environment, such as selecting screen savers, adding hardware, or changing desktop colors.

Copy   To duplicate.

Cut   To remove an item and store it in the Windows Clipboard.

Defragmentation   The process of reorganizing portions of files scattered throughout a disk and making those file portions contiguous. Used to help speed up processing time.

Desktop   The background on which all other elements of Windows 98 appear. Items on the desktop can be hidden, moved, and removed.

Dialog Box   A window that requires intervention by the user to provide information needed to complete or confirm an operation.

Disk Cleanup   A utility that automates the removal of old files, downloaded files, and cached files from your system.

Disk Defragmenter   A utility that reorganizes a disk to place all portions of files in contiguous order.

Disk Drive   A device that holds, reads, and writes information to and from storage media such as disks, tapes, or CDs. A hard drive is commonly called the "C" drive, designated as C:\. A floppy drive reads and writes to 5 $\frac{1}{4}$- or 3 $\frac{1}{2}$-inch disks, and is commonly designated as the "A" drive. As other drives are added to a computer, the operating system usually assigns the next unused letter of the alphabet to identify that drive. As a matter of practice, Network Administrators assign F:\ as the designated personal network drive.

Docking station   Hardware that a laptop can be connected to, containing power connections, connections for peripherals, and sometimes network connectors.

Domain   On the Internet, the last part of an Internet address (for example, .gov and .com). In networks, a group of connected computers that share the same security system, so a user has to use only one ID and one password to be able to access resources within the domain.

DOS   See *MS-DOS.*

Drag and drop   A procedure that uses a mouse to move objects to a new position onscreen by pointing to the object, pressing and holding the left mouse button, moving the object to the desired location, and dropping the object by releasing the mouse button.

DriveSpace   A utility that compresses the files on a disk to make more free space.

DVD   Digital Video Disc. A new CD storage medium with much higher storage capacity than a CD-ROM.

Email   Messages sent electronically over a network, an intranet, or the Internet.

Executable File   The file used to start a program. Executable files can be identified by their icon, which typically matches the logo of the software product and has a file extension of .EXE.

Explorer   See *Windows Explorer* and *Internet Explorer.*

Extranet   A group of interconnected intranets. Companies doing business with one another may form extranets in order to share certain types of information. See also *Intranet.*

FAT16   A file-allocation system older than FAT32 that limits the maximum size of a hard drive to 2GB. It allocates about eight times the amount of space to a file as the FAT32 system. See *FAT32.*

FAT32   A new file-allocation system available only with Windows 98 that utilizes less space per file than previous systems, resulting in a larger disk space capacity.

Favorites   A Windows folder used to store shortcuts to frequently visited files, folders, and Web addresses.

File   A set of information or data such as a document or a program or a graphic. Files require names and file extensions.

File Allocation Table (FAT)   A way to control the allotment of disk space utilized for each file.

File Attributes   Characteristics assigned to files (read-only, archive, system, hidden).

File extension   A three-letter abbreviation following a filename that describes the type of file (such as TXT for text, DOC for document, XLS for Excel spreadsheet, and so forth).

File Manager   A Windows 3.1 feature that allows users to view the contents of folders. Replaced by My Computer and Windows Explorer in Windows 98.

File Transfer Protocol (FTP)   A protocol designed for transferring large messages (files) between two points on the Internet, providing error-checking functions so that the entire data file arrives intact.

Floppy Drive   See *Disk Drive.*

Folder   A directory or container for files and programs.

Formatting   In disk management, formatting divides a disk into tracks and sectors, so the operating system can find and identify the files stored on the disk. In word processing, formatting refers to the assignment of characteristics to a document or font, such as bolding a font, or selecting a page orientation.

Fragmentation   The distribution of parts of a file over different areas of a disk. Over time, as a disk is used, spaces are created where files have been deleted. When new files are added, they are put into these spaces. However, if the file is larger than the space, other parts of it are scattered across the disk, filling other spaces. The file is therefore fragmented.

Frame   The areas that divide a browser window into sections so that several Web pages can be viewed at the same time.

Gig   See *Gigabyte.*

Gigabyte A storage measure equaling 1,024 megabytes, commonly expressed as 1,000 megabytes.

Graphical User Interface (GUI) An operating-system environment that represents software programs through the use of graphics, such as icons and pictures. Graphical User Interface supports the use of a mouse.

Handle The small boxes that appear around a selected object, such as a graphic image. Dragging a handle resizes a selected object.

Hard Drive See *Disk Drive.*

Hidden A file attribute usually applied to system files to make them invisible when viewing files and folders. This prevents the user from accidentally deleting or changing the files that are hidden.

Hit A match between search parameters and information found on a home page on the Internet. The more specific the search parameters, the smaller the number of "hits" returned.

Home page The first page that displays when a user visits an Internet or intranet site. The home page of a site usually contains a company logo and links to the other pages within the site.

Host Drive A designation applied to a portion of a disk when DriveSpace compresses files and stores them in a host drive. This is not a true drive, simply a designation applied to that portion of the disk.

HTML (Hypertext Markup Language) A collection of instructions or tags that tell a browser program how to display a document, as in when to bold or italicize text. HTML tags typically appear embedded within a document, set apart from the document text by angle brackets. For example. <B> means display the text that follows as boldface; </B> means turn off the boldface for the text that follows.

Hyperlink A block of text (usually colored and underlined) or a graphic which represents a connection to another place in a document or a separate document. Clicking on the hyperlink opens the document to which it is linked.

Hypertext Special text contained in a Web page that, when clicked on, takes the user to a related Web page. Hypertext often appears as blue underlined text, changing to purple text when clicked on.

Hypertext Transfer Protocol (HTTP) Defines how HTML files are sent and received over the Internet. See also *HTML*.

Icon Pictures that represent programs, folders, files, printer information, and computer information in both Windows 98 and Windows applications.

Image map A special kind of graphics link that contains several embedded pointers. Different areas of the image map contain different links to different Web pages or sites.

IMAP server A type of incoming email message server. IMAP is short for Interactive Mail Access Protocol. See also *POP3 server*, *Email*, and *SMTP server*.

Internet A worldwide conglomeration of computer networks that can communicate with one another. See also *Web*.

Internet Explorer Microsoft's Web browser.

Internet Protocol (IP) The system that defines the "location," or IP address, of the networks which comprise the Internet. See also *TCP/IP*.

Intranet A company's computer network working with software that lets it route HTML documents. The documents can be read on the company network using a Web browser. An intranet can span the globe, connecting offices of a large corporation. See also *Extranet*.

ISP Short for Internet Service Provider, a company that provides access to the Internet.

Java An interpreted programming language developed by Sun Microsystems. A Java program is delivered, in textual, compressed, or tokenized form, from an Internet server to a computer, where a Java interpreter or "Java virtual machine" (such as the one which comes with Internet Explorer) interprets and executes that program—just as though it were stored on the user's own hard disk. Java makes possible the transmission of logical and often user-tailored content (such as a desktop stock ticker), whereas HTML, by contrast, is merely a system for the format and display of text and graphics.

K or KB   See *Kilobyte*.

Keyboard shortcut   See *Shortcut Keystroke*.

Kilobyte   A storage measure equaling 1,024 bytes, commonly expressed as 1,000 bytes.

Laptop   A portable computer that can run on batteries. Some portable computers are also referred to as "Notebooks."

Legacy Program   Used to describe programs designed to run with an older operating system such as Windows 95, Windows 3.1, or MS-DOS.

Link   A pointer to a block of data, graphic, or a page in an external file. On the Web, a link can reference another Web page, a file, or a program, such as a Java program.

Local Area Network (LAN)   A network that connects a group of computers that are within an immediate area, such as the same building, and are connected to one another by network cable.

Log On/Log Off   Attaching to and detaching from a network. Logging on usually requires the user to enter a username and password.

Mailing lists   Services, generally automated, which send newsletters or similar material to an email address on a regular basis. Some email messages which are meant to be shared among a group of recipients are distributed through a mailing list server.

Mapping   A method of assigning a drive letter to represent a path to a network computer or file server that includes the computer name, volume (if a file server), directory, and any subdirectories leading to a folder.

Maximize   To increase the size of a window to full screen to view the entire contents of the window.

Meg   See *Megabyte*.

Megabyte   A storage measure equaling 1,048,576 bytes, commonly expressed as 1,000,000 bytes.

Menu   A list of related commands, organized in logical groups, that are used to perform tasks in Windows and Windows applications.

MIME Acronym for Multipurpose Internet Mail Extensions. An Internet standard that permits data transfer. An Internet browser or Internet mail viewer associates a MIME type with a file type, which gives information about which program should run when the file is opened over the Internet.

Minimize To decrease a window to a button on the taskbar.

Modem A piece of hardware, either internal or external, that allows one to send data via the telephone lines.

Monospace Font A font (typeface) whose characters are each the same width and take the same amount of space on a document. For example, "W" takes up the same space as "I." See also *Proportional font*.

MS-DOS Acronym for Microsoft Disk Operating System. An operating system program that interprets instructions to and from computer software and hardware. MS-DOS is text-based and does not use a graphical user interface.

MS-DOS command line The string of text and any accompanying switches that instruct the operating system. Commands on the command line include Copy, Print, and Format.

MS-DOS prompt The indicator on the MS-DOS command line that directs the operating system to the location that a command should be performed, such as a disk and directory: C:>.

Multimedia A combination of two or more mediums, such as sound, fixed pictures, moving pictures, and animation.

Multitasking The ability to run more than one program at a time.

My Computer An icon on the desktop that represents the contents of the computer on which it resides, including the files found on a hard drive, floppy and CD drives, applications, and folders.

NetMeeting A component that facilities the use of the Internet for free, private long distance calls. With NetMeeting and the appropriate equipment, one can share an electronic whiteboard, perform video conferencing, or share applications over an Internet application.

Network A group of computers and peripheral devices that are connected and can communicate with one another, allowing people to share information and resources. See also *LAN, Internet, Intranet, and Extranet*.

Network Drive   See *Disk Drive*.

Network News Transfer Protocol (NNTP)   A protocol used in newsgroup communication. See also *UseNet*.

Newsgroups   Public discussion groups on the Internet. Messages are posted to the newsgroup and can be read and responded to by others. Outlook Express can act as a newsgroup reader. See also *NNTP server, Thread,* and *Post*.

NNTP server   A server that handles newsgroup messages using NNTP, or Network News Transfer Protocol. See also *Newsgroups*.

Notebook   See *Laptop*.

Online Services icon   A desktop icon that runs a Wizard designed to make signup for an Internet service provider quick and easy.

Operating System   Software that controls the hardware of a computer and interprets the instructions from the software and operating systems to the hardware.

Outlook Express   A program that works with Internet Explorer for the purpose of sending email, participating in chat groups, and working in newsgroups over the Internet.

Pane   A portion of a window, usually divided from the remainder of the window by a movable border.

Partition   A division of a disk (usually a hard disk) that acts as a separate disk and has its own drive designation.

Password   A series of letters or numbers or combination of both used to log in to a computer, Windows, or a network.

Paste   A function that takes data that has been cut or copied from one document and places it into another.

Path   The full name of a file combined with the drive letter, folder, and subfolders that make up its specific location. For example, the spreadsheet file JanTax.xls is located in the January subfolder of the 1st Quarter folder, which is a subfolder of the My Documents folder that resides on the C: drive. The full path for this file is C:\My Documents\1st Quarter\January\JanTax.xls.

PC Card A card-sized, removable device for laptop computers frequently used for modem and network adapters. When the user plugs the device in, Windows 98 Plug and Play detects the device and loads the appropriate driver to use the device.

Peer-to-Peer A network that allows each computer in the network to access files on any other computer in the network. All people using the network store their files on their own computers.

Pixel One of the small "dots" that make up the screen. Each one is colored separately, but together they form the picture on the screen.

Plug and Play A set of specifications (such as a protocol) that allows the operating system and a computer to automatically detect hardware added to the system when the system is turned on, by reading the device ID and loading and initializing the device drivers. It also notifies applications that the device is available.

Pointer An onscreen icon that represents the computer's mouse, trackball, touchpad, or other selecting device. Use it to select items and choose commands.

POP3 server One type of incoming email server. POP is short for Post Office Protocol. See also *Email, IMAP server,* and *SMTP server.*

Pop-up menu A menu which appears when an item is right-clicked. Also called a shortcut menu.

Post To place a message in a newsgroup. See also *Newsgroup* and *Thread.*

Program A list of instructions to the computer coded to accomplish a specific task or group of tasks, such as an operating system or application.

Program Manager A Windows 3.1 feature that allowed users to view a list of installed programs. Replaced by the Start button and Taskbar in Windows 98.

Properties The distinct options or settings applied to an item.

Proportional font A font (typeface) whose characters are of different widths. For example, in a proportional font, "W" takes up more space than "I." See also *Monospace font.*

Protocol A set of rules that governs the transmission of data over the Internet. See *File Transfer Protocol, HyperText Transfer Protocol, Internet Protocol, Network News Transfer Protocol, Telnet,* and *Transmission Control Protocol.*

Proxy server   A computer that acts as a client in the server/client connection, through which information is passed before it is sent to the real client. Proxy servers are used to improve access time on the Internet, by caching frequently requested information. Proxy servers can also be used to prevent unauthorized access.

Push technology   A method that allows the server to send information to a client without a client request.

Read-Only   A file attribute that prevents the user from changing the file, although the file can be viewed, without saving the file to another name.

Recycle Bin   A Windows 98 folder that stores deleted files. Files in the Recycle Bin are not removed from your disk until you empty the Recycle Bin.

Registration   The association between a file and its originating application that allows the user to click and open a file and its application simultaneously.

Restore   To convert backed-up files to their original state and, if desired, their original location.

Save   To store a file on a disk, tape, or CD-ROM.

Save As   A menu selection used to save a file while giving the file a new name or location.

ScanDisk   A Windows utility that checks a disk for damaged files.

Search engine   A special program that allows users to find information on the Internet by typing in a key word or phrase. The search engine searches the Internet for pages containing the key word or phrase. The search engine then returns a list of Web addresses to the browser which are active links to pages on which the key word or phrase was found.

Server   A computer whose purpose is to store files or programs and provide file, program, and resource access to clients.

Shortcut, Desktop   An icon representing a program, printer, or file often placed on the Desktop for quick access to frequently used items.

Shortcut Keystroke   A keystroke or combination of keystrokes that allows a task to be performed more quickly and simply, without using a mouse.

Shortcut Menu See *Pop-up menu*.

Shut down The recommended Windows command used to exit Windows prior to turning off a computer.

Single-click option See *Web Style*.

SMTP server An outgoing email message server. SMTP is short for Simple Mail Transfer Protocol. See also *Email, IMAP server*, and *POP3 server*.

Standby A hibernation mode which keeps battery-powered computers available for use, but conserves power consumption. The monitor and hard disk are turned off during standby. This is also referred to as *suspend*.

Start Button A button on the Windows 98 taskbar that displays a menu from which applications, documents, programs, and Windows options can be accessed as well as Help and Windows shutdown menus.

Start page The first page displayed on Internet Explorer. From this page, one can access other Web sites.

Status bar The bar across the bottom of the window that describes the contents of the window, such as free space, number of objects or files in a window, and so on.

Submenu A secondary menu which appears when a primary menu item is selected.

Subscription A Web page, channel, or Active Desktop Item whose information is updated on a computer at preset intervals determined by the user. Subscriptions also apply to newsgroups. See also *Channel, Active Desktop Item,* and *Newsgroups*.

Surfing Browsing the Internet; similar to browsing or "surfing" channels on cable TV.

Suspend A hibernation mode, which keeps battery-powered computers available for use, but conserves power consumption. The monitor and hard disk are turned off during standby. This is also referred to as *Standby*. Suspend is a command on the Start Menu.

Swap File An area of the hard disk set aside to supplement RAM. See *Virtual Memory*.

System Administrator   The person who oversees and manages a network. The administrator can grant a user permission to access certain files and resources, troubleshoot problems with the network, and control each computer on the network. The administrator has the ability to track each user's activities on the network.

System Files   Files that are necessary to run the Windows 98 operating system.

Task Scheduler   A Windows 98 utility program that allows Windows 98 to automatically perform selected tasks, such as backing up.

Taskbar   A bar at the bottom of a window that contains the Start button, any open application or window buttons, and the time. Clicking a taskbar button opens the window or application it represents.

TCP/IP   See *Transmission Control Protocol*. This term stands for Transmission Control Protocol/Internet Protocol.

Telnet   A protocol that defines how one computer can act like a terminal on another. Using a telnet program, one can log on to another computer and run programs on it, just as though they were sitting at its own console.

Thread   The display of related documents or email messages in outline form. A thread displays the order of new documents or newsgroup messages and their replies form a thread, which, when read, forms a discussion.

Tile   A Windows option that displays all open windows at the same time, so that they appear side by side (vertically), or one on top of the other (horizontally).

Toolbar   A bar in a window that displays graphic tool buttons that represent shortcuts to various menu commands.

Transmission Control Protocol (TCP)   The protocol that defines how data should be sent from point to point over the Internet. Following TCP protocol, data is broken into packets which are flushed through the Internet in the general direction of their recipient. There, they are collected and reorganized into their original sequence. Because TCP and IP protocols work hand in hand, people refer to them together as TCP/IP.

Uniform Resource Locator   See *URL*.

URL (Uniform Resource Locator)   A pointer to the location of an object, usually the address of an Internet resource. URLs conform to a standard syntax which generally appears as follows: [protocol]://[host].[domain], such as www.mcp.com.

UseNet   A network of NNTP servers, which provides access to Internet newsgroups. A news reader, such as Outlook Express News, is necessary to view and send newsgroup messages. See also *Network News Transfer Protocol*.

Username   The name by which one is identified to the computer or network.

Virtual Memory   A swap file created when additional RAM is needed for a program or document. Some of the program code and data are swapped temporarily to a special file on the hard disk called a swap file. This swap file, or virtual memory, isn't visible but allows the computer to run more programs at the same time than RAM would normally allow.

WAIS (Wide Area Information Server)   The first widely used system for cataloging information and files on the Internet, in which the catalog can be *queried* using simple, everyday language. A user places a query to a WAIS database, and the WAIS server responds with a listing of files or other data which the server concludes best responds to the query.

Web   The *World Wide Web* (or just *Web*) is a component of the Internet. It is a collection of HTML documents accessible through the Internet.

Web Address   See *URL*.

Web browser   A software program that allows users to read and download documents on the Web, use hyperlinks, receive email, and access newsgroups.

Web Help   The latest Windows 98 technical support available from a Web site, accessed through the Help menu.

Web Page   One of the HTML documents that makes up the World Wide Web.

Web Site   A group of related Web pages.

Web Style   A Windows 98 option that changes how objects are selected in Windows. When Web style is turned on, a single-click opens objects, and pointing to objects, selects them.

WebBot   Object inserted into a Web page which allows viewers to perform tasks such as searching a Web site.

Window A boxed area in which programs, files, folders, drives, icons representing programs are viewed. Files of folders and other elements.

Windows Clipboard A Windows function that allows data to be cut or copied from one file, stored on the clipboard, and then transferred to another file.

Windows Explorer A Windows feature designed to display drives, folders, and files. Unlike My Computer, everything is contained in one window. The list of all drives and folders on a system or network is on the left, and the contents of the selected folder or drive are on the right.

Windows Fine Tune Wizard A utility that schedules tasks to clean up unnecessary files on a hard disk, scan for disk errors, and defragment a disk.

Windows NT A Microsoft operating system, similar in many ways to Windows 98, that has separate server and workstation versions.

Wizard An interactive mini-program, designed to assist users in a particular feature or function of the software or operating system.

Workgroup A group of people working together and sharing computer data, often over a company intranet.

Working offline Working with Internet-related documents while disconnected from the Internet.

Workstation A computer used for work by an individual. Workstations can be standalone computers, or networked computers (see also *Client*).

Index

A

accelerator keys, 131, 535
accessibility options for
physically challenged users
automatic timeouts, 276
bounce keys, 275
color settings, 275
font sizes, 274
icon size, 275
MouseKeys, 276
scroll bars, 275
sound sentry, 275
sticky keys, 275
text size, 275
toggle keys, 275
Accessibility Properties dialog box, 277
Accessibility Settings Wizard
accessibility options, 273-276
launching, 273
accessing
Control Panel, 175-177
from desktop, 175-177
from Explorer, 175-177
from taskbar, 175-177
files (Network Neighborhood), 479-482
folders (Network Neighborhood), 479
Start menu properties, 208-209

Accessories menu commands, Fax, 533
activating Web-style option, 444-445
Active Desktop Item (Internet Explorer 4.0), 535
push technology, 397-398
subscribing, 397-398
methods (Web pages), 392-393
active windows, 286
ActiveMovie player
compatible file types, 317
launching, 317
ActiveX control, 535
Add Active Channel Content dialog box, 395
Add Echo command (Effects menu), 315
Add Favorite dialog box, 209, 377
Add New File Type dialog box, 129
Add New Hardware (Control Panel), 177
Add New Hardware Wizard, 219-220
Add or Remove Fonts (Control Panel), 178
Add or Remove Programs (Control Panel), 178
Add or Switch Screen Savers (Control Panel), 178

Add Printer Wizard, 267-268
network printers, adding, 486-488
Add to Favorites command (Favorites menu), 209, 377
Add/Remove Programs icon (Control Panel), software installation methods, 216-217
adding
files (My Briefcase), 500-501
fonts, 254-255
hypertext links in Web pages (FrontPage Express), 435-436
items to toolbars, 202
modems to system, 240-242
network printers (Network Administrator), 486-488
programs to Start menu, 205-208
sites
local intranet zone, 389-390
restricted sites zone, 389
trusted sites zone, 389
text to graphics (Paint), 308-310
Web pages to Favorites folder (Internet Explorer 4.0), 377-378
Windows 98 components, 220-222

Address Bar
  Explorer, 108-109
  My Computer, 78
Address Book
  address groups, 417
  address information,
    entering, 415-417
  email
    composing messages,
      417-418
    unread status, 418
**Address toolbar (Internet
  Explorer 4.0), 348**
**addressing email (Outlook
  Express), 413**
**Adjust System and Program
  Sounds (Control Panel), 179**
**Adjust the Settings for Your
  Mouse (Control Panel), 178**
**adjusting page margins
  (WordPad), 302-303**
**airport regulations, laptop
  computers**
  pilot interference, 498
  X-ray machines, 498
aligning text (WordPad), 301-302
AltaVista Web site, 370
Always On Top taskbar, 199
anti-virus programs, FAT32
  drive conversion warning, 161
AOL NetFind Web site, 369-370
applications
  adding to Start menu, 205-208
  automatic start-ups, configur-
    ing, 212
  data, sharing, 320-321
  document files, 127
  .EXE file extension, 184
  executable file extensions
    (DOS), 526-527
  executing
    under non-DOS manage-
      ment, 529
    under non-Windows
      management, 529
  exiting, 284
  files
    associated types, 128-131
    categorizing, 61-63
  hard disks, removing, 218
  launching
    DOS, 525-527
    My Computer, 70

multimedia
  Entertainment menu, 312
  Windows 98 location, 311
multiple open windows,
  navigating between, 288-290
non-virtual machine (DOS),
  528-529
opening, 281-282
.PIF extension, 526
removing from Start menu,
  207-208
shortcuts
  creating, 183-187
  launching, 186
stops responding scenario,
  261-262
toolbar buttons, 32-33
troubleshooting, uninstalling
  process, 218
virtual machine (DOS), 528
window appearance, 283
windows, switching between,
  288
archive file attributes, 123-124
**Arrange Icons command (View
  menu), 65, 106**
arranging desktop
  icons, 187-188
  windows, 285-287
**As Web Page command (View
  menu), 103**
**associating sounds with system
  events, 234-235**
**Attributes command (Image
  menu-Paint), 307**
**Attributes dialog box (Paint),
  307**
**audio, configuring for multi-
  media devices, 235-237**
Auto Hide taskbar, 199
**automatic application start-ups,
  configuring, 212**
**automatic timeouts, physically
  challenged users, 276**

B

**background colors, modifying
  (Internet Explorer 4.0), 375-376**
background graphics
  inserting
    folders, 80-81

backing up data, 136-142
  entire hard drive, 263
  restoring, 142-145
  task scheduler, 145-149
  versus copying, 135
**Backup Job Options dialog
  box, 141**
**Backup Progress dialog box,
  139, 142**
Backup Utility
  backup settings
    data compression, 140-142
    drive location, 140-142
    overwriting files, 140-142
  installing, 140
  job status, viewing, 142
  launching, 136-142
Backup Wizard dialog box, 136
**battery alarms (laptop comput-
  ers)**
  critical, 493
  low, 493
**battery power (laptop comput-
  ers)**
  Power Meter indicator,
    490-491
  status mode, 490-491
  suspend mode, 490-491
  traveling tips, 496
**blind carbon copies (Bcc:), email
  (Outlook Express), 413**
**blocking site access (Internet
  Explorer 4.0), 390-391**
bookmarks, 436, 535
**Boolean arguments, search
  engine support, 364**
boot, 536
**boot menu, viewing options
  (DOS), 530-531**
boot sector viruses, 259
booting DOS
  cold method, 524
  direct method, 524-525
  prompt, 520
  prompt directly, 531-532
  warm method, 524
borders (windows), sizing, 27-28
**bounce keys, accessibility
  options, 275**
Briefcase menu commands
  Split from Original, 504
  Update All, 504
  Update Selection, 504

Browse for Folder dialog box, 88, 111
browsing Web
  via Explorer, 453-454
  via My Computer, 453-454
bulletin boards
  (HyperTerminal)
  defined, 439
  dialing into, 442
  fees, 442
  login process, 442
  maintenance, 439
  private online service, 442
  purpose, 439
  software downloads, 442
bytes, 536
  file sizes
    gigabytes, 121-122
    kilobytes, 121-122
    megabytes, 121-122

C

caches, 536
  defined, 356-358
  Internet Explorer 4.0 data, 356-358
  sizes, 356-358
  Web pages
    display speeds, 386-387
    offline viewing, 357
call waiting, disabling
  (HyperTerminal), 442
canceling subscriptions
  (Internet Explorer 4.0), 402-403
carbon copies (cc:), email
  (Outlook Express), 413
cascading windows, 285-286
  horizontally, 71
  vertically, 71
categorizing
  files
    by client names, 63
    by date, 63
    by software, 61
    criteria, 61
  Start menu into submenus, 208-209
CD Music, configuring, 235-237
CD Player, 312
  hardware requirements, 315
  launching, 315

no sound, troubleshooting, 316
  volume control, 316
centered text, 302
certificates, 536
Change Desktop Colors and
  Background (Control Panel), 178
Change Regional Settings
  (Control Panel), 179
Change Settings for Multimedia
  Devices (Control Panel), 178
Change Settings on Your
  Keyboard (Control Panel), 178
Change Windows Password
  dialog box, 224-225
changing network passwords, 465
Channel bar (Internet
  Explorer 4.0), 536
  categories, 393-394
  displaying, 393-394
  logos, 395-396
  surfing, 393-394
channels, 6
  offline viewing, 397
  subscribing
    Internet Explorer 4.0, 394-396
    methods (Web pages), 392-393
  subscription modifications, 399-402
    applets, 401
    images, 401
    manual updates, 402
    schedule, 402
    sound, 401
    update KB limits, 401
  unsubscribing, 402-403
  update options, 395
  work offline options, 403-404
Character Map dialog box, 256
Character Map utility, 256-257
check boxes
  activation, 55
  deactivation, 55
checking
  file statuses (My Briefcase), 502-503
  system properties, 214
children, Internet blocking
  applications
  Cyberpatrol, 391
  Cybersitter, 391

Kinder Guard, 391
  Net Nanny, 391
Clear command (Documents
  menu), 211
clearing
  Documents list from Start
    menu, 211
  print queue, 272
clicking
  hypertext on Web pages, 334-335
  mouse, 15-16
  toolbar buttons, 32-33
client/server networks, 458-459, 536
clients, 536
  file categorization, 63
  software
    email, 332
    newsgroups, 332
    Web browsers, 332
Clipboard
  contents, viewing, 292
  cut, copy, and paste func-
    tions, 291-292
  installing, 292
  potential memory problems, 295
clock, property options
  AM/PM, 200
  month, 200
  taskbar, 199-200
  time zone selection, 200
  year selection, 200
Close command (Control
  menu), 284
Close command (File menu), 30, 113
Close Program dialog box, 261
closing
  Explorer, 113
  Network Neighborhood, 465
  windows, 30-31
cold booting (DOS), 524
color palette (Paint)
  fill colors, 305
  outline colors, 305
colors
  accessibility options for
    physically challenged
    users, 275
  hypertext appearance, 334
  modifying on desktop, 189-190

schemes (desktop), 190
setting number of, monitors, 232-233
command buttons, 50, 56
commands
  accelerator keys, 131
  Accessories menu, Fax, 533
  Briefcase menu
    Split from Original, 504
    Update All, 504
    Update Selection, 504
  Contents menu, Trouble-shooting, 528
  Control menu, Close, 284
  Documents menu, Clear, 211
  Drive menu
    Compress, 156
    Uncompress, 159
  Edit menu
    Copy, 294
    Cut, 84
    Invert Selection, 82
    Paste, 84, 294
    Paste Special, 327
    Select All, 82
    Undo, 83
  Effects menu
    Add Echo, 315
    Reverse Play, 315
    Speed of a Sound File, 314
  Favorites menu
    Add to Favorites, 209, 377
    Manage Subscriptions, 399
    Organize Favorites, 210, 379
  File menu
    Close, 30, 113
    Create Shortcut, 87, 119, 184
    Delete, 85
    Empty Recycle Bin, 93
    Exit, 284
    Files or Folders, 110
    Find, 87
    Folder Options, 101
    Install New Font, 255
    Print, 268
    Rename, 86, 118
    Restore, 93
  File menu (WordPad), Page Setup, 302
  Format menu (WordPad), Font, 300-301
  grayed-out, 35

Insert menu
  Object, 326
  Picture, 326
keyboard shortcuts, 36-37
  Copy (Ctrl+C), 84
  Cut (Ctrl+X), 84
  Paste (Ctrl+V), 84
New menu
  Folders, 64
  Shortcut, 185
Printer menu
  Pause Printing, 271
  Purge Print Jobs, 272
Programs menu, StartUp, 212
selecting, effect of
  action, 35
  dialog boxes, 35
  feature launches, 35
  submenus, 35
separator lines, 36
Settings menu
  Folder Options, 8, 72, 104
  Printers, 267
  Taskbar & Start Menu, 204
Start menu
  New Folder, 206
  Run, 522
  Shut Down, 21
toolbar buttons, executing, 32-33
View menu
  Arrange Icons, 65, 106
  As Web Page, 103
  Customize this Folder, 79
  Folder Options, 36, 72, 104
  Internet Options, 375
  Line Up Icons, 65, 106
  Refresh, 66
  Status Bar, 25, 69
  Toolbars, 68, 77
companies
  extranets, 335-336
  intranets, 335-336
components
  adding, 220-222
  disk management tools, 220-222
  online service options, 220-222
composing email messages
  Address Book, 417-418
  Outlook Express, 412
Compress command (Drive menu), 156

compressed files (Sound Recorder), 315
compressed volume file (CVF), 537
compressing
  disk space, 156-157
  drive settings, 157
Compression Agent Settings dialog box, 158
CompuServe PPP Connection (Dial-Up Networking), 509
computer viruses
  defined, 258
  infection process, 258-259
  Norton Antivirus (Symantec), 260
  potential damage, 258-259
  preventing, 259-260
  proliferation of, 259
  software, 259-260
  types
    boot sector, 259
    macro, 259
    program file, 259
    VirusScan (McAfee Associates, Inc.), 260
computers
  docking stations
    docked status, 489-490
    undocked status, 489-490
  locating (Network Neighborhood), 475-477
  undocking, 489-490
Configure Your Modem (Control Panel), 178
Configure Your System for Networking (Control Panel), 179
configuring
  applications for automatic startups, 212
  dial-up connections
    Connection Wizard, 340-344
    Dial-Up Networking, 506-507
  email options (Outlook Express), 406-409
  HyperTerminal connections, 440-441
  keyboard
    character repeat, 237-238
    repeat delay, 237-238

laptops, power management settings, 491-492
monitors
  multiple setup, 233-234
  video options, 229-233
mouse
  click rates, 238-239
  left hand versus right hand, 238-239
  pointer speed, 238-239
multimedia devices
  audio, 235-237
  CD Music, 235-237
  MIDI, 235-237
  video, 235-237
multiple monitors
  number of colors, 234
  physical arrangement, 234
multiple users for single computer, 226-228
newsgroup options (Outlook Express), 406-409
passwords, 224-225
sound options, 234-235
connecting to Web sites (Internet Explorer 4.0), 354-356
Connection Description dialog box, 440
Connection Wizard
  configuration options (Outlook Express), 406-409
  dial-up connections (Internet Explorer 4.0), 340-344
  ISP selection (Internet Explorer 4.0), 339-340
connections (HyperTerminal)
  configuring, 440-441
  creating, 440-442
Content view (online Help), 40-41
contents, viewing
  Clipboard Viewer, 292
  folders, 65-66
Contents menu commands, Troubleshooting, 528
Contents view (Help feature), displaying, 41-42
context sensitivity, 537
Control menu commands, Close, 284
Control Panel
  accessing, 175-177
  features, 175-177
    Add New Hardware, 177
    Add or Remove Fonts, 178

Add or Remove Programs, 178
Add or Switch Screen Savers, 178
Adjust System and Program Sounds, 179
Adjust the Settings for Your Mouse, 178
Change Desktop Colors and Backgrounds, 178
Change Regional Settings, 179
Change Settings for Multimedia Devices, 178
Change Settings on Your Keyboard, 178
Configure Your Modem, 178
Configure Your System for Networking, 179
Find System Information, 179
Manage the Use of Your Power Resources, 179
Modify Internet Settings, 179
Set Accessibility Options, 177
Set or Change Passwords, 179
Set the System Date and Time, 178
Set Up for Dialing Out, 179
Set Up Mail and Fax, 179
screen savers, selecting, 180-182
controlling print jobs, 271-272
converting drives
  Drive Converter (FAT32), 160
  to FAT32 systems, 159-160
Copy command (Ctrl+C), 294
Copy command (Edit menu), 294
Copy Disk dialog box, 169
copying
  Explorer files, 116-117
  files
    drag-and-drop method, 84
    to floppy disks, 85, 117
    versus backing up, 135
  floppy disks, 169-170
  folders, cut and paste method, 85
  graphics between same applications, 294

text
  between different applications, 294-295
  between same applications, 294
corrupted files, repairing, 164-165
cover sheets, designing (Microsoft Fax), 534
Create Hyperlink dialog box, 435
Create Shortcut command (File menu), 87, 119, 184
creating
  connections (HyperTerminal), 440-442
  custom toolbars for taskbar, 200-203
  desktop patterns, 191-192
  desktop shortcuts to Web pages, 385
  drawings (Paint), 307-308
  files
    date/time stamps, 123
    shortcuts, 86-87, 119
  folders
    Explorer, 63-65
    My Computer, 63-65
  HTML folder pages, 449-452
  links in documents, 322-325
  multiple user profiles, 226-228
  new folders (My Briefcase), 500
  passwords, 224-225
  shortcuts, 183-187
    Network Neighborhood, 464
    right mouse button, 185
  sound effects (Sound Recorder), 314-315
  startup disks, 264
  Web pages, 80
    FrontPage Express, 431-432
  Web searches (Internet Explorer 4.0), 365-368
Crtl+Alt+Del combination, rebooting warning, 261-262
CSLIP UNIX Connection (Dial-Up Networking), 509
Ctrl+C (Copy) command, 294
Ctrl+V (Paste) command, 294
curing computer viruses, 259-260

Custom Settings dialog box, 72, 106

Customize this Folder command (View menu), 79

Customize this Folder dialog box, 79

customized toolbars
Address, 200-203
Desktop, 200-203
Links, 200-203
Quick Launch, 200-203

customizing
folder appearance, 79
start pages (Internet Explorer 4.0), 382-384

cut and paste method, folders
copying, 85
moving, 83-84

Cut command (Edit menu), 84

Cyberpatrol, 391

Cybersitter, 391

D

daily scheduling, data backup, 147

data
backing up, 136-142
task scheduler, 145-149
caches
Internet Explorer 4.0, 356-358
sizes, 356-358
cut, copy, and paste functions (Clipboard), 291-292
embedding
advantages, 325
disadvantages, 325
linking
advantages, 322
disadvantages, 322
links, creating, 322-325
modems, transmission of, 240
restoring, 142-145
sharing between applications, 320-321

date/time
file creation, 63, 123
queries, Web search engines, 364-365

default programs, selecting (Internet Explorer 4.0), 391

defragmentation, 537
hard disks, 153-155

Defragmenting dialog box, 154

Delete command (File menu), 85

deleting
files
temporary Internet files, 152
types, 132-133
folders, 85-86
hidden, 101
fonts, 255
old email (Outlook Express), 420
print jobs, 272
text (WordPad), 298-299

designing cover sheets (Microsoft Fax), 534

desktop
classic style (Windows 95), 8
colors
modifying, 189-190
schemes, 190
fonts, modifying
color, 194-195
size, 194-195
icons
arranging, 187-188
custom properties, 187
drag-and-drop printing, 272
horizontal alignment, 187
large, 188
left alignment, 187
moving windows, 29
patterns, creating, 191-192
shortcuts, placing, 184
themes
modifying, 192-193
selecting, 192-193
wallpaper, selecting, 190-191
Web-style option
activating, 444-445
appearance, 444-445
window clutter, 71
windows
arranging, 285-287
cascading, 285-286
minimizing, 287
tiling, 286-287
Windows 98 appearance, 13
differences for Windows 3.1 users, 8-10
differences for Windows 95 users, 3-7

desktop shortcuts, creating to Web pages, 385

Desktop Themes dialog box, 192

Desktop toolbar, 200-203

Device Manager
device configurations, 247
functions, 246-247
hardware information
driver, 248-249
general, 248-249
printing, 249
resources, 248-249
settings, 248-249
plug-and-play concept, 246-247
searching hardware information, 247-249

Dial-Up Connection Name dialog box, 342

dial-up connections (Dial-Up Networking)
activating, 510
advanced options, 510
configuring, 506-507
modifying, 508-510

dial-up connections (ISPs)
configuring (Connection Wizard), 340-344
features, 338

Dial-Up Networking
dial-up connections
activating, 510
advanced options, 510
configuring, 506-507
modifying, 508-510
remote access features, 505
server type access
CompuServe PPP Connection, 509
CSLIP UNIX Connection, 509
NRN NetWare Connect, 510
PPP Windows 98, 510
SLIP UNIX Connection, 510
settings
modem selection, 507-508
remote computer ID, 507-508
telephone numbers, 507-508

dialing into bulletin boards (HyperTerminal), 442

dialing properties
area codes, 243
call waiting disabled, 243
calling card PIN number, 243
country selection, 243
dialing prefixes, 243
modems, modifying, 242-244
remote locations, 244
**Dialing Properties dialog
box, 242**
dialog boxes
Accessibility Properties, 277
Add Active Channel Content,
395
Add Favorite, 209, 377
Add New File Type, 129
Attributes (Paint), 307
Backup Job Options, 141
Backup Progress, 139, 142
Backup Wizard, 136
beeping indication, 48
Browse for Folder, 88, 111
Change Windows Password,
224-225
Character Map, 256
Close Program, 261
components
check boxes, 49, 55
command buttons, 50, 56
list box, 49
list boxes, 54
option buttons, 49, 54-55
property sheets, 57
radio buttons, 50
tabs, 50, 57
text boxes, 49, 52-54
What's This? feature,
49, 51-52
varying complexities, 49-50
Compression Agent Settings,
158
Connection Description, 440
Copy Disk, 169
Create Hyperlink, 435
Custom Settings, 72, 106
Customize This Folder, 79
Defragmenting, 154
Desktop Themes, 192
Dial-Up Connection Name,
342
Dialing Properties, 242
Disk Cleanup, 151
Display Properties, 230
Edit File Type, 132
Email Server Names, 342

File Corrupted, 165
Find, 90, 110
Find: All Files, 87, 476
Find: Computer, 476
Folder Options, 72, 104
Format, 169
functions, 48
Insert Object, 326
Internet Email Address, 342
Internet Mail Account, 342
Internet Mail Logon, 342
Internet Options, 375
Keyboard Properties, 237
Microsoft Backup, 136
Modem Properties, 242
Modems Properties, 240
Multimedia Properties, 236
New Action, 130
New Toolbar, 202
Open Backup Job, 140
Organize Favorites, 210
Page Setup (WordPad), 302
Paste Special, 327
Pattern, 192
Pattern Editor, 192
Phone Number, 341
Power Management
Properties, 491
Properties, 125
Remove Shortcuts/Folders,
207
Select Program Folder, 206
Set Up Your Internet
Connection, 341
Setup Options, 341
Shut Down Windows, 262
Sounds Properties, 234
Surface Scan Options, 161
System Properties, 247
Taskbar Properties, 198, 204
User Name and Password,
342
User Settings, 227
varying complexities, 49-50
direct booting (DOS), 524-525
prompt, 531-532
**Direct Cable Connections for
laptops, 494-495**
**disabling call waiting
(HyperTerminal), 442**
disaster planning
backing up data, entire hard
drive, 263
startup disks, creating, 264

disconnecting drive mapping,
484
Disk Cleanup dialog box, 151
**Disk Cleanup Utility, launch-
ing, 151-152**
Disk Defragmenter
configuration options,
154-155
launching, 153-155
disk drives, 537
**disk space, monitoring (My
Computer), 92-93**
disks
converting, Drive Converter
(FAT32), 160
Disk Cleanup Utility
launching, 151-152
space calculations, 151-152
FAT management system, 159
"holes," 152
maintenance overview,
150-151
management overview,
150-151
ScanDisk
features, 161
launching, 161
sectors, repairing, 162
space
compressing, 156-157
DriveSpace Utility, 155
maintenance, 150-151
**Display Properties dialog box,
230**
displaying
files
Explorer options, 101-102
properties, 124-126
folders
My Computer, 73-74
Web-style option, 447-448
Network Neighborhood
large icons, 468-471
small icons, 468-471
two-pane view, 474
workgroups, 459-461
online contents help
Contents view, 41-42
Index view, 42-44
Search view, 44-46
print queue, 271
single folder, Web-style
option, 448-449

toolbars (Internet Explorer
4.0), 349
Web pages (Internet Explorer
4.0), 386
windows
as Web-style appearance,
103-107
in Windows 95 style,
103-107
docking stations, 489-490, 538
document files, 127
documents
creating links, 322-325
multimedia files in docu-
ments, 317
pasted data, embedding,
326-328
saving (WordPad), 303-304
**Documents menu commands,
Clear, 211**
domains, 538
extensions
.com, 353
.edu, 353
.gov, 353
.mil, 353
.net, 353
.org, 353
URL address components,
353
DOS
applications
executable file extensions,
526-527
installing, 527
launching, 525-527
non-virtual machine,
528-529
virtual machine, 528
backward compatibility with
Windows 98 file names, 522
boot menu, viewing options,
530-531
cold booting, 524
.COM file extension, 526-527
configuration files, 521
direct booting, 524-525
.EXE file extension, 526-527
FAT management system, 159
file names
conversion to Windows
98, 120
illegal symbols, 521-522
length, 521-522

.LNK file extension, 526
.PIF file extension, 526
prompt
booting, 520
direct booting, 531-532
launching, 522-523
screen appearance, 520
upgrade process, 517-518
use with Windows interfaces,
520
warm booting, 524
Windows sessions, launching,
523
double clicking mouse, 15-16
**downloading files from Web
pages, 380-381**
drag-and-drop method
embedding, 328
files
copying (Explorer), 116
moving (Explorer), 115
folders
copying, 84
moving, 83
programs, adding to Start
menu, 207
drag-and-drop printing, 272
on networks, 486
dragging mouse
objects, 16
Solitaire game, 16
**drawings, creating (Paint),
307-308**
**Drive Converter (FAT32),
launching, 160**
**drive mapping (Network
Neighborhood)**
disconnecting, 484
launching, 483-484
Drive menu commands
Compress, 156
Uncompress, 159
drivers for printers, 267
drives
compression designations
artificial, 157
host, 157
converting
Drive Converter (FAT32),
160
FAT32 systems, 159-160
icons (My Computer), 67
uncompressing, 159

DriveSpace Utility
Compression Agent, 157
drive compression, 156-157
uncompressing, 159
features, 155
launching, 156-157
maximum drive compression,
157
UltraPack compression, 157
when to use, 155
DVD (Digital Video Disc), 538
**DVD Player, Entertainment
menu, 312**
**Dynamic Data Exchange (DDE)
protocol, 131**

E

Edit File Type dialog box, 132
Edit menu
commands
Copy, 294
Cut, 84
Invert Selection, 82
Paste, 84, 294
Paste Special, 327
Select All, 82
Undo, 83
Explorer menu bar, 109
My Computer menu bar, 76
Network Neighborhood
menu bar, 473
**editing Web pages (FrontPage
Express), 432-433**
**effects, sound (Sound Recorder),
314-315**
Effects menu commands
Add Echo, 315
Reverse Play, 315
Speed of a Sound File, 314
email (Outlook Express)
Address Book
address entries, 415-417
address groups, 415-417
address components, 405-406
addressing, 413
carbon copies, 413
composing, 412
Address Book, 417-418
configuring options, 406-409
deleting, 420
file attachments, 415
paperclip icon, 419
formatting, 414
graphic insertion, 415

IMAP (Internet Message
Access Protocol), 406
monitoring intervals, 419
newsgroup messages, 405-406
POP (Post Office Protocol),
406
priority status, 415
public key encryption, 415
reply options, 419-420
saving, 414
sending, 412-414
SMTP (Simple Mail Transfer
Protocol), 406
spellchecking, 415
unread status, 418
**Email Server Names dialog box
(Connection Wizard),
342embedding**
advantages, 325
disadvantages, 325
drag-and-drop method, 328
objects, 325-326
overview, 325
pasted data in documents,
326-328
**Empty Recycle Bin command
(File menu), 93**
emptying Recycle Bin, 92-93
**Entertainment menu, multi-
media applications**
CD Player, 312
DVD Player, 312
Interactive CD Player, 313
Media Player, 313
Sound Recorder, 313
Trial Programs, 313
Volume Control, 313
WebTV for Windows, 313
**error messages, network logon
procedures, 12-13**
Excite Web site, 369
.EXE file extension, 184
executing
applications
in DOS non-virtual
machine, 528-529
in DOS virtual machine,
528
under non-DOS manage-
ment, 529
under non-Windows
management, 529
commands from toolbar
buttons, 32-33

dial-up connections (Dial-Up
Networking), 510
Exit command (File menu), 284
exiting
applications, 284
Outlook Express, 410
Windows 98 Safe Mode, 262
WordPad, 303
Explorer
Address Bar, 108-109
closing, 113
Contents pane, 106
files
copying, 116-117
deleting, 117-118
display options, 101-102
moving, 115-116
searching, 110-113
selecting, 114-115
shortcut creation, 119
tree structure, 99-100
folders, creating, 63-65
functions, 96
HTML folder pages
creating, 449-452
graphic backgrounds,
inserting, 452-453
icons
drives, 99-100
folders, 99-100
menu bar
Edit, 109
Favorites, 109
File, 109
Go, 109
Help, 110
View, 109
opening, 96-97
toolbars
All Folders, 98-99
Channels, 98-99
Favorites, 98-99
History, 98-99
Search, 98-99
Web browsing capabilities,
453-454
Web-style option
appearance, 445
customizing, 446-447
windows, pane divisions,
97-98
extensions, files, 128-131
extranets, 335-336, 538

F

FAT (File Allocation Table), 539
FAT16 systems, 159
FAT32 systems
anti-virus programs, drive
conversion warning, 161
drives, converting, 159-160
**Favorites folder (Internet
Explorer 4.0), Web pages**
inserting, 377-378
managing, 379-380
opening, 378-379
Favorites menu commands
Add to Favorites, 209, 377
Manage Subscriptions, 399
Organize Favorites, 210, 379
**Fax command (Accessories
menu), 533**
fax transmissions
laptops, standby mode, 494
sending (Microsoft Fax),
533-534
file allocation table, *see* **FAT**
file association
versus file registration,
127-128
Windows 3.1, 127
file attachments (email), 419
File Corrupted dialog box, 165
file extensions, 539
File menu
commands
Close, 30, 113
Create Shortcut, 87, 119,
184
Delete, 85
Empty Recycle Bin, 93
Exit, 284
Files or Folders, 110
Find, 87
Folder Options, 101
Install New Font, 255
Page Setup (Paint), 302
Print, 268
Rename, 86, 118
Restore, 93
Explorer menu bar, 109
My Computer menu bar, 76
Network Neighborhood
menu bar, 472
**file registration versus file
association, 127-128**
File Transfer Protocol (FTP), 333

files
access control (Network
Neighborhood), 479-482
adding (My Briefcase),
500-501
attributes
archive, 123-124
hidden, 123-124
read-only, 123-124
system, 123-124
backing up versus copying,
135
categorizing
by client names, 63
by date, 63
by software, 61
criteria, 61
copying
cut and paste method, 85
drag-and-drop method, 84
Explorer, 116-117
floppy disks, 85, 117
versus backing up, 135
date/time creation, 123
deleting, 85-86
Explorer, 117-118
program downloads, 152
temporary Internet files,
152
display options (Explorer),
101-102
DOS naming rules
illegal symbols, 521-522
length, 521-522
downloading from Web
pages, 380-381
drive mapping (Network
Neighborhood), 483-484
embedding, 325-326
locating, 87-90
Network Neighborhood,
475-477
moving
cut and paste method,
83-84
drag-and-drop method, 83
Explorer, 115-116
naming
character limit, 120
DOS guidelines, 120
illegal characters, 120
long name considerations,
120-121
properties, viewing, 124-126

removing
selected status, 93
total removal, 93
renaming, 86, 118-119
Restore Wizard, set options,
144-145
restoring, 142-145
Recycle Bin, 93-94
scattered effect on hard disk,
repairing, 152-155
searching (Explorer), 110-113
selecting (Explorer), 114-115
sharing (Network Neighborhood), 479-482
shortcuts, creating, 86-87, 119
sizes
gigabytes, 121
kilobytes, 121
megabytes, 121
status checks (My Briefcase),
502-503
sync link removal (My
Briefcase), 504
System File Checker, 164-165
types
Dynamic Data Exchange
(DDE) protocol, 131
icons, modifying, 133-134
modifying, 131-132
Quick View, 131
registering, 128-131
removing, 132-133
updating (My Briefcase),
503-504
**Files or Folders command (File
menu), 110**
Find command (File menu), 87
Find dialog box, 90, 110
**Find System Information
(Control Panel), 179**
**Find: All Files dialog box, 87,
476**
Find: Computer dialog box, 476
**fine-tuning monitor resolutions,
231-232**
fixed-width fonts, 375
floating toolbars, 203
floppy disks
copying, 169-170
files
copying, 117
copying to, 85
formatted versus
unformatted, 167

formatting, 167-169
Copy Systems Files Only
option, 168
Full option, 168
name or label, 171
process, 167
Quick option, 168
storage size, 167
transferring (My Briefcase),
501
**Folder Options command (File
menu), 101**
**Folder Options command
(Settings menu), 8, 72, 104**
**Folder Options command (View
menu), 36, 72, 104**
**Folder Options dialog box,
72-75, 104**
folder pages (HTML)
creating, 449-452
graphic backgrounds,
inserting, 452-453
removing customization, 453
folders
access control (Network
Neighborhood), 479
appearance, customizing, 79
background graphics,
inserting, 80-81
contents
details, 65
large icons, 65
lists, 65
small icons, 65
viewing, 65-66
copying
cut and paste method, 85
drag-and-drop method, 84
Explorer, 116
creating, 63-65
My Briefcase, 500
customization, removing, 81
deleting, 85-86
Explorer, 117-118
display options
Details, 106-107
Large Icons, 106-107
Lists, 106-107
My Computer, 73-74
Small Icons, 106-107
drive mapping (Network
Neighborhood), 483-484
Folder Options dialog box,
74-75

hidden, deleting, 101
moving
  cut and paste method, 83-84
  drag-and-drop method, 83
  Explorer, 115-116
naming conventions (Network Neighborhood), 478
opening (My Computer), 69
renaming, 86, 118-119
searching (Explorer), 110-113
selecting (Explorer), 114-115
sharing (Network Neighborhood), 478-479
Web-style appearance (My Computer), 71-72
Web-style option, displaying, 447-449
Windows 98 screen appearance, 15
Folders command (New menu), 64
Font command (Format menu-WordPad), 300-301
fonts
  accessibility options for physically challenged users, 274
  adding, 254-255
  Character Map utility, 256-257
  characteristics
    case, 251-252
    effects, 251-252
    size, 251-252
    type style, 251-252
    width, 251-252
  decorative, 251
  defined, 251
  folders, viewing, 252
  missing, troubleshooting, 252
  modifications to color, 194-195
  modifications to size, 194-195
  modifications to style, 194-195
  removing, 255
  sans serif, 251
  searching, similarity option, 253-254
  selecting (Internet Explorer 4.0), 375
  serif, 251
  symbols, 251

Format dialog box, 169
Format menu commands, Font, 300-301
Format toolbar (FrontPage Express), 428-429
formatting
  email (Outlook Express), 414
  floppy disks, 167-169
    Copy Systems Files Only option, 168
    Full option, 168
    name or label, 171
    process, 167
    Quick option, 168
  text (WordPad), 300-301
  Web pages (FrontPage Express), 433
Forms toolbar (FrontPage Express), 431
fragmentation, 539
frames, 436, 539
FrontPage Express
  Format toolbar, 428
    buttons, 428-429
  Forms toolbar, 428
    buttons, 431
  HTML coding, 431-432
  launching, 427-428
  Standard toolbar, 428
    buttons, 429-430
  Web pages
    creating, 431-432
    editing, 432-433
    graphics insertion, 436-437
    hypertext links, 435-436
    page properties, 434-435
    text formatting, 433
  WebBots, inserting, 437-438
FTP (File Transfer Protocol)
  defined, 539
  links, 360

G

G-Guide Web site, 318
gigabytes, 540
Go menu
  Explorer menu bar, 109
  My Computer menu bar, 76
  Network Neighborhood menu bar, 473
Gopher
  Internet protocol, 333
  links, 358-359

graphic links, 358
graphics
  copying between same applications, 294
  handles, 437, 540
  in email (Outlook Express), 415
  inserting into folder views, 80-81
  pasting between same applications, 294
  selecting for copying or moving, 294
  Web pages (FrontPage Express), 436-437
grayed-out commands, 35

H

handles (graphics), 437, 540
hard disks
  backing up entirely, 263
  removing applications, 218
hardware
  Add New Hardware Wizard, 219-220
  device configurations, caution in changing, 247
  device information, printing, 249
  information, locating, 247-249
  installing, 218-220
  lack of detection from Windows 98, 219-220
  minimum system requirements (Windows 98), 515-516
  multimedia requirements, 311
  plug-and-play concept (Device Manager), 218-220, 246-247
  requirements for CD Player, 315
Help feature
  online contents
    Contents view, 40-41
    Index view, 40-41
    Search view, 40-41
  types
    Index, 39-40
    online contents, 39-40
    Search, 39-40
    Web Help, 39-40
  Web Help, 46-47

Help menu
 Explorer menu bar, 110
 My Computer menu bar, 77
 Network Neighborhood
  menu bar, 473
Help toolbar buttons
 Back, 40
 Forward, 40
 Hide, 40
 Options, 40
 Web Help, 40
hidden file attributes, 123-124
hidden folders, deleting, 101
hiding taskbar, 19, 198-199
History folder
 time settings (Internet
  Explorer 4.0), 374
 Web pages, viewing, 372-374
hits, 540
"holes" in hard disks, 152
home pages, 540
 Internet Explorer 4.0, 346-347
host drive, 540
HTML (Hypertext Markup
 Language), 333, 540
 defined, 431
 documents, *see* Web pages
 folder pages
  creating, 449-452
  graphic backgrounds,
   inserting, 452-453
  returning to standard
   appearance, 453
 hypertext component, 335
HTTP (Hypertext Transfer
 Protocol), 333, 541
hyperlinks, 11, 540
HyperTerminal
 bulletin boards
  dialing into, 442
  overview, 439
 call waiting, disabling, 442
 connections
  configuring, 440-441
  creating, 440-442
 launching, 440
hypertext, 361, 541
 appearance, 334-335
 clicking in Web pages,
  334-335
 HTML notations, 335
 Web pages, adding, 435-436
Hypertext Markup Language,
 see **HTML**

I

icons, 541
 accessibility options for
  physically challenged users,
  275
 desktop
  arranging, 187-188
  custom properties, 187
  drag-and-drop printing,
   272
  horizontal alignment, 187
  large, 188
  left alignment, 187
 file types, modifying, 133-134
 My Computer, 68
 shortcuts, appearance, 184
 Windows 98 screen appearance, 14
image map links, 361-362, 541
images, selecting for copying or
 moving, 294
IMAP (Internet Message Access
 Protocol), 406
 server, 541
importing old addresses
 (Outlook Express), 410
Include WebBot, 437-438
Index view (Help feature),
 displaying
indirect access (ISPs), online
 services
 America Online, 337-338
 CompuServe, 337-338
 MSN, 337-338
Infoseek Web site, 370
Insert menu commands
 Object, 326
 Picture, 326
Insert Object dialog box, 326
inserting
 background graphics in
  folder views, 80-81
 graphic backgrounds in
  HTML folder pages, 452-453
 graphics for Web pages
  (FrontPage Express),
  436-437
 text (WordPad), 298-299
 WebBots (FrontPage Express),
  437-438
insertion point, moving
 with keyboard (WordPad),
  298
 with mouse (WordPad), 298

Install New Font command (File
 menu), 255
installation options
 (Windows 98)
 compact, 518-519
 custom, 518-519
 portable, 518-519
 typical, 518-519
installing
 Backup Utility, 140
 Clipboard Viewer, 292
 DOS applications, 527
 hardware, plug-and-play
  concept, 246-247
 new fonts, 254-255
 new hardware, 218-220
  troubleshooting, 219-220
 printers, 267-268
  from manufacturer's
   disks, 268
 software
  Add/Remove Programs
   icon (Control Panel),
   216-217
  automatic setup, 216-217
  Run menu, 216-217
 TV Viewer, 318
 Windows 98 on MS-DOS
  systems, 517-518
IntelliKeyboard, 239
IntelliMouse, 239
Interactive CD Player, 313
Internet
 clients, role of, 332
 defined, 331
 newsgroups, reading feature
  (Outlook Express), 421
 protocols
  development, 332
  File Transfer Protocol
   (FTP), 333
  Gopher, 333
  HTML, 333
  HTTP, 333
  Internet Protocol (IP), 333
  NNTP (Network News
   Transfer Protocol), 334
  Telnet, 333
  Transmission Control
   Protocol (TCP), 333
 servers, role of, 332
 TCP/IP (Transfer Control
  Protocol/Internet Proto-
  col), 457
 Web component, 331

Internet Connection Wizard, 7
**Internet Email Address dialog
box, 342**
Internet Explorer 4.0, 6, 332
Active Desktop Item,
subscribing, 397-398
automatic disconnections, 404
background colors, modifying, 375-376
caches, 356-358
Channel bar
categories, 393-394
displaying, 393-394
logos, 395-396
channels, subscribing, 394-396
connection information,
345-346
Connection Wizard
dial-up connections,
340-344
features, 339
ISP selection, 339-340
default programs, selecting,
391
desktop shortcuts, creating,
385
Favorites folder, Web sites
additions, 377-378
opening, 378-379
fonts, selecting, 375
History bar, 373
History folder, time settings,
374
home page, 346-347
languages, selecting, 376
launching, 345
Links toolbar, 384-385
push technologies, 397-398
Search bar, 368-369
search methods
whole Web, 363-365
within Web page, 365
within Web site, 365
security zones
custom security, 388-389
high security, 388-389
Internet, 387
local intranet, 387
low security, 388-389
medium security, 388-389
restricted sites, 387
trusted sites, 387
sites, access blocking, 390-391
start pages, 346-347
customizing, 382-384

subscriptions
canceling, 402-403
modifying, 399-402
updating, 403
text, resizing, 375
toolbars
Address, 348
displaying, 349
Links, 348
Standard, 348
Web pages
display options, 386
display speeds, 386-387
file downloads, 380-381
navigating, 351
subscribing, 392-393
Web searches, creating,
365-368
Web sites
connecting, 354-356
subscribing, 396-397
work offline, 346, 403-404
**Internet Mail Account dialog
box, 342**
**Internet Mail Logon dialog
box, 342**
**Internet Options command
(View menu), 375**
Internet Options dialog box, 375
Internet Protocol (IP), 333
Internet Service Providers,
see **ISPs**
intranets, 335-336, 457, 541
**Invert Selection command (Edit
menu), 82**
ISPs (Internet Service Providers)
selecting via Connection
Wizard, 339-340
service levels
dial-up access, 337-338
indirect access, 337-338
persistent connection,
337-338
versus online services, 338

J - K

Java, 541
justified text, 302
keyboard
shortcut combinations
commands, 36-37
menu commands, 35
text boxes, editing keys, 53

**Keyboard Properties dialog
box, 237**
keyboard shortcuts, commands
Ctrl+C (Copy) command,
84, 294
Ctrl+V (Paste) command,
84, 294
keyboards
configuring character rates,
237-238
Intelli-keyboard, 239
language options, 238
kilobytes, 542
Kinder Guard, 391

L

**labeling floppy disks during
formatting process, 171**
languages
options for keyboards, 238
selecting (Internet Explorer),
376
laptops
airport regulations (FAA), 498
pilot interference, 498
X-ray security, 498
battery alarms
critical, 493
low, 492-493
battery power
Power Meter indicator,
490-491
standby mode, 490-491
suspend mode, 490-491
My Briefcase
features, 499-500
opening, 499-500
networks, cable connections,
494-495
power management settings,
configuring, 491-492
standby mode and fax
transmissions, 494
theft protection guidelines,
497
traveling tips
battery supply, 496
local ISP access numbers,
495
peripherals and supplies,
496-497
protective case, 495-496
**Launch Outlook Express (Quick
Launch toolbar), 18**

launching
   Accessibility Settings Wizard, 273
   ActiveMovie player, 317
   applications
      from My Computer, 70
      shortcuts, 186
   Backup Utility, 136-142
   CD Player, 315
   Character Map utility, 256-257
   dial-up connections (Dial-Up Networking), 510
   Disk Cleanup Utility, 151-152
   Disk Defragmenter, 153-155
   DOS
      applications, 525-527
      prompt, 522-523
      Windows sessions, 523
   Drive Converter (FAT32), 160
   drive mapping (Network Neighborhood), 483-484
   DriveSpace Utility, 156-157
   FrontPage Express, 427-428
   HyperTerminal, 440
   Internet Explorer 4.0, 345
   Maintenance Wizard, 165
   Media Player, 316-317
   Microsoft Fax, 533
   online contents help
      Contents view, 41-42
      Index view, 42-44
      Search view, 44-46
   Outlook Express, 410, 422
   Restore Wizard, 142-145
   ScanDisk, 161
   Scheduled Task Wizard, 145
   Sound Recorder, 313
   System File Checker, 164
   Web Help, 46-47
   WebTV for Windows, 318
   see also opening
left-aligned text, 302
legacy programs, 542
Line Up Icons command (View menu), 65, 106
linking
   advantages, 322
   disadvantages, 322
   example, 322
   TV Viewer to programming site, 318

links, 542
   appearance on Web pages, 358
   creating, 322-325
   documents, creating, 322-325
   modifying, Links toolbar (Internet Explorer 4.0), 384
   types
      FTP, 360
      Gopher, 358-359
      graphic, 358
      hypertext, 361
      image map, 361-362
      mailto, 360-361
      Web pages, 358
Links toolbar, 200-203, 384-385
   Internet Explorer 4.0, 348
   My Computer, 78
list boxes, 54
local intranet zone, sites, adding, 389-390
local ISP access numbers, laptop traveling tips, 495
local printers, 267
locating
   computers (Network Neighborhood), 475-477
   files, 87-90
      Network Neighborhood, 475-477
   hardware information, 247-249
logging off networks, 465
logging on networks
   error messages, 12-13
   via Network Neighborhood, 461
logins versus passwords, 223-224
low battery alarm, setting (laptops), 492
Lycos Web site, 370

M

macro viruses, 259
mailing lists, 542
mailto links, 360-361
Maintenance Wizard
   launching, 165
   schedule settings, 165-166
Manage Subscriptions command (Favorites menu), 399

Manage the Use of Your Power Resources (Control Panel), 179
managing
   disks, maintenance overview, 150-151
   Web pages (Favorites folder), 379-380
mapping, 542
   drives, 483-484
Maximize button, window size, 24-26
maximizing window size, 26-27
Media Player
   file types, 316-317
   launching, 316-317
   multimedia applications, 313
megabytes, 542
menu bars
   commands, directory structure, 33
   My Computer
      Edit menu, 76
      File menu, 76
      Go menu, 76
      Help menu, 77
      View menu, 76
   Network Neighborhood
      Edit menu, 473
      File menu, 472
      Go menu, 473
      Help menu, 473
      View menu, 473
menu commands
   context-sensitivity, 33-34
   grayed-out, 35
   keyboard shortcuts, 35
   mouse, selecting, 34-35
   separator lines, 36
   use of, practicing, 36
menus
   commands, context-sensitivity, 33-34
   defined, 33
   elements
      check mark, 36
      ellipsis, 36
      option bullet, 36
      separator lines, 36
      submenu arrow, 36
   pull-down, 34
   shortcut, 33-34
      displaying, 37

messages, newsgroups
posting (Outlook Express), 425
reading (Outlook Express), 424
Microsoft Backup dialog box, 136
Microsoft Fax
cover sheets, designing, 534
faxes, sending, 533-534
Group 3 fax compatibility, 533
Windows 98, implementing, 533
Microsoft Start Page, 382-384
Microsoft Windows 98 Help site
registration verification control, 47
Web Help, 46-47
MIDI (musical instrument digital interface), configuring, 235-237
MIME (Multipurpose Internet Mail Extensions), 130
Minimize button, 24, 27
minimizing windows, 26-27, 287
minimum system requirements (Windows 98), 515-516
missing fonts, troubleshooting, 252
Modem Properties dialog box, 242
modems, 543
adding to system, 240-242
creating connection (HyperTerminal), 440-442
defined, 240
detected status, 241
dialing
into bulletin boards (HyperTerminal), 442
properties, modifying, 242-244
installation process, 240-242
miscellaneous properties
baud rates, 244-245
connection settings, 244-245
ports, 244-245
speaker volume, 244-245
PCMCIA PC cards, 241
port designations, 242
undetected status, 241

Modems Properties dialog box, 240
Modify Internet Settings (Control Panel), 179
modifying
background colors (Internet Explorer 4.0), 375-376
Backup Utility settings, 140-142
cache settings, Web page display speeds, 386-387
desktop
colors, 189-190
font appearance, 194-195
themes, 192-193
dial-up connections (Dial-up Networking), 508-510
file types, 131-132
folders, display options, 74-75
icons for file types, 133-134
links, (Links toolbar), 384-385
modems
dialing properties, 242-244
miscellaneous properties, 244-245
monitor resolution, 230
Network Neighborhood, display choices, 468-471
passwords, 225-226
screen resolution from taskbar, 232
sound, volume controls, 235
Start menu properties, 204-205
subscriptions (Internet Explorer 4.0), 399-402
taskbar size, 197
monitoring
email status (Outlook Express), 419
hard disk space (My Computer), 92-93
monitors
colors, setting number of, 232-233
multiple setup
configuring, 233-234
uses, 233
PCI graphics adapters, 233
pixels, 229
resolution
fine-tuning, 231-232
modifying, 230
standard pixel count, 229

screen savers, functions, 180
video options, configuring, 229-233
monthly scheduling, data backup, 147
mouse
configuring
click rates, 238-239
left hand versus right hand, 238-239
pointer speeds, 238-239
IntelliMouse, 239
multiple objects, selecting, 16
objects, dragging, 16
options
clicking, 15-16
pointing, 15-16
right-clicking, shortcut menus, 33-34, 185
Solitaire, dragging practice, 16
text, selecting, 293
MouseKeys, accessibility options for physically challenged users, 276
moving
files, drag-and-drop method, 83
folders, cut and paste method, 83-84
insertion point
with keyboard (WordPad), 298
with mouse (WordPad), 298
scroll bars, 29
taskbar, 19, 196-197
windows on desktop, 29
MS-DOS
FAT management system, 159
screen appearance, 520
upgrade process, 517-518
multimedia applications, Entertainment menu
CD Player, 312
defined, 311
DVD Player, 312
hardware requirements, 311
Interactive CD Player, 313
Media Player, 313
Sound Recorder, 313
Trial Programs, 313
Volume Control, 313
WebTV for Windows, 313

multimedia devices, configuring, 235-237
Multimedia Properties dialog box, 236
multiple files, selecting, 82-83, 114-115
multiple monitors, configuring, 233-234
  monitor arrangement, 234
  number of colors, 234
  screen resolution, 234
multiple objects, mouse selection, 16
multiple open windows in same application, 288-290
multiple computer users, configuring, 226-228
Multipurpose Internet Mail Extensions, *see* MIME
multitasking, 11, 543
My Briefcase
  features, 499
  files
    adding, 500-501
    replace, 502-503
    status checks, 502-503
    sync link removal, 504
    up-to-date, 502-503
    updating, 503-504
  floppy disks, transferring, 501
  new folders, creating, 500
  opening, 499-500
  out-of-sync files, 503-504
My Computer
  applications, launching, 70
  drive icons, 67
  folders
    creating, 63-65
    display options, 73-74
    opening, 69
    Web-style appearance, 71-72
  function, 67
  hard disk space, checking, 92-93
  HTML folder pages
    creating, 449-452
    graphic backgrounds, inserting, 452-453
  icons, 67-68
  menu bar
    Edit menu, 76
    File menu, 76

Go menu, 76
Help menu, 77
View menu, 76
opening, 67
toolbars
  Address Bar, 78
  Links, 78
  standard buttons, 77-78
  Text Labels, 78
Web browsing capabilities, 453-454
Web-style option
  appearance, 445
  customizing, 446-447
window appearance
  address bar, 68-69
  menu bar, 68-69
  status bar, 69
  title bar, 68-69
  toolbar, 68-69
Windows 98 screen appearance, 14

N

naming
  files
    character limit, 120
    DOS guidelines, 120
    illegal characters, 120
    long name considerations, 120-121
  floppy disks during formatting process, 171
  folders (Network Neighborhood), 478
  network printers, 488
NASA Web site, 355
navigating
  between multiple open windows in same application, 288-290
  Web pages
    Internet Explorer 4.0, 351
    previously viewed, 372-374
Net Nanny, 391
NetMeeting, 6
Network Administrator
  Network Neighborhood, 460-461
  network printers, adding, 486-488

Network Neighborhood
  access privileges, 461
  closing, 465
  computers, locating, 475-477
  display choices
    large icons, 468-471
    small icons, 468-471
  drive mapping, 483-484
  files
    access control, 479-482
    locating, 475-477
    sharing, 479-482
  folders
    access control, 479
    sharing, 478-479
  functions, 459
  menu bar
    Edit menu, 473
    File menu, 472
    Go menu, 473
    Help menu, 473
    View menu, 473
  Network Administrator, 460-461
  network printers, browsing, 488
  networks, logging on, 461
  opening, 462
  passwords, 461
  printers, sharing, 483
  shared resources
    drives, 463-464
    functions, 459-461
    printers, 463-464
  shortcuts, creating, 464
  toolbar buttons, 471-472
  toolbars, 462-464
  two-pane view, 474
  user names, 461
  window elements, 462-464
  Windows 98 screen appearance, 14
  workgroups, displaying, 459-461
network paths, Uniform Naming Convention (UNC), 390
network printers, 267
  adding, 486-488
  naming, 488
  selecting, 488
Network Redirector, print files
  to local printer, 485-486
  to network printer, 485-486

networks
advantages, 459
cable connections for laptops, 494-495
defined, 457-458
Dial-up Networking, 506-507
drag-and-drop printing, 486
features
communication protocols, 457-458
hardware connections, 457-458
Internet, TCP/IP (Transfer Control Protocol/Internet Protocol), 457
logging off, 465
logging on, 461
error messages, 12-13
passwords, administrative rules, 465
peer-to-peer, 458-459
roles
clients, 458-459
servers, 458-459
New Action dialog box, 130
New Folder command (Start menu), 206
New menu commands
Folders, 64
Shortcut, 185
New Toolbar dialog box, 202
newsgroups, 544
configuring options (Outlook Express), 406-409
content warning, 421
list retrieval (Outlook Express), 422
messages
posting, 425-426
reading, 424-425
threaded, 425
Outlook Express, launching, 422
reading functions, 421
subscribing, 421-423
unsubscribing, 422-423
NNTP (Network News Transfer Protocol), 334
server, 544
non-contiguous multiple files, selecting, 82-83
non-virtual machine (DOS), 528-529

Norton Antivirus (Symantec), 260
NRN NetWare Connect (Dial-Up Networking), 510

O

Object command (Insert menu), 326
objects, 321
dragging mouse, 16
embedding, 325-326
handles, 437
offline viewing
of channels, 397
of Web pages via caches, 357
online contents help, displaying
Content view, 40-42
Index view, 40-44
Search view, 40-41, 44-46
types, 39-40
online services
benefits, 337
software, 339
trial periods, 337
versus ISPs, 338
online services icon, 14
Open Backup Job dialog box, 140
open documents, opening applications, 281-282
open multiple windows, system loads, 25
opening
applications
from open documents, 281-282
from program groups, 281-282
Character Map utility, 256-257
Explorer, 96-97
My Briefcase, 499-500
My Computer, 67-69
Network Neighborhood, 462
Paint, 305
Recycle Bin, 91-92
Web pages (Internet Explorer 4.0), 378-379
windows, 25-26
WordPad, 296-297
see also launching
option buttons
choice selection, 54-55
dialog boxes, 54-55

Organize Favorites command (Favorites menu), 210, 379
Organize Favorites dialog box, 210
organizing submenu entries in Start menu, 209-211
Outlook Express, 6
Address Book, 415-417
Draft folder, 411
email
addressing, 413
carbon copies, 413
composing, 412
configuring, 406-409
deleting, 420
file attachments, 415, 419
formatting, 414
graphic insertion, 415
monitoring intervals, 419
overview, 405-406
priority status, 415
public key encryption, 415
reply options, 419-420
saving, 414
spellchecking, 415
exiting, 410
Folder Bar, 412
Inbox, 411-412
launching, 410, 422
newsgroups
configuring options, 406-409
list retrieval, 422
messages, posting, 425-426
messages, reading, 424-425
reading function, 421
subscribing, 422-423
unsubscribing, 422-423
old addresses, importing, 410
Outbox, 411-412
Outlook Bar, 412
Sent/Deleted Items, 411-412
window appearance, 411-412
Windows 98 screen appearance, 14
Outlook Express Mail, 332
Outlook Express News, 332

P

page margins, adjusting (WordPad), 302-303
Page Setup command (File menu-WordPad), 302
Page Setup dialog box (Paint), 302
Paint
   drawings
      creating, 307-308
      saving, 310
   elements
      color palette, 305
      tools, 305, 307
   exporting to other programs, 305
   opening, 305
   text, adding to graphics, 308-310
   Text tool, insertion point, 308
   toolbox
      ellipses, 307
      fill color, 307
      line color, 307
      line width, 307
panes, 544
   Explorer, 97-98
   Network Neighborhood, displaying, 474
paperclip icon, email file attachments, 419
partitions, 544
passwords
   administrative rules, 465
   character length, 225
   lowercase versus uppercase, 225
   modifying, 225-226
   Network Neighborhood, 461
   purpose, 223-224
   removing, 226
   screen savers, setting, 181-182
   selecting, 465
   setting up, 224-225
   versus logins, 223-224
Paste command (Ctrl+V), 294
Paste command (Edit menu), 84, 294
Paste Special command (Edit menu), 327
Paste Special dialog box, 327
pasted data, embedding in documents, 326-328

pasting
   graphics between same applications, 294
   text
      between different applications, 294-295
      between same applications, 294
      WordPad, 299
Pattern dialog box, 192
Pattern Editor dialog box, 192
patterns, desktop, 191-192
Pause Printing command (Printer menu), 271
pausing print queue, 271
PC Card, 545
PCI graphics adapters, 233
PCMCIA PC cards, 241
peer-to-peer networks, 458, 545
   printer-sharing (Network Neighborhood), 483
performing Windows 3.1 tasks under Windows 98, 9
peripherals, laptops, traveling tips, 496-497
persistent connections (ISPs)
   company use, 338
   network logons, 338
Phone Number dialog box (Connection Wizard), 341
physically challenged users, accessibility options
   automatic timeouts, 276
   bounce keys, 275
   color settings, 275
   font sizes, 274
   icon size, 275
   MouseKeys, 276
   scroll bars, 275
   sound sentry, 275
   sticky keys, 275
   text size, 275
   toggle keys, 275
Picture command (Insert menu), 326
pixels, 229, 545
   monitor adjustments, 230
placing
   multimedia files in documents, 317
   shortcuts on desktops, 184
playing sounds
   from Media subfolder, 234-235
   Sound Recorder, 314

plug-and-play
   hardware installation, 218-220
      troubleshooting, 219-220
   installing hardware, 246-247
   PCMCIA PC cards, 241
pointer, Windows 98 screen appearance, 15
pointing mouse, 15-16
POP (Post Office Protocol), 406
pop-up menus, 545
port designations for modems, 242
posting newsgroup messages (Outlook Express), 425-426
Power Management Properties dialog box, 491
Power Meter indicator (taskbar), 490-491
PPP Windows 98 (Dial-Up Networking), 510
preventing computer viruses, 259-260
previously viewed Web pages, navigating, 372-374
Print command (File menu), 268
print jobs, 270
   controlling, 271-272
   deleting, 272
print queue
   clearing, 272
   displaying, 271
   functions, 270-271
   pausing, 271
   renaming, 271
Printer menu commands
   Pause Printing, 271
   Purge Print Jobs, 272
printers
   drag-and-drop printing, 272
   drivers, 267
   error messages, troubleshooting, 270
   installing, 267-268
      from manufacturer's disks, 268
   local, 267, 485-486
   network, 267, 485-486
      drag-and-drop printing, 486
   print jobs, 270
   print queue, 270-271
   sharing (Network Neighborhood), 483
   stalled, troubleshooting, 271

Printers command (Settings menu), 267
printing
from applications on networks, 485-486
hardware information (Device Manager), 249
program file viruses, 259
program groups, opening applications, 281-282
programming, linking WebTV for Windows, 318
programs
adding to Start menu, 205-208
automatic start-ups, configuring, 212
hard disks, removing, 218
removing from Start menu, 207-208
stops responding scenario, 261-262
troubleshooting, uninstalling process, 218
see also applications
Programs menu commands, Start Up, 212
properties
accessing (Start menu), 208-209
files, viewing, 124-126
modifying (Start menu), 204-205
setting (Recycle Bin), 94-95
Properties dialog box
Statistics page, 125
Summary page, 125
property sheets
dialog boxes, 57
tab selections, 57
proportional fonts, 375, 545
protocols (Internet)
defined, 332, 458
development, 332
File Transfer Protocol (FTP), 333
Gopher, 333
HTML, 333
HTTP, 333
Internet Protocol (IP), 333
NNTP (Network News Transfer Protocol), 334
Telnet, 333
Transmission Control Protocol (TCP), 333
URL address components, 352

proxy servers, 546
public key encryption (Outlook Express), 415
pull-down menus, 34
purchasing software guidelines
CD as source, 215
disk media, 215
manufacturer recommendations, 214
system requirements, 213
Windows 98 compatibility, 213
Purge Print Jobs command (Printer menu), 272
push technology, 546

Q - R

Quick Launch toolbar, 200-203
Launch Internet Explorer Browser, 18
Launch Outlook Express, 18
Show Desktop, 18
View Channels, 18
Quick Links, 384
quick rebooting, 217
Quick View files, 131
radio buttons, 50
RAM (random access memory)
defined, 215
minimum system requirements for Windows 98, 515-516
random access memory, *see* **RAM**
read-only file attributes, 123-124
reading newsgroup messages (Outlook Express), 424-425
rebooting
quick method, 217
Windows 98 (Crtl+Alt+Del warning), 261-262
recording
software serial numbers, 216
sounds (Sound Recorder), 313-314
Recycle Bin
all files, removing, 93
appearance
empty, 91-92
full, 91-92
drive location, 91
emptying, 92-93

files
deleting, 117-118
restoring, 93-94
folders, deleting, 85-86
functions, 91
maintenance frequency, 150
opening, 91-92
properties, setting, 94-95
selected files, removing, 93
window appearance, 92
Windows 98 screen appearance, 14
reducing window clutter, 71
Refresh command (View menu), 66
registering files, 127-128
types, 128-131
registration (files), 546
Remove Shortcuts/Folders dialog box, 207
removing
all files (Recycle Bin), 93
customization from HTML folder pages, 453
file sync links (My Briefcase), 504
file types, 132-133
folder customization, 81
fonts, 255
passwords, 226
programs
from Start menu, 207-208
hard disks, 218
selected files (Recycle Bin), 93
shortcut icons, 186
toolbars, 203
Rename command (File menu), 86, 118
renaming
files, 86, 118-119
print queue, 271
shortcuts, 185
repairing
corrupted files, 164-165
disk sectors, 162
files, scattered effect on hard disk, 152-155
replying email messages (Outlook Express), 419-420
resizing
taskbar, 197-198
text (Internet Explorer 4.0), 375
toolbar buttons (Internet Explorer 4.0), 385
window borders, 27-28

resolution, monitors, 231-232
restarting
    computer after new software
        installations, 217
    Windows 98, 262
Restore command (File
    menu), 93
Restore Wizard
    file replacement, 144-145
    media selection, 144-145
restoring
    backup files to hard disk,
        142-145
    files, 142-145
        from Recycle Bin, 93-94
    window size, 26-27
restricted sites zone, sites,
    adding, 389
retrieving (Outlook Express)
    email messages, 418
    newsgroup lists, 422
Reverse Play command (Effects
    menu), 315
right-aligned text, 302
right-clicking mouse, shortcut
    menus, 33-34
Run command (Start menu), 522

S

Safe Mode
    exiting, 262
    restarting, 262
sans serif fonts, 251
saving
    documents (WordPad),
        303-304
    drawings (Paint), 310
    email (Outlook Express), 414
ScanDisk
    advanced options, 163
    launching, 161
Scheduled Task Wizard,
    launching, 145
scheduling
    data backup, 145-149
        frequency setting, 147-149
    Maintenance Wizard, utility
        settings, 165-166
schemes (desktop color), 190
screen appearance (Windows 98)
    desktop, 13
    folders, 15
    icons, 14

My Computer, 14
Network Neigborhood, 14
online services icon, 14
Outlook Express, 14
pointer, 15
Recycle Bin, 14
taskbar, 14
screen resolution
    modifying
        from taskbar, 232
        monitors, 230
    monitors, 231-232
screen savers
    functions, 180
    security passwords, 180-182
    selecting, 180-182
scroll bars
    accessibility options for
        physically challenged
        users, 275
    contents, viewing via, 28-29
    moving, 29
Search bar (Internet Explorer
    4.0), 368-369
search engines, 546
    Boolean arguments, 364
    date/time queries, 364-365
    defined, 363
    differences among competi-
        tors, 365
    query syntax, 364-365
    types
        AltaVista, 369-370
        AOL NetFind, 369-370
        Excite, 369-370
        Infoseek, 369-370
        Lycos, 369-370
        Yahoo!, 369-370
Search view (Help feature)
    Customize Search Capabili-
        ties, 45
    displaying, 44-46
    Maximize Search Capabili-
        ties, 45
    Minimize Database Size, 45
    words or phrases, 46
Search view (online help), 40-41
Search WebBot, 437-438
searching
    computers (Network
        Neighborhood), 475-477
    files, 87-90, 110-113
        criteria, 89-90
        Network Neighborhood,
            475-477

fonts, similarity option,
    253-254
hardware information
    (Device Manager), 247-249
with Internet Explorer 4.0
    whole Web, 363-365
    within Web page, 365
    within Web site, 365
security
    laptops, theft protection
        guidelines, 497
    passwords
        creating, 224-225
        modifying, 225-226
        purpose, 223-224
        removing, 226
    site access blocks (Internet
        Explorer 4.0), 390-391
    zones (Internet Explorer 4.0),
        387
Select All command (Edit
    menu), 82
Select Program Folder dialog
    box, 206
selecting
    colors for desktop, 189-190
    default programs (Internet
        Explorer 4.0), 391
    desktop
        colors, 189-190
        themes, 192-193
        wallpaper, 190-191
    files
        Explorer, 114-115
        multiple, 82-83
        non-contiguous multiple,
            82-83
        single, 82-83
    fonts (Internet Explorer 4.0),
        375
    graphics for copying or
        moving, 294
    ISPs via Connection Wizard,
        339-340
    languages for Internet
        Explorer 4.0 viewing, 376
    menu commands with
        mouse, 34-35
    multiple objects with
        mouse, 16
    network printers, 488
    objects with mouse, 15-16
    schemes (desktop color), 190
    screen savers, 180-182

text
for copying or moving,
293
WordPad, 299
wallpaper from Web pages,
191, 386
sending
email messages (Outlook
Express), 412-414
faxes (Microsoft Fax), 533-534
separator lines in menu
commands, 36
serial numbers, software,
recording, 216
serif fonts, 251
Set Accessibility Options
(Control Panel), 177
Set or Change Passwords
(Control Panel), 179
Set the System Date and Time
(Control Panel), 178
Set Up for Dialing Out (Control
Panel), 179
Set Up Mail and Fax (Control
Panel), 179
Set Up Your Internet Connection dialog box , 341
setting
accessibility options
physically challenged
users, 273-276
properties, 277-278
clock properties for taskbar,
199-200
data backup by frequency
(Task Scheduler), 147-149
dial-up connections, 340-344
Dial-up Networking
modem selection, 507-508
remote computer ID,
507-508
telephone numbers,
507-508
Disk Defragmenter, configuration options, 154-155
laptops, low battery alarm,
492
Network Neighborhood,
access privileges, 461
number of colors for
monitors, 232-233
Recycle Bin properties, 94-95
ScanDisk, advanced options,
163

screen savers, passwords,
181-182
taskbar properties, 199
time settings, History folder
(Internet Explorer 4.0), 374
toolbars, display options, 202
Web page properties
FrontPage Express,
434-435
graphics options, 386
setting up passwords, 224-225
Settings menu commands
Folder Options, 8, 72, 104
Printers, 267
Taskbar & Start Menu, 204
Setup Options dialog box, 341
sharing
computers, multiple user
profile configurations,
226-228
data between applications,
320-321
files (Network Neighbor-
hood), 479-482
folders (Network Neighborhood), 478-479
printers (Network Neighborhood), 483
Shortcut command (New menu),
185
shortcut key combinations,
commands, 36-37
shortcut menus, displaying, 37
shortcuts
appearance, 183
creating, 183-187
Network Neighborhood,
464
for files, creating, 86-87, 119
function, 183
icons, 184
removing, 186
launching applications, 186
on desktops, placing, 184
renaming, 185
right mouse button, creating,
185
Show Clock taskbar, 199
Show Desktop, 18
Show Small Icons taskbar, 199
Shut Down command (Start
menu), 21
Shut Down Windows dialog
box, 262

similar fonts, searching, 253-254
single files, selecting, 82-83
sites (Web)
access blocking (Internet
Explorer 4.0), 390-391
adding
local intranet zone,
389-390
restricted sites zone, 389
trusted sites zone, 389
AltaVista, 370
AOL NetFind, 369-370
Excite, 369
G-Guide, 318
Infoseek, 370
Lycos, 370
Microsoft Hardware Com-
patibility List, 516
Microsoft Windows 98 Help,
46-47
NASA, 355
Yahoo!, 369
sizing
taskbar, 197-198
window borders, 27-28
SLIP UNIX Connection (Dial-
Up Networking), 510
SMTP (Simple Mail Transfer
Protocol), 406
server, 547
soft shutdowns, 20
software
computer viruses, cure and
protection, 259-260
files, categorizing, 61
installation methods
Add/Remove Programs
icon (Control Panel),
216-217
automatic setup, 216-217
Run menu, 216-217
installation preparations
closure of other programs,
215-216
license agreement, 215-216
RAM check, 215-216
serial numbers, 215-216
operating system backups,
263
purchasing guidelines
CD as media, 215
disk media, 215
manufacturer recommen-
dations, 214

system requirements, 213
Windows 98 compatibility, 213
serial numbers, recording, 216
Solitaire, mouse-dragging practice, 16
Sound Recorder
compressed sound files, 315
launching, 313
sounds
effects, 314-315
playing, 314
recording, 313-314
sound sentry, accessibility options for physically challenged users, 275
sounds
effects (Sound Recorder), 314-315
events, associating, 234-235
playing
from Media subfolder, 234-235
Sound Recorder, 314
recording (Sound Recorder), 313-314
volume, modifying, 235
Sounds Properties dialog box, 234
Speed of a Sound File command (Effects menu), 314
spellchecking email (Outlook Express), 415
Split from Original command (Briefcase menu), 504
stalled printers, troubleshooting, 271
Standard toolbar
FrontPage Express, 429-430
Internet Explorer 4.0, 349-350
standby mode (laptops), 494, 547
Start button, tasks
documents, 17
Eject and Suspend, 17
Favorites folder, 17
Find feature, 17
Help feature, 17
Log Off, 17
programs, 16
settings, 17
Shut Down, 17
Windows Update, 16

Start menu
commands
New Folder, 206
Run, 522
Shut Down, 21
Documents lists, clearing, 211
Favorites submenus, 210
programs
adding, 205-208
removing, 207-208
properties
accessing, 208-209
modifying, 204-205
submenus, categorizing, 208-209
Start Menu Organizer Wizard, 7
start pages, 346-347, 547
customizing, 382-384
starting, *see* **activating Web-style option; executing; launching**
StartUp command (Programs menu), 212
startup disk, creating, 264
StartUp folder, automatic program start-ups, 212
Status Bar command (View menu), 25, 69
sticky keys, accessibility options for physically challenged users, 275
submenus
categorizing Start menu, 208-209
in Favorites (Start menu), organizing, 210-211
subscribing (Internet Explorer 4.0)
Active Desktop Item, 397-398
channels, 394-396
methods (Web pages)
Active Desktop Items, 392-393
channels, 392-393
Web sites, 392-393
newsgroups, 421-423
Web pages, 392-393
Web sites, 396-397
subscriptions, 547
canceling, 402-403
modifying, 399-402
updating channels, 403
Surface Scan Options dialog box, 161

surfing Web, 333, 547
Channel bar (Internet Explorer 4.0), 393-394
suspend mode, 547
swap file, 547
switching
between applications
via taskbar, 288
via window clicking, 288
between windows, 70
symbols (Character Map utility), 256-257
sync links, removing (My Briefcase), 504
system events, associating sounds, 234-235
system file attributes, 123-124
System File Checker, 7, 164
system properties, checking, 214
System Properties dialog box, 247

T

tabs, 50, 57
Task Scheduler Wizard tabs, 7
Schedule, 148
Settings, 148
Task, 148
taskbar
applications, switching between, 288
clock, setting, 196-200
custom toolbars, creating, 200-203
hiding, 19, 198-199
icon appearance, 196-197
moving, 19, 196-197
open applications, 196-197
position of, 196-197
properties
Always on Top, 199
Auto Hide, 199
Show Clock, 199
Show Small Icons, 199
screen appearance, 196-197
screen resolution, modifying, 232
sizing, 197-198
viewing options, 20
Windows 98 screen appearance, 14
Taskbar & Start Menu command (Settings menu), 204

Taskbar Properties dialog box, 198, 204
tasks
  data backup
    frequency setting, 147-149
    scheduling, 145-149
  Windows 3.1, performing under Windows 98, 9
Telnet protocol, 333, 548
text
  accessibility options for physically challenged users, 275
  adding to graphics (Paint), 308-310
  aligning (WordPad), 301-302
  centered, 302
  copying
    between different applications, 294-295
    between same applications, 294
    WordPad, 299
  deleting (WordPad), 298-299
  formatting (WordPad), 300-301
  inserting (WordPad), 298-299
  justified, 302
  left-aligned, 302
  pasting
    between different applications, 294-295
    between same applications, 294
    WordPad, 299
  resizing (Internet Explorer 4.0), 375
  right-aligned, 302
  searching on Web pages, 370-371
  selecting
    for copying or moving, 293
    WordPad, 299
text boxes
  dialog box components, 49, 52-54
  editing within, 53
  I-beam pointer, 52
  keyboard options, 53
  text replacement, 52
theft protection, laptop guidelines, 497

themes (desktop), selecting, 192-193
threaded messages (newsgroups), 425
threads, 548
tiling windows, 286-287
Timestamp WebBot, 437-438
Title bar, 24
toggle keys, accessibility options for physically challenged users, 275
toolbar buttons
  dependent on application, 32-33
  Network Neighborhood, 471-472
  resizing (Internet Explorer 4), 385
toolbars
  display options, 202
    Internet Explorer 4.0, 349
  Explorer, 107-108
  floating, 203
  items, adding, 202
  removing, 203
  standard buttons (My Computer), 77-78
  taskbar, customized, 200-203
  viewing, 68
Toolbars command (View menu), 68, 77
transferring to floppy disks (My Briefcase), 501
Transmission Control Protocol (TCP), 333
traveling with laptops
  battery charger, 496
  local ISP access numbers, 495
  peripherals and supplies, 496-497
  protective case, 495-496
tree structure (Explorer), 99-100
Trial Programs, multimedia applications, 313
troubleshooting
  CD Player, no sound, 316
  fonts, missing, 252
  hardware installation, 219-220
  printers
    error messages, 270
    stalled, 271
  programs, uninstalling process, 218

Windows 98 , emergency startup disk, 264
Troubleshooting command (Contents menu), 528
trusted sites zone, sites, adding, 389
typing URLs, 354-356

U

UltraPack compression (DriveSpace Utility), 157
Uncompress command (Drive menu), 159
uncompressing drives, 159
Undo command (Edit menu), 83
undocking laptops, 489-490
Uniform Naming Convention (UNC), 390
Uniform Resource Locators, *see* **URLs**
uninstalling programs, 218
unsubscribing
  channels, 402-403
  newsgroups (Outlook Express), 422-423
Update All command (Briefcase menu), 504
Update Selection command (Briefcase menu), 504
updating
  channel subscriptions, 403
  My Briefcase files, 503-504
upgrading
  from MS-DOS, 517-518
  from Windows 3.1, 517
  from Windows 95, 516-517
URLs (Uniform Resource Locators), 549
  address components
    directory, 353
    domain names, 353
    protocol, 352
  appearance, 352
  bookmarks, 436
  typing, 354-356
UseNet newsgroup, 549
User Name and Password dialog box, 342
user profiles, multiple, configuring, 226-228
User Settings dialog box, 227

V

video options, configuring
monitors, 229-233
multiple setup, 233-234
multimedia devices, 235-237
View Channels, 18
View menu
commands
Arrange Icons, 65, 106
As Web Page, 103
Customize This Folder, 79
Folder Options, 36, 72, 104
Internet Options, 375
Line Up Icons, 65, 106
Refresh, 66
Status Bar, 25, 69
Toolbars, 68, 77
Explorer menu bar, 109
My Computer menu bar, 76
Network Neighborhood
menu bar, 473
viewing
address bars, 69
Backup Utility, job status, 142
boot menu configurations,
530-531
Channel bar, 395-396
Clipboard Viewer contents,
292
file properties, 124-126
folder contents, 65-66
font folder, 252
Status bar, 25
taskbar, 20
toolbars, 25, 68
Web pages, History folder,
372-374
window contents via scroll
bars, 28-29
windows content by
details, 29-31
large icons, 29-31
list, 29-31
small icons, 29-31
virtual machine (DOS), 528
virtual memory, 549
**VirusScan (McAfee Associates,
Inc.), 260**
Volume Control, 235, 313, 316

W - Z

**WAIS (Wide Area Information
Servers), 549**
wallpaper
options
center, 191
stretch, 191
tile, 191
Web pages, selecting, 191, 386
warm booting (DOS), 524
Web (World Wide Web)
as part of Internet, 331
creating searches, 365-368
hypertext technology, 331
search engines
Boolean arguments, 364
capability differences, 365
date/time queries, 364-365
query syntax, 364-365
surfing, 333
Web browsers, 549
Web Help
Help feature, 39-40
launching, 46-47
Web pages, 549
adding to Favorites folder,
377-378
creating, 80
FrontPage Express,
431-432
desktop shortcuts, creating,
385
display speeds (Internet
Explorer 4.0), 386-387
editing (FrontPage Express),
432-433
Favorites folder, managing,
379-380
files, downloading, 380-381
frames, 436
FrontPage Express, 427
FTP links, 360
Gopher links, 358-359
graphic links, 358
graphics insertion (FrontPage
Express), 436-437
graphics options, setting, 386
History folder (Internet
Explorer 4.0), 372-374
hypertext, clicking, 334-335,
361
FrontPage Express,
435-436

image map links, 361-362
links
appearance, 358
types, 358
mailto links, 360-361
navigating (Internet Explorer
4.0), 351
offline viewing, 357
page properties (FrontPage
Express), 434-435
previously viewed, navigating, 372-374
start pages, customizing
(Internet Explorer 4.0),
382-384
subscribing (Internet Explorer
4.0), 392-393
text, searching, 370-371
text formatting (FrontPage
Express), 433
wallpaper, selecting, 191, 386
WebBots
functions, 437-438
inserting, 437-438
Web sites
AltaVista, 370
AOL NetFind, 369-370
child security
Cyberpatrol, 391
Cybersitter, 391
Kinder Guard, 391
Net Nanny, 391
connecting via Internet
Explorer 4.0, 354-356
defined, 549
Excite, 369
G-Guide, 318
Infoseek, 370
Lycos, 370
Microsoft Hardware
Compatibility List, 516
Microsoft Windows 98 Help,
46-47
NASA, 355
subscribing
Internet Explorer 4.0,
396-397
methods (Web pages),
392-393
URLs, typing, 354-356
Yahoo!, 369
Web-style option
activating, 444-445
customizing, 446-447

displaying
folders, 447-448
for single folder, 448-449
Explorer, 445
My Computer, 445
WebBots, 549
functions, 437-438
inserting (FrontPage Express),
437-438
types
Include, 437-438
Search, 437-438
Timestamp, 437-438
WebTV for Windows
installing, 318
launching, 318
programming, linking to, 318
**weekly scheduling, data
backups, 147**
windows
active, 286
address bar
Explorer, 97-98
My Computer, 68-69
applications
multiple open, 288-290
switching between, 288
arranging on desktop, 285-287
borders, sizing, 27-28
cascading, 71, 285-286
closing, 30-31
cluttered appearance,
reducing, 71
contents
opening, 25
view options, 29-31
display options
Web-style appearance,
103-107
Windows 95 style, 103-107
elements
borders, 24
Close button, 24
Control Menu button, 24
files, 24
folders, 24
Internet Explorer 4.0,
347-348
Maximize button, 24
Menu bar, 24
Minimize button, 24
Scroll bar, 24
Status bar, 24

Title bar, 24
toolbar, 24
Maximize button, 26
menu bar
Explorer, 97-98
My Computer, 68-69
Minimize button, 27
minimizing, 287
moving on desktop, 29
open applications, appearance of, 283
opening, 25-26
pane divisions (Explorer),
97-98
Restore button, 26
scroll bar functions, 28-29
size
maximizing, 26-27
minimizing, 26-27
restoring, 26-27
switching between, 70
tiling, 286-287
title bar
Explorer, 97-98
My Computer, 68-69
Windows 3.1
desktop comparison with
Windows 98, 8-10
FAT management system, 159
file associations, 127
tasks, performing under
Windows 98, 9
upgrade process, 517
Windows 95
desktop
classic style, 8
comparison with
Windows 98, 3-7
DOS appearance, 520
FAT management system, 159
upgrade process, 516-517
Windows 98 new features
versus
channels, 6
disk management
utilization, 7
full window dragging, 7
Internet Connection
Wizard, 7
Internet Explorer 4.0, 6
multiple display support
for PCI machines, 6
NetMeeting, 6
Outlook Express, 6

Start Menu Organizer
Wizard, 7
System File Checker, 7
Task Scheduler, 7
television reception
capability, 7
unified driver model, 6
Windows Tune-Up
Wizard, 7
Zones, 6
Windows 98
Backup Utility, launching,
136-142
components, adding, 220-222
configuring for multiple
users, 226-228
Crtl+Alt+Del warning,
rebooting, 261-262
desktop
classic style, 8
differences for Windows
3.1 users, 8-10
differences for Windows
95 users, 3-7
DOS
applications, launching,
525-527
backward compatibility
with file names, 522
configuration files, 521
FAT management system, 159
Hardware Compatibility Test
Microsoft Web site, 515-516
installation options
compact, 518-519
custom, 518-519
portable, 518-519
typical, 518-519
Microsoft Fax, configuring,
533
minimum system require-
ments, 515-516
new features
channels, 6
disk management
utilization, 7
full window dragging, 7
Internet Connection
Wizard, 7
Internet Explorer 4.0, 6
multiple display support
for PCI machines, 6
NetMeeting, 6
Outlook Express, 6

Start Menu Organizer
Wizard, 7
System File Checker, 7
Task Scheduler, 7
television reception
  capability, 7
unified driver model, 6
Windows Tune-Up
  Wizard, 7
Zones, 6
operating system
  hyperlinks, 11
  multitasking capa-
    bilities, 11
print options, 269
restarting, 262
screen appearance
  desktop, 13
  folders, 15
  icons, 14
  My Computer, 14
  Network Neighbor-
    hood, 14
  online services, 14
  Outlook Express, 14
  pointer, 15
  Recycle Bin, 14
  taskbar, 14
shutdown options
  DOS restart mode, 20
  restarting computer, 20
  soft, 20
  total, 20
upgrades
  from MS-DOS, 517-518
  from Windows 3.1, 517
  from Windows 95, 516-517
Windows DOS sessions
  icon selection, 523
  launching, 523
Windows Messaging, 332
Windows Tune-Up Wizard, 7
WordPad
  documents, saving, 303-304
  exiting, 303
  features, 296
  Format bar, 301
  Help feature, 297
  insertion point
    moving with keyboard,
      298
    moving with mouse, 298

opening, 296-297
page margins, adjusting,
  302-303
screen elements, 297
text
  aligning, 301-302
  copying, 299
  deleting, 298-299
  formatting, 300-301
  inserting, 298-299
  pasting, 299
  selecting, 299
text-wrapping, 296
versus other word processing
  programs, 296
**work offline options (Internet
Explorer 4.0), 403-404**
workgroups, 550
  displaying (Network
    Neighborhood), 459-461
workstations, 550
  client/server networks,
    458-459
  peer-to-peer networks,
    458-459
  sharing, 226-228

Yahoo! Web site, 369